THEY CAME FROM MISSOURI

THE HISTORY OF MISSOURI HEIGHTS COLORADO

Anita McCune Witt

Copyright © 1998 by Anita McCune Witt

All rights reserved. No part of this book may be reproduced or transmitted in any form or by any means, electronic or mechanical, including photocopying, recording, or by any electronic storage or retrieval system – except by a reviewer who may quote passages to be printed in a magazine or newspaper – without permission of the author.

Gran Farnum Printing and Publishing, Inc.
3401 Grand Avenue
Glenwood Springs, Colorado 81601
(970) 945-9605

ISBN 0-9649593-3-X

Manufactured and printed in the United States of America

REMEMBRANCES OF MISSOURI HEIGHTS

"We heard that when the men had arrived from Missouri, Dr. Clagett, my brother Victor Thompson, Jerome Stovall, and Carl Hill, that they had named the high mesa up above the Roaring Fork "Missouri Heights." It was named when we arrived there in 1914." **Blanch (Thompson) Smith**, Homesteader on Missouri Heights

"Although I hated Missouri Heights and its isolationism, I loved its children. They had a rough time -- picking potatoes, skimping on clothes and managing their meager resources carefully. However, they were very intelligent, very creative and just plain nice. I truly enjoyed my years of teaching on Missouri Heights." **Betty Jane (Kreutz) Floyd**

"Our father was a unique individual. He loved putting water in places it had never been to make things grow!" **Helen (Holmes) Bond**, daughter of Harleigh Holmes, builder of the Missouri Heights Reservoir in 1912

"One time a woman was exclaiming over Mount Sopris and the view. My dad looked her right in the eye and said, 'You can't eat the god-damned scenery.'" **Margaret (Marks) Harris**

"I remember how hard the wind blew on the Heights. I'd feed stock and the hay wound up at the neighbors." **Bud Fender**

"I was almost expelled once at Catherine School. The outhouse was old and dilapidated, with cracks in the side of it. One time I waited until the teacher had gone in and sat down, and I fished a little willow branch in there and tickled her butt! S'─────── in big trouble." **Lael Hughes**

"I remember when I went to Luby School up on the Heights. When kids accidentally wet their pants, they had to stand in front of the old wood stove until they dried out, while the rest of us snickered and made faces at them when the teacher wasn't looking." **Betty (Fender) Prichard**

"I remember my mother describing the absolute bottom of desolation. One day, after she had done a large washing and hung everything to dry, the cow got out of the pen and knocked the clothes line down, dropping the entire wash in the mud. It must have taken a special kind of courage to face the problems and difficulties that presented themselves." **Dr. O.T. "Jim" Clagett**

"Nettie and I did the plowing, the disking, raking and mowing of the hay and everything. We could both drive a two or a four-horse team, and I sang the whole time I was driving those horses. I'm sure they heard me a mile away singing for all I was worth. I sang Red River Valley, Home on the Range, and the Yellow Rose of Texas at the top of my lungs!" **Elvira "Tootie" Artaz**

"I remember Rosezella "Rosie" Gould and my sister Betty Jane used to catch big bull frogs at the reservoir. They would crack the frogs' heads on the wagon tongue, cut off their legs and fry them. They tried to get me to eat them, but I wouldn't." **Helen Kreutz**

"My maternal grandmother "Lizzie" (Curtis) was somewhat of a medicine woman and midwife. She helped people through the flu, smallpox and other ailments. Her husband, James William, made coffins, and if Lizzie couldn't cure them -- he buried them." **Virginia (Callicotte) Cordiel**

"The area where Catherine Store is today, in 1998, was called Catherine after Judge Edward Stauffacher's wife, Mary Catherine. The Stauffacher's ran the post office from their home, which is still there today on the southeast side of Highway 82 and County Road 100." **Charles "Chuck" Harris**

WRITTEN SOURCES

Colorado and Its People, Leroy R. Hafen, Ph.D., LTT D., Lewis Historical Publishing Co., Inc., N.Y.

Roaring Fork Valley, Len Shoemaker, Aspen Historical Society, 1958.

Pioneers of the Roaring Fork Valley, Len Shoemaker, 1965.

Carbondale Pioneers, Edna Sweet, 1947.

Progressive Men of Western Colorado, A.W. Bowen & Co., 1905, Chicago, Ill.

The Democratic Roosevelt, Roxford G. Tugwell.

Portrait and Biographical Record, Chapman Co., 1889.

America's Country Schools, Andy Guliford, University Press of Colorado, 1996.

THANKS TO...

Garfield County Court House: Clerk, Recorder's Office, Clerk of the Court, and County Clerk - Pat Cerise.

Carbondale Town Clerk - Suzanne Cerise.

Silt Historical Society and Museum - Ruth Chaffee.

New Castle Historical Society - Edna Sample.

Glenwood Historical Society - Willa Soncarty.

Church of Jesus Christ, Latter Day Saints, Genealogy Department - Bonnie Terilamis.

John H. Luby - son of Judge William H. Luby, Eagle, Colorado.

Colorado Department of Transportation.

Bureau of Land Management, Glenwood Springs, Colorado - George Allen and Dan Sokal.

Valley Journal, Carbondale, Colorado.

The Glenwood Post, Glenwood Springs, Colorado.

The Denver Public Library, Western History Division.

Gordon Cooper Library, Carbondale, Colorado.

Basalt Library, Basalt, Colorado.

Glenwood Springs Branch Library, Glenwood Springs, Colorado.

ASCAP - American Society of Composers, Authors, and Publishers.

BMI - Broadcast Music, Inc.

The Harry Fox Agency, Inc.

The Song Writers Guild of America.

SONY-ATV Music Publishing.

Wynonna, Inc.

Sears, Roebuck and Co. Archives - Vicki Cwiok.

AND SPECIAL THANKS TO...

The Fender Family:
Rokie, Myrlene, Ruth, Gary and Linda,
Roberta and Marvin, and Harold.

Donna Fasi, Gary Fender, and Mike Strang
for maps and deeds.

Dean Frazer
Professor of History, Santa Rosa Junior College,
Santa Rosa, California.

Lisa and Jim MacDonald

Chris Kelly & Jim Rathell

Peter Fitzsimmons

Jim Lenzke
Old Cars News Weekly.

Chris Chacos

Vi Farmer
who spent many months typing, scanning, and
giving me encouragement and support.

I dedicate this book to the people who lived it, and who were kind enough to spend countless hours telling me their stories and rummaging through long forgotten records, dusty boxes, and faded picture albums.

Their ancestors, parents, and some of those I spoke with came by ship, by foot, by horse, and mule and oxen, by covered wagon, and railroad box car, from all over the world, ultimately to settle on the high mesa above the Roaring Fork Valley. They are the true pioneers of this country, and of this state – and I am so proud to call them my dear friends.

Cattle Creek and the Crystal Springs areas are included in this work because of their close proximity, and because the lives of the people who lived there were so intertwined with those living on Missouri Heights. The histories of Cattle Creek and Crystal Springs families are too wonderful to be forgotten.

– A. Witt

TABLE OF CONTENTS

FOREWORD

SECTION I – MAPS

Missouri Heights and Cattle Creek 1
1884 2
1888 3
Government Surveys 4
1888, by sections 5
First Road from El Jebel 9
Family Arrivals 1884 - 1950 10

SECTION II – THE FAMILIES

Needham – 1882 17
Stauffacher – 1884 18
Heuschkel – 1884 30
Sanborn/Holgate – 1885 39
Waters – 1886 48
Hotz – 1889 56
Miller – 1889 63
Curtis/Callicotte – 1889 70
McNulty, Thomas – 1890 85
McNulty, Patrick – 1890 97
McLean – 1894 102

Desert Land Act and Homestead Act 117

Harris, William – 1900 119
Harris, Charles – 1900 136
Blue – 1902 142
Martin – 1907 150
Yeoman – 1908 161

Fisher Cemetery 170

Holmes – 1911 173
Fender, Ira – 1914 184
Clagett – 1914 198
Smith – 1914 211

Sewing Club 227

Green – 1914 229
Renftle – 1916 236

Cowen – 1917 244
Fender, Orville – 1918 255
Gould – 1920 261

Watson Colony – 1920..271
Turner – 1948 275

Loesch – 1920 277
Artaz – 1922 280

Cream Separator..289

Kreutz – 1926...290

"Misery" Heights – 1929 297

Jammaron – 1930...299
Lyons – 1934 308
Hughes – 1934 315
Bair – 1934 325
Holcomb – 1935...330
Diemoz – 1938 334
Long – 1941 338
Bianco – 1942..343
Sterrett – 1943..350
Marks – 1944...357
Sirola – 1944 360
Higginbotham – 1946 368
Young – 1946...371
Fender, Harold – 1950 375

SECTION III – ONE ROOM COUNTRY SCHOOLS

Catherine School..379
Upper Cattle Creek School 391
Lower Cattle Creek School 404
Crystal Springs School 407
Blue Creek School 419
Luby School...423
Missouri Heights School 440

SECTION IV – MISSOURI HEIGHTS WATER 463

SECTION V – SUBDIVISIONS 477

FOREWORD

Back in the 1960s and '70s, my old friend and neighbor, John McNulty, worked my land up on Missouri Heights. He drove an old, green, dilapidated 1946 John Deere tractor, held together with barbed wire, bent nails and shoe leather, and it was broken down about half the time. The other half, it worked pretty darn well, and he brought in a couple cuttings of good alfalfa hay.

He always brought his lunch with him, which consisted of a can of Eagle brand evaporated milk, a baloney sandwich, and usually a package of those little donuts covered with powdered sugar. He'd stash the can of evaporated milk in the irrigation ditch to keep it cool, and put his lunch in the shade of the scrub oaks and go to work in the field.

One day he was just sittin' there under the oaks, having his lunch, when he looked down and found a genuine arrowhead starin' him right smack in the face. He was so happy, he couldn't wait to show it to me, and after a lot of haggling and carrying on, I finally begged it off him. My old friend is gone now, but I still have that arrowhead today in 1998, and every once in awhile I put it in my pocket and walk the ranch with my dog, Sadie, and just think about things.

I think about the Indian, most probably a Ute, though it could have been an Arapahoe, who either shot or dropped the arrowhead. I imagine how the land must have looked to him back then, so open and peaceful and quiet, with no subdivisions, no paved roads or telephone lines. Even though it has changed dramatically, some things are still the same. If he looked south from my place, he saw Mount Sopris in all its beauty, just exactly as it looks today; to the north and northeast, Red Table Mountain with its gentle slopes, contrasting rugged terrain and vast acreage of forest land of aspen and tall pines; to the east, Basalt Mountain, which might have been his hunting ground of meandering deer and elk trails, dense timber stands, rich meadows of tall grasses, and flowing, natural creeks; to the west, Sunlight Mountain, Sunlight Peak, Twin Peaks, and Baldy Mountain. All sights I never tire of, can't get enough of, even after thirty years. It's Missouri Heights, with all its beauty and history, and yes, even with all its changes, one of the most beautiful places on earth.

SECTION I

MISSOURI HEIGHTS MAPS

MISSOURI HEIGHTS
Township 7 South, Range 87 West of the Sixth Principal

Approximately four miles wide, and five to six miles long.

1884

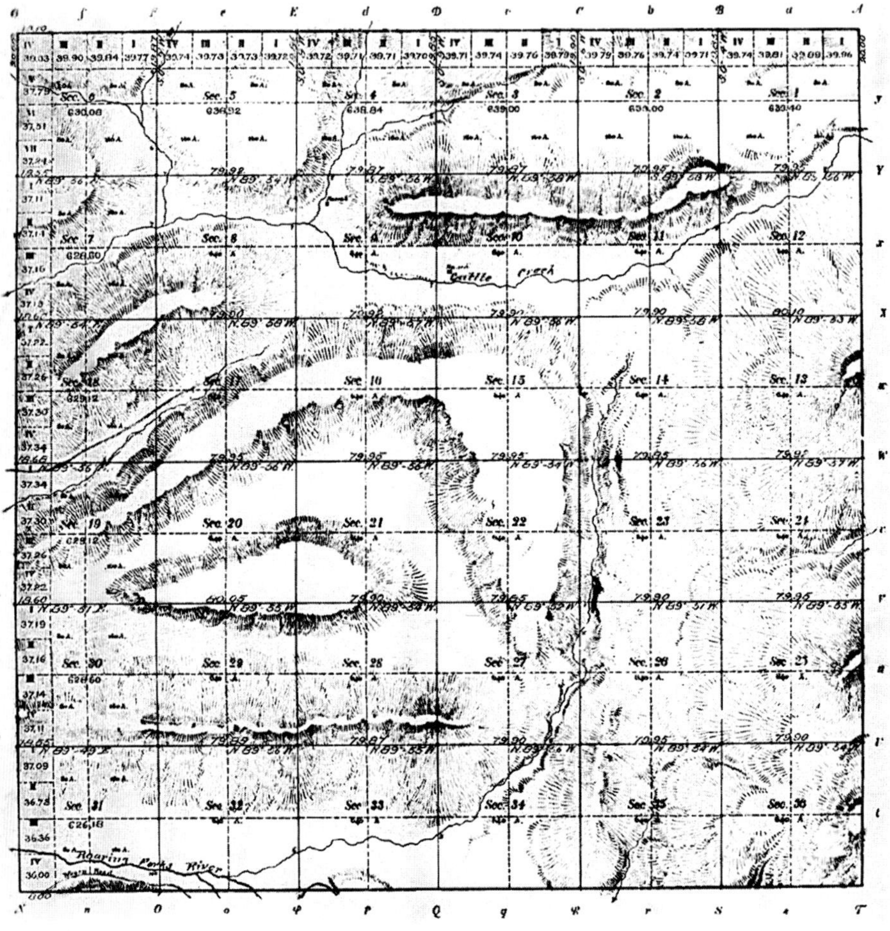

Bureau of Land Management (BLM) records show that the first Government Land Office survey map was developed March 19 - 29, 1884 by Samuel G. Rhoads.

1888

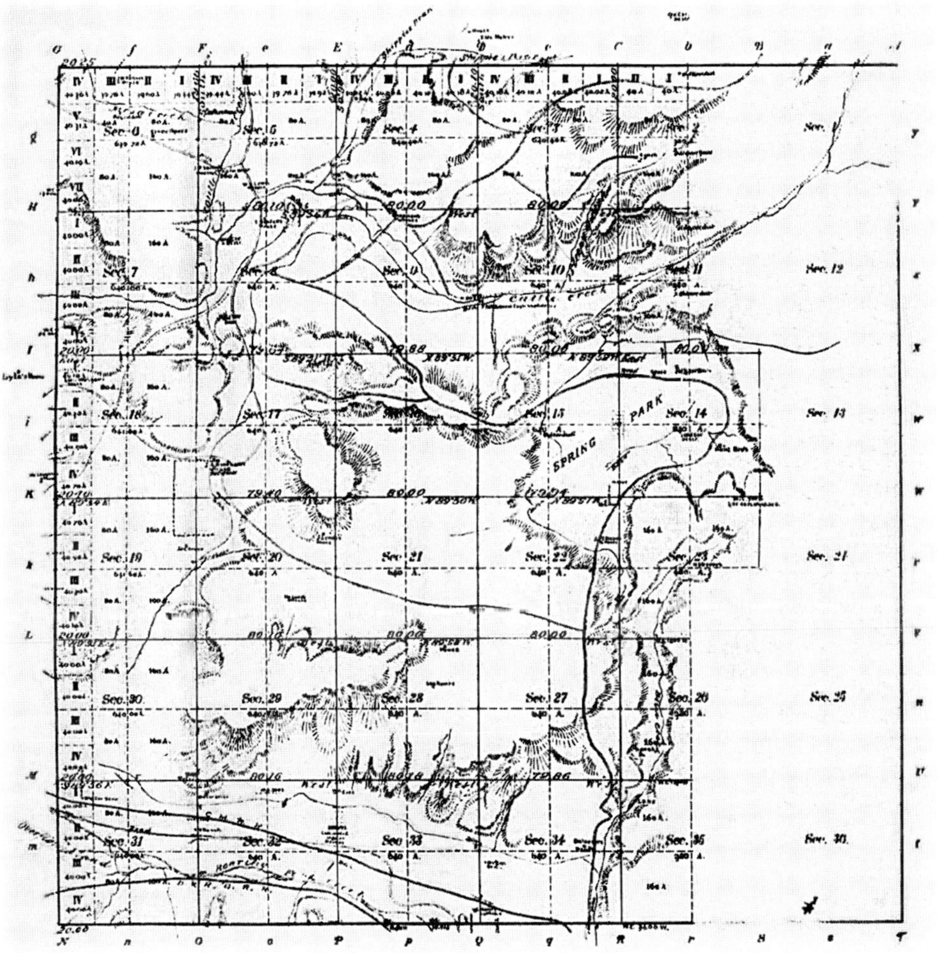

*The second Government Land Office map was developed
July 9 - 24, 1888 by Leonard Cutshaw.*

GOVERNMENT SURVEY

The object of the government survey was to create a checkerboard of identical squares covering a given area. The largest squares measure 24 miles on each side, and are called "quadrangles." Each quadrangle is further divided into sixteen squares called "townships" whose four boundaries each measure six miles and run north-south and east-west. A column of townships running north-south is called a "range" and is numbered numerically east and west according to its distance from the principal meridian. There are now 36 principal meridians located in different parts of the United States. In most of Colorado, ranges lie west and are numbered from the 6th principal meridian. The 6th principal meridian is located near Lincoln, Nebraska, and is 402 miles due east of Colorado Boulevard in Denver, Colorado.

A township is six miles square, or 36 square miles. Townships are numbered north and south from the base line. Each square mile which is equivalent to 640 acres is designated as a section. Sections within a township are numbered from the northeast corner, following a back and forth course, until the last section in the southeast corner is reached. For purposes of land description, sections are commonly divided into half sections containing 320 acres, quarter sections containing 160 acres, etc. Land acreage descriptions are then generally made by referring to a particular quarter of a particular quarter of a particular section located within a particular township or tier either north or south of a particular base line, and either east or west of a particular meridian.

A section is the smallest subdivision usually surveyed by government surveyors, and at each section corner there is a marker known as "Survey Monument."

1888

Government Land Office Map, Northwest Section

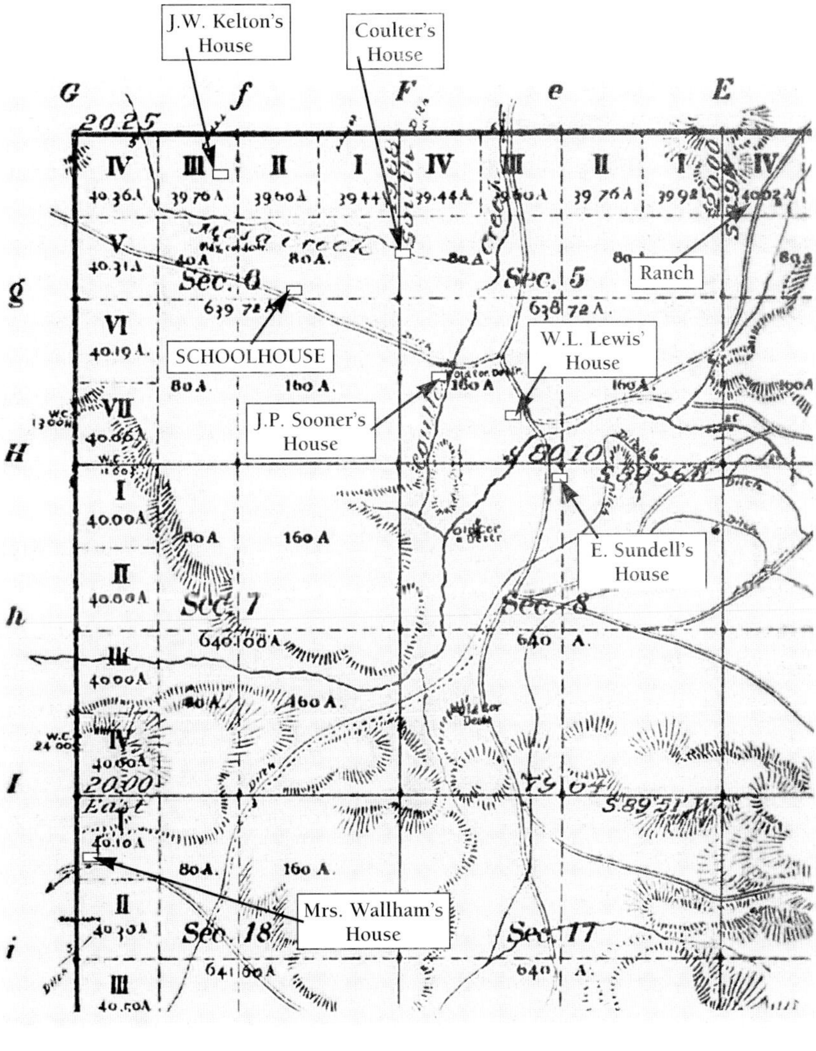

1888
Government Land Office Map, Northeast Section

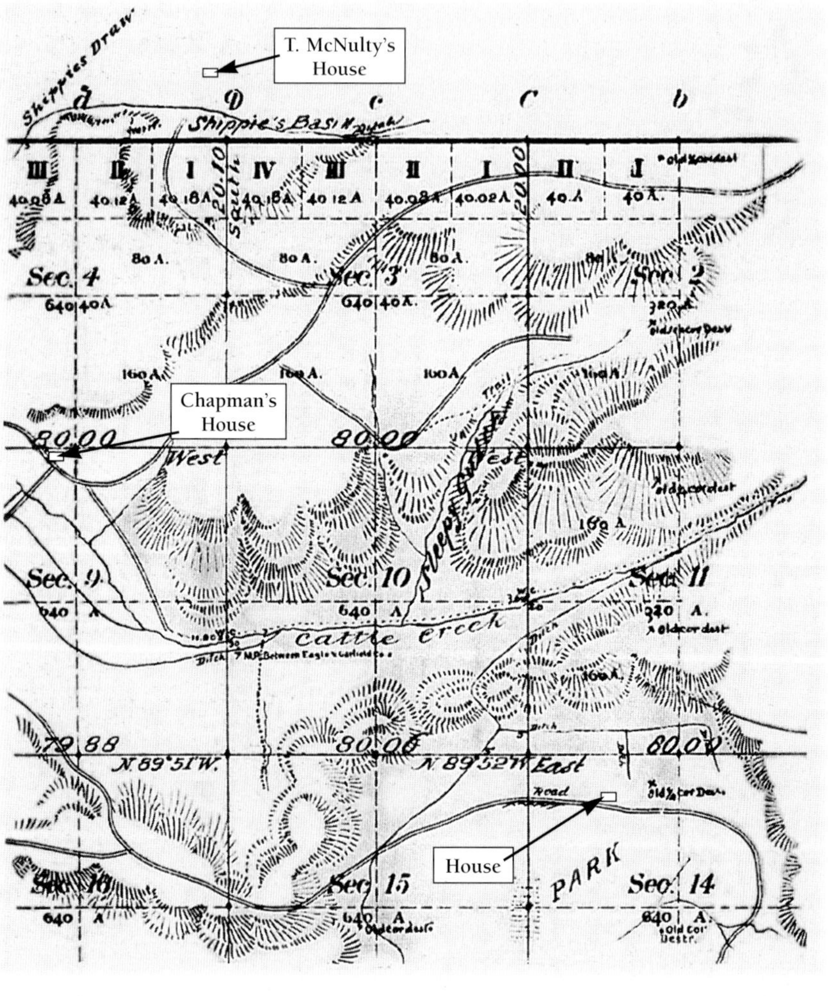

1888
Government Land Office Map, Southwest Section

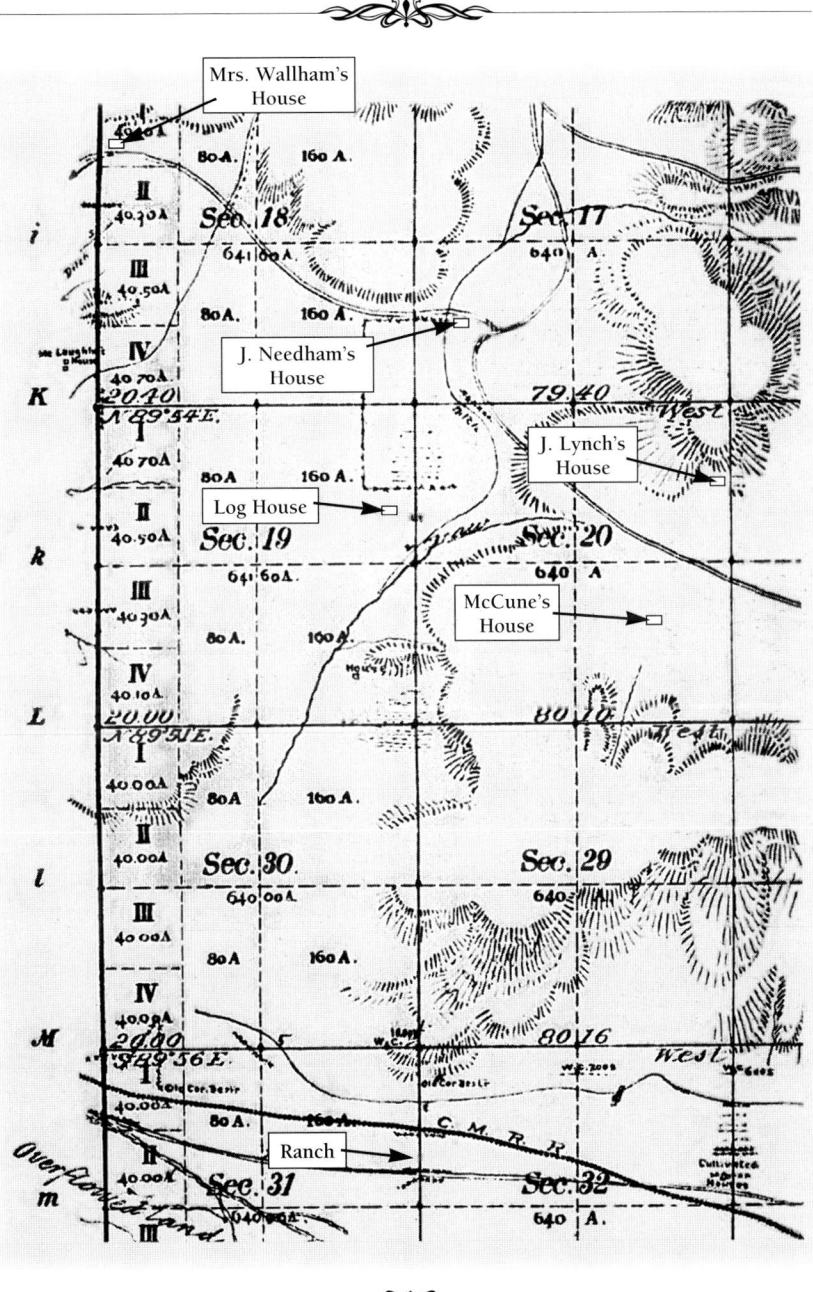

1888
Government Land Office Map, Southeast Section

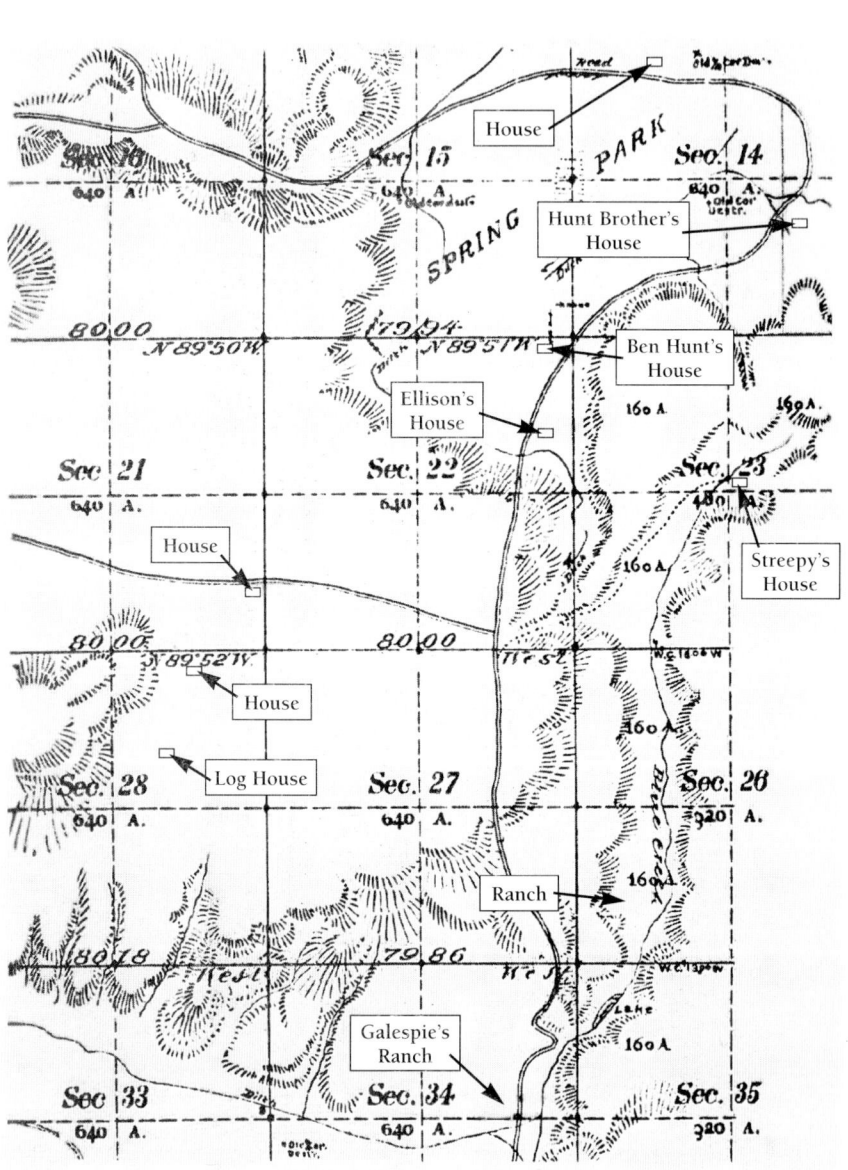

FIRST ROAD

From El Jebel to Missouri Heights

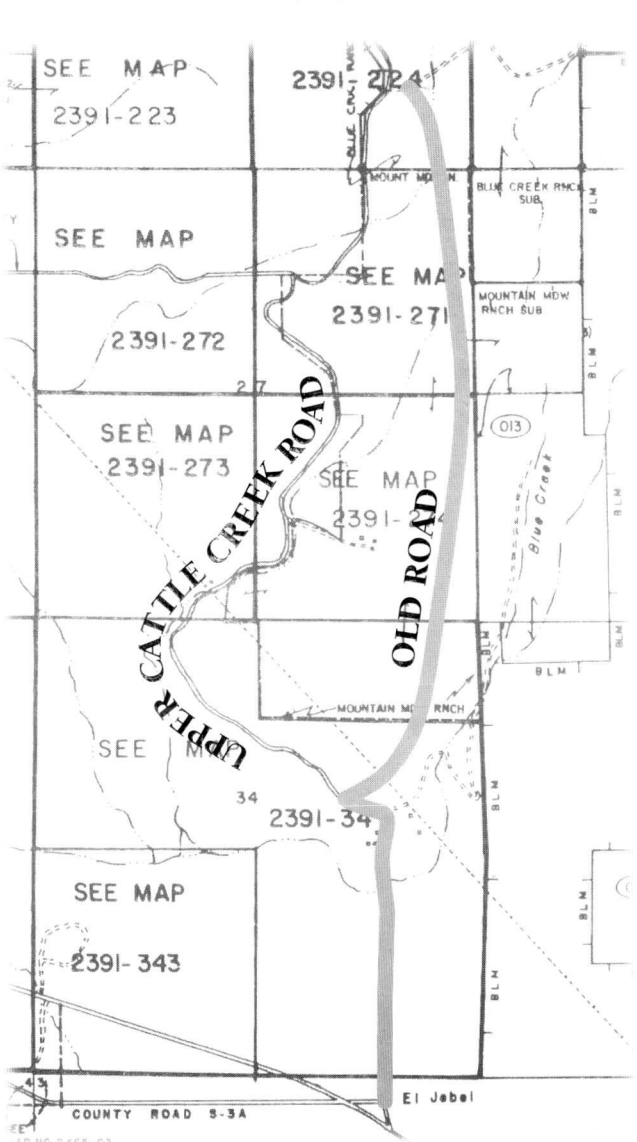

Map indicates the path of the first road (Old Road) which led up to Missouri Heights from El Jebel in the late 1800s. It was a very steep, rough, rocky road; wagon wheel tracks can still be seen in the rocks in some places along the route in 1998. Later, in the late 1920s and early 1930s, another road up to Missouri Heights was built in segments, and called Upper Cattle Creek Road. Map courtesy of Noel Crawford.

DATES OF FAMILY ARRIVALS

The following three maps indicate locations where families settled in the Missouri Heights and Cattle Creek areas, and the approximate year of their arrival. Family histories, later in this book, give the exact year of their arrivals and other details. Unfortunately, there were many other families who settled in the area whose histories and descendants cannot be found.

1884 - 1900

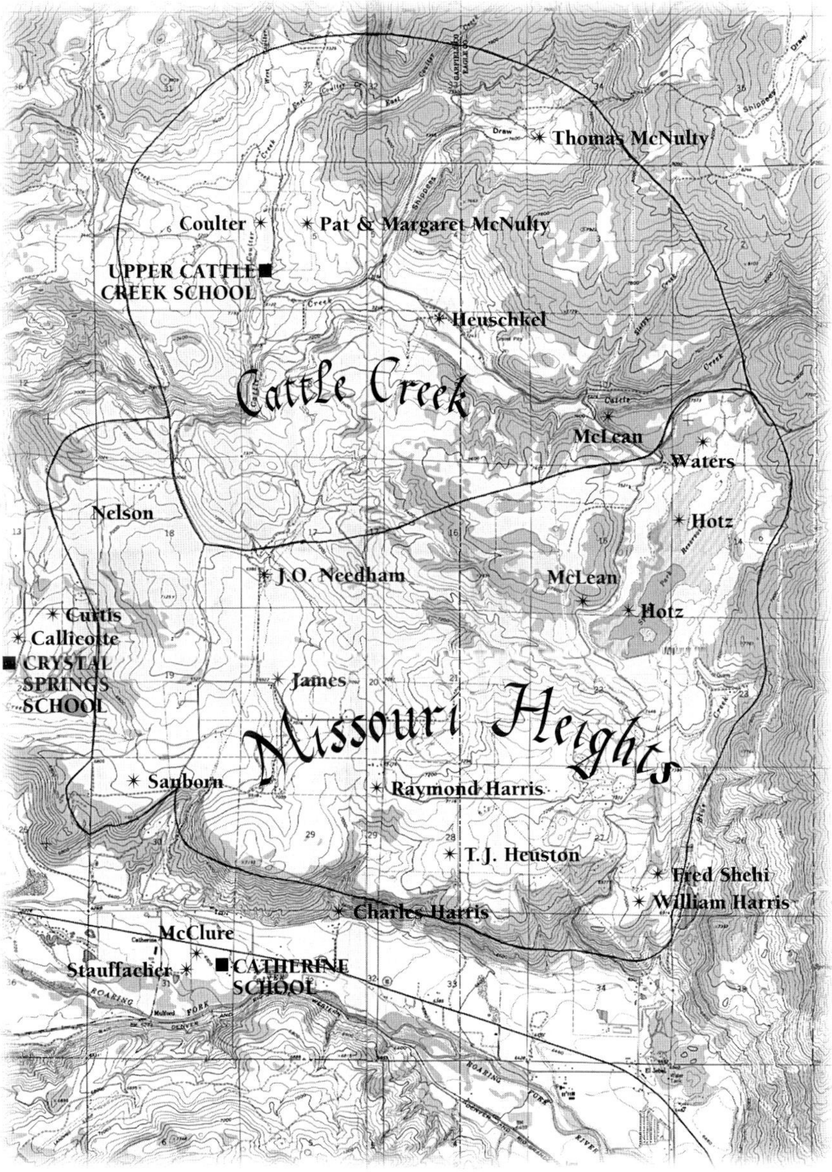
Thomas McNulty
Coulter
Pat & Margaret McNulty
UPPER CATTLE
CREEK SCHOOL
Heuschkel
Cattle Creek
McLean
Waters
Nelson
Hotz
J.O. Needham
McLean
Curtis
Hotz
Callicotte
CRYSTAL
SPRINGS
SCHOOL
James
Missouri Heights
Sanborn
Raymond Harris
T.J. Heuston
Fred Shehi
William Harris
Charles Harris
McClure
Stauffacher
CATHERINE
SCHOOL

1902 – 1927

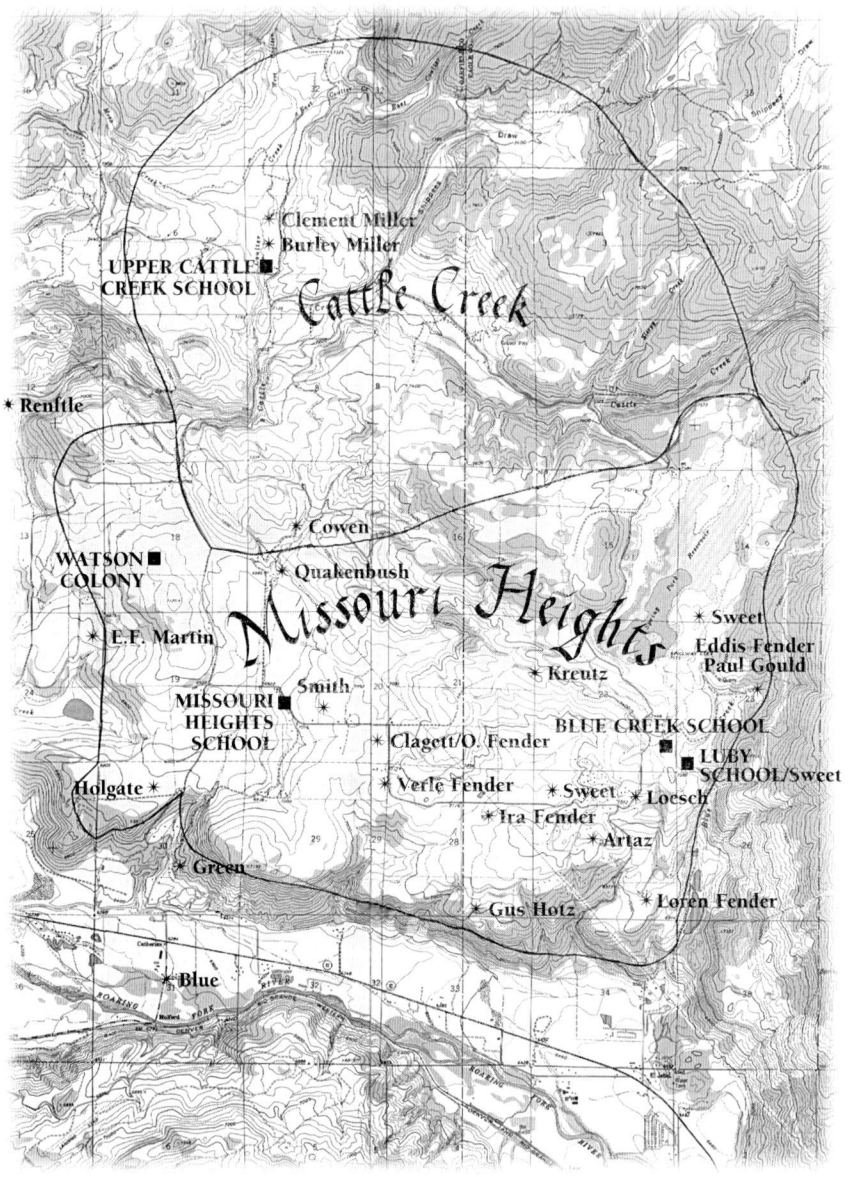

1930 - 1950

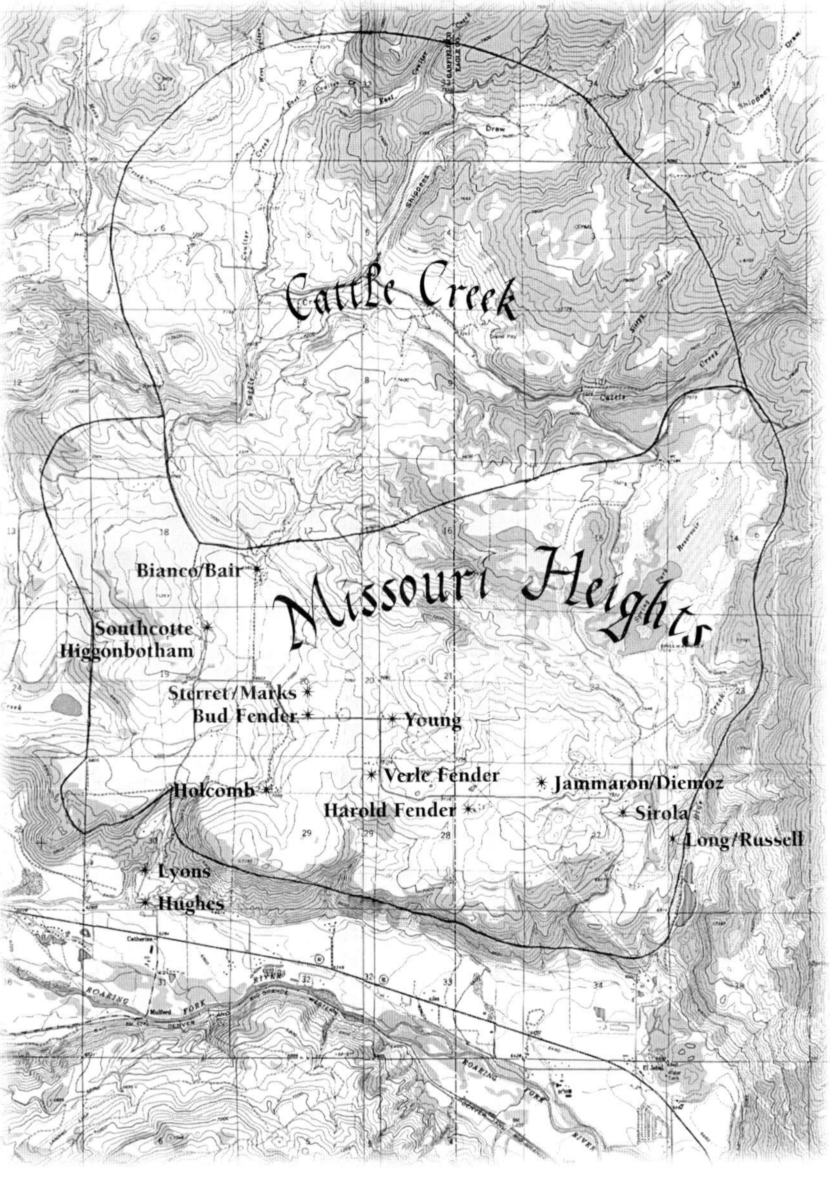
Cattle Creek
Missouri Heights
Bianco/Bair
Southcotte
Higgonbotham
Sterret/Marks
Bud Fender
Young
Verle Fender
Jammaron/Diemoz
Holcomb
Harold Fender
Sirola
Long/Russell
Lyons
Hughes

SECTION II

THE FAMILIES

JAMES NEEDHAM – 1882

James Needham was one of the first homesteaders on the high mesa which would one day be called Missouri Heights. His name appears on some of the 1882 government records.

The only information and history about Needham was found in Edna Sweet's book *Carbondale Pioneers* ©1947:

"James Needham was born in Canada and raised in Pennsylvania. He married Cyrene Underwood, from St. Louis, in 1876. In 1879 they came to Leadville where James was a miner. He also worked in the mines at Red Cliff."

In 1882, he moved down the Roaring Fork Valley and homesteaded the land on the high mesa which is the Mike and Kit Strang ranch in 1998.

"It is believed that the original homestead house which still stands today was built by Needham. James had two brothers who came to Colorado, Ike and Wilson. Ike's wife, Kate, taught school in Carbondale."

A Place Called Catherine
THE STAUFFACHER FAMILY - 1884

Judge Edward Stauffacher
1851 - 1935

Mary Catherine (Geiger) Stauffacher
1853 - 1935

The Children of Judge Edward and Mary Catherine Stauffacher:

1. Edward............................1876
2. Bennett...........................1879
3. Arthur............................1880
4. Clyde...................1882 - 1924
5. Edith..............................1884
6. Katie..............................1886
7. Ernest.............................1889
8. Mary...............................1891
9. Clara..............................1893
10. Anna..............................1894
11. Lester............................1896
12. Edna..............................1898

A Place Called Catherine
THE STAUFFACHER FAMILY

Judge Edward Stauffacher's parents were Anton and Anna (Stauffacher) Stauffacher, Anna being of the same last name. They were both born in Matt, Canton Glarus, Switzerland. They married and immigrated to America early in life, locating in Green County, Wisconsin. Their children were:

1. Jacob 1835
2. Mathias (1) 1837
3. Mathias (2) 1889
4. Anton, Jr...................1841
5. Isaiah........................1842
6. John A. 1847
7. Edward.....................1851
8. Anna Margaret 1852
9. Barbara 1854
10. Mary Ann 1856

Lorraine Purdue, grandniece of Judge Edward explains the title 'Judge': "In Switzerland it was an old tradition that the seventh son of a seventh son be given the title of 'Judge.' I have checked the family records, and it is so; Edward was the seventh son, and so was his father."

Edward was born near Monroe, Green County, Wisconsin, on March 6, 1851. He became a dairy farmer, and developed a dairy and cheese enterprise. On January 1, 1875, he married Mary Catherine Geiger, also a native of Switzerland. Her parents were Leonard and Mary (also a Stauffacher) Geiger, from Switzerland.

In the spring of 1880 the family moved to Aspen, where Judge Edward engaged in mining claims. Although he was financially unable to develop what claims he located, he did lease them to other parties and ultimately received $20,000 for his efforts. In 1884 the family moved down the Roaring Fork Valley, and the Judge homesteaded a 260-acre tract of land, consisting of the four corners where County Road 100 and Highway 82 are located today in 1998.

In 1884 there were no railroads, only meandering country roads between farms. The Colorado Midland Railroad and the Denver Rio Grande came to the Roaring Fork Valley in 1887. The tracks for the Midland passed to the north side of the Stauffacher home, while the

Rio Grande tracks were to the south, along the Roaring Fork River. It is assumed that Judge Stauffacher named the Colorado Midland whistle stop at the junction of the four corners "Catherine," after his wife, Mary Catherine.

In 1892, Judge Stauffacher applied for a U.S. Post Office to be located in the Stauffacher home, and also named the Post Office "Catherine."

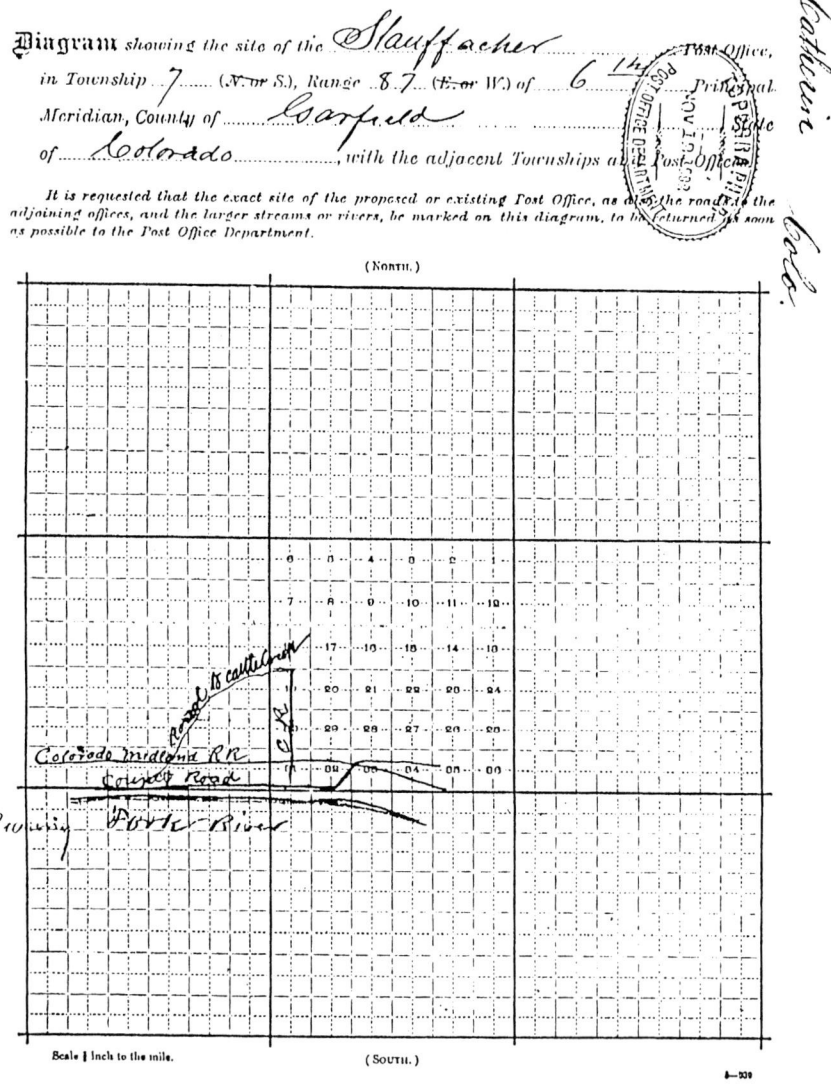

Post Office Department location paper 1892.

No. 1011.   (LOCATION PAPER.)

Post Office Department,

OFFICE OF THE FOURTH ASSISTANT POSTMASTER GENERAL,
APPOINTMENT DIVISION.
WASHINGTON, D. C., APR 5 1892 ......, 18

SIR: Before the Postmaster General decides upon the application for the establishment of a post office at _Stauffacher_, County of _Garfield_, State of _Colo._, it will be necessary for you to carefully answer the subjoined questions, get a neighboring postmaster to certify to the correctness of the answers, and return the location paper to the Department, addressed to me. If the site selected for the proposed office should not be on any mail route now under contract, only a "Special Office" can be established there, to be supplied with mail from some convenient point on the nearest mail route by a special carrier (see section 7.11, Postal Laws and Regulations of 1887), for which service a sum equal to two-thirds of the amount of the salary of the postmaster at such office will be paid by the Department.

You should inform the contractor, or person performing service for him, of this application, and require him to execute the inclosed certificate as to the practicability of supplying the proposed office with mail, and return the same to the Department.

Very respectfully,

E. J. Rathbone
Fourth Ass't Postmaster General.

To Mr. _Edward Stauffacher_
care of the Postmaster of _Carbondale_, who will please forward to him.

STATEMENT.

The proposed office to be called _Stauffacher_ _Catherine_

☞ Select a short name for the proposed office, which, when written, will not resemble the name of any other post office in the State. ☜

It will be situated in the _N.W._ quarter of Section _31_, Township _7_, (North or South), Range _87_ (Number West), in the County of _Garfield_, State of _Colorado_.
It will be on or near route No. _165,032_, being the route from _Aspen Junction_ to _Glenwood Springs_, on which the mail is now carried _Fourteen_ times per week.
Will it be directly on this route?—Ans. _Yes_
If not, how far from it?—Ans. ____ To be supplied from ____
If not on any route, is a "Special Office" wanted?—Ans. ____
The name of the nearest office to the proposed one, on one side, is _Carbondale_.
Its distance is _Ten and two_ miles in a _South Westerly_ direction from the proposed office.
The name of the nearest office, on the other side, is _Sheamer_.
Its distance is _Seven_ miles in a _Easterly_ direction from the proposed office.
The name of the other nearest office to the proposed one is _Aspen Junction_.
Its distance by the most direct road is _Eight_ miles in a _South Easterly_ direction from the proposed office.
The name of the most prominent river near it is _Roaring Forks_.
The name of the nearest creek is _Cattle Creek_.
The proposed office will be _One Half_ miles from said river, on the _North_ side of it, and will be _Five_ miles from said nearest creek, on the _South_ side of it.
The name of the nearest railroad is _Colorado Midland R.R._
If on the line of or near a railroad, on which side will the office be located; how far from the track; and what is, or will be, the name of the station?—Ans. _The office will be located one half mile of Railroad_ ____
If it be a village, state the number of inhabitants.—Ans. ____
Also, the population to be supplied by the proposed office.—Ans. _75 to 80 Ranchmen_
A diagram, or sketch from a map, showing the position of the proposed new office, with neighboring river or creek, roads, and other post offices, towns, or villages near it, will be useful, and is therefore desired.
A correct map of the locality might be furnished by the county surveyor, but this must be without expense to the Post Office Department.

ALL WHICH I CERTIFY to be correct and true, according to the best of my knowledge and belief, this _25_ day of _April_, 1892.
(☞ Sign full name.) _Edward Stauffacher_ Proposed P. M.

I CERTIFY that I have examined the foregoing statement, and it is correct and true, to the best of my knowledge and belief.

J. F. Woodward
Postmaster at _Carbondale_
Garfield Co. Colo.

(OVER.)

APR 30 1892

Catherine, Colorado

A post office was established November 23, 1892, with daily mail service at Catherine, Colorado. It was named for Catherine, the wife of Judge Edward Stauffacher. It was on their ranch about three miles east of Carbondale. The name of the post office and train stop was chosen by the Judge.

– *From the Avalanche Echo newspaper.*

Ed. Stauffacher

To Ed. Stauffacher belongs honor as the originator of a new industry in these valleys. It requires not alone enterprise but considerable courage to branch forth in a new and untried path in this county, but this Mr. Stauffacher has done and success has trodden in his footsteps. Two years ago all the cheese used in the Grand Valley was produced and shipped in from abroad – today the cheese fac-

tory established at Catherin by Ed. Stauffacher supplies the home demand. Thus he not only creates a demand for the milk produced on his neighbors' ranches, but he keeps the money circulating in our midst.

Mr. Stauffacher was a resident of the "badger" state during the years of '75, '76 and '77 where he was the successful proprietor of a cheese factory in that state of dairies. In the course of his travels through the West, he became imbued with the belief that this section afforded excellent opportunities for the successful making of cheese. On his return he disposed of his Wisconsin plant and for awhile located at Aspen. Confirmed in his belief, he moved to Catherin, but it was not 'til the spring of '93 that he was in a position to erect a modern cheese factory. This was done then and since the day of its completion, it has been kept buy making that cheese which is now so familiar in the households of the Grand Valley.

The factory is modern in all of its departments, and has a capacity of 360 gallons of milk per day. During the past year it has utilized some 1200 lbs. of milk daily, but this year Mr. S. hopes to be able to obtain twice that quantity with a corresponding increase in the output of cheese. The machinery is all of the very best, and is adapted to making "Swiss," "brick" or "limburger" cheeses. At present cheese is made once every day but with an increased supply of milk, his year will see it made twice a day. The factory pays 1 cent per pound for milk, this distributing quite a neat sum each year amongst the neighboring farmers, while the cheese made from it is of the full cream variety and readily sells for 15 cents per pound.

So excellent is the cheese produced and so large the demand for it, that Mr. Stauffacher finds it almost impossible to keep with his orders. He proposes to increase his force as soon as the supply of milk is forthcoming when he will be able to more satisfactorily supply the demand. At present he has made no effort to do more than supply the local markets of Carbondale, Aspen, Glenwood and New Castle, but with enlarged facilities the "Catherin" cheese will soon take its place in all the markets of the state of Colorado.

– *From the Avalanche Echo newspaper, 1893.*

CATHERIN.

Catherin is the center of a fertile country containing some of the most enterprising ranchmen in the county. The farms are very productive, agriculture and the raising of small fruit is a flourishing industry while stockraising is carried on to a large extent. The large dairy and cheese factory there has started the farmers to raising the finest stock and their produce is taken for the manufacture of cheese. Small fruits such as strawberries, raspberries, etc., are grown successfully and are as good as a bank account to any man that goes into the business.

In the vicinity of Catherin post office there are a number of beautiful and will tilled ranches. Stockraising is a growing industry.

– From the Avalanche Echo newspaper special edition, 1893.

The Post Office was established November 23, 1892, from the Stauffacher home, with daily mail service. From 1889 until 1892, Benjamin Harrison of Ohio was the 23rd president of the United States. Both Eagle and Garfield counties were established in Colorado in 1883.

In 1893 Judge Stauffacher opened his own dairy and cheese factory, directly west of the Stauffacher family home, which today in 1998, is the Preshana Horse Farm. The new business was called The Catherine Cheese Factory, and was a very modern, well-equipped facility in its time.

From the beginning, the Catherine Corner was a significant landmark for the residents of the area which would one day be called Missouri Heights. Many of them traveled to Colorado on the

Left photo: Mathias "Uncle Matt." Right photo: the Stauffacher family, left to right, Mary Catherine, Mathias "Matt," Judge Edward, and eight of the Stauffacher children.

Hoesly-Stauffacher reunion in Monticello, Wisconsin, 1902. Judge Stauffacher, far left of second row with the young boy.

Colorado Midland Railroad, with all of their worldly possessions packed into chartered boxcars. The Catherine Stop was where many people unloaded, packed up their wagons and buggies, saddle horses and mules, and started up the hill to their newly acquired properties.

Their mail was picked up and received at the Catherine Post Office in the Stauffacher home, where Judge Edward and Mary Catherine were postmaster and postmistress. Missouri Heights farmers sold their cream and dairy products to Judge Edward at the Catherine Cheese Factory, and for many, those transactions were their only source of cash money until crops were harvested.

In the book *Portrait and Geographical Record*, published by Chapman Company in 1889, Judge Edward's political beliefs are stated, "He is a believer in Populist principles and always votes with the People's Party, although in former years he was a Republican. In 1896, he was elected to his present office of Commissioner, in which capacity he has given excellent service."

In 1896, Edward Stauffacher was elected Garfield County Commissioner. He is first mentioned in the *1891 - 1899 County Commissioners Record Book B*, page 480, excerpts:

"January 12, 1897, Proceedings of the Garfield County Board of County Commissioners met pursuant of adjournment of the morning session at 2 o'clock p.m. Present commissioners Wm. L. Smith, G.P.A. Kimball, E. Stauffacher, and County Clerk Frank Tanghurbough."

"Upon motion of Commissioner Stauffacher, Dr. M. Dean was appointed County Physician for the year 1897."

"Upon motion of Commissioner Kimball, John Wessick was appointed Janitor for the year 1897."

"Upon motion of Commissioner Stauffacher, George E. Taboo was appointed Road Overseer of Roads, District #1; Wm. Murtle, District #2; L.R. Abudson, District #5, and E. Triffer, District #3."

"Upon motion of Commissioner Stauffacher, the salary of Road Overseers was fixed at $2.50 per day, and $1.00 per day for team."

"Upon motion of commissioner Stauffacher, the appointment of H.G. Isaacs as Deputy Sheriff was in approval."

Very few people can remember the Stauffachers in 1998. Varoqua "Rokie" Fender remembers them with fondness, "I was only seven years old in 1915, when we came to Colorado from Missouri. I don't know why, but while my dad, Ira, built our house up on the Heights we lived in a cabin at the old Stauffacher place. They were wonderful to us, and made us feel welcome and comfortable. I remember Mathias. Us kids called him 'Uncle Matt' and he was always nice to us. They gave us free apples and potatoes the whole time we lived there."

Ruth (Gould) Zancanella: "I remember my parents speaking of the Stauffachers. My dad really liked Judge Edward. I remember them saying how nice and congenial the Stauffachers were."

Len Shoemaker mentioned Judge Stauffacher in his book *Roaring Fork Valley*. "Edward Stauffacher, a rancher who lived a few miles east of Carbondale, secured a post office in 1892, which was called Catherine. He was appointed its postmaster on November 23, and ran the office until he left that part of the country. He also constructed a cheese factory, and ran it in connection with his ranch. He was a Dutchman and belonged to a group who called themselves The Sons of Herman. Annually, he held a picnic in a cottonwood grove near his home, and the Colorado Midland Railroad ran a special train from Aspen for the occasion. The people who attended danced, drank beer and usually fought with each other before the picnic ended."

Edward is listed in the County Commissioners' meetings from 1897 until January 9, 1900. Proceedings of the *Board of County Commissioners Book C*, 1899 - 1910, page 75 excerpt: "January 9, 1900. It being in the course of events that our chairman Ed Stauffacher is about to retire from the Board of Commissioners,

Stauffacher

Commissioner Monrow asks that the clerk enter up on the records without the chairman in any way acting, that chairman Stauffacher has at all times acted impartially, fairly, and with ability in the discharge of his duty, and to the entire satisfaction of the Board."

Edward sold the four corners, 260 acres, at the Catherine intersection, to George and Mae Blue in 1902. It is not known where the Stauffachers went after selling the four corners, but Edward owned land in various locations throughout the Roaring Fork Valley, and his brother, Matt, owned a large parcel of land northwest of the Catherine intersection. Edward was recorded as the Vice President of the Roaring Fork Potato Growers Association in 1910, and the Stauffacher family is listed in the 1920 Garfield County census records. It is believed they left Colorado in the 1920s for California.

From the content of a letter, it is assumed the Stauffachers had grown weary of the cold Colorado winters. The letter, from Judge Stauffacher in Wilmington, California, was written to his sister, Barbara (Stauffacher) Hoesly, who lived near Monticello, Wisconsin, and dated March 30, 1931. In his letter, he said that he was eighty years old, with medical problems. He also wrote about the economic struggles of the United States in the 1930s.

Mary Catherine died January 24, 1935, and Edward died November 21, 1935. They are buried in the Wilmington, California cemetery.

> Wilmington, Calif. March 30-1931
>
> Dear Sister and all
>
> I receaved the letter that Mrs. Wilbert Hoesly wrote me. and will try to scribble you a few lines at least. and hope this will find you all as well as can be expected. under the circumstences. we are all quite well althow not young anymore. the 6 th of last march was my 80. birthday of coarce you are a few years younger. but probably feels as old as I do althow I have ben under the weather this winter for a couple of months. was in bed. with liver troubles. gravel or stones. in the liver. but am all over that now and feeling all O.K. again. Can get around all right have a little rhumatis. in one of my feoot but so I cant get around all right without any trouble if you only could get around as well would be glad to hear it you bet Rudy is 2 or 3 years older then I asked you once but you did not say what his age was. when was his birthday and in what year was he born. hope he is feeling well as I am tell him. I would like to run a rase with him anyhow just to see if he could beat me. that would be fun anyhow. well we have had a fine winter this.

Page one of Judge Stauffacher's letter to his sister Barbara Hoesly.

It should also be noted that Mary Ann (Stauffacher) Norder (sister to Edward), born in 1856, is buried on a mountainside in Aspen, Colorado. Mathias "Matt" Stauffacher (Edward's brother, who lived at Catherine) died in 1922, and is buried at Wilmington, California.

Please note that in various writings, the name "Catherine" is sometimes spelled "Catherin."

It is also to be noted that after the cheese factory was closed, the building was converted into apartments. It is mentioned that Harleigh

Page two of Judge Stauffacher's letter to his sister Barbara Hoesly.

Holmes and Jerome Stovall lived there while the Missouri Heights reservoir was being constructed.

Excerpts from <u>Roaring Fork Valley</u> by Len Shoemaker, courtesy of the Aspen Historical Society.

Excerpts from the Garfield County Commissioners' meetings courtesy of Garfield County Courthouse.

With special thanks to the Stauffacher family: Lorraine Purdue, Vivienne Williams, fellow historians.

When I'm feelin' tired,

Elijah takes my arm.

He says, "Keep on goin'

Hard work never did a body harm."

And when I'm really troubled

And I don't know what to do

Granny whispers, "Just do your best,

We're awful proud of you."

GUARDIAN ANGELS
By: John Jarvis, Don Schlitz, and Naomi Judd

Copyright © 1985 Plugged In Music.
All rights administered by Sony/ATV Music Publishing,
8 Music Square West, Nashville, TN 37203.
All Rights Reserved. Used by Permission.
Copyright © Wynona, Inc. Used by Permission.
Copyright © Harry Fox Agency. Used by Permission.

THE FRANK HEUSCHKEL FAMILY - 1884

Frank Heuschkel
1853 - 1922

Josepha (Roberts) Heuschkel
1852 - 1920

THE FRANK HEUSCHKEL FAMILY

Frank left Saxony, Germany, as a young boy to avoid being drafted into the German army. He joined a whaling fleet when he was twelve or thirteen years old. He hunted whales, sailing all over the Arctic Ocean and around Hawaii. Later, he owned his own ship, and was one day shipwrecked off the coast of America near Georgia. He lived there for awhile, and never returned to the sea or to Germany.

Around 1867 he journeyed to Leadville, Colorado, where he worked in the mines. Austin Heuschkel, his grandson, son of Tom, remembers what his father told him about how Frank and Josepha met. "Josepha's father and brother had come from England and lived in Leadville where they ran a blacksmith business. Frank became acquainted with them, and while visiting at their house saw a picture of Josepha. At that time she lived in England. He wrote to Josepha in England, and asked her to marry him. She consented by return mail, came to the U.S. in 1880, and they were married in Leadville the same year."

They had seven children: Ellen, William, John, Ernastina, Alta, Bertha, and Tom.

Frank and Josepha left Leadville in 1882 and came to the Roaring Fork Valley. Austin Heuschkel recalls, "They went to Glenwood and at that time the town had one store and Chief Colorow and his tribe were camped near the hot springs. My grandfather told my father that when he went back to Glenwood a little later he saw Indians but never again together as a tribe."

The Heuschkels looked the area over and finally settled up on the high mesa above the Roaring Fork. In 1884 they homesteaded 320 acres east of what is the McNulty place today in 1998, on Cattle Creek, near the area that would be called Missouri Heights. The cabin which Frank built on his land still stands in deterioration on the McNulty place today.

Later, the family partnership bought the neighboring William Chapman place of 320 acres, directly west of their homestead. Chapman had homesteaded the land in the middle 1800s. A stone house was built by the Heuschkels on the property and the family lived there for many years.

Above and right:
The cabin built by Frank Heuschkel in 1884.

Below:
A view of the Heuschkel place in 1910, showing the stone house in which they lived.

1 - Bertha, 2 - Alta, 3 - Ernastina, and 4 - Tom Heuschkel.

Josepha died in 1920, and Frank died in 1922. They are buried at Rosebud Cemetery in Glenwood Springs. After Frank died, his son, Will, sold the lower section (the old Chapman place) to John McNulty in 1940. In 1942 John McNulty bought the upper section (the original Heuschkel homestead). John Heuschkel, Frank's son, bought the McLean place from John McLean in 1932. It was located next to the Hotz ranch, near the reservoir.

Frank and Josepha Heuschkel with their children.

THE THOMAS HEUSCHKEL FAMILY

Thomas Henry Heuschkel
1891 - 1968

Beryl Vernice (Smith) Heuschkel
1902 - 1989

Thomas and Beryl were married September 1, 1919. They had five children: Austin, Vern, Margaret "Peggy," Ernestine Beryl, and Donald Gene. Thomas and Beryl's first home was the old stone house which had belonged to Frank and Josepha. Two of their children, Austin and Vern, were born there. In 1921 the family moved to Cottonwood Pass, and in 1930 they moved to Cattle Creek three miles up from the Lower Cattle Creek School, which was located on the south side of the 1998 intersection of Highway 82 and 113 Road.

Left photo, left to right: Austin and Vern Heuschkel.
Right photo, children in front row, left to right: Don, Peggy, and Ernestine Heuschkel.

Austin and Vern went to school in Glenwood Springs first, and then to Lower Cattle Creek School. Margaret "Peggy" went to first, second and third grades at Lower Cattle Creek School.

Peggy (Heuschkel) Sholes remembers, "My teachers were Marie Roberts, first grade; Charlene Roberts, second grade; and Marie again in the third grade. They were sisters, and they were always real nice. My brothers, Austin and Vern, went from fifth to eighth grade there. Our classmates were Helen Tanner, Mike Bianco, Dorothy Sievers, and her brother, Clyde."

Peggy continues, "I remember when we put Epsom salts in Dad's coffee one day. He spit and sputtered and looked around the table at us five kids. We all acted very innocent!

"One time the game warden came to our house. I was just a little thing, and was standing by my dad as they talked. The game warden looked my dad in the eye and asked, 'Seen anyone shootin' grouse around here?' My dad shook his head 'no.' [I said,] 'Oh, remember,

Left to right: Donald, Peggy, Vern, Ernestine and Austin Heuschkel.

Daddy, you brought some home in your boots the other day!

"I also remember how much us kids loved Johnnie McNulty. He always went to town on Saturday nights, and Sunday morning we would find candy bars for each of us in the mailbox!"

Austin remembers, "We used to ride the old work horse with the harness on. One day, Peggy, Ernestine and me were all on. Peggy kicked him in the flanks, he bucked, and I went sailing right off.

"We raised Burbank potatoes on my dad's place. When I was in the seventh grade, I had to sort potatoes all winter long in the potato cellar. Dad would harvest six to seven railroad car loads, and load them at the Catherine whistle stop. They went all over the U.S.

"We also had seventy milk cows and a contract to provide all the dairy products to the Colorado Hotel in Glenwood Springs. My job was to bring the cows in to milk, and then put them back out to graze.

"There were card parties at peoples' farms, and dances at the schoolhouses. Folks would fix up their sleighs in the winter time with blankets and hot rocks to go to the dances.

"When I was older, I worked with the road grading crew. Joe Ottobe drove the four horse team, John McNulty was the blade man, and in the summer I was up ahead with a pitchfork getting rocks off the road. I made $3 a day, and back then that was big money."

The Heuschkel ranch.

Austin bought the old Tremble place in 1939. He owned 980 acres, including 320 acres of what would one day become Panorama Estates. He had 500 head of cattle, raised hay, grain, and pigs. He sold the ranch in 1968 to Mr. Duboise, but ran it until 1980. It is the Cattle Creek Ranch in 1998.

History of the Land Owners

William Chapman homesteaded 320 of the original acres in the 1880s.

Frank and Josepha Heuschkel homesteaded 320 of the original acres in 1884.

Will Heuschkel acquired the combined homesteads in 1922 for a total of 640 acres.

John McNulty acquired the 640 acres in two equal portions, 320 acres in 1940, and the remaining 320 acres in 1942. He also homesteaded additional land, ultimately owning nearly 2,000 acres.

Gary and Sara Lillian (Wendy) McNulty....1973......542 acres

Elana McNulty..1998......400 acres
  Pleasant Valley Ranch

I've got a hundred-sixty acres in the valley

I've got a hundred-sixty acres of the best

Got an ole stove there

That'll cook three square

And a bunk where I can lay me down to rest.

I've got a hundred-sixty acres full of sunshine

I've got a hundred-sixty million stars above

Got an old paint hoss

I'm the guy who's boss

On the hundred-sixty acres that I love.

– Written by David Kapp
©David Kapp, with permission from Anneliese Kapp

THE SANBORN FAMILY – 1885

Anna Burney (Gale) Sanborn
1844-1928

THE SANBORN FAMILY

Anna B. "Gale" Sanborn was born at Amesburg, Massachusetts, in 1844. She married James Frank Sanborn of Tabor, Iowa, in 1862. They came to Colorado in 1879, locating in California Gulch. In 1885 they moved to Aspen. They homesteaded 160 acres of land on the high mesa (which would later be called Missouri Heights) above the Roaring Fork River.

James Frank Sanborn atop a haystack (left) on the 160 acres. The land was reached by taking an abrupt left at the crest of the hill on Catherine Road and then 1/4 mile.

The legal description of their land reads as follows: "The SE 1/4 of the SE 1/4 Section 24TP7 s., Rg 88W. and the SE 1/4 of the SW 1/4 and Lot 4, Section 19 and Lot 1, Section 30 Tp7 s., RG87 W. 6th P.M. – containing 160 acres more or less."

The marriage ended and Anna B. became the owner of the 160 acres, although she lived in Aspen most of the time. Anna B. was a member of the Eastern Star Lodge of Aspen. She was a self-taught artist, an excellent knitter, and did perfect needlework.

Anna B. deeded the land to her daughter, Anna Emma, who was married to Robert Roberts. According to one of her descendants, Cora (Holgate) Natal, "Anna E. definitely ruled the roost! I remember

Anna E. (Sanborn) Roberts

the story about the tobacco plant. Someone brought it to her as a gift, and it was rather pretty, with blooms on it. When she heard it was a tobacco plant, it went straight to the pig pen! She was a good hearted lady though, and if anyone needed help, Anna E. was right there!"

Anna E. did not live on her mother's 160 acres, but in Brush Creek near Aspen. She, in turn, deeded the land to her daughter, Wynona, who married Fred Holgate. In 1913 they moved to the 160 acres and worked the land.

Anna B. and Anna E. are buried in the Red Butte Cemetery in Aspen.

THE HOLGATE FAMILY

Fred Huntington Holgate
1875-1944

Wynona Ethel (Roberts) Holgate
1890-1933

THE HOLGATE FAMILY

Fred Holgate was raised in Denver, Colorado, and graduated from West Denver High School in 1874. He moved to Marble and worked for the Marble Company, then became a carpenter and worked on construction jobs in various places. Wynona Roberts worked in the kitchen and waited tables in the boarding house in Marble, earning $5 a week. They met at the boarding house and became sweethearts.

Fred and Wynona Ethel Roberts were married July 17, 1910, in Glenwood Springs. They had five children: Naomi, Cora, Lenore, Owen, and Robert "Bob." Fred and Wynona lived in Marble until 1913, when they moved to the 160 acres on the high mesa which Wynona had inherited from her mother, Anna E. Sanborn. The house they lived in at Marble was picked up and moved to the 160 acres on the mesa. The house had two rooms, and two more rooms made from stones gathered from the ranch were added.

Three of the Holgate children: Naomi and Robert (rear), and Lenore in front.

Cora (Holgate) Natal remembers, "Most of the 160 acres was sagebrush, which they cleared. The land was very fertile and grew good crops of grain, potatoes, and hay. One year they had a better than average spud [potato] crop, and the prices were so high they made some money. In the '20s there were dry years when the reservoir didn't have much water, and crops were not plentiful.

"There were a few beef cattle, my dad's brand was $\overline{\underline{\text{O}}}$ (Lazy H-O), and a few milk cows. My mother peddled butter and buttermilk in Carbondale. There were a few chickens and turkeys. At Christmas time the turkeys were dressed to sell for Christmas dinners. They

Mary Ferguson, Missouri Heights School teacher, with Cora Louise Holgate in front of a 1928 Chevrolet.

also raised a few hogs. There were four horses on the ranch, three for work and one saddle horse. There were fruit trees: apple, plum and apricot, and it was quite beautiful in the spring when they were in bloom.

"The community of farmers built the Missouri Heights School in 1917 under the guidance of my father, who was a carpenter. Later, they built the teachereage (teacher's living quarters) and then a coal storage unit. Some of the teachers were Vera (Patterson) Kyner, Mary Ferguson, Eva Ravoux and Susorine (Diemoz) Bon.

In order to pay for the school, dances were held, and everyone came and enjoyed them. I remember Jim Clagett and Eddis Fender played saxophone, and my mother, Wynona, played piano. We all brought food and Mama ground up chicken for sandwich meat.

"Mom and Dad bought a Model T Ford, and Bob drove it to the high school in Carbondale. The Ford didn't last very long, and there was no car until Bob bought one of his own.

"My father was a member of the Independent Order of Oddfellows of Carbondale, and mother was a member of the Seven Stars Rebekah Lodge #91 of Carbondale.

"After the harvest was finished, Carbondale celebrated Potato Day. Mother would sort potatoes in the potato cellar down to the best six or eight. There was a county extension agent who showed her what to look for in prize potatoes. In 1932 we won eight blue ribbons, three white [3rd place], and one second place. Also in 1932 we won a second prize ribbon at the Colorado Springs pure seed show."

The following is a postcard which Wynona wrote to her mother Anna E. in Brush Creek near Aspen:

"I can't come up as the threshers are coming Tues. or Wed., and I will have to help get the grain in between now and then. The machine is at Prices' tonight, and have Laudenklos' and Blues,' and then us – and our grain is still in the field. Will keep Fred and I busy getting it in as he has to make a trip to town for coal and sacks. Gee – wish I could but it will hit me just at the wrong time, I'll be so busy I can't see straight!"

Threshing the grain.

Cora (Holgate) Natal says, "I remember my parents sitting at the kitchen table (which I still own) at night with us children. Dad would read *The Denver Post* and Mom would read a magazine or a book while we did our school work, all by the light of a gasoline lamp.

"My parents were very sweet and loving, in fact, so much so that they probably spoiled us kids. They were both quite active in the community. My father had a reputation as being a very honest man."

Wynona Holgate died in 1933. Fred H. Holgate died in 1944. They are buried in White Hill Cemetery at Carbondale, Colorado.

Robert "Bob" Holgate married Blanche Whitbeck on November 10, 1934. They had four children: Claude Robert, Kenneth James, Wynona, and Janice.

Blanche (Whitbeck) Holgate remembers, "I was only sixteen years old when I married Bob, and we moved up to the Holgate place. Bob's mother had just passed away, and I took over the house for her, taking care of Fred (Bob's father), Cora, and Owen (Bob's younger siblings), myself and my new husband. I was too young and too dumb to know just how difficult it all was. We had no water, and no electricity, and I cooked what I could cook on the old wood stove.

"One of the stories Bob loved to tell was the very first time I tried to bake bread on that old wood stove. Well, the bread came out so hard, no one could even dream of eating it. Bob gave it to the dogs, and the dogs buried it! We've laughed about that story for years.

"There were wonderful card parties on the Heights. We would go to someone's house and stay all night long, laughing, playing cards and having a good time. We'd put all the kids to sleep, and the next morning the women would get the kids fed and dressed and off to school, while the men went home to milk.

"Our neighbors were the Virgle Holcomb family, Helen and Louie Stott, the Fenders, Charles Olivers, Elmer Bair, Gracie Cowen and others.

"We also had dances at the Missouri Heights School, and the Upper Cattle Creek School. Everyone brought food and we partied all night.

"We lived off and on at the Heights until 1948, when we bought the Catherine Store and ran it for seven years. We bought it from Chuck and Bobbie Harris, and sold it back to them in 1953.

After Bob's dad, Fred, died in 1944, the land went into an estate, and we then sold to John Mulford in 1958.

History of the Land Owners

Anna B. Sanborn .... 1885 .... 160 acres

Anna E. Roberts .... early 1900s .... 160 acres

Wynona (Roberts) Holgate .... 1913 .... 160 acres

Bob and Blanch Holgate .... 1948 .... 160 acres

John Mulford .... 1958 .... 160 acres

Katrina and Courtney Barnes .... 1960 .... 400 acres

A. Guy and Martha Crouch .... 1982 .... 400 acres
(Los Pinoñes de Crouch)

DeeDee and Bob Ray .... 1989 .... 200 acres
(Subdivided Los Pinoñes)

Patsy and Tony Hirsch .... 1998 .... 53 acres

There's a place where mother nature's

Got it all together

She knows just when to let wild flowers bloom

Somehow she always seems to know

Exactly what she's doin'

And the Lord saw fit to furnish elbow room.

Have you ever been down to Colorado

I spend a lot of time there in my mind

And if God doesn't live in Colorado

I bet that's where he spends most of his time.

COLORADO
By: Dave Kirby
Copyright © 1975 Sony/ATV Songs LLC.
All rights administered by Sony/ATV Music Publishing,
8 Music Square West, Nashville, TN 37203.
All Rights Reserved. Used by Permission.

THE THOMAS WATERS FAMILY
1886

Thomas Waters
Unknown - 1920

Katherine (Kennedy) Waters
Unknown - Unknown

Thomas was born in County Wicklow, Ireland. He married Katherine Kennedy in 1864 and came to the U.S. in 1880. He located in Leadville, Colorado, where he worked in the mines.

Thomas and Katherine had eight children: Mary, Andrew, Thomas, Patrick, Henry, Ann, Katherine, and Bridgett.

In 1886, he homesteaded 160 acres on Cattle Creek, bordering what would later be called Missouri Heights. His land was situated due north of where the Missouri Heights Reservoir is today in 1998. He raised hay, grain, potatoes and vegetables, cattle and horses.

No. 75934.

Last Will and Testament

I, Thomas Waters, of Cattle Creek, Garfield County, Colorado, duly realizing the uncertainty of life, and being of sound mind, memory and judgement, do hereby make, declare and publish this my last will and testament, hereby revoking all former wills, in manner and form following, to-wit:

First, I direct that upon my death my remains be interred in a manner befitting my station in life and the condition of my estate.

Second:: – I direct that the expenses of my last illness, the expenses of my funeral, and my just debts be paid, recourse being first had of my personal estate, and that not being sufficient then to my real estate.

Third: — To my beloved children Patrick Waters, Henry Waters, Ann Parmer, Katherine Blue and Bridget Waters, I leave my paternal blessing, and no property, this from no ill-feeling toward them, but for the reason that I am under many obligations to my children, Mary Andrew and Thomas, and realize that they, of all my children, need and deserve all of the property I may leave.

Fifth: – I hereby nominate and appoint my said son Patrick Waters, the sole Executor of this my last will and testament, to serve without bond.

In testimony whereof I have hereunto set my hand and seal in the presence of the witnesses below named, this 19th day of December, A. D. 1908.

Witness to mark:	his Thomas (x) Waters (Seal) mark
A. L. Beardsley	
Anna Preti	

Signed, sealed, declared and published by the said Thomas Waters as and for his last will and testament in the presence of each of us, who, at his request and in his presence, and in the presence of each other, have attested the same and subscribed our names as witnesses hereto.

                                        Amos P. Ralston
                                 Residing in Cattle Creek, Colo.

                                        Albert L. Coulter
                                 Residing at Glenwood Springs, Colo.

                                          IN THE COUNTY COURT.

THE PATRICK WATERS FAMILY

Patrick James Waters
1870 - 1949

Nellie (Nickle) Waters
1892 - 1981

Patrick James homesteaded another 160 acres next to his father's land on Cattle Creek. The land bordered the McLean ranch, the properties being separated by the county road. He married Nellie Nickle in December of 1918. Their children were: Theo Leone (a half sister), Andrew Ray, Ethel Alma, Patrick George, and Jerry. Patrick raised hay and grain, beef and dairy cattle and pigs. Nellie had a large vegetable garden.

Ethel (Waters) Heuschkel: "My mother, Nellie, and Ethel McLean were best friends from when they attended grade school in Redstone, until the day they died. They grew up and married, and became neighbors on the Heights. As their children were born, each helped the other give birth.

Ethel McLean (left) and Nellie Waters with Agnes (front) and baby Ethel.

Gould, McLean and Waters children.

The Upper Cattle Creek School.

"I went to school in Glenwood for the first three grades. After that, I went to the Upper Cattle Creek School until I graduated from the eighth grade. My teachers were: Edwina Sheehan, Sylvia Shellhamer, and Katherine Senor. I loved Katherine Senor so much.

"We rode our horses to school, which was three and a half miles from home. Our horses were: Scraggles, Strip, and Rusty.

"There were usually twelve or thirteen kids in school. My schoolmates were Alden Haff, Billy and

Left to right; back row: Patrick, baby Ethel, and Nellie. Front row: Theo, Tom and Andrew.

Left to right, back: Tom and Andrew; front: Pat, father Patrick, baby Jerry and Ethel.

Margie Blue, the Grems children, and the Blacks, the Mocks, and Viola Miller. I remember on a cold winter day we would start off on our horses from home. John McNulty lived about half way and we would stop there to warm up. Johnnie or whoever happened to be there would have hot chocolate ready for us. We would warm up by the stove, and then John would boost us back up on our horses, and we'd ride on to school!

"I'm sure things were not easy for my parents on the Heights, but growing up there was a lot of fun for us kids. There were always dances at the Upper Cattle Creek School. As soon as we were old enough we would learn to dance. For us girls it meant that our first dancing partner and teacher was our dad.

"When we were older there were card parties and surprise parties. We would all go to someone's house and wait and hide before they got home from town or wherever. It was always after dark, and when they walked in we'd all jump out and yell and scream 'Surprise!,' scaring them half to death. Then, we would dance and party all night.

"I'll never forget when we surprised Johnnie McNulty one winter night. We told him the party would be at another house, but we knew he was going to town, and would stop by home to change clothes, so we decided to surprise him instead. He finally came home and the lights were all out and we were all hidden under beds and behind chairs and wherever. I can still hear him muttering to himself about how that ole stove was still warm. Well, we all screamed and jumped out and he loved every minute of it. He didn't even take his overshoes off – he just started dancin'. That was Johnnie!"

Austin Heuschkel, who married Ethel Waters in 1992 remembers, "One Halloween night Johnnie McNulty and his friends were up to no good. The next morning, my dad woke up and went out to milk. He opened the barn door and found all the milk cows decked out in work harnesses. He never said a word to anyone, but just waited until someone let it slip – and they did – and, of course, the initiator was Johnnie McNulty!"

Ethel, "Another Halloween, Johnnie and his friends somehow, some way, put a whole spring wagon up on top of the schoolhouse [The Upper Cattle Creek Schoolhouse]. Who in the world knew how they got it up there, but they did. It was Johnnie McNulty, John Walsh, and John Nickeles!"

A spring wagon.

Patrick and Nellie are buried in Rosebud Cemetery in Glenwood Springs.

History of the Land Owners

Thomas Waters .... 1886 .... *homesteaded 160 acres*
Andrew Waters .... *160 acres*
Patrick Waters .... *160 acres*
Oscar Cerise .... 1944 - 1998 .... *650 acres*

Some of the information about the Waters family is taken from the book <u>Progressive Men of Western Colorado</u>, Published in Chicago by A.W. Bowen and Co. ©1905.

A hundred year old photograph

Stares out from a frame

and if you look real close

You'll see

Our eyes are just the same.

I never met them face to face

But I still know them well

From the stories

My dear grandmother tells.

GUARDIAN ANGELS
By: John Jarvis, Don Schlitz, and Naomi Judd

Copyright © 1985 Plugged In Music.
All rights administered by Sony/ATV Music
Publishing, 8 Music Square West, Nashville, TN 37203.
All Rights Reserved. Used by Permission.
Copyright © Wynona, Inc. Used by Permission.
Copyright © Harry Fox Agency. Used by Permission.

THE HOTZ FAMILY – 1889

Seated, left to right:
Lizzie Hotz Hammel, 1877-1926; Martin G. Hotz 1847-1924 – Father;
Augustine V. Hotz, 1893-1964; Mary Hotz, 1848-1918 – Mother;
Clara Hotz Mall 1876-1918.

Standing, left to right:
Adele Hotz 1890-1906; Ben Hotz; George Hotz 1879-1924;
Joseph Hotz 1884-1961; Mary Theresa "Mamie" Hotz 1888-1968.

Picture circa 1905

Martin G. Hotz
1847-1925

Mary Hunt Hotz
1848 - 1918

THE HOTZ FAMILY

Martin G. Hotz was born in 1847, and raised in Baden, Germany. His father was Valentine Hotz, who died in 1858, and his mother was Elizabeth Hotz, who died in 1866. Valentine was a prosperous and skillful farmer in Baden. The family was of Catholic religion, and they had six children.

Martin attended school for nine years in Baden, Germany, and also worked the family farm. When he was nineteen years old he learned the trade of a cooper – a maker of wooden barrels. He came to the United States in 1872, locating in St. Louis, Missouri, and continued his trade as a cooper there.

On September 3, 1874, he married Mary Hunt of St. Louis, Missouri. Her parents, Anton and Frances Hunt, were also born and raised in Baden, Germany, and were also of the Catholic faith. They came to the United States shortly after their marriage, settled in St. Louis, and that is where Mary Hunt was born and raised.

Martin G. came to Colorado in 1889 by way of Leadville and Aspen, where he lived for short periods of time. At that time he was the only survivor of his Baden, Germany, family. Martin came to the Roaring Fork Valley in 1889 and took over or pre-empted a claim of 160 acres up on the mesa seven miles northwest of Basalt. It was called the Spring Park Ranch, and he paid $4,800 to John A. Hunt (his wife's brother). It is presumed that John A. Hunt homesteaded the land. John's brother, Ben, also homesteaded land nearby.

The deed reads: "All of ranch in what is known as Spring Park together with all of the improvements consisting of stables, dwelling, horse grainery, barn and out buildings, all fencing."

The description of the land is as follows: "The south 1/2 N.W. 1/4 and the N. 1/2 of S.W. 1/4 of section 14 of Township R.87 West of 6th Meridian."

Martin bought and homesteaded the land adjoining the 160 acres and the farm grew to 800 acres. Some of the land was bought from a White, one of the first homesteaders on the mesa. The spring on the original property was a great source of water for the Hotz farm. The Hotz family lived in the dwelling mentioned in the deed until 1904 or 1905, when a fine house was built, a larger farm house with many rooms.

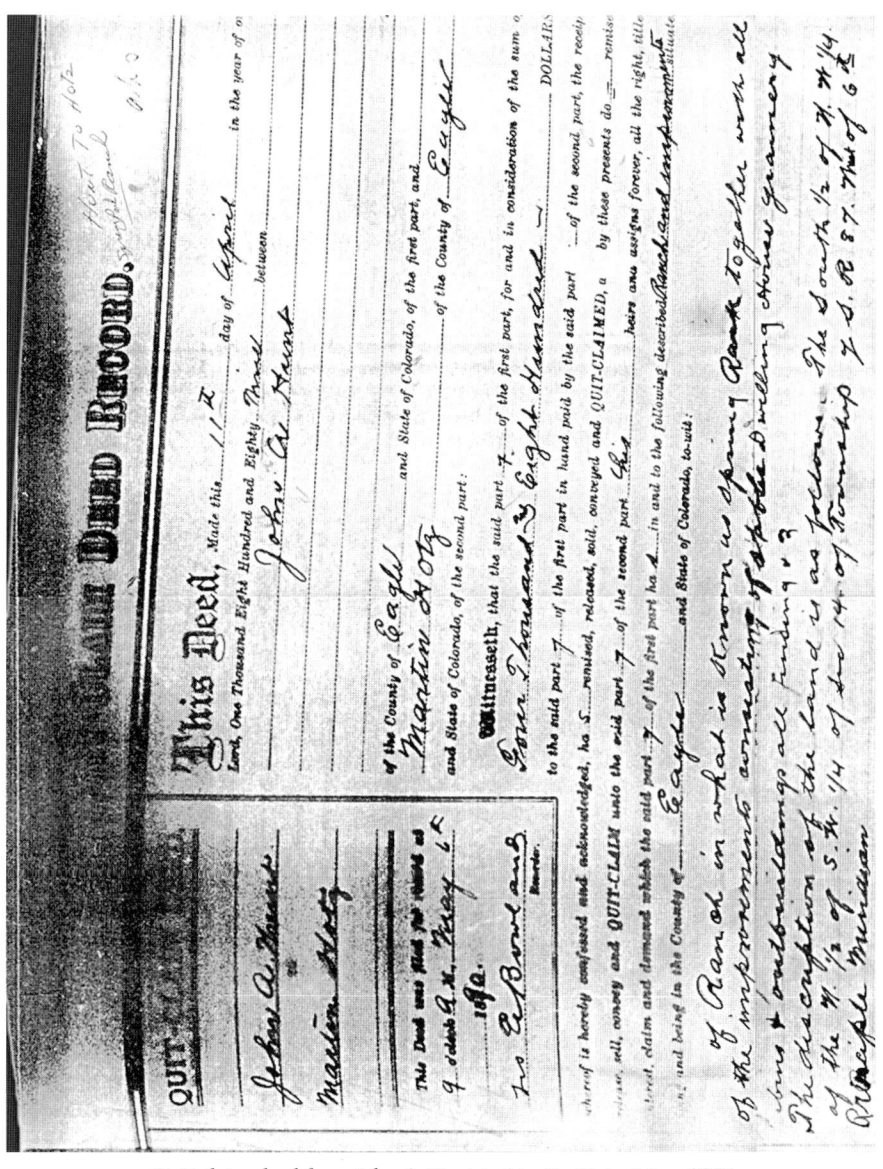
Quit claim deed from John A. Hunt to Martin Hotz. May, 1890

Martin and Mary had eight children: Clara, Elizabeth, George, Benjamin, Joseph, Mary Theresa "Mamie," Adele, and Augustine. It is said that two additional children, two tiny babies, were born and buried on the ranch.

Martin, like his father, Valentine, was an industrious and successful farmer, and eventually 700 acres of the land was under cultivation. He raised purebred cattle, fine horses, hay, oats, barley, potatoes, and huge amounts of vegetables. He was described in the book *Progressive Men of Western Colorado*, published in 1905, as "one of the extensive and successful stock growers and ranchmen of Garfield County." He was a zealous Republican, and belonged to the St. Joseph and the St. Nicholas beneficial societies.

Martin was a staunch believer in hard work and all of the children worked many hours in the fields, plus whatever household duties they were given by their mother.

Marian Hotz, who was married to one of Martin G. Hotz's descendants, remembers some of the family stories in 1998:

"My husband's grandfather, who was Martin G. Hotz from Germany, kept a firm hand on his family. They worked from dawn 'til dusk in the fields. Even so, there was time for fun. The boys had fine horses back then, and horse racing was one of their greatest pleasures. They also rode to Carbondale for dances and parties. For the girls there were quilting parties and church activities. With a family of ten, you can imagine the tremendous amount of cooking and baking, washing on a washboard, sewing and mending, soap making and cleaning that had to be done. The two oldest girls married quite late, and the youngest girl, Adele, died at sixteen years of age on the ranch. No one could remember what she died of."

It is noted in the book mentioned previously, *Progressive Men of Western Colorado*, that around 1900 the Hotz boys started operating a threshing outfit, and were successful with it. It is also evident that the Hotz family were considerate neighbors, as several families on the mesa mention in their histories that one of the Hotz boys or their father helped them clear the land, cultivate, and build various structures on their farms.

In 1911 Martin sold a large portion of his land to Harley Holmes, who with his partner, Jerome Stovall, started construction of the reservoir in the summer of 1912. The company, which still provides irrigation water in 1998, was called the Carbondale Reservoir and Irrigation Company. The Hotz house, which sat where the reservoir is today, was picked up and moved in 1911, using horses and skids, to another location near Missouri Heights, and is still there today in 1998.

Austin Heuschkel recalls, "The house was moved out in 1911 by the Tremble family, and is on what is called the Cattle Creek ranch today in 1998. It was disassembled into pieces because the road was too narrow to move it whole. The pieces were numbered and coded, so it could be put back together properly."

Martin gave some of his sons parcels of land from the main ranch, and other land that he owned on the mesa. He and Mary moved to Glenwood Springs, where Martin ran a livery stable and delivery service. Mary died in 1918, and Martin died in 1925. All of the family are buried at Rosebud Cemetery in Glenwood Springs, except for Benjamin who is buried in Denver.

With special thanks to Marian Hotz, who was married to Martin G. Hotz, son of Joseph Hotz, son of Martin G. Hotz from Germany.

<u>Progressive Men of Western Colorado</u> *compiled and published 1905 by A.W. Bowen & Co., Chicago, Illinois.*

History of the Land Owners

The original 160 acres was homesteaded by John A. Hunt in the 1880s, and increased to 800 acres during the time it was owned by the Hotz family.

John A. Hunt	*160 acres*	*1880s*
Martin Hotz		*1889*
Harley Holmes		*1911*
John & Uriah McLean		
Mulford		
Albert and Laura Grange		
Grange		
HLEM		*1996*
Spring Park Ranches		*1998*

The family home which was built in 1904 or 1905 stands in all its beauty on the Cattle Creek Ranch located on Coulter Road at 113 Road.

THE HOTZ FAMILY

Martin G. Hotz
1847-1925

Mary (Hunt) Hotz
1848 - 1918

Children:
George Henry, Benjamin, Joseph Arthur,
Augustine, Elizabeth, Clara, Adele, Mary Theresa "Mamie"

<u>George Henry</u>
Pansy Callahan }

<u>Benjamin</u>
Mary } Augustine

<u>Joseph Arthur</u> } Thelma Lucille → Thelma Lucille } Allen
Adelbert Bowles } Arthur
Phyllis

<u>Mary Catherine</u> } Martin George → Martin George } Martin G., Jr.
Marian Jacobs } Mary Jo

<u>Augustine</u>

<u>Elizabeth</u>
Dominick Hammel } Laura, Marie, and Katherine

<u>Clara</u>
Louie Mall } John, Frank, Catherine, Ann

<u>Adele</u>

<u>Mary Theresa "Mamie"</u>

THE MILLER FAMILY - 1889

Clement and Susan on their wedding day, June 8, 1905.

Clement Wilbur Miller
1879 - 1951

Susan Acenith (Cantrell) Miller
1887 - 1935

THE MILLER FAMILY

John Smith Miller, his wife, Jerusha Diena, and their six children left Lawrence County, Missouri, in 1889 in a covered wagon bound for Colorado. Somewhere along the route they transferred all their belongings, including their horses, into a railroad boxcar and mother, father, and all six children climbed inside. They arrived in the Roaring Fork Valley and settled on a ranch in Spring Valley. Their seventh child, Lena, was born there.

Viola (Miller) Waters remembers a story about her grandfather, John Smith, "It was not easy to get to church on Sundays, so people gathered at each others' houses to worship. My grandfather was not a preacher, but nonetheless, he loved to preach. I remember being told that he preached up a storm and even pounded on the makeshift pulpit as he spoke."

The John Smith Miller family, left to right, standing: Eva, Ery, Clement, Burley, Cora. Seated: John Smith, Jerusha, Addie, Little Lena.

When the boys were older they bought land on Cattle Creek, one-half mile north of the Upper Cattle Creek Schoolhouse. Clement and Burley had their adjoining ranches there, near the Pat and Margaret McNulty place.

The Miller brothers had 166.23 acres, and they raised hay, oats, barley, and some potatoes, and eventually developed a large herd of white-faced Hereford cattle. The cattle were driven to Carbondale each fall to be shipped to Denver and sold. They also kept about twenty head of horses, some for work in the fields, and some for transportation.

When Clement was 24 years old, he married 18 year-old Susan Acenith Cantrell, on June 8, 1905. The couple lived on the Cattle Creek ranch. Clement and Susan had four children: Grace, born in 1906; Nellie, born in 1908; Harold, born in 1914, and Viola, born in 1922.

Viola: "Before I was born my mother and father made butter and sold it in

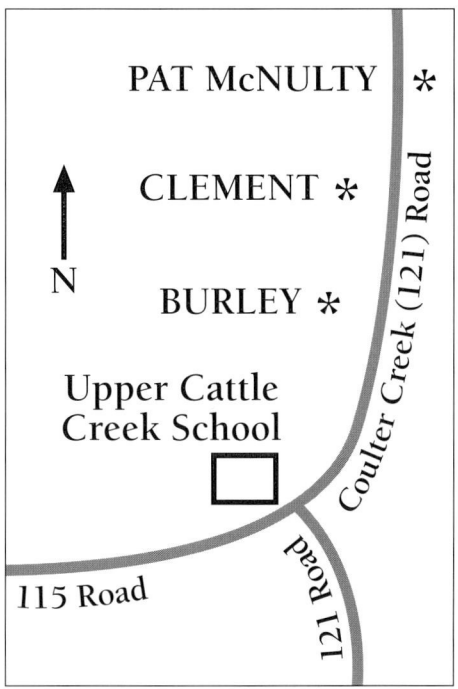

Left to right: Nellie, Susan, and Grace in 1914.

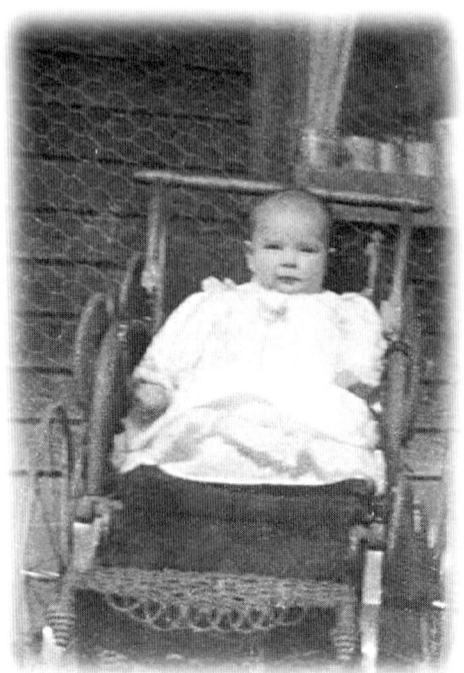

Harold Miller, 1914. *Viola Miller, 18 months old, 1924.*

Harold and Viola Miller at the Upper Cattle Creek School.

Left to right: unknown child, Clement, Susan and Burley, with a 1922 Starr automobile.

Glenwood Springs. I can remember when we used to crate eggs and sold them to the J.S. Woody store in Glenwood. He would give us credit toward our grocery bill. We also sold cream at the creamery on Cooper Street.

"My mother baked all the time and I remember how good everything tasted. My brother, Harold, took care of me, and I followed him everywhere. Sometimes he tried to lose me!

"All of us kids went to Upper Cattle Creek School, and my father was always a member of the School Board. My parents came to all of our programs and meetings.

"One of our neighbors was Bob Leyerley, and he was real hard of hearing. You had to really yell loud at him. He also talked to himself a lot. I remember one time, I was out near the house and saw him riding by on his horse. My mother's wash was hanging on the line and I heard Bob talking to himself, 'That woman wears out Clement's clothes washing them!'

"We had many school parties and dances. Sometimes we went over to the Missouri Heights School for dances. We would always go somewhere on Saturday nights, either to a dance or to a neighbors to a party.

"My mother died when I was thirteen years old and it hurt me terribly. I was just about ready to graduate eighth grade from Upper Cattle Creek School, but I didn't attend the graduation exercises. I ended up taking an exam in Glenwood Springs to get my diploma. Mrs. Alma Harris was the county supervisor, and she gave me the exam. I remember how sympathetic and kind she was.

"My father had me board with friends in Glenwood Springs to go to high school. My father was a good man, very gentle and kind. I can remember if I got out of line, all he had to do was say, 'Viola,' in a certain tone, and I shaped right up. I don't remember him ever spanking me. He was a hard worker, very strong and muscular. My mother was a very quiet, loving person.

Bob Leyerely.

"Burley, my father's brother, married Lottie and they had two children, Roy and Ila Mae. After we were grown, my father sold out to John Heuschkel, and moved to Glenwood. Burley sold out to Mary McNulty Squires, and moved to Carbondale. My people are all buried in the Rosebud Cemetery in Glenwood Springs."

History of the Land Owners
A.L. Coulter homesteaded the land in the 1800s

Miller brothers Ery, Clement, Burley..............1902.....................166.23 acres
*   Burley to Clement Miller...........................1923..*
*   Clement Miller additions..........................1931..........................320 acres*
*   1932..........................160 acres*
*   Clement Miller additions...*
Clement Miller to John Heuschkel.................1949.......................1500 acres
Burley Miller to Mary McNulty Squires..........1949..........................240 acres
John Heuschkel to Virgil & Joyce Gould.........1961................lower 540 acres
Mary McNulty Squires to Harley Squires.......1958..........................240 acres
Harley Squires to James & Hensley Peterson..1972..........................240 acres

The Clement Miller home in 1998.
County Road 121 (or Coulter Creek Road).

The Burley Miller home in 1998.
County Road 121 (or Coulter Creek Road).

THE CURTIS FAMILY – 1889

JAMES WILLIAM CURTIS
1842 - UNKNOWN

ELIZABETH "LIZZIE" ANNE (MCCANSLAND) CURTIS
1846 - 1941

THE CURTIS FAMILY

James William left his homeland, Nova Scotia, and came to the United States on a ship, first working as a cabin boy, and then learning cabinet making and scroll work while en route. Scroll work was a tedious art whereby fancy designs were cut into wood with a scroll saw. James had three brothers who were all medical doctors, and one sister named Beth. It is believed they all came to the U.S. around 1860.

Elizabeth Anne was born and raised in Maine, where it is believed she and James met and married. James traveled to Leadville in 1879, in search of gold and silver. In 1880, Elizabeth Anne "Lizzie" joined him in Leadville, where she taught school.

James traveled over Independence Pass and stopped at a small lake seven miles from Aspen, where he started placer mining. He built a one room cabin and returned to Leadville for his family. There, he bought several burros and an Indian pony to make the trip back to the cabin.

Grandma McCansland, Elizabeth's mother, had brought the children out from Maine to their parents. There were Rex, Hattie, Alice, and a young girl that Elizabeth had adopted in Maine.

To make the trip, James tied two children, each in a gunny sack, on each side of a burro. Alice cried bitterly as she was put in the gunny sack and begged to walk with her grandmother. She was only four and a half years old, and she and grandmother walked the whole way. Elizabeth Anne rode the Indian pony side saddle, and carried a baby in her arms, with tiny Rex strapped behind the saddle. At one point the pony stepped

Grandma McCansland.

The Curtis family's Crystal Springs home in the early 1900s.

in a hole and Elizabeth Anne jumped off, broke the straps which held her son, and kept him from being stomped by the flailing pony.

At the new homesite they built a much larger dwelling and opened a way station where travelers were fed and lodged, and animals could be cared for. Elizabeth Anne and her mother cooked on two sheet iron stoves for the travelers – sometimes as many as fifty at a time. Elizabeth Anne baked her own bread, cooked for the crowd, tended her children, and taught them as if they were in school.

Elizabeth Anne and James had a baby girl in 1883, who lived only two years. After that, another daughter, Judith Ann, was born.

Around 1895, Elizabeth Anne's health declined and they closed the way station and moved to Aspen. In Aspen, James went back to his early training and helped build the Jerome Hotel, his contributions being cabinet making and scroll work which can still be seen and admired today in 1998.

Later, they moved on down valley and eventually lived on the high mesa on Crystal Springs, right on the edge of what would become Missouri Heights. The Curtis Ranch was located up 103 Road, north of Highway 82, about two and a half miles, on the right.

Lizzie was somewhat of a medicine woman and midwife. People came to her for care. She helped people live through the flu and smallpox and other ailments; James William made coffins, and if Lizzie couldn't cure them, he buried them.

James and Elizabeth Anne were an extraordinary couple who not only raised their own children, but adopted and raised four orphans. Even so, Elizabeth Anne was active in the community, and took a keen interest in politics.

Lizzie was the first school teacher at the Crystal Springs School in 1889 or 1900; before that she had taught students in her home on the Crystal Springs ranch. She had received her degree at Colby University in Watterville, Maine.

When James died, he was buried beneath the lilacs of his beloved mountain home. Elizabeth Anne moved to California with her son, Rex, and daughter, Hattie, and lived to be ninety-five years of age.

Some of the Curtis history was taken from Edna Sweet's book <u>Carbondale Pioneers</u>, ©1947.

Lilacs and Mount Sopris on Crystal Springs. Photo by Ron Martin.

CERTIFICATE OF CITIZENSHIP

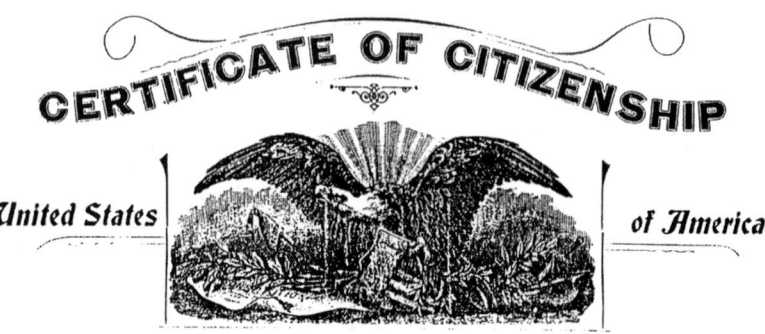

United States   **of America**

STATE OF COLORADO, } ss.   In the County Court,
County of Garfield   June Term, 1906.

BE IT REMEMBERED, That on the 29th day of August, in the year of our Lord One Thousand Nine Hundred and Six, personally appeared before the Hon. A. L. Beardsley, Judge of the County Court of the County of Garfield and State aforesaid (the same being a Court of Record, having and exercising common law jurisdiction, a Seal and a Clerk), sitting judicially for the dispatch of business at the Court House in Glenwood Springs, in the County aforesaid, JAMES W. CURTIS, an alien, of lawful age, and applied to the said Court to be admitted to become a Naturalized Citizen of the United States of America, pursuant to the directions of the Act of Congress of the United States, entitled "An Act to Establish an Uniform Rule of Naturalization, etc.," passed April 14, 1802, and the Acts subsequently passed on that subject, and to the directions of the Act of Congress entitled "An Act to Regulate the Immigration of Aliens into the United States," approved March 3, 1903. And the said alien having thereupon produced to the Court record testimony showing that he has heretofore reported himself, and filed his declaration of his intention to become a Citizen of the United States, according to the provisions of the said several Acts of Congress, and the Court being satisfied, as well from the oath of the said alien as from the affidavit of Charles M. White and William Cardnell that the said alien has resided within the limits and under the jurisdiction of the United States for at least five years last past, and at least one year last past within the State of Colorado, and that during the whole of that time he has behaved himself as a man of good moral character, attached to the principles contained in the Constitution of the United States, and well disposed to the good order and happiness of the same; and two years and upward having elapsed since the said alien reported himself and filed his declaration of his intention aforesaid, and the Court being further satisfied from the affidavits of said alien and his said witnesses, that he does not disbelieve in and is not opposed to all organized government, and is not a member of or affiliated with any organization entertaining and teaching such disbelief in or opposition to all organized government, or who advocates or teaches the duty, necessity or propriety of the unlawful assaulting or killing of any officer or officers, either of specific individuals or of officers generally, of the Government of the United States, or of any other organized government, because of his or their official character; that he has not knowingly aided or assisted or connived or conspired with any person or persons to allow, procure or permit any alien who is an idiot, an insane person, or one who has been declared insane by any lawful authority within five years previous to his arrival, or one who has epilepsy, or one who is a pauper, or one who is likely to become a public charge or a professional beggar, to enter the United States, or any territory subject to the jurisdiction thereof; that he has not landed or permitted to be landed any alien at any other time or place than that designated by the Immigration officers of the United States; that he has not by himself or another, brought, landed, or imported, or attempted to bring, land or import into the United States any alien who is afflicted with a loathsome or dangerous contagious disease, or one who has been convicted of a felony or other crime or misdemeanor involving moral turpitude, or one who is a polygamist, or any woman or girl for the purposes of prostitution; that he has not held or attempted to hold any woman or girl for the purposes of prostitution in pursuance of such illegal importation; that he has not aided or abetted the importation of any person or persons in violation of the terms of the Contract Labor Laws of the United States; and that he has not violated any provision of an Act of Congress, entitled "An Act to regulate the immigration of aliens into the United States," approved March 3, 1903; and the said affidavits reciting and affirming the truth of every material fact requisite for naturalization, having been recorded, and he having now here in open Court taken and subscribed the oath required by law to support the Constitution of the United States, and to renounce and abjure all allegiance and fidelity to every foreign Prince, Potentate, State or Sovereignty whatever, and particularly all allegiance which he may in anywise owe to Edward VII, King of Great Britain, whereof he was heretofore a subject;

IT IS THEREUPON CONSIDERED, ORDERED AND ADJUDGED BY THE COURT, That the said JAMES W. CURTIS be admitted to all and singular the rights, privileges and immunities of a naturalized Citizen of the United States, and that the same be certified by the Clerk of this Court, under the seal of said Court accordingly.

By order of the Court.

IN TESTIMONY WHEREOF, The seal of the said Court is hereunto affixed this 29th day of August, One Thousand Nine Hundred and Six, in the 129th year of our Independence.

(Seal)   A. L. Beardsley, Clerk.

By Judge and Acting Clerk Deputy.

Lizzie and her daughter, Judith Ann, became well known for their medical knowledge. Although neither received formal medical education, they both acted as doctor, nurse and midwife when medical attention was needed in the community. The following letter, written by Dr. Charles Courtney Curtis (a brother of James William), is an example of some of the knowledge acquired by Lizzie and eventually handed down to Judith Ann:

Los Angeles, Calif.
April 21, 1906

Dear Sister Lizzie,

Your letter of the 16th just now received.

In almost every case of erysipelas give Belladonna three grain and Arsenicum three grain in alternation and dissolve an ounce of Sulphate of Soda in one pint of hot water. Dip cotton cloths in this and apply them to the parts afflicted. Change them often. Baptisia and Rhustox three grain are other remedies to be thought of.

In cases of pregnancy, give Caulophyllin second in alternation with Cimicifriga three grain once in four hours, commencing two weeks before labor is expected. Olive oil is good to apply to the abdomen and the bowels should always be kept in healthy condition. The most certain remedy is to have the old man sleep in the barn. I was pleased to receive William's letter a few days ago, but it made me feel very gloomy to think he did not feel like taking his chances for eternity in this golden state of flowers and sunshine. Of course, he might live in some canyon and become a nature man by digging out a hole in the ground and spending his nights there, or he might live in San Diego and put himself in Sophie's care. She'd see to it that he attended church often and went to prayer meetings once or twice a week. If he will do this, I think he can come with a reasonable assurance of safety. You see, he is so liable to stray away, and as an additional precaution, you might keep a string tied to him.

Since you are determined to take the risk of coming here, what is the date that we may look for you? We all are practically well now and are doing very satisfactory. I had a very pleasant call from Judith and Miss Foster while in San Diego. Tell William this letter is for him as well as yourself. The earthquake and fire at San Francisco has almost wiped out the city. The conditions are horrifying. Much love from each of us to you all.

Your brother,
C.C.C.

Los Angeles,
Cal,
April 21, 1906

Dear Sister Lizzie,
 Your letter of the 16th just now received. In almost every case of Erysipelas give Belladonna 3x and Arsenicum 3x in alternation and disolve an ounce of Sulphate of Soda in one pint of hot water. Dip cotton cloths in this and apply them to the parts afflicted. Change them often. Baptisia and Rhus tox 3x are other remedies to be thought of. In cases of pregnancy give Caulophyllin 2nd in alternation with Cimicifuga 3x once in 4 hours, commencing two weeks before labor is expected. Olive oil is good to apply to the abdomen and the bowels should always be kept in a healthy condition. The most certain remedy is to have the old man sleep in the barn. E

I was pleased to receive Wm's letter a few days ago, but it made me feel very gloomy to think

he did not feel like taking his chances for eternity in this golden state of flowers and sunshine. Of course he might live in some kanyon and become a nature man by diging out a hole in the ground and spending his nights there or he might go to live in San Diego and put himself in Sophias care. She see to it that he attended church often and went to prayer meeting once or twice a week. If he will do this I think he can come with a reasonable assurance of safety. You see he is so liable to stray away, and as an additional precaution you might keep a string tied to him. Since you are determined to take the risk of coming here what is the date that we may look for you? We all are practically well now and are doing very satisfactory. I had a very pleasant call from Judith and Miss Foster while in San Diego. Tell Wm this letter is for him as well as yourself. The earth quake and fire at San Francisco has almost wiped out the city. The conditions are horofying. much love from each of us to you all.
Your brother C. C. R.

THE WILLIAM CALLICOTTE FAMILY

William Riley Callicotte
1847 - 1921

Duley Ann (Akin) Callicotte
Unknown - 1925

William Riley walked from his home in Clarinda, Iowa, to Leadville, Colorado, in the late 1800s. He walked beside a family in a covered wagon, and he kept a diary of his trip which is still intact and owned by his granddaughter, Lucille (Maxfield) Bogue, in 1998.

William Riley went to Leadville to inquire about a teaching position at the local school. After looking over the situation, he accepted the job, and sent for his family. The students, especially the older boys, were quite difficult.

Virginia (Callicotte) Cordill, William's granddaughter, remembers, "My grandfather heard about the problems with the big, older boys. They had held one of the teachers out of a window and broken both his legs. So, he [William] took a six-foot stove poker with him on the first day of classes. He walked in, laid it ceremoniously on his desk, and faced the class looking directly from one trouble maker to the next and said, 'I hope I won't need to use this!' The boys gave him no trouble. To this day, I have his former students tell me, 'If not for your grandfather, I would never have straightened my life out and made something of myself!' That makes me feel very proud."

On weekends, William worked as a surveyor of mining claims in Leadville. His granddaughter, Lucille, remembers this story. "One night a lynching party came to his house, all set to hang him. One of his school boys had been in a fight, got beaten up by another student, and instead of telling the truth, told his father that Professor Callicotte had beaten him. The boy's father was a rough miner, and he was out for revenge. As luck would have it, William Riley was not at home, and when things cooled down, the boy told the truth, but it was a close call!"

The Callicotte family later moved to Aspen and William Riley started a fish hatchery. He took office as Fish Commissioner and Game Warden on April 5, 1893. Commissioner Callicotte spoke to Governor Waite about the problems he found when taking over the office. "The difficulties with which I undertake this work seem insurmountable. There are but few fish stock (fish of sufficient age and size to produce eggs), there were no previous reports giving data with regard to difficulties to be overcome at the various locations of hatcheries. These had to be learned by experience. With civilization came the sportsman, the market fisher, the fish hog, the dynamiter, the sawmill, the placer, the irrigation ditch – all sources of destruction to fish. These have done their deadly work, until many of our streams have not a fish left to tell the story." Mr. Callicotte recommended that no fishing be allowed before July 1, and the fishing season should close November 1. He was the commissioner until 1896. William later became a lobbyist, and once ran for the U.S. Senate.

Lucille remembers, "My grandfather had high hopes of 'cleaning things up' in government. I was nine years old when he ran for the Senate on the Independent ticket. He didn't win, but even at that age I was impressed with his high ideals. He was truly a great, noble man."

William and Duley Ann had five children: True, Pearl, Maude, Jessie, and Ellen. William had several brothers, two of whom were engineers on the Colorado railroads, which entitled William's family to free passage, allowing them to travel more easily between Aspen and Denver, where they lived and spent time.

William started the State Humane Society for Children and Animals, and taught related classes at the Teacher's College in Greeley, Colorado, commuting between Denver and Greeley in his Model A Ford.

The exact year is not known, but William filed for land on Crystal Springs, 500 acres near the high mesa which would later be called Missouri Heights. He helped survey for the Spring Park Reservoir in hopes of encouraging the surrounding farmers to unite in the effort toward building a reservoir. The venture did not materialize, and later, in 1912, Harleigh Holmes created the Carbondale Irrigation and Reservoir Company.

Virginia (Callicotte) Cordill: "My grandfather died saving someone's life. He was in Denver, at the capitol building, and ironically enough, the president of Greeley College had parked his car on Capitol Boulevard, and didn't put on the hand brake. The car started to roll and pick up speed, headed right for a group of people on the sidewalk. My grandfather ran to push a girl out of the way, and was hit. He was killed when the car ran over him."

THE JESSE CALLICOTTE FAMILY

Jesse Callicotte
1887 - 1967

Judith Ann (Curtis) Callicotte
1887 - 1971

Jesse and Judith Ann were both born at the Curtis Way Station, seven miles above Aspen. They did not know each other until much later in life. Jesse's father, William Riley Callicotte, was an educator and entrepreneur in Denver, and the family lived in both Denver and Aspen. Judith Ann grew up in Aspen, but was sent to high school and college in California, where she received a teaching degree.

When she came back to Colorado, she followed her mother, Lizzie's, footsteps and taught school at the Crystal Springs School. She met Jesse Callicotte, and they fell in love. They were married in 1912. Jesse rode a horse to Glenwood Springs to pick up his wedding suit.

He had built a log cabin and piped in running water on his father's land on the mesa between Cattle Creek and Crystal Springs, next to what would later be called Missouri Heights. The young couple moved in, and they were the first of the family to actually work the land. Jesse homesteaded three other parcels of land, eventually owning 600 acres. At one point, they lived in Carbondale for awhile, and Jesse ran a mail route.

Judith Ann also learned medicine and healing from her mother, Lizzie. People came to her often for medical help.

Their children were: Ralph, Steve, Dale, Virginia, and Dee. In 1918, the family left Colorado and moved to California to get away from the 1918 Spanish flu epidemic. Steve Callicotte remembers, "When the flu scare was over, we drove back to Colorado in a Model T Ford. I was only five or six, and we ate prickly pear cactus fruit coming back. I can remember that ride so clear – like it was yesterday."

Virginia (Callicotte) Cordill: "All of us kids went to the Crystal Springs School. It sat right where my driveway is in 1998, and meets the road [County Road 103] about one and three-quarter miles up from Highway 82. By the time I went there, mother had stopped teaching and my teachers were: Miss Weller, my favorite; Addie Atley, and my aunt Maude (Callicotte) Maxfield. Aunt Maude was my father's sister. All of us kids but Dee graduated eighth grade from Crystal Springs School.

"One time I was all set to throw a snowball at a boy, when the teacher called us inside, so I just took the snowball with me, hoping I'd have a chance while the teacher wasn't looking. Well, I didn't get the chance. The snowball melted and I was embarrassed because it looked like I'd had an accident.

"We used to play Tarzan and swing from the piñon trees. They weren't great swinging trees, and one day my cousin fell and busted his head. Someone took him to Dr. Tubbs down in Carbondale, and he had twenty-nine stitches. When Mom heard, that was the last of our Tarzan games.

"My sister, Dale, and I delivered our little sister, Dee. Dr. Tubbs didn't make it on time, so my Mom very calmly told us what to do. I can still hear her saying, 'Now this is what will happen next, and this is what to do.' We did as we were told, and pretty soon we had a new baby sister named Dee.

The Callicotte family with friends and relatives, left to right, back row: Herman Huntington, Gladys H. Reed, Alice Huntington, Ralph Huntington, Willard Reed, Jesse Callicotte, James William Curtis. Center row: Maxine Huntington, Dale Callicotte, Jean Huntington, Ralph Call, Lizzie Curtis. Front row: Virginia Callicotte, Willadear Reed, Merly Reed, Steve Callicotte.

"In 1931, my brother, Ralph, and I contracted polio. Mama treated us, and I remember how bad we hurt. Mama dipped sheets in boiling water and wrapped them around us. It relieved the pain. Mama didn't know it then, but she learned later that the same treatment was given in hospitals.

"My parents were very musical and we had a song-fest almost every night. My mother played piano and Dad played the accordion. Kids don't know what they're missing today. We had so much fun! My brother, Steve, became a musician, too. One time he won the first place trophy for playing the tuba in the band contest at Provo, Utah."

Jesse lost some of the land when it went into foreclosure, but in 1926 Judith Ann inherited 240 acres nearby, from her mother, Lizzie Curtis. Steve worked the land and raised hay, grain, and potatoes. He also had a small herd of cattle. His brand was ⌸ (Double Three-Quarter Box).

Later, in 1968, Steve became a water commissioner, and held that position until 1988. He was in charge of District 38, which included all of Missouri Heights and everything on the Roaring Fork drainage from Glenwood Springs to Independence Pass.

Steve says, "It [The District] had more ditches in it than any other district in the state! It was my job to divide up water, keep everyone happy, and stay alive to accomplish it."

Steve also found time to be a musician, and played guitar and piano in a group called "The Sopris Six." The members of the group were: Henry Schucher, coronet; Rose Creton, accordion; Butch Druy, drums; Walt Lawrence, banjo; Howard Wolf, saxophone; Steve Callicotte, guitar and piano. Steve recalls, "The group played on weekends for dances and parties anywhere they would have us. We played at schools, the Elks and the Oddfellows, hotels, barbeques, and wherever. Many Missouri Heights residents danced the night away to the music of the Sopris Six."

THE THOMAS McNULTY FAMILY - 1890

Thomas McNulty
1860 - 1932

Mary (Judge) McNulty
1864 - 1929

THE THOMAS McNULTY FAMILY

Thomas and Mary McNulty were potato farmers in County Mayo, Ireland. They left Ireland in the late 1800s after the potato famine, and immigrated to the United States to make a better life. They first settled in Leadville, where Thomas was a miner. Later, they moved to Aspen, where Mary worked as a secretary to an attorney. Eventually, they moved on down to the Roaring Fork Valley, and homesteaded land up on Cattle Creek, near what would one day be called Missouri Heights. They raised potatoes, alfalfa, hay, oats, barley and livestock. Their cattle brand was MC-N. They also owned a ranch between Carbondale and Glenwood Springs called the Red Canyon Creek Ranch.

Thomas and Mary's children were James "Jim," Tom, John Anthony, Margaret, and Anna Harriet. Tom was an engineer on the Midland Railroad. He married Elizabeth Shay. Margaret became a school teacher and taught in several schools on the Western Slope of Colorado, including Emma and Canyon Creek. Anna Harriet found her way to Chicago where she worked as a chef and governess for wealthy families. Anna also did charity work for the Trinity Baptist Church and School in Chicago, volunteering time and aid to the less fortunate. Anna was very frugal, saved her money, and when she came back to Colorado, she acquired several parcels of land on Missouri Heights, Cottonwood Pass, and in Glenwood Springs. John Anthony and Jim were farmers, and lived their lives on the Cattle Creek property.

Mary died at 65 years of age at the McNulty Red Canyon Creek Ranch between Carbondale and Glenwood Springs, on what is Highway 82 today in 1998. She was helping feed cattle in the winter, slipped from the wagon, and fell onto a pitchfork.

Thomas and Mary lived on the land until their deaths. They are buried in Rosebud Cemetery in Glenwood Springs.

Photograph taken at Mary McNulty's funeral in 1929.

Left to right, back row: Al Donegan (married to Margaret), Mrs. Shay (Elizabeth's mother), Elizabeth (married to Tom), Anna, John Anthony, Thelma (married to Jim).

Left to right, second row: Little Margaret (Margaret's daughter), Tom (married to Elizabeth), Thomas (father), Jim.

Left to right, children in front row: Steven (Margaret and Al's son), Joanna (Thomas and Elizabeth's daughter), Anna Mae (Margaret and Al's daughter).

History of the Land Owners

Thomas and Mary McNulty homesteaded the land in the late 1800s

Jim and Thelma McNulty	1932
Jim and Louise McNulty	1962
Harold Fender	1963
Trudy Pete	1998

John McNulty
1901 - 1993

When you invited John to dinner, you never knew just what you'd get
'Cause he seldom came all by himself, he usually brought a pet.

He drove his 'ol white pick-up truck with Sweet William in the back
A big, white billy goat he was with his saddle all intact.

His horns were big, thick handlebars with bells tied at the tips,
And on the saddle was a scabbard; he was decked out for all his trips.

Or it might be Baby Beaver,
Who John had saved and called his own,
He chewed through walls and dammed doorways
In John's dilapidated home.

He had a big pet turkey, Ayatollah Khomeini was his name
He rode with John in the pick-up truck and he was beautiful and tame.

His dog, named Mike, would climb a tree,
John would laugh and shake his head.
And he had an old black Angus bull
That would lie down and play dead.

There were geese that walked all in a row
And they did whatever John said,
A trout named Henrietta, who would swim right up for bread.

How he loved to entertain his friends,
He'd laugh and his eyes would shine
As his pets went through their antics, he was truly in his prime.

He lived life to its fullest, joked and laughed right to the end.
I was lucky to have known him, John McNulty, my old friend.

– Written by A.W.

THE JOHN McNULTY FAMILY

John Anthony McNulty
1901 - 1993

Mary (Johnston) McNulty
1910 -

THE JOHN McNULTY FAMILY

Mary's parents were Frank and Cora Eda (Wyers) Johnston. Frank was from Cheyenne, Wyoming, and Cora Eda from Fort Collins, Colorado. Frank and Cora Eda lived on Missouri Heights for a couple years, including 1914, when Mary was four years old. Their place was southeast of the Missouri Heights Schoolhouse. They found the winters to be too cold, and moved to Rifle.

John's parents were Thomas and Mary (Judge) McNulty, from Ireland. John was raised on Thomas and Mary's farm on Cattle Creek. John loved life, and was a great source of fun for his friends and neighbors. He was always up to some prank like putting horse harnesses on a neighbor's milk cows, placing an entire spring wagon on the roof of the Upper Cattle Creek Schoolhouse, instigating parties and dances and get-togethers. The people of Cattle Creek and Missouri Heights loved him, and speak of him with great joy.

Frank and Cora Eda Johnston

No one loved John more than the children. Peggy (Heuschkel) Sholes was raised on Cattle Creek and remembers, "John went to town every Saturday night to a dance or a movie or something. Us kids all knew that every Sunday morning we would find candy bars or Cracker Jacks left in the mailbox for us. That was John!"

John and Mary met through Willis and Eunice (Johnston) Kissee (Mary's sister), who lived on the McNulty ranch, where Willis worked as a hired hand. Mary came to visit, met John, and they became sweethearts.

John McNulty in his 1930 Model A Ford Standard Phaeton.

They married in 1935 in Fairplay, Colorado. Mary's older sister, Alice, lived in Fairplay, where her husband worked in the mine. Alice stood up with the couple to be married. A year later, they were married again in the Catholic Church in Glenwood Springs to satisfy John's Irish family. John and Mary's two children were Gary Keith and Elana Coreen.

John bought the 640-acre Frank Heuschkel homestead from Will Heuschkel in 1940 and 1942. There they raised hay, oats, barley, and potatoes. John also had Hereford cattle. His brand was ⌣8 (Quarter-Circle-Eight). There was a natural gravel pit on the land which he and his son, Gary, developed into a business. Scorio-pumice rock was sold throughout the area for constructing roads and driveways, among other things. Mary and John divorced in 1958, and John and Gary continued working the ranch and gravel pit for many years.

Elana and Gary McNulty.

Anita Witt: "I was a neighbor of John's for years; John was most certainly the epitome of a real character. It's absolutely true that his dog, Mike (a female), climbed a tree. John strategically nailed boards up the tree's trunk to give her footholds, and then taught her to climb. John retrieved discarded pop cans along the road on his horse. Mike went with him, picking up

John with his female dog, Mike, retrieving pop cans.

the pop cans in her mouth, standing on her hind legs, leaning against the horse and handing the cans to John. It's also true that the geese walked in a line, sometimes in the 4th of July parade in Aspen, and sometimes up a plank to the back of John's flatbed truck, where kernels of corn awaited them. The trout, named Henrietta, did come when it was called; and the beaver, "Baby Beaver," ate through walls and dammed up doorways with shoes, papers, rags, cans, and anything else it could find laying around the old farm house. Baby Beaver often came to my house on Missouri Heights with John, Gary, and Elana for dinner.

"I remember one Thanksgiving Day when John and Gary brought Baby Beaver. They also brought a child's play pen for him to

Left: Baby Beaver with John. Right: Don Witt, Baby Beaver, John and Gary McNulty.

sit in while we enjoyed dinner. Baby Beaver happily chewed on willow branches and watched us.

"Sweet William, the goat, was a sight to behold, decked out in his kid's saddle, bells on his horns, a scabbard, ski goggles, and sometimes a bright scarf around his neck. One time Sweet William got sick and had to stay in a stall at Dr. Dewell's Veterinary Clinic on Highway 82. We all tacked up get well cards on the walls, and John was so pleased.

"The turkey, Ayatollah Khomeini, was quite beautiful especially when he fanned his feathers and strutted his stuff. He often rode in the old white pick-up, on the passenger's side, beside John.

The goat, Sweet William, and John McNulty.

"Many people will smile and remember sitting in the main room of John's old dilapidated farm house and being told to cover their eyes with their hands, while John hurried out the door. He was after a surprise, and he nearly shook with anticipation, as his guests waited, full-grown adults with their hands covering their eyes like little children. In a few minutes, the floor would begin to shake under their feet, and the room filled with a distinct odor quite familiar to farm people. When at last they were allowed to look, there stood the big Hereford bull, Señor Francisco Franco, Jr., looking around the room with big eyes, and John rocking on his heels with pride and excitement. It really happened!

"I saw John often, until his death in 1993. Laura Van Dyne and I went to the nursing home in Fruita, Colorado, where he spent his last years. He was so happy to see us, and wanted to hear all the news about the Heights. He was quite a jokester right to the end. He'd carry his aluminum walker up off the floor with one hand to make the nurses laugh, and he still wanted to party! If I had not brought my guitar he would ask me to play the piano. I'd say, 'Well... I don't really play the piano...' and he'd answer, 'Just plunk on it, it won't matter.' When we finally had to leave, he would watch us from the window until we were out of sight."

Gary worked the land with John for many years. Today, in 1998, Elana McNulty carries on the McNulty ranching tradition. Elana and Mary McNulty (who is 88 years old in 1998) still own 400 acres of the original ranch now known as The Pleasant Valley Ranch.

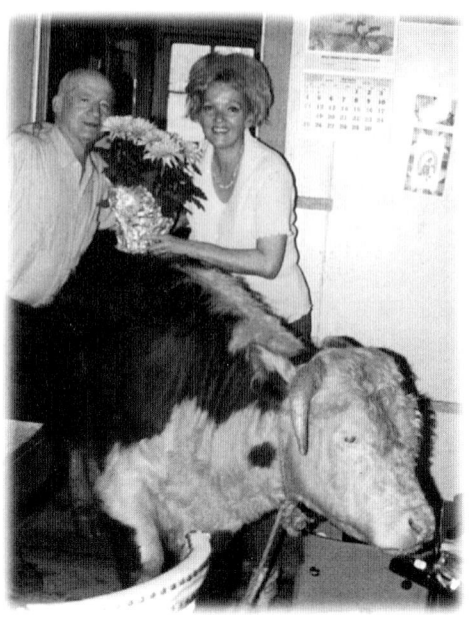

Señor Francisco Franco, Jr. with John McNulty and Anita Witt in John's farm house.

Gary McNulty.

History of the Land Owners

William Chapman homesteaded 320 of the original acres in the 1880s.

Frank and Josepha Heuschkel homesteaded 320 of the original acres in 1884.

Will Heuschkel acquired the combined homesteads in 1922 for a total of 640 acres.

John McNulty acquired the 640 acres in two equal portions, 320 acres in 1940, and the remaining 320 acres in 1942. He also homesteaded additional land, ultimately owning nearly 2,000 acres.

Gary and Sara Lillian (Wendy) McNulty ....1973......542 acres

*Elana McNulty..1998.....400 acres
Pleasant Valley Ranch*

Obituaries
John Anthony McNulty

Mass will be held for John Anthony McNulty of Fruita at 11 a.m. this Friday, June 25, at St. Stephen's Catholic Church in Glenwood Springs. The Reverend John Brady will officiate.

Mr. McNulty died Monday, June 21, 1993, at Family Health West in Fruita. He was 91.

He was born November 19, 1901, in Cattle Creek to Tom and Mary McNulty, who immigrated to American in the 1800s from Ireland. He attended school in Cattle Creek.

Mr. McNulty ranched what is now known as Pleasant Valley Ranch, which was Ute Indian territory when he was born.

He married Mary G. Johnston in 1935 in Fairplay, Colorado. They later divorced.

Mr. McNulty belonged to the Knights of Columbus, and loved riding horses and fishing, and in his younger years rode in rodeos.

He was preceded in death by two brothers, Tom and Jim McNulty, and two sisters, Anna McNulty and Margaret Donegan.

Survivors include a son, Gary McNulty of Missouri Heights; a daughter, Elana C. McNulty of Battlement Mesa; and two grandchildren.

Martin Mortuary in Grand Junction is in charge of arrangements.

THE THOMAS McNULTY FAMILY

Thomas McNulty
1860 - 1932

Mary (Judge) McNulty
1864 - 1929

Children
Jim, Tom, John Anthony, Margaret, and Anna.

Jim
Thelma LaForce } Louise, James → James, Mary } Mark, Shelia

Tom
Elizabeth Shay } Joanna, Cecila

John Anthony
Mary Johnston } Gary Keith, Elana Coreen → Gary Keith, Sarah "Wendy" } Katie, Megan

Margaret
Al Donegan } Anna Mae, Margaret, Sharon

Anna

THE PAT McNULTY FAMILY
1890

PATRICK McNULTY
1862 - 1924

MARGARET McNULTY
1864 - 1938

Pat and Margaret came from Ireland to the United States in the late 1800s. They were not related to the Thomas and Mary McNulty family which also hailed from Ireland.

The wedding day of Charles and Josephine Coryell.

Josephine with young Pat (baby unknown).

Pat and Margaret homesteaded 255 acres on Cottonwood Pass, on Cattle Creek. Their children were: Catherine Esther, Martin, Mary, and Josephine. Catherine and Mary both became school teachers, and Mary taught at the Upper Cattle Creek School.

All four children homesteaded additional land near their parents, living alone for seven months as required by the Federal Homesteading Regulations. Mary was quoted as saying, "That's why we were able to homestead the land, because it was nearby. It wasn't far to go for anything we needed."

Mary taught school in the area, and in 1936, when she was fifty years old, met Harley Squires, who was twenty-five. Two years later, they were married and bought a ranch near the old McNulty homestead, which was the old Burley Miller place.

Josephine married Charles Coryell, and they adopted a son, Pat. Pat lived part time at the old homestead with his grandmother, Margaret, and attended Upper Cattle Creek School. Pat worked the ranch with his uncle, Martin, for several years, and in 1948 he bought the old Ralston place, which adjoined the McNulty homestead. In 1972, James Peterson bought both properties, about 700 acres, and still owns them today in 1998.

It is mentioned in the Dr. Oscar Clagett history that he bought his land, 360 acres, from Pat and Margaret McNulty, who had homesteaded the land and built a rough cabin, which the Clagetts lived in until their new home was built in 1914.

It is also mentioned in the Frank and Blanch Smith history that the Clagetts were invited to Christmas dinner at the Pat and Margaret McNulty home in 1914, and that Martin McNulty (son of Pat and Margaret) gave the Clagett children the horse named George Pokey Legs, which they all rode together to Catherine School.

Left to right: Charles Coryell and dog, Catherine, and Mary.

Rosary Service for C.E. McNulty Will be Friday

A rosary service for Catherine Esther McNulty will be held at the Farnum chapel Friday evening, August 16, at eight o'clock.

She was killed in an auto accident six miles south of Glenwood Springs Wednesday night, August 14, 1957, at 7:40 p.m.

Funeral services will be held at St. Stephen's Catholic church at 9 a.m. The Reverend C. E. Kessler will officiate, and burial will be in the Rosebud cemetery in Glenwood Springs. Farnum Mortuary is making the arrangements.

Miss McNulty was born May 23, 1897 at Cattle Creek, and spent her lifetime farming in that area. She was a graduate of Garfield County High School, and the University of Colorado at Boulder. She taught chemistry in Glenwood Springs four years, in Del Norte five years, and in Alamogordo, New Mexico for a year.

Surviving are a brother, Martin McNulty, Carbondale; two sisters, Mrs. Mary Squires, Carbondale, and Mrs. Josephine Coryell, Glenwood Springs.

Her affiliations were with St. Stephen's Catholic Church, Catholic Daughters of America, Legion of Mary, and the Third Order of the Franciscans.

History of the McNulty Land

Pat and Margaret McNulty homesteaded the original 225 acres in the late 1800s.

Catherine McNulty	1940	225 acres
Mary (McNulty) Squires	1958	225 acres
Harley Squires	1984	225 acres
James and Hensley Peterson	1972	225 acres

History of the Ralston Land

The father of the Ralston family homesteaded the original 410 acres in the late 1800s.

Ira Ralston (son)	1905	410 acres
Catherine and Martin McNulty	1919	410 acres
Pat and Adeline Coryell	1948	410 acres
James and Hensley Peterson	1972	410 acres

The Pat and Margaret McNulty homestead cabins (above) and barn (right) in 1998.

The Ralston homestead, restored, in 1998.

Grandpa – everything is changing fast

They call it progress, but I don't know.

Grandpa – let's wander back into the past,

Paint me a picture of long ago.

GRANDPA (TELL ME 'BOUT THE GOOD OLD DAYS)
By: Jamie O'Hara

Copyright © 1985 Sony/ATV Tunes LLC.
All rights administered by Sony/ATV Music Publishing,
8 Music Square West, Nashville, TN 37203.
All Rights Reserved. Used by Permission.

THE JOHN W. McLEAN FAMILY
1894

JOHN WILLIAM McLEAN
1843 - 1913

MARY E. (MILLER) McLEAN
UNKNOWN - 1928

THE JOHN W. McLEAN FAMILY

John William McLean was born May 10, 1843, in Middlesex County, Ontario, Canada. His ancestors came from Scotland. In the middle 1800s his family settled in Halls Station, Missouri, where John William joined the Union Army in 1865. He enlisted as a musician in Company C, 51st Missouri Regiment. We know that he played the violin (a talent he passed on to his son, John Martin) but we do not know if he also played other instruments.

#1745 Ute Series. Elial U. Miller.

It is presumed that John met Mary E. Miller in Missouri. They were married February 5, 1867, in Rushville, Missouri. It is believed their four children, Uriah, Elial, Mary, and John Martin, were born in Missouri. In 1890 they moved to Colorado, lived in various places, until 1894 when they came to the Roaring Fork Valley to the high mesa which would one day be called Missouri Heights. Mary's brother Elial U. Miller had preceded them to Colorado and homesteaded land on the high mesa.

In 1895 Elial U. Miller sold the 160 acres to his sister Mary E. McLean for $1,000.00.

Eagle County, Colorado
Abstract of Title

Elial U. Miller

to

Mary E. (Miller) McLean

Book 45, Page 318, March 11, 1895
Warranty Deed
March 9 - 1895
Conveying W 1/2 of Sec. 11 tp 7
SR 87 W. 160 acres

John William and Mary bought and homesteaded more land adjoining the original 160 acres, as did their son, John Martin McLean. They bought a 160-acre ranch which had been homesteaded by A.P. Spaunkle. Their land holdings bordered the Hotz and McNulty ranches.

Agnes (McLean) Dye, John and Mary's granddaughter remembers, "When Grandma [Mary] died in 1928 they put her body in the kitchen of my parents' home on the ranch. They wouldn't let us kids go in there, but she was there two or three days, and then our neighbor, John McNulty, came and got her in a wagon and took her to the Basalt Sairview Cemetery."

In 1911 Harleigh Holmes bought 90.3 acres of the McLean property to build the Carbondale Reservoir and Irrigation Company.

John William died in 1913. Mary died in 1928. They are both buried in the Basalt Sairview Cemetery.

John William and Mary's house on the original 160 acres. 1909.

Department of the Interior
GENERAL LAND OFFICE
4—121
Form approved by Comptroller of Treasury
January 9, 1913.

RECEIPT

No. 2409892

U. S. LAND OFFICE, Glenwood Springs, Colo. March 29, 1920
                                                    (Date.)
RECEIVED of   John M. McLean   Carbondale, Colorado
                (Name.)   (Address.)
EIGHT &--25/100 Dollars, in connection with
HOMESTEAD FINAL PROOF   UTE   SERIAL No. 09026
    (Kind of application and act under which made.)

Purchase money,		acres, at $	per acre.	
Purchase money, excess area.		acres, at $	per acre.	
Fees				
Commissions on	160	acres, at $ 1.25	per acre.	6 00
Testimony fees,	1000	words, at 22½	cents per 100 words.	2 25
Contest fees,		words, at	cents per 100 words.	
Transcripts of records,		words, at	cents per 100 words.	
Interest, $	from	to	at %.	
		(Inclusive)		
Surplus amount tendered				
plats	, at $	each		
			Total	8 25

H. Holmes, Receiver of Public Moneys.

This Receipt is evidence only of the receipt of the amount indicated, and must be issued at the time the money is received, without regard to the subsequent allowance or rejection of the application, entry, etc., due notice of which will be given.
In case of error in this Receipt, notify the Receiver of Public Moneys where issued, and the Commissioner of the General Land Office, Washington, D. C., in writing to the local land office or the General Land Office concerning the application or entry in connection with which this Receipt issued, always give the above Serial Number and the Receipt Number.

NOONAN AND NOONA, ATTY AT LAW, GLENWOOD SPRINGS,

Form 8—10M—1-29

Estate No.....................

Receipt **N⁰ 47553**

County Court of........EAGLE............County.

RECEIPT FOR INHERITANCE TAX
OFFICE OF THE TREASURER OF
THE STATE OF COLORADO

$ 10.00   Denver, Colo. AUGUST 7, 1929

Received of ......JOHN MCLEAN, ADM.,

of the estate of........MARY MCLEAN........, deceased,

........TEN AND NO/100........ Dollars

for Inheritance Tax and fees for examination and issuance of waiver, as itemized below, due to the State of Colorado from said estate, pursuant to an order of the Hon...A K ETHL........, Judge of the County Court of......EAGLE........County. Date of death of decedent...DEC 23, 1928.....

Value of property, gross..$ 6,000.00.....deductions....$ 830.00.....net..$ 5,170.00.....

Description of property:

E½ SW¼ OF SEC. 11, T 7 S R 87 WEST OF THE 6TH P.M. AND
W½ SW¼ OF SEC. 11, T 7 S R 87 WEST OF THE 6TH P.M. AND
NW¼ NW¼ AND LOTS 2 AND 4 OF SEC. 14, AND THE E½ NE¼ OF SEC.
15, T 7 S R 87 WEST, LESS AND EXCEPT THE FOLLOWING
PORTIONS,
38.34 ACRES THEREOF CONVEYED TO JOHN M MCLEAN BY A WARRANTY
DEED RECORDED AS DOCUMENT NO 32640, IN BLK 79, PAGE 566,
OF THE RECORDS OF EAGLE COUNTY, COLO., WITH PROPORTIONATE
ITCH AND WATER RIGHTS (MONARCH).
THAT PART OF THE 3 PARCEL OF LAND ABOVE DESCRIBED WHICH WAS
CONVEYED TO THE CRABONADLE IRRIGATION CO., CONTAINING
90.3 ACRES, $4 000 00

LOTS A AND B, IN BLK 10, TOWN OF MARBLE, GUNNISON COUNTY, COLO   200 00
THE FOLLOWING LODE MINING CLAIMS, PITKIN COUNTY, COLO.
THE DOUBLE DECKER, DOC. NO. 63040. THE GYPSON, DOC. NO 62041,
THE GROUND HOG, DOC. NO 62039,   THE MARY MCNUMBER 1, BOOK 100,
              AT PAGE 201,
THE MARY MCNUMBER 2, BOOK 100, PAGE 199,
THE MARY MCNUMBER 3, BOOK 100, PAGE 200,
THE SUN FLOWER, BOOK 107, PAGE 294,
THE MORNING GLORY, BOOK 107, PAGE 292.   EST. VALUE.   1 500 00
CASH AND MISC. PERONSAL PROPERTY   300 00
                                                                $6 000 00
Tax fixed by order of court - - - $
Interest - - - - - - - - - $
Fees, examination and waiver - - $ 10 00
Total - - - - - - - - - - $
Discount - - - - - - - - - $
     Grand Total - - - - - $ 10 00

W. D. MacGinnis
Treasurer of the State of Colorado

By W C Bate
                Deputy

THE JOHN M. McLEAN FAMILY

John Martin
1880 - 1942

Ethel LaVeta (Batt) McLean
1891 - 1980

THE JOHN M. McLEAN FAMILY

The first home of John Martin and Ethel LaVeta, built on John's father's ranch.

John Martin was born in Halls Station, Missouri, in 1880, and came to Colorado in the late 1800s with his family.

He married Ethel LaVeta Batt in 1909. For a time they lived outside of Carbondale at Penny Hot Springs, where two of their five children, Morace and William, were born. John and Ethel moved to the family ranch on the high mesa above the Roaring Fork and built their first house on John's father's land, where their other three children, Charles, Agnes, and Donald, were born.

Ethel on a fine looking horse at the McLean ranch.

Agnes at eight years old, and Donald, three years old.

Agnes (McLean) Dye recalls, "Our neighbor, Nellie Waters, and my mother, Ethel, were the best of friends and had been since they were girls. Nellie always came to the house to help my mother when her children were born. My mother did the same for her in return. We always laughed because my Mom had to work harder – Nellie had twice as many kids!"

John Martin raised wheat and hay on the land. He had a few head of cattle, and also work and riding horses. His work team's names were Scraggles and Snip. Ethel, like all farmers' wives, tended a huge garden.

Ethel and John Martin with Morace and baby Bill.

This is to Certify, That Agnes McLean **is this day**

PROMOTED

From the 3rd. Grade of the Course of Study, to the 4th. Grade

Issued from School District { Name or Number } 12 County Garfield

Date of Promotion May 20, 1932

Katherine L. Craig, County Superintendent / State Superintendent

Rachel B. Woods, Teacher

Local Superintendent

Garfield COUNTY
PUBLIC SCHOOLS
1931 — 1932

District No. 12
Report of Agnes McLean
Grade Third
Rachel B. Woods, Teacher.

Parent or guardian is requested to examine this report carefully and to acknowledge its receipt by signing below. Kindly return at once.

SIGNATURE OF PARENT OR GUARDIAN

September Mrs. John McLean
October Mrs. John McLean

Agnes (McLean) Dye remembers, "I went to Luby School for three years: first, second, and third grades. For some reason I never learned to print, but only to write. It was the old Palmer Method of writing we were taught. We practiced on lined paper and I remember we had to stay in the lines. The 'L's' were clear to the top of the line, the 'G's' clear to the bottom. We learned reading, writing, arithmetic, and phonics to pronounce words correctly. I can still remember sounding out my name, Agnes, as 'Ag–ga–nes'! In 1931 and '32 my teacher was Rachel B. Woods.

METHOD OF GRADING
A+ = 95–100
A = 90–95
B+ = 85–90 E—Excellent   Grade from 90 to 100
B = 80–85   G—Good   Grade from 75 to 90
C+ = 75–80 F—Fair   Grade from 60 to 75
C = 70–75   P—Poor   Grade below 60

ATTENDANCE STUDIES	1st Mo.	2nd Mo.	3rd Mo.	4th Mo.	5th Mo.	6th Mo.	7th Mo.	8th Mo.	9th Mo.	1st Exam.	2nd Exam.	3rd Exam.	Average
Days Present	28	30	27	25½	30	30							
Days Absent	½	0	3	4½	0	0							
Times Tardy	0	0	0	0	0	0							
Reading	B+	B	B	B+	A	A							B+
Writing	A	A	A	A	A	A							A
Arithmetic	A	B	B+	B+	B+	B+							B+
Spelling	A+	A+	A+	A+	A+	A+							A+
Geography	B+	A	A	A+	A+	A							A
Gram. & Lang.	B+	B	B+	C+	B+	B+							B+
U. S. History	A	A	A	A	A	A							A
Physiology													
Agriculture													
Music													
Colo. History													
Civics													
Drawing	A	A	A	A	A								A
Health	A	B+	A	A	A								A
Nature	A	A	A	A	A								A

N. B. This Mark X is placed opposite to trait to which attention is called.

PERSONAL CHARACTERISTICS	1st Mo.	2nd Mo.	3rd Mo.	4th Mo.	5th Mo.	6th Mo.	7th Mo.	8th Mo.	9th Mo.	10th Mo.
INTEREST										
Excellent	X	X	X							
Good										
Fair										
Poor										
HABITS										
Excellent	X	X	X							
Good										
Fair										
Poor										
CITIZENSHIP										
Excellent	X	X								
Good			X							
Fair										
Poor										
HEALTH	X									
Excellent	X		X	X						
Good										
Fair										
Poor										

"We rode horseback five miles to school. I remember one time my horse, Scraggles, bucked me right off, but it didn't hurt me.

"Desmond Harris was a real little kid, too little for school, but he came anyway. He liked to make pictures and lines on the blackboard. At that time the teacher was Mrs. Potter, and she was mean. She smoked cigarettes, but didn't want anyone to know. She kept sneaking to the outhouse to have a smoke, and then she wouldn't let us kids go out there to use the toilet. Poor little Desmond begged to go, and she wouldn't let him, and he wet his pants every day. He felt so bad and so did the rest of us because we all wet our pants, too. I had to ride my horse home with wet pants. Well, my Mom and Dad soon got the drift of this and they went to school and straightened Mrs. Potter out. It never happened again. To this day when I see Desmond Harris I think about mean ol' Mrs. Potter!

"My older brother, Morace, loved school so much. He became ill, but didn't want to miss school, and went each day until he could no longer physically handle it. By the time he was diagnosed with sugar diabetes, it was too late, and he died when he was only eleven years old.

Left to right: Bill, Chuck (inside car), Morace, and Ethel McLean with their Model T Ford. Photo taken in 1920.

"Our teachers were Rachel B. Woods, Josiphrine Trout, and Olla Jacobs. Our neighbors were the Renftles, the Millers, Nellie and Pat Waters, and John and Mary McNulty.

"In those days, the game warden used to come to the ranches unannounced to see if he could catch anyone poaching [killing game out of season]. Of course, we all were, that's the only way we got by. Our neighbor, John McNulty, would come warn us when he learned the game warden was on the way. He came over to warn us one day, and found no one at home, so he went into the meat house and took the buckskin [deer] and elk pieces out and hid it all in our grain bin. He carefully covered it up so it couldn't be seen, then, knowing the first thing my Mom would do when she got home was start dinner, he put small pieces of wood in the old cook stove, wrote a note about where he'd hidden the meat, and put it under the lid of the stove. He knew Mom would look under there to start the fire. The message was 'Meat covered up in the grain bin!' John was a great neighbor, he warned everyone!

"It would take all day to go to town, Carbondale and back. We went in a horse and buggy in the summer, and a horse and sled in the winter. The stores were Witcheys, Baggetts, Pings, Dinkles, and IGA. I remember Baggetts had a big sack of candy for a nickel – I loved that!

"We went to dances at the Upper Cattle Creek School and the Missouri Heights School. I remember, in the winter, Mama would heat rocks all day long on the wood stove and then put them in blankets to wrap around us kids in the sled. There were also card parties every Saturday night at someone's house. They played a card game called 500.

"My mother, Ethel, played piano, and I still have her piano in my home today. My daddy played violin. He learned from his father. They played for us kids, and sometimes at church.

"I remember when we had to churn the cream to make butter. We didn't want to, especially, so Dad made up a song that helped. We churned up and down to the beat, 'Ginger bum, butter come. Peter's waiting at the gate for a butter cake.' It seemed like the butter came faster when we sang!

Dash Churn.

Common Dash Churns. A long handle goes through the cover at the top, with a dasher at the bottom which is worked up and down inside the churn.

	Price, each.	Per doz.
No. 16952. 3 gallon dash churn	$0.56	$6.00
No. 16953. 4 gallon dash churn	.70	7.56
No. 16954. 5 gallon dash churn	.85	9.13
No. 16955. 6 gallon dash churn	.96	10.37

Dash Churns, Striped Cedar, With Brass Hoops.

No. 16957. 4 gallons.	Price, each	$1.30
No. 16958. 5 gallons.	Price, each	1.45
No. 16959. 6 gallons.	Price, each	1.59

Left photo, left to right: two types of butter churns.
Right photo: the description of a churn similar to the one used by the McLean family from a Sears, Roebuck and Co. catalog.

"We had no refrigerator so the cream was kept in the pantry. The cream had been separated from the milk, and my mother liked it to be somewhat sour when we made butter from it. We used a wooden churn which held about three gallons of cream. We didn't put the whole three gallons of cream in the churn, but just the amount mother knew she needed. Mother or Dad would pour it in the churn, and Dad would start singing 'the butter song' as he moved the wooden plunger (or stick) up and down. The stick had a wooden cross on the end which fit down into the churn. Dad would start to churn and sing:

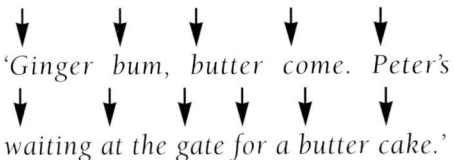

'Ginger bum, butter come. Peter's waiting at the gate for a butter cake.'

"Hearing that song was enough to make us kids get interested, and we'd come to help. Dad would let us take over, and we'd sing our hearts out and churn. Sometimes we'd get to going too fast and Dad would say, 'Calm down now – go easy!' I can still hear the splash-splash of the cream as we sang. We were having fun and the time went by. In fifteen or twenty minutes the cream had turned to butter!"

Agnes (McLean) Dye in 1997, displaying the butter churn she used as a child.

"Some butter churns were smaller and worked by turning the handle. Even later, too late for us kids, the churns were electric and the churning was done automatically! The work was well worth it. Nothing in the world tasted better than homemade butter on my mom's freshly baked homemade bread!

"My dad, John Martin, and his brother, Martin, inherited the ranch from grandfather John William. Uriah, my uncle, never married. In 1932 my father developed sugar diabetes, and sold out. They sold the complete ranch to John Heuschkel for $5,000 and we moved to Carbondale.

John Martin died in 1942. Ethel LaVeta died in 1980. They are buried in Hill Crest Cemetery on White Hill near Carbondale.

History of the Land Owners

E.U. Miller	1890	homesteaded 160 acres
Mary (Miller) McLean	1895	160 acres
John William and Mary McLean	late 1800s	260 acres
John Martin McLean	1915	homesteaded 160 acres
John Martin and Uriah McLean	1918	
John Heuschkel	1932	
Albert Grange		
Grange		
HLEM		
Spring Park Ranches	1998	Nine homes

THE MCLEAN FAMILY

John William McLean
1843 - 1913

Mary E. (Miller) McLean
Unknown - 1928

Children

Elial........................died at age 11   Mary........................died at birth
Uriah............................unknown   John Martin.............1880 - 1942

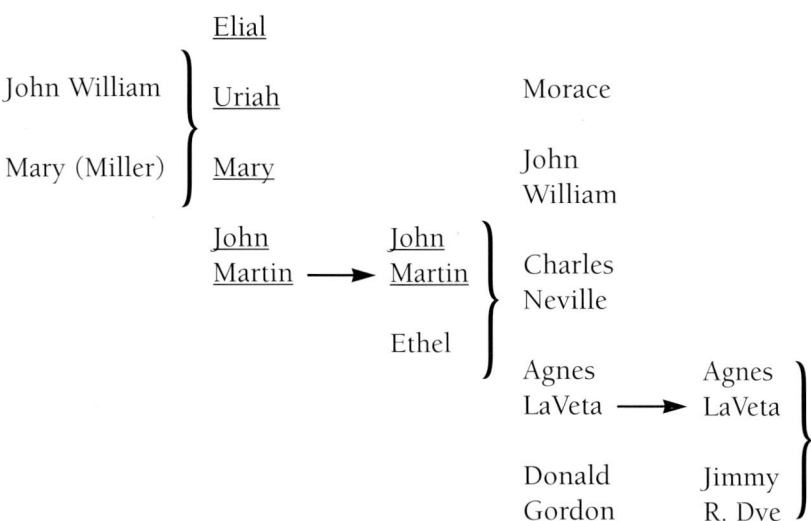

1877 DESERT LAND ACT

The Desert Land Act authorized disposition of a 640-acre tract of arid public land at $1.25 an acre to homesteaders upon proof of reclamation of lands by irrigation. Difficulties of reclamation subsequently reflected by more than ten relief acts by Congress to aid aspiring settlers. In 1891, area limitation was reduced to 320 acres of desert lands.

1862 HOMESTEAD ACT

The Homestead Act authorized unrestricted settlement on public lands to all settlers, requiring only residence, cultivation, and some improvement of a tract of 160 acres. Any person was eligible who was head of a family or had reached the age of 21, who was a citizen or intended to become one, and who did not own as much as 160 acres. After living on the land and farming it for six months, he could buy the homestead at $1.25 an acre, but, after five continuous years, he could apply for and receive a patent or title to the 160 acres for a filing fee of $15.

Originally passed by Congress on May 20, the Homestead Act was later amended to increase area limitations under certain conditions. Subsequent liberalizations of the act were in accord with prevailing philosophy that public lands should be given free to bona fide farmers and stockmen, whose homesteads would ultimately become permanent settlements. While the once vital act served its original purpose of stimulating settlement of the nation, it was destined for an active life of only about seventy years – when there no longer were enough public lands suitable for homesteading and capable of supporting a farm family.

Grandpa, tell me 'bout the good 'ol days,
Sometimes it seems like this world's gone crazy.
Grandpa, take me back to yesterday,
When the line between right and wrong
Didn't seem so hazy.

Lovers really fell in love to stay,
Stand beside each other come what may,
A promise really somethin' someone kept,
Not just something they'd forget.
Families really bowed their heads to pray,
Daddy's really never go away.
Whoa, whoa, Grandpa,
Tell me 'bout the good 'ol days.

GRANDPA (TELL ME 'BOUT THE GOOD OLD DAYS)
By: Jamie O'Hara

Copyright © 1985 Sony/ATV Tunes LLC.
All rights administered by Sony/ATV Music Publishing,
8 Music Square West, Nashville, TN 37203.
All Rights Reserved. Used by Permission.

THE WILLIAM HARRIS FAMILY
1900

WILLIAM HENRY HARRIS
1858 - 1933

MOLLIE (CAREY) HARRIS
1865 - 1927

THE WILLIAM HARRIS FAMILY

William H. Harris was born July 16, 1858, in Clinton County, New York. His parents were William and Catherine (Janes) Harris, natives of Monmouthshire, England. They had nine children. The family moved to Wisconsin, where William H. was raised. He worked on the family farm, and also at a stave factory (where narrow iron or wooden strips were made for placing around barrels to hold them together) before coming to Colorado.

Mollie (Carey) Harris was the daughter of Michael and Mary (Gleason) Carey, natives of Ireland who emigrated to America and settled in the copper region of Michigan. There, Michael acquired valuable mining interests. Later they moved to Leadville where Michael had several productive claims.

Irena (Harris) Arbaney remembers, "My grandfather, William H. Harris came to Colorado in July of 1881. He followed his brother, Charles Harris, who had arrived in 1880. It is said that Charles was the first white man to settle in the El Jebel area.

"William H. came to Colorado with Jack Morgan, commonly known as 'Black Jack.' They crossed Independence Pass with blankets packed on their backs. They built a cabin along the way. Because they feared Indians, they made holes in the cabin walls through which to shoot, but were never attacked.

"William H. took up a squatter's claim on 160 acres which was then part of the Ute Indian Reservation opened for white settlement in 1881, following the Meeker Massacre of 1879. This land parallels the Roaring Fork River, between Emma and Carbondale. This 160 acres would become the nucleus of the ranch which, with subsequent purchases, eventually grow to 860 acres. He raised hay, grain, fruit, potatoes, and large herds of cattle and horses. The ranch was well supplied with water from its private ditches. William H. sold hay for $160 a ton in Aspen. He and his brother, Charles, were two of the 17 men who built the road around the mountain near Emma, which is today part of Highway 82 between El Jebel and Basalt."

On January 26, 1884, William H. Harris became the first person to take out a marriage license in Garfield County. He made the transaction in Glenwood Springs. On January 31, 1884, he married Mollie Carey; it was the first marriage recorded at St. Mary's Catholic Church in Aspen, Colorado.

Their children were: Irene, 1887 - 1898; Bryon, 1885 - 1895; William Albert, 1887 - 1946; Ralph, 1889 - 1973; Raymond, 1892 - 1975.

The first marriage license issued in Garfield County, taken out by William H. Harris on January 26, 1884, in Glenwood Springs.

William H. Harris with his short horn bull which took first prize at the Denver Stock Show in 1905. His brand was "HK."

Irena (Harris) Arbaney recounts, "The Ute Indians came from Meeker, Colorado, to attend the fair, which was held on the south side of Glenwood Springs, Colorado. The fairgrounds were later made into a golf course, then a residential district.

"My grandfather was a good friend of the Indians and was sent to the reservation to get them to come to the fair. They brought their ponies in cattle cars. The Indians pitched their tents, as the fair lasted a week.

"The Indian ponies were 'very fast' and my dad (Ralph Harris) got to ride with the Indians in some of the races. Riding bareback was great fun for a young boy, especially to be riding an Indian pony. Grandfather Harris had two fast ponies and the Indians used them to compete in the races."

"These Ute Indians came from Meeker in 1910 to attend the fair. This picture of the Utes and W.H. Harris with Mr. Kelly was taken in front of the Kelly Building in Basalt, Colorado, which was built in 1900."

The family house on the El Jebel ranch.

Harvesting potatoes on William H. Harris' El Jebel ranch.

Threshing hay at the Harris' El Jebel ranch.

For reasons no one remembers, William H. sold the Emma ranch and bought acreage in El Jebel. It was located on both sides of what is Highway 82 today, including the Blue Lake Subdivision and property owned by Capitol Peak Outfitters, Sandy and Steve Rieser. The potato cellar built by William H. still stands today, only a few feet from Highway 82 on the south side.

Ralph and Alice (McCarthy) Harris wedding picture, April 18, 1911.

In 1919, William H. and Mollie sold the El Jebel ranch to Roger Darien and moved to Missouri Heights, homesteading 1,200 acres called the Mountain Meadows ranch. Their son, Ralph, and his wife, Alice (McCarthy) moved to the Heights with them.

McCarthy-Harris Wedding

One of the happiest wedding parties that ever came to Glenwood was the Harris-McCarthy party this Tuesday morning, that the wedding of Ralph Harris of Basalt and Miss Alice McCarthy of Carbondale might be solemnized by the Rev. Father Carrigan of the Catholic church. In the party were only the immediate friends and relatives of the contracting parties. The ceremony was performed at 9 o'clock. The trip to this city was made by the parents of the bride and groom.

The groom is the son of Mr. and Mrs. W. H. Harris of Basalt, and is one of the model young men of Eagle County. Being already "back to the soil," he bids fair to become one of the most prosperous ranchers in Western Colorado. The bride is the charming daughter of Mr. and Mrs. Dan McCarthy of the Carbondale country. Mr. McCarthy is one of the leading ranchers of that section. The prosperity of the two families is best attested by their bank accounts and ability to travel the hills and valleys in modern autos.

Following the ceremony in which W. J. Oulds was best man and Miss Ella McCarthy, sister of the bride, was bride's maid, the wedding party enjoyed breakfast at Martin's Cafe. The young people have taken rooms in the Everett block and will spend a few days here before returning to their ranch home near Basalt. They have the best wishes of a host of admiring friends.

4—407 a-ty.

The United States of America,

Desert Lands.

Ute Series.

Certificate No. 267.

To all to whom these presents shall come, Greeting:

WHEREAS, ——— WILLIAM H. HARRIS ———————————————

has deposited in the GENERAL LAND OFFICE of the United States a Certificate of the Register of the Land Office at Glenwood Springs, Colorado, ———— whereby it appears that full payment has been made by the said William H. Harris ————————

according to the provisions of the Act of Congress of the 24th of April, 1820, entitled "An Act making further provision for the sale of the Public Lands," and the acts supplemental thereto, for the south half of the northwest quarter, the north half of the southwest quarter, and the southeast quarter of Section twenty-seven in Township seven south of Range eighty-seven west of the Sixth Principal Meridian, Colorado, containing three hundred twenty acres,

according to the Official Plat of the Survey of the said lands, returned to the GENERAL LAND OFFICE by the Surveyor General, which said Tract has been purchased by the said William H. Harris:

NOW KNOW YE, That the UNITED STATES OF AMERICA, in consideration of the premises, and in conformity with the several Acts of Congress in such case made and provided, HAVE GIVEN AND GRANTED, and by these presents DO GIVE AND GRANT, unto the said William H. Harris ——————————————————————————— and to his heirs, the said Tract above described; TO HAVE AND TO HOLD the same, together with all the rights, privileges, immunities, and appurtenances, of whatsoever nature, thereunto belonging, unto the said William H. Harris ————————————— and to his heirs and assigns forever; subject to any vested and accrued water rights for mining, agricultural, manufacturing, or other purposes, and rights to ditches and reservoirs used in connection with such water rights, as may be recognized and acknowledged by the local customs, laws, and decisions of courts, and also subject to the right of the proprietor of a vein or lode to extract and remove his ore therefrom, should the same be found to penetrate or intersect the premises hereby granted, as provided by law; and there is reserved from the lands hereby granted, a right of way thereon for ditches or canals constructed by the authority of the United States.

In testimony whereof I, Theodore Roosevelt , President of the United States of America, have caused these letters to be made Patent, and the seal of the General Land Office to be hereunto affixed.

GIVEN under my hand, at the City of Washington, the twentieth day of August , in the year of our Lord one thousand nine hundred and seven and of the Independence of the United States the one hundred and thirty-second.

By the President: *Theodore Roosevelt*

By *F. M. McLean* , Secretary,

Recorder of the General Land Office.

Recorded Miscellaneous , Vol. 635, Page 331.

Act of April 24, 1820, an abandoned credit system for buying public lands. Minimum price fixed at $1.25 an acre, and minimum unit of sale 80 acres. Public lands initially offered by district land offices at pre-announced, scheduled public auction. Then, if unsold, lands available for purchase at minimum price on first come, first served basis.

The apple tree planted by William H. Harris in 1919 as it appears in 1998 on Dr. George Dewell's place.

Irena (Harris) Arbaney, daughter of Ralph and Alice, remembers, "In 1919, the El Jebel ranch was sold to Roger Darien, and my grandparents, William H. and Mollie, and my parents, Ralph and Alice, myself and my brother, Ralph Vincent, moved to Missouri Heights, homesteading 1,200 acres. I remember living in a tent for awhile, while my father was having a home moved from Basalt to the ranch. Our grandfather's home was located where Dr. George Dewell lives today in 1998. An apple tree which my grandfather planted still lives today in 1998. 'The woods,' as we called it, part of the ranch across from my grandfather's home, was a source of fire wood, piñon nuts, and where we herded the cows.

In 1998, 'the woods' has been divided into subdivisions: The Purchard, Los Piñones, and Aspen Mesa.

"There was an Indian grave in the woods. The Indians put several poles from limb to limb high in the trees, and lay their dead on the poles to let the body wither away. It had been torn apart by someone who undoubtedly did not know what it represented."

Their crops on the Heights were hay, grain, oats, and, of course, potatoes. They also raised cattle and horses. William's brand was HK (H connected K) and Ralph's brand was ||= (Eleven Two Bars).

Ralph and Alice lived in the house which is owned by Caroline and Patrick Murphy today in 1998. There was a large potato cellar to the west of the house. It was demolished and covered, and is buried beneath the lawn in 1998.

Irena says, "The potatoes were sorted and taken to Hook's Spur by sled in the winter, and loaded into a railroad car. (Hook's Spur is near Emma, past Willets Lane, over Hook's Bridge, to the right on Hook's Lane, and 1/8 of a mile on the left.) Many trips were made to fill the car. The farmers took great pride in their potato crops, and on Potato Day my dad would clean and polish 32 uniform potatoes to put on display, and be judged at the Carbondale Potato Celebration Day. He won many first prize ribbons. The women took vegetables to be judged. A free barbeque was held at noon, the parade at 10 a.m., and the dance at the Independent Order of Odd Fellows hall in the evening. What fun was had by all, and everyone looked forward to next year!"

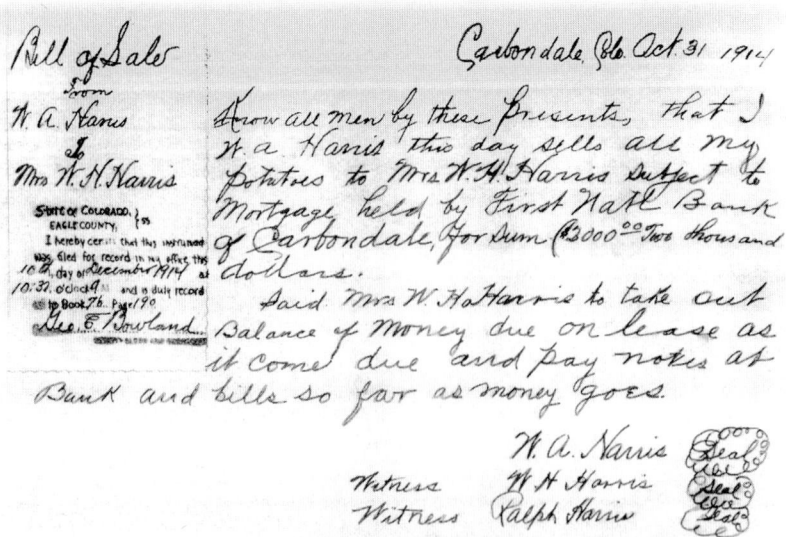

Harris potato deal.

William H. Harris, at the wheel of a 1909 Buick, at the Hotel Glenwood.

Irena continued, "My grandfather (William H.) and my father (Ralph) and many of the farmers on the Heights dug trenches and laid pipe from Blue Creek to have drinking water in their homes, as well as troughs in the barn for the horses. Our mother, Alice (wife of Ralph Harris), did the usual things. She raised chickens, turkeys, had a big garden, and every two weeks she attended the Literary Sorosis Club.

"We went to country dances at the Missouri Heights School. Every housewife brought food and lunch was served at midnight. Everything was free!

"My brother, Vincent, and I attended Luby School, which was named for Judge Luby of Eagle, Colorado. I won spelling and oratorical contests and went to Gypsum to compete with other schools in the district. I won a medal, third place in the oratorical contest. The subject was 'The Three C's of Education: Character, Culture and Citizenship.'

"My baby brother, Desmond, was born on the Heights in 1925, and on June 16, 1936, I was married to Laurent Arbaney at St. Mary's Catholic Church in Aspen, where my grandparents were married in 1884."

Irena (Harris) Arbaney and Laurent Arbaney, June 16, 1936.

Desmond Harris recalls, "For six years I herded milk cows for Dad up on our home on the Heights. I'd saddle my horse, Trinket, and take the cows out in the morning to graze, and then go get them again each evening and bring them home. One day, my big brother, Vincent, got a Model A Ford, and sometimes I'd get the cows out on the road by foot, and then push them on home with the Model A behind them.

"I remember once I was playin' at being a cowboy, and I roped one of the milk cows. My horse, Trinket, started backing up like he was supposed to do, but then he wouldn't stop. He pulled me and the cow backwards right through the barbed wire fence!

"I went to Luby School for eight years. We had a lot of fun there and there was a stepping structure called a fence stile to get over the fence to school. This picture is some of the kids who went to Luby.

Luby School fence stile.

"We used to sleigh ride down the road from Missouri Heights in the winter. It was great fun.

"I remember seeing my grandfather, William H., sitting in a wheelchair when he got old. One of his legs had been taken off by Dr. Hopkins, and I felt sorry for him.

"This is me and my horse, Cayuse, in 1936.

Desmond Harris.

"In 1939 my father, Ralph, my mother, Alice, and my brother, Vincent, and I moved to Glenwood Springs. Part of the Mountain Meadows ranch, where my grandfather homesteaded, was eventually sold to Loren and Glafrie Fender, and to John and Victoria Sirola."

Mollie (Carey) Harris died in 1927. William H. Harris died in 1933. They are buried in Sairview Cemetery in Basalt, Colorado.

Alice (McCarthy) Harris died in 1944. Ralph Harris died in 1973. They are buried in Rosebud Cemetery in Glenwood Springs.

History of the Land Owners

Mountain Meadow Ranch was homesteaded by William H. and Mollie Harris in the early 1900s. When sold, they split it into several portions:

Lower:
Fred Shehi ....early 1900s
Loren and Glafrie Fender 1939
Harold and Ruth Fender 1953
Dr. George and Ruth Dewell 1966
Gary and Linda Fender 1971
Mountain Meadows Subdivision 1977
Ruth Fender 1979

Upper:
Ralph and Alice Harris 1934
John and Victoria Sirola 1942
Donald Witt and George Thurman 1964
Dick Meeker 1969
Red Table Acres Subdivision:
John Wicks 1973
Bob Sewell 1975
Homeowners 1977
Donald H. and Anita L. Witt.............................1967 - 1993
Anita L. Witt 1998

The Woods Subdivisions:
The Purchard, Los Piñones, and Aspen Mesa

It is with heartfelt gratitude that I thank Irena (Harris) Arbaney for this wonderful, rich history of the William H. Harris family. Irena worked diligently for many years compiling the history of her family for her descendants. In 1998 she is a resident of the Valley View Nursing Home in Glenwood Springs, Colorado. Time has faded her recollections of life on Missouri Heights, but I do believe that somewhere deep in her soul, the memories whisper and linger on. – Anita Witt

Some of the William H. Harris history is taken from the book <u>Progressive Men in Colorado</u>.

Last Will and Testament

I, William H. Harris, of the county of Eagle, in the State of Colorado, being of sound and disposing mind and memory, do now make, publish and declare this as and for my last will and testament, in manner and form as follows, to-wit:

1. It is my wish and desire that out of and from the estate by me left, be first paid all my just debts and liabilities, including those expenses contingent upon my last sickness and burial.
2. After the payment of my just debts and liabilities as aforesaid, I give and devise unto my son, Ralph Harris, all my real property, forever, wheresoever situate, including my Mount Basalt Ranch, which is located about 9 miles Northeast of the Town of Carbondale, Colorado.
3. I give and bequeath unto my son, Albert Harris, the sum of One ($1.00) Dollar in money.
4. I give and bequeath unto my son, Raymond Harris, 2 of my cows, and he shall have any two that he might select.
5. I also give and bequeath unto my said son, Ralph, all my horses, farming machinery, tools, implements and equipment.
6. I give and bequeath unto my grand-daughter, Irene Harris, of Carbondale, Colorado, the Newman piano which is located in the dwelling on the said ranch.
7. I give and bequeath unto my daughter-in-law, Alma Harris, and my granddaughter, Isabel Harris, share and share alike, all my books and also the book case which is located in the said dwelling.
8. I give and bequeath unto my daughter-in-law, Alice Harris, of Carbondale, Colorado, the china closet with chinaware contained therein, located in the said dwelling.
9. I give and bequeath my writing desk which is located in the said dwelling, to my said son, Ralph.
10. I give and bequeath to each of my grand-children, William Paul Harris, Isabel Harris, Vincent Harris, Irena Harris and Desmond Harris, 2 cows, each, to be selected by the executor hereinafter named, as he shall deem fit.
11. I give, devise and bequeath all the rest, residue and remainder of my property real, personal and mixed unto my said son, Ralph, forever, howsoever the same may be evidenced and wheresoever situate.

It is my wish and desire that my said, son Ralph Harris, be appointed as the executor of this my last will and testament, and I request that he be not required to give bond.

IN WITNESS WHEREOF, I have hereunto set my hand and seal this 13th day of March, A.D. 1934.

William H. Harris   (SEAL)

Signed, sealed, published and declared by the above named testator, WILLIAM H. HARRIS, as and for his last will and testament, in our presence and in the presence of each of us, who, at his request and in his presence and in the presence of each other have subscribed our hands and seals as witnesses of the due execution of said above last will and testament.

George L. Winters   (SEAL)
Residing at Glenwood Springs, Colorado

C. W. Darrow   (SEAL)
Residing at Glenwood Springs, Colorado

C. H. Darrow   (SEAL)
Residing at Glenwood Springs, Colorado

CARBONDALE IS SPUD CENTER

Carbondale continues to be not only the potato center of Colorado, but those who have traveled extensively and who have been close observers do not hesitate to pronounce it the peerless spud producing territory of the world.

Not only does that splendid section in the vicinity of Carbondale, the Roaring Fork and Crystal river valleys hold first rank in the way of yield, but the potatoes grown in that section are of such superior quality that they find a ready sale in the best markets of the world and usually at an advance in price over the product of other localities.

The State Agricultural college this year made several tests on some experimental plots of the Sweet ranch with such satisfactory results that the work will be continued next year.

This work was under the special direction of Professor Fitch who superintended the plowing and planting and made several visits to the tracts during the growing season, and estimated the percentage of stand and the general conditions, making copious notes for future reference.

The land was not manured nor treated with commercial fertilizer and the cultivation and care was the same as given by Mr. Sweet to his own field of 85 acres. While Mr. Sweet on a considerable portion of his land had a yield of 250 sacks to the acre and while there are fields after field in the Carbondale section that will yield from 200 to 225 sacks, the college tract gave enormous yield of 38,200 pounds, or 332 sacks or about 633 bushels per acre. — *Glenwood Post, Saturday, Oct. 15, 1910.*

CARBONDALE SPUDS ARE ON EXHIBITION

Succulent Tubers, Beef and Coffee Served Barbecue Style to Great Crowds Last Saturday

The citizens of Glenwood and surrounding towns who journeyed to Carbondale last Saturday deemed it a great treat to be able to look in on the splendid exhibit of wealth producing tubers, especially when they realized that by their presence and their interest in the event they were giving encouragement to an industry that is yet in its infancy, but which is destined soon to become the great and overpowering industry of western Colorado. It is but a few years since the farmers of the Carbondale district turned their attention from the long horned steers and the alfalfa fields to the culture of the succulent spud and they have since made it a study and a business and advanced in the science of its production until today Carbondale potatoes are known the world over and find ready sale at advanced prices among people who know a good article and want the best that can be produced.

Time was when the farmers, in the Carbondale country as well as elsewhere, paraded their potatoes for their size and freakish irregularities. but they were soon made to understand by buyers and consumers that not mammoth proportions, but uniformity of size, smoothness of surface and quality of texture are the things to be aimed at in producing a popular and practical potato.

With these suggestions before them, the farmers of Carbondale set about in an intelligent manner to breed potatoes just as they had set out to breed horses and cattle of a certain type.

All the various disadvantages were studied, combatted and overcome, the questions of seed selection, planting, cultivation, irrigation, harvesting and and marketing – all these have engaged the intelligent consideration of the Carbondale farmers for years until today it is a science with them as is in but few places in the United States, while the ideal climatic conditions and the splendid irrigation advantages combine with scientific application to make potato production in this section the leading and most profitable rural industry in Colorado.

Ask any one of a dozen prominent potato growers in the vicinity of Carbondale to give you a story on the potato. Pick up an ordinary spud and engage him in conversation about it. He can give you its history and pedigree, trace its family tree, or vine, back a century and tell you all about its cousins and its uncles and its aunts. Then he will tell you the good qualities of this especial variety and also recount its weaknesses and tell you what is being done right in the Carbondale section to breed the vices out of that particular potato and make it more self-respecting and more admired by the housewife so that people of discriminating tastes can look it in the eye without apologizing for its poor appearance.

And if you don't believe the appearance of the ordinary field potato can be wonderfully improved by careful seed selection and proper cultivation you should have been at Carbondale last Saturday.

LIST OF COMMITTEE AWARDS

Early Ohio White Potatoes – Early Ohio – H.L. Edgerton, first.

Medium Early White – Chas. Downing, Sherman Bros., first; Russett burbank, Joseph Laudendklos, second; same, Jos. Carnahan, third; Snowflake, Crystal River Land Company, fourth; Russett Burbank Samuel Bowles, fifth.

Medium Early Red – Rose Seddling, H. L. Edgerton, first; George Sievers, second; same, John Laudendklos, third; Early Red Ohio,

H.L. Edgerton, fourth; Bliss Triumph, John Laudendklos, fifth.
Late Red – Peachblow, Crystal River Land Company; first; Red McClure, W.H. Harris, second; same, Big Four Ranch, third; same Frank Berthod, fourth; same, George Sievers, fifth.
Late White – Rural New Yorker, H.L. Edgerton, first; Peerless, Crystal River Land Company, second; Valley Prize, same, third; Up to Date, Leo Leonhardy, fourth; White McClure, W.H. Harris, fifth.
Best Five Boxes – H.L. Edgerton, first.
Best Single Box – Crystal River Land Company, Peachblows, first; Sherman Bros., Charles Downing, second; W.H. Harris, Red McClures, third; John Laudendklos, Russett burbank, fourth; H.L. Edgerton, Rose Seedlings, fifth.
Best Exhibit at Show – Crystal River Land Company, first; Sherman Bros, second; Harry Shuttleworth, third; John Laudendklos, fourth, H.L. Edgerton, fifth.
Best Box Seed Potatoes – Harry Shuttleworth, Red McClures, first; Samuel Bowles, Russett, Burbanks, second; Sherman Bros., Chas. Downing, third; big Four Ranch, Red McClures, fourth; H.L. Edgerton, Peachblow, fifth.
Bliss Triumph Seed – John Laudendklos, first; Russett, seed, Samuel bowles, second; Gold Coin, seed, Samuel Bowles, second; gold Coin, seed, Big Four Ranch, third; Red McClure, seed, Crystal River Land Company, fourth; White McClure, seed, Sherman Bros., fifth.
Best Freak Potato – W.H. Harris.
Best Sack Market Potatoes – Harry Shuttleworth, first; Big Four Ranch, second.
Best Display Home Prepared Fruit – Mrs. Estella Pings, first; Mrs E.S. Shadle, second.
Best Display Homemade Butter – Mrs. James Fatkins, first; Mrs. Tim Doyle, second.
Winners in Bread Contest – Mrs. Samuel Bowles, first; Mrs. Beulah May Hawk, second; Mrs. Edna Trout, third; Mrs. Fatkins, fourth; Mrs. Z.B. Kiggins, fifth; Mrs. Estella Pings, sixth; Mrs Budd, seventh.
Grain and Vegetables
Best Thirty Pounds Oats – John Forclay, first; C.L. Fuller, second.
Best Thirty Pounds Wheat – C.L. Fuller, first.
Best Three Heads Cabbage – H.I. Gardner, first; Crystal River Land Company, second.
Best Sugar Pumpkin – Crystal River Land Company, first; H.L. Edgerton, second.
Best Field Pumpkin – Crystal River Land Company, first.

– *Glenwood Post, Saturday, Oct. 29, 1910.*

THE CHARLES HARRIS FAMILY
1900

Charles H. Harris
1852 - 1925

Rosetta (Noble) Harris
1858 - 1934

THE CHARLES HARRIS FAMILY

Charles H. Harris was a brother of William H. Harris. Charles came to Colorado in May of 1880, and was believed to have been one of the first white men in the Roaring Fork Valley. He and Thomas Cannon crossed the Continental Range over Cottonwood Pass to Aspen. Then, the area had only a few log cabins and tents.

Charles and Thomas left their wagon on the east side of the range, as there was no wagon road to Aspen, and set out down the Roaring Fork Valley to try to find a suitable location for ranching and stock raising. Charles and Thomas stuck their stakes in the valley, where they found wild hay growing in abundance on land which, in 1998, is the Dakota Subdivision on Highway 82.

Charles H. Harris' grandson, Charles "Chuck" Harris believes his grandfather started with 160 acres and later bought out his partner and other early settlers.

Charles H. Harris said, "When we located our ranch, we stuck our stakes so as to take in about six miles of the valley, but in the summer of 1881, settlers came in so fast that by fall they had us boiled down to our present location.

"We made our living hunting and fishing. In the month of August 1880, there was a kind of rough road built to Aspen. I made a trip to Buena Vista and bought some provisions: a scythe (an implement used for mowing by hand, with a long, curving blade fastened at an angle to a long handle), a snath (a scythe handle), and a couple of hay forks. I got my wagon this trip and went as far as Aspen with great difficulty. We stored our provisions in our cabin at Aspen and went to the ranch in the valley to put up hay. We put up about twenty tons in September of 1880. We then went to Aspen after more grub and found our cabin broken into and everything taken. We had to have more grub, and no money to buy it with. We started back down to the ranch and went fishing. We caught and dressed 250 pounds of trout. It was then cold enough nights to keep them. We packed them in grass, loaded them on our broncs and went to Aspen.

Charles H. Harris.

"We made another trip to Buena Vista and sold the fish for fifty cents per pound. We brought more grub and potatoes to our ranch to keep an eye on it, because it was worth money in those days. Most of the potatoes were planted the next spring, being the first lot of potatoes grown in Garfield County and on the Western Slope of Colorado. In the winter of 1880 and 1881, we put in our time hunting and baling hay, packing meat and hay to Aspen on ponies and jacks. We got $100 per ton for it [hay]."

In 1882 Cannon sold out and Charles H. Harris stayed on the land. He married Rosetta Nobel from Iowa on January 19, 1886. In her book *Carbondale Pioneers*, Edna Sweet tells how Charles and Rosetta met: "Rosetta Nobel was one of the first teachers in Aspen. She and another lady teacher landed at Independence, one of the first three mining camps high in the upper valley of the Roaring Fork on Independence Pass." The first three mining camps were Ute City, which eventually became the town of Aspen, Independence, and Ashcroft.

"The teachers landed at Independence in the evening and were told that a trapper had just brought in a huge bear, so, of course, they were filled with curiosity to see the mighty hunter. He was not a handsome man, but a large one, and in his rough clothes with coonskin cap, he was formidable looking. Rosetta's companion remarked, 'Good Lord, he wouldn't have to shoot a bear, it would frighten to death just to look at him!' However, romance was in the air that night, and the trapper, Charles Harris, and Miss Nobel began their courtship, which led to marriage."

They had five children: Nettie, Ruth, Dora, Ambrose Vern, and Clara Beth. Although Charles H. and Rosetta did not live on Missouri Heights, he did buy and sell land there. It is noted in the Fender history that Ira Fender bought 160 acres from Rosetta and Charles in 1914.

Charles "Chuck" Harris, grandson to Charles H. remembers some of the history his grandfather and father, Ambrose, shared with him. "The area where Catherine Store is [today in 1998] was called 'Catherine' after Judge Edward Stauffacher's wife, Mary Catherine. The Stauffachers ran the post office from their home, which is still there in 1998, on the southeast side of Highway 82 and County Road 100. It sets 3/8 of a mile south of Highway 82, adjoining County Road 100. I think the post office opened around 1892.

Rosetta (Noble) Harris.

"The Colorado Midland tracks were right where Highway 82 is today, and the Catherine Corner was a whistle stop. The train would slow way down as it approached the corner, the conductor would toot the whistle and Ed would throw on a sack of mail as another sack of mail was thrown off. Then the train moved on up the line to Aspen, repeating the process. I'm pretty sure the post office closed in the early 1900s."

Chuck Harris lived on his grandfather's ranch (which in 1998 is operated by Richard Cerise), until he was four years old. "My grandmother, Rosetta, was a rather quiet person, but everyone was welcome at the ranch. People were always asked to stay over night when traveling up and down the valley. My grandfather raised huge amounts of potatoes. There was a certain amount of disease – blight – that hit the potato industry in the valley and up on the Heights, but it wasn't the whole cause of the decline of potato production. Prices got lower, fewer people could be found to pick, and it was just too much hard work for the money!!"

Chuck Harris owned Catherine Store at various times through the years. He tells the history of the store, and the corner of Highway 82 and County Road 100, which was an important landmark to all

Missouri Heights residents. "A Mr. Hoagland bought the corner about 1930 and built the original place. It was up on stilts because of the railroad grade, which put the land down in a hole. Then, a Mr. Adamson bought it, built on, and sold gas and cigarettes. He had two pretty daughters, and all the men stopped in to look at them. Next, my wife's brother, Lewis Glassier, bought the place. At that time it was a one room shack with a partition. Lewis filled in the bottom land around the place and added two rooms. He made a real store out of it and sold a lot of groceries.

"Then, in 1942, my wife, Bobbie, and I bought it with about a third of an acre and ran it until we sold out to Bob and Blanche Holgate (Fred Holgate's son). Bobbie and I bought it back in 1953 from the Holgates, tore it down and rebuilt the present structure in 1958, which still stands today in 1998. We sold to Anthony "Tony" Baudino and Kenneth Maurin. Tony and his wife, Jeanette, and her sister, Bonnie, ran the store for about four years, and sold it to the present owners, Eddie and Lael Hughes. That's the history of Catherine Store.

"I still remember, when I owned the store I would get mail addressed to Catherine, Colorado."

Some of the history of Charles H. Harris is condensed from the book Progressive Men of Colorado *, and the newspaper* The Carbondale Item, *and the book* Carbondale Pioneers *by Edna Sweet.*

Eddie and Lael Hughes, owners of Catherine Store in 1998.

THE CHARLES HARRIS FAMILY

Charles H. Harris
1852 - 1925

Rosetta (Noble) Harris
1858 - 1934

Children

Annetta "Nettie"	1887 - 1972	Ambrose Vern	1891 - 1987
Ruth	1888 - 1889	Clara Beth	1895 - 1929
Dora	1890 - 1935		

<u>Annetta "Nettie"</u>

<u>Ruth</u> - died in infancy

<u>Dora</u>
Mr. Johnson } Dorothy Jane

<u>Ambrose Vern</u>
Alvina Dickson } Charles "Chuck" → Charles "Chuck" Margaret "Bobbie" Glassier } Alvin Adele, Glen Charles

<u>Clara Beth</u>
Elmer Kunke } One child, died in infancy

THE GEORGE BLUE FAMILY - 1902

The Blue family circa 1920. Left to right, standing: Bess, Earl, and Lloyd; seated: George, Daisy, and Mae.

GEORGE BLUE
1868 - 1951
ROSA MAE (SCOTT) BLUE
1877 - 1953

George and Mae Blue came from Clay Center, Kansas, in a covered wagon to the Roaring Fork Valley in either 1900 or 1901. They had four children, Lloyd, Daisy, Earl, and Bess. In 1902, George bought the four corners at Catherine, 260 acres, from Ed Stauffacher, at the intersection of what is Highway 82 and 100 Road in 1998. At that time the Catherine School was located east of the corner where Catherine Court Trailer Park, owned by Ed Dreager, is today in 1998. There was nothing else there but the Colorado Midland railroad tracks. A man named Newton Lance had given a 100-foot strip of his land for the tracks in 1886.

THE LLOYD BLUE FAMILY

Lloyd Blue
1895 - 1966

Mary Catherin (Gallunaw) Blue
1893 - 1969

THE LLOYD BLUE FAMILY

In the late 1800s W.L. Grubb homesteaded 415 acres north of what is Highway 82 today in 1998, from 100 Road west, up to the Clifford Cerise ranch. He sold to Daniel McCarthy in 1904, and in 1921, McCarthy sold to Mary Catherin Blue. The land is still the Blue Ranch today, and is owned by Dee and Jean Blue. Although the Blues lived near rather than on Missouri Heights, other family members owned land on the Heights, and the Blues became a part of Missouri Heights history.

Lloyd and Mary were married in 1923, and had two sons, Jean and Harold.

Jean Blue: "My dad raised potatoes, grain and hay. He also had around 300 head of beef cattle, Herefords, which were on the ranch in the winter, and grazed up on Placita Range near Redstone and Lilly Lake in the summer. He also ran a flock of sheep, about 150, and in the '30s they used to graze where the old Carbondale landfill was located. I remember a story my dad told me that happened when he was grazing cattle up by Redstone. Mrs. Osgood [Mrs. John Cleveland Osgood, whose husband built the Cleveholm mansion, also known as Redstone Castle] owned a cabin on the property where Dad grazed the cattle. One of Dad's riders used the cabin once in awhile. For some reason Mrs. Osgood didn't like the forest ranger in the area, and she told my dad not to ever let him use the cabin. Well, he did use it, and he and my dad got into a huge argument over it. My dad had a quick temper and when it was all over, he lost his grazing rights up there. My dad did have a nasty temper, but he also forgot and forgave easily.

"My mother, Mary, was a quiet lady, but also a very talented musician. I don't know where she learned, but she played piano and violin quite well. My parents held big community dances right here on the ranch, first in the barn, and then, when the barn was full of hay, they danced in the ranch house. The ranch house was the original homestead on the place, and it's still here today in 1998. My mother played and sometimes other musicians joined her. Many on Missouri Heights came to the dances and sometimes she played the music for dances at the schools on Missouri Heights. I remember, if someone asked her to play a song she didn't know, she would say, 'Hum a few bars.' Once she heard that, she played the song.

"One of my happiest memories of when I was a kid was about my grandmother on my mother's side, Nora Gallunaw. She lived with us at the ranch off and on. My brother, Harold, and I made ourselves a vehicle out of an old buggy frame. We put a pair of little wheels on the back, and some old big cultivator wheels on the front. It didn't have any brakes, but we rigged up a rope attached to the axle to steer with. We sat on each side and pushed with our feet. On a steep downhill road we didn't have to push. It was great fun when Grandma Gallunaw would get right on that thing, and ride with us. There was a real steep road on the ranch, and that's where we took Grandma. It must have been a sight, with us two boys and Grandma in her long skirts, flying down the road, laughing and hanging on for dear life, and trying to steer that contraption around curves. We never crashed, but we came close."

History of the Land Owners

W.L. Grubb homesteaded the original 415 acres in the late 1800s.

Daniel McCarthy .... 1904 .... 415 acres
Mary C. Blue .... 1921 .... 415 acres
Dee and Jean Blue .... 1998 .... 415 acres

THE JEAN BLUE FAMILY

JEAN AND DEE (REINWAND) BLUE

Jean was raised on the ranch and well remembers the potato crop and the work involved.

Jean: "The potatoes were mostly Burbanks. They were forked into the sorter, and the sorter was moved back and forth, letting the culls drop out. The culls smaller than one and a half inches, were fed to the pigs. The number one potatoes were of good size, over and inch and a half, with no sunburn, no cracks, no knots, bruises, or worm holes. The number two potatoes did have knots and cracks, but not much else. Sometimes we sold the little ones for seed, but mostly fed them to the pigs. I remember the late '30s. We had 20,000 sacks of potatoes worth twenty-five cents a sack. The government sent out men who came in and sprayed the spuds with purple paint so we couldn't sell them. It was supposed to raise the price up, but it didn't help much.

"My mother, Mary, was the secretary for the government Prisoners of War Organization in the area. The prisoners were held at the old CCC camp in Glenwood Springs."

The CCC (Civilian Conservation Corps) was a part of President Roosevelt's New Deal; young men from all over the country were organized and paid to work for the government in the areas of forestry, prevention of soil erosion, flood control and national park upkeep. That was in the 1930s, when millions of Americans were out of work, and the country was in the worst economic depression in its history. When the country began to prepare for World War II in 1941, the CCC was disbanded.

Jean continues, "The old CCC barracks had not been torn down in Glenwood, so they were used to house the German prisoners of

A Boggs potato sorter used in the 1930s and 1940s.

Doorway (above) and interior (below) of a potato cellar on the Blue Ranch, 1998.

war. The prisoners were sent here to pick potatoes in the Roaring Fork Valley, and they were made to pick in an unusual fashion. Men were started at both ends of twelve rows of potatoes, and picked toward each other. When they got to the middle, they walked across the field to the next twelve rows and picked from the opposite direction. This was done because it was easier to guard them. The guards were armed with 30-caliber carbine rifles.

"My brother, Harold, and I went to the Crystal Springs School. I remember two teachers, Maude (Callicotte) Maxfield, and Art Bogue.

"In 1918 the Colorado Midland Railroad shut down, and a year or so after that my father, Lloyd, helped to pull up the tracks for the new road that would one day be Highway 82."

The final environmental impact statement for State Highway 82, Carbondale East, Colorado Department of Highways (1981) states, "For the most part, State Highway 82 follows the original Colorado Midland Railroad alignment through the Roaring Fork Valley. In 1918, the Colorado Midland ceased operations between Glenwood Springs and Aspen and their right of way was subsequently acquired by the State in 1920. In the twenties, this right of way was converted to a dirt road which was maintained by grading, rolling, and oiling. Between 1935 and 1938 the first bituminous paving was done, using the old roadbed as part of the sub-base.

"Improvement of State Highway 82 began back in the late 1950s and continued through the 1960s. At that time, projects were prepared in short segments of between two and four miles and then constructed, proceeding up the Roaring Fork Valley from Glenwood Springs. The northerly twelve miles of State Highway 82 were improved to four-lane standards in this manner during the 1960s and early 1970s."

Jean continues, "My first wife, Lorine (Cerise) and I lived in the last box car left at the Catherine stop in 1945. We had an old wood stove, and it got mighty cold in there on a winter morning. We used to scrape the ice from the walls. We eventually got electricity and even a phone. We lived in the box car from 1946 until 1960. Then we moved it up to the ranch and finally over to my brother's place on Missouri Heights. It's still up there today, but it's in shambles."

Lorine and Jean had one son, Bruce. Jean lost both Lorine and Bruce to cancer.

Jean and Dee Reinwand were married in 1975, and live on the Blue ranch today in 1998.

THE MARTIN FAMILY – 1907

ELFES "E.F." THEODORE MARTIN
1872 - 1965

KATHERINE "KATIE" PAULINE (MALLOW) MARTIN
1876 - 1962

THE MARTIN FAMILY

Elfes "E.F." Martin married Katherine "Katie" Mallow on November 6, 1895. They had two sons, Guy and Glenn. The Martins came to Colorado in 1902 from Salina, Kansas. The Chris Nelson family came with them. Chris was married to Katherine's sister.

The Martins' son, Guy, was one year old when they arrived, and for awhile they lived in the beautiful brick home which still stands on Willet's Lane and is a part of the Happy Day Ranch today in 1998.

Later, both families bought property on Cattle Creek, near what would one day be called Missouri Heights. The Nelson land was near the Martin land, and Chris built a huge barn where community dances were held. The Martins' 473.21 acres of land were bought from A.B. Foster; land which Merrill Harvey McLachlin had homesteaded in 1892. It was located about two and a half miles from what is now Highway 82, up 103 Road, on the right.

The Crystal Springs was the closest source of domestic water for the Martins and their neighbors. It was first called "The Vance Springs," later "The Kelly Spring" and eventually "The Crystal Springs."

Ted Martin, grandson to Elfes, remembers, "My grandfather, E.F., told me how they would take a wagon with several cream cans to get their water before they had a well. Everyone always said it was the best water they ever tasted and still is today in 1998. Back then, my grandfather said they kept a tin cup hanging at the springs. At that time the County Road 103 was at a much lower level and it was boggy around the springs.

Glenn Martin (born 1905) at age three.

No. 311433 WARRANTY DEED 67/539

This Deed, Made this 12th day of August in the year of our Lord one thousand nine hundred and Seven, between A. B. Foster of the County of San Diego and State of California, of the first part, and Elfes T. Martin of the County of Garfield, and State of Colorado, of the second part;

WITNESSETH, That the said party of the first part, for and in consideration of the sum of Twelve Thousand DOLLARS, to the said party of the first part in hand paid by the said party of the second part, the receipt whereof is hereby confessed and acknowledged, has granted, bargained, sold and conveyed, and by these presents does grant, bargain, sell, convey and confirm unto the said party of the second part, his heirs and assigns forever, all the following described lot or parcel of land, situate, lying and being in the County of Garfield and State of Colorado, to-wit: Lots Six (6) Twelve (12) Section thirteen (13) and Lot one (1) Section Twenty four (24) Township Seven (7) South of Range Eighty eight (88) West of the Sixth P.M. also Lots one (1) Two (2) Section Nineteen (19) and Lots four (4) Seven (7) Eleven (11) Twelve (12), and the N½ of SE¼, Section Eighteen (18) in Township Seven (7) South of Range Eighty Seven (87) West 6 P.M. containing 473.21 acres more or less; together with first party's interest in and to the C. and M. Ditch and water right, and any and all ditches and water rights owned by first party and used in connection with said lands.

TOGETHER With all and singular the hereditaments and appurtenances thereunto belonging, or in anywise appertaining, and the reversion and reversions, remainder and remainders, rents, issues and profits thereof; and all the estate, right, title, interest, claim and demand whatsoever, of the said party of the first part, either in law or equity, of, in and to the above bargained premises, with the hereditaments and appurtenances.

TO HAVE AND TO HOLD The said premises above bargained and described, with the appurtenances, unto the said party of the second part, his heirs and assigns forever. And the said A. B. Foster party of the first part, for himself, his heirs, executors and administrators, do covenant, grant, bargain and agree to and with the said party of the second part, his heirs and assigns, that at the time of the ensealing and delivery of these presents he is well seized of the premises above conveyed, as of good, sure, perfect, absolute and indefeasible estate of inheritance, in law, in fee simple, and has good right, full power and lawful authority to grant, bargain, sell and convey the same, in manner and form aforesaid, and that the same are free and clear from all former and other grants, bargains, sales, liens, taxes, assessments and incumbrances, of whatever kind or nature soever Except a promissory note for $1,000, and Trust Deed given to secure same to the Logan Investment Company, dated September 1st, 1906 which second party hereby assumes and agrees to pay when due and the above bargained premises in the quiet and peaceable possession of the said party of the second part, his heirs and assigns, against all and every person or persons lawfully claiming or to claim the whole or any part thereof, the said party of the first part shall and will WARRANT AND FOREVER DEFEND.

IN WITNESS WHEREOF, The said party of the first part has hereunto set his hand and seal the day and year first above written.

Signed, Sealed and Delivered in Presence of

A. B. Foster (Seal)

STATE OF COLORADO, } ss.
County of Garfield }

I, Charles M. Taylor a Notary Public in and for said County, in the State aforesaid, do hereby certify that A. B. Foster personally known to me to be the person whose name is subscribed to the annexed deed, appeared before me this day in person, and acknowledged that he signed, sealed and delivered the said instrument of writing as his free and voluntary act for the uses and purposes therein set forth.

(NOTARIAL SEAL)

Given under my hand and Notarial seal, this 12th day of August A.D. 1907.
My commission expires January 9th 1911.

Charles M. Taylor
Notary Public

Filed for record the 2nd day of December A.D. 1907, at 1:30 o'clock P.M.
___ P. ___ Recorder.
By ___ Deputy.

Deed, 1907: A.B. Foster to Elfes T. Martin, 473.21 acres for $12,000.

Ron Martin, E.F.'s great grandson, remembers, "E.F. and Katie raised potatoes as did many in the area, and would some years ship a full railroad car himself. He raised hay, grain, and for many years had a threshing machine and steam engine, and ran a threshing operation for neighbors and farmers in the Roaring Fork Valley. Katie was a wonderful cook, and loved to feed the threshing crew. When it was her turn to cook and feed the crew, she would pester E.F. to learn every item the other women had prepared, so she could out-do them. It wasn't unusual for her to throw out a pie or cake if it wasn't just perfect, and make another. One day she had the table all set and ready for the threshing crew to come in and sit down when one of the dogs chased a pet goat into the house. It jumped on the table and proceeded to demolish her beautiful table setting. They got rid of the goat!"

The Elfes Martin cattle brand and ear mark was issued January 7, 1903.

Ron Martin: "E.F. was an extraordinary horseman and it was a good thing because he often told about the broncs they had for teams when they did field work. He had many fine teams, one a matched pair of grays named Dolly and Tango."

			779-C 7289-37 18926-47 21407-57	3306-62 3059-82 87 92			16300
DATE						BOOK	PAGE
Jan	7	1903	E. T. Martin,			M8	399
			Carbondale, Garfield Co				
			TRANSFERS				
Nov	30	1945	Lee Berges, Carbondale, Garfield Co			16	636
May	27	1964	Harold Lee Berges, ~~Carbondale, Illns~~			32	101
~~Rt 2, Brt 105, Glenwood Spgs. 81601~~					Garfield Co		
			~~Rt 1, Box 25,~~ Carbondale, 81623				
			1840 Upper Cattle Ck Rd				
Jan.	27	1989	Richard A. &Karen		L.Haff,46535 Hwy 6&24,	92	321-
			Glenwd.Spgs,		81601, Garfield Co.		322
FORM X-64							

Elfes with his work team.

The boys, Guy and Glenn grew to manhood on the ranch. Guy married Bulah Tremble and they had one son, Theodore "Ted" Winfield.

Ted Martin: "I was born at my mother's family home, at the Tremble place, which is the Cattle Creek Ranch today in 1998, at the intersection of Cattle Creek Road 113 and Coulter Creek Road. I was born in [what was originally] the Martin Hotz family home, which was disassembled and moved to the Tremble place in 1911, when

The Martin family, left to right: Guy, Glenn, unknown, E.F., and Katherine.

Harleigh Holmes was getting ready to build the big reservoir on the Hotz land. The house has been remodeled and is quite beautiful today. I was born there in 1917.

"My mother, Bulah, died when I was two years old, and my grandparents, E.F. and Katherine, and my father, Guy, raised me. In 1926, when I was nine years old, my grandfather ordered a pre-cut Sears and Roebuck house, and it arrived on the train. After the house was assembled and was being painted, I noticed a can of white paint in the basement. I also saw a gray cat that happened to be there, too. Well, I dunked that cat in the paint, and when Grandma saw it, she asked, 'What happened?' I told her I guess it had fallen in the cream can! Well, the poor cat lost all its hair, and its skin turned blue and stayed that way for a long time – but it lived!

"I can still remember riding my grandfather's thresher. I loved to sit up there and feel it rock back and forth. The women always prepared a real delicious dinner for us. My uncle, Glenn, cut that old thresher up when World War II erupted and the government needed steel. After that, we got a rubber-wheeled thresher, and then a more modern combine."

Ron Martin: "When the telephone became available everyone was on a party line, and the phone would ring a different number of rings

The Hotz family home, moved to the Tremble place in 1911.
The Cattle Creek Ranch in 1998.

The Westly
No. P13085 "Already Cut" and Fitted
$2,614.00

Sears, Roebuck and Co.

FIRST FLOOR PLAN

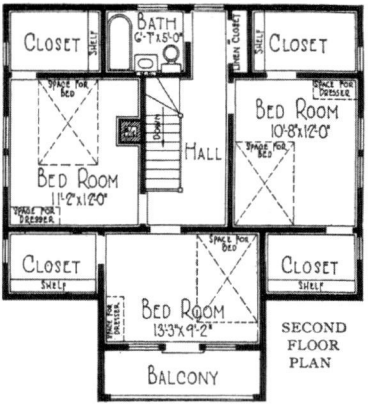

SECOND FLOOR PLAN

The Westly is a high grade two-story home, retaining the architectural beauty of a modern bungalow. Built everywhere. Every customer satisfied. Praiseworthy letters from Westly owners tell of the fine interior arrangement, beautiful woodwork, our approved "Honor Bilt" ready-cut system of construction, and of savings even as high as $1,500.00.

Exterior. Sided with narrow bevel clear cypress siding in first story; dormer, roof & second story covered with best grade thick cedar shingles. Large front porch, 30 by 8 ft. Porch can be screened or glazed.

FIRST FLOOR. **The Living Room.** An attractive feature is the open stairway that leads to the second floor. A coat closet with a mirror door is near the stairway. Furniture can be attractively arranged because of space. There are two windows at the side and one window at the front.

The Music Room. French doors connect with the living room. This music room is sometimes used for a bedroom instead. Has a double window at the side and a high sash looking over the space for piano at the rear.

The Dining Room. A wide cased opening connects the living room and dining room. Space for a complete dining set, including a buffet. Two side windows and one front window provide light and air.

The Kitchen. A swinging door connects with dining room. The space for sink, range, table and chair is laid out to save steps for the housewife. One side window and one rear window furnish light and cross ventilation. The pantry has five roomy shelves and a window.

A door from the kitchen opens into the rear porch, which has stairs to basement and to grade.

SECOND FLOOR. **The Bedrooms.** Stairs from the living room lead directly into a well lighted hall. This hall connects with the three bedrooms, bathroom and linen closet. The three bedrooms are all of good size. The front bedroom has a door to balcony. Each bedroom had two windows and a spacious clothes closet with a window. One bedroom has two clothes closets.

The Basement. Space for furnace, laundry and storage.

Height of Ceilings. First floor, 9 ft., floor to ceiling. Second floor, 8 ft., floor to ceiling. Basement 7 ft., floor to joists.

WHAT OUR PRICE INCLUDES: At the price quoted we will furnish all the material to build this seven-room house.

[for each different phone number], so they all knew if someone was being called. Katie loved to listen in, but she wasn't the only one, and the people on the line could hear one receiver after another being picked up. Finally, there were so many people listening in that the line got weak and full of static, and no one could hear!"

Chris Nelson, who had moved his family to Colorado with the Martins, also owned land along 100 Road (across from the fire station today in 1998). Many of the Missouri Heights residents remember the dances held in the Nelsons' big barn. Ted still remembers how the crowd enjoyed themselves. His dad, Guy, often called square dances.

Ted Martin: "The old county road used to go from Road 105 straight on up to Road 100, and part of it was on my grandfather's place. It isn't used today in 1998. One time a fellow was hauling down a big load of logs from Basalt Mountain, and he couldn't hold the load back when he hit the low grade on that road. The whole thing got away from him, and he had to jump free. Several horses were killed when they hit the old bridge on that road. It was a bad time.

"I remember my dad, Guy, worked for Harleigh Holmes

Ted and his guitar on the steps of the Martins' Sears Roebuck home.

Katie with great grandson Ronald on sheep.

Sunday Morning, November 15, 1959

Glenwood Pair Has 64th Anniversary

The 64th wedding anniversary of Mr. & Mrs. E.T. Martin; 1959.

GLENWOOD SPRINGS – They met at a party, sunny-haired Katie Mallon and a young farmer named E.F. Martin.

A date was made for him to call at her home the next Sunday and on November 6, 1895, they exchanged wedding vows in the parlor of her parent's home in Salina, Kansas. The pretty bride helped cook the turkey dinner that served forty guests. Mrs. Martin's wedding gown was a dove-gray taffeta trimmed in pink and she wore a hat of the same material.

Sixty-four years is a long time to remember, but Mr. Martin recalls with pride the lovely team of horses and shining rig he used in courting his wife when the country school was the center of entertainment. There on Sunday they attended church and sang together; Wednesday was prayer meeting and song-fest; Friday or Saturday, debates, in which everyone took part, spell-downs and ciphering matches.

Mr. and Mrs. Martin came to Basalt on February 7, 1902, to find the winter open and relatively warm after blizzards in Kansas. They lived in that area for only about two years before moving to the Crystal Springs district near Carbondale, where they farmed for forty-nine years.

Five years ago they retired and moved to Glenwood Springs.

Mrs. Martin's housekeeping is as neat as a starched linen napkin, and her nice needle craft is in evidence everywhere.

Their family consists of two sons, Guy and Glenn, both of Glenwood Springs, and four grandchildren.

A grandson and his wife, Mr. and Mrs. Ted Martin, held a family party in their honor last Sunday. They were presented with a huge anniversary cake and gift by the family.

during the construction of the Carbondale Reservoir in 1912. I used to go over and watch, as it was a real sight to see all the men and horses and equipment working.

"My father's brother, Glenn, married Vernice Maxfield, who was related to the Callicottes. Vernice's mother, Maude, was my first grade teacher at the Crystal Springs School. The school was right where the County Road 103 is today, about one and three-quarter miles up from Highway 82. It was just a short way from my grandfather's ranch. Mary Ferguson was my fourth grade teacher. When I went to high school in Carbondale, I rode a horse for the first two years. The first year, I rode old Shorty, and the second year I rode a horse Dad rented from a dude outfit in Glenwood Springs. After that I was able to ride with someone in a car.

"When cars became available, my grandfather bought a Model T. I guess he drove it pretty fast because people used to say, 'Watch out for Mr. Martin on the road.' I guess he really went scootin' down those roads. Then, he bought an Oakland, a Scripts Booth, and a 1926 Olds. He'd drive the Olds along the irrigation ditches to check them."

Ron Martin: "In his later years, E.F. sold off part of his land – the parcel where Laura Van Dyne lives today in 1998. We don't know who he sold it to, but he never got paid. We've always heard how Katie never let him forget it."

Ted married Lucille Harris, and they had three children: Ronald, Marvin, and Scheryl. When Ron was ten or twelve years old, his parents were out for a Sunday drive and Ted let Ron take the wheel, driving up the road to E.F. and Katie's. Ron made the turn in to the driveway but accidentally kept on turning and drove right through the fence and the garden. E.F. looked out the window and said, "Some damn fool just drove right into my garden!" He didn't know it was his own great-grandson.

Katherine died in 1962, and Elfes died in 1966. They are buried in Rosebud Cemetery in Glenwood Springs.

Glen and Ted both went into the excavating construction business and built many of the roads, ditches, and easements in Garfield County, Haystack Mountain, Basalt Mountain, Red Tables, and on the Flattops. Ted started his own business in 1946, and fifty-one years later there are still Martins in the excavating business. His

The Martins' Sears Roebuck home in 1998.

sons, Ronald, Marvin, and grandsons, Gary and Larry, continue the family tradition of running heavy equipment.

Some years after the ranch was sold, Ronald and a friend got their car stuck in the snow up Cattle Creek. They walked to John McNulty's for help. Of course, John planned to help but he asked Ron to go down to the barn to harness his horses to pull them out. Ron said he didn't know how, and John shook his head and sighed. Then he looked at Ron and said, "You're E.F. Martin's grandson, and you don't know how to harness?"

Bob and Betsy Schenck live on what was once part of the Elfes Martin place. The bunk house that Elfes built is a part of the Schenck home today in 1998. The Crystal Springs is located near the 103 Road on the Ronald and Margie Martin land in 1998.

History of the Land Owners

Merrill Harvey McLachlin homesteaded 473.21 acres in 1892.

A.B. Foster..................1900..........473.21 acres
Elfes Martin..................1907..........473.21 acres
Bob Lewis ....
Oscar Cerise..300 acres
Cerise Family..................1998................300 acres

THE JOHN YEOMAN FAMILY
1908

John Yeoman

Janie (Nichols) Yeoman

John and Janie Yeoman came to Aspen in June of 1885 from the mining camp of Rosita, Colorado. The Yeomans were originally from Missouri. They came to Aspen because of the silver boom, and traveled in covered wagons along with several other families, all related by marriage: the Hiram Shoemakers, the Berriers, the Lees, the Jeff Nichols family, the Mays, and a cowboy named Bill Taylor.

Jeff Nichols and John Yeoman drove horse teams, Berrier a span (pair) of mules, May a yoke (a wooden frame by which two draft animals are joined at the heads or necks for pulling together) of milk cows, and Lee and Shoemaker, yokes of oxen. Jeff Nichols had 150 head of range stock, twenty milk cows, and fifteen head of horses, which were all driven by Taylor and Nichols.

The group traveled north through Silver Cliff, toward the Arkansas River Valley, northwest to Hayden Creek, and stopped at John Hayden's way station to buy supplies and rest the animals. Moving on, they endured a long, difficult trip across the Sangre de Cristo Range, and reached the San Luis Valley Road. From there, north over Poncha Pass, 9,000 feet high, and onto Maysville and up the Arkansas River Valley to St. Elmo and Tin Cup Pass, 10,500 feet high. They passed Mirror Lake and entered the Taylor River Valley.

Len Shoemaker, Hiram Shoemaker's son, remembered the trip in his book *Pioneers of the Roaring Fork Valley*: "Their strenuous struggle through the snow on Tin Cup Pass had fatigued (almost exhausted) the teams and yokes, and a long rest was necessary. The women washed and mended clothes, and the girls gathered wild flowers which grew in great profusion all over the area, and all of them visited the few tumbled down shacks and houses which stood nearby. There was one good floor in one of the houses, they cleaned it out, Nichols got out his fiddle, and they all danced quadrilles [square dances].

"The travelers moved out, going over Taylor Pass at 11,900 feet, in July. The snow was higher than the tops of the covered wagons. We moved on down Express Creek toward Ashcroft and into Aspen.

"Aspen was a beehive of industry when we arrived, pedestrians, horseback riders, vehicles, wagons and jack trains came and went in all directions. Hundreds of miners working round the clock in their ceaseless round of drilling, shooting and mucking to take out valuable ores, trudged back and forth to the mines. Silver was king – and he and his cohorts were riding wide and handsome over that fair city of 5,000 inhabitants."

John and Janie Yeoman and their daughter, May, settled near El Jebel, and a son, John "Elvie" Alva was born in 1886.

THE "ELVIE" YEOMAN FAMILY

John "Elvie" Alva Yeoman
1886 - 1967

Mattie (Pitts) Yeoman
1887 - 1953

Elvie and Mattie Yeoman owned two parcels of land near Missouri Heights. The "Upper Place" as they called it was on Upper Cattle Creek at the base of Hoiser and Basalt mountains. They homesteaded 160 acres between Yeoman Creek and Iola Creek, with Hoiser on the north, and Basalt Mountain to the south.

The Gordan Ratcliff place, 160 acres, was northwest of Yeoman's, and Dave Thompson's 160 acres was due west. Dave Thompson was Mattie's stepfather, and was called "Grandad" by the Yeoman children, David (1909 - 1930), Opal (1912 - 1987), and Richard (1915 - 1994).

The "Lower Place" was also on Cattle Creek, two miles east of where Highway 82 is in 1998, on the right.

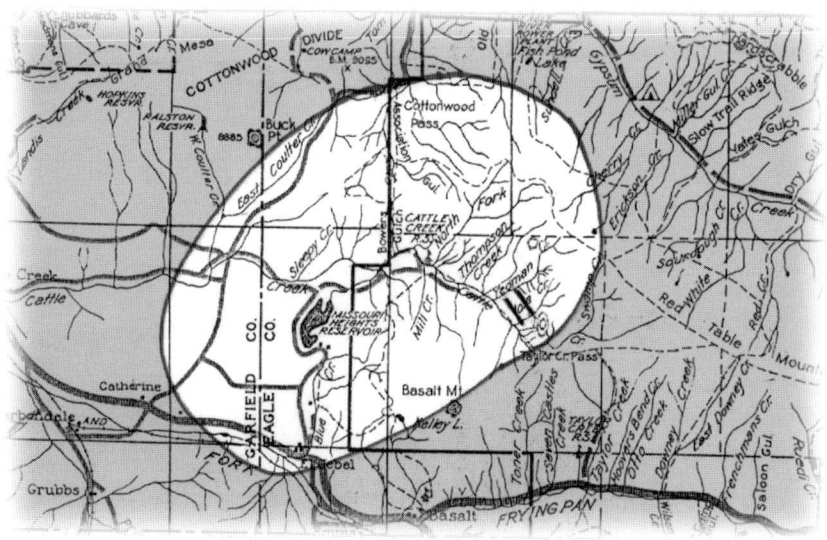

Dave Thompson was Mattie's stepfather. He had a son by another marriage, Matt. Dave was "Grandad" to the Yeoman children, Matt was "Uncle Matt."

The Yeomans did not live directly on the Heights, but they were very much a part of the community, and well thought of by everyone. In her book *My Corner of Colorado*, Opal (Yeoman) Scott wrote with such love for her family, and appreciation of her life in the high country. "I'll never forget moving! One of my earliest recollections is moving. My folks owned a homestead way up in the mountains and my grandad owned a place down on the creek in addition to a homestead one mile from my folks. So he and my uncle stayed up in the hills the year around and we used the 'Lower Place' in the winter so us kids could go to school.

Grandad Dave Thompson.

"I think I remember first moving up – as that was the biggest thrill. Winter was behind us – and some morning at dawn the three of us kids and my uncle would climb up on our horses and start moving thirty or forty head of loose cattle and that many horses east. Amidst much running and hollering and noise we'd get them all started. We always had one leader horse and one leader cow. This meant they knew where they were going and took the lead. It was up to us to keep the rest of the cattle in line and we always seemed to – with the help of three or four dogs, as excited as we were.

"We had every mile of road named. When we got as far as the 'Iron Spring' we'd all rest and get a drink before tackling the long, long 'Renftle Grade,' which seemed endless but now is like a small rise. Then up the 'Cattle Creek Canyon.' At the 'Coulter Creek' bridge the small calves would be tiring and the going would be lots slower but the thrill of getting closer was beginning to take over the thrill of starting. Next the 'Mailboxes' would be behind us, then past the 'Cottonwood Pass' turnoff and at the 'Cattle Creek' crossing we'd gather all the stock up on the hillside to feed and rest. Then, the creaking wagons, three of them, Mama in one, Daddy in another, and Grandad in another, would be there. We'd all dismount and take the bit out of our horses' mouths so they could feed and drink, then we'd eat. Boy, was the food good! I can't remember what we had besides cold biscuits but I can still remember how good it was.

"Then came the task of getting the cattle on the move again. The horses would be too willing as they knew and loved the high country. The baby calves were another thing; they'd usually be lying down and had to be raised, each and every one. Then, a gradual grade up to the 'Reservoir.' There, life began again, for we could see the aspens in their pale, new leaves and it would be real, it was just ahead. The road wound two or three miles along the reservoir's edge, then we were in the 'Oaks' but, by then the babies would really be tired, some of their legs just couldn't go on – so my older brother and my uncle would load them in front of my younger brother and myself and one each with them on their horses and we'd keep moving until the wagons caught up with us again, which they always did in the 'Oaks.' Then, we'd transfer the calves to one of the wagons. That posed another problem – keeping the worried mother cows on the move. They needed to be convinced their babies were alright every once in awhile, so they would dash back to the wagons bawling the loudest any cows had ever bawled.

"Finally – the top of the 'Long Grade.' There would be early spring in all its glory. Dog tooth violets making a carpet to the very edge of the snow. The most beautiful yellow I have ever seen. The wagons would pull ahead here. There was no holding back now – we had all seen spring – it was here. Summer and the green, green hills would be coming soon. So, on down the grade. Red columbines everywhere and every now and then a huge clematis vine, clinging to a small white and pale green quakie. Then, the beaver dams. It was always muddy there – deep, black, thick mud. By then our saddle horses were tired so we were walking, giving them a rest. Boy, those beavers were sure busy last winter. Look how high the old dams were, and look at the new ones! At last, back on dry ground and through the 'Flats' and the top of the 'Short Grade' and the Ranger Station, still partly buried in snow. Now, we had to be careful not to push the herd – let them take their time, because there was a sheer drop of a hundred feet over the bank and no place else to go – so how carefully we moved them. Well, that was made and I can't remember one accident there.

"Now we were in the 'Bear Trap.' Tall, tall, black pines, new tender skunk cabbages poking through the black earth, and a really, truly bear trap – a three-cornered one made out of logs.

"By now it was getting dark, and the air had still a trace of winter in it – but how thrilling to breathe it, even if my teeth were chattering and my stomach didn't know if it would ever get anything again.

"The gate at last – left open by the wagons. Everything turned loose, and how well they knew it. They scattered in every direction and the dogs romped and played around the horses – ran ahead and came back. Then, the lighted windows of Grandad's. Someone with a lantern coming out. We'd go to the barn, unsaddle, and turn our horses loose, then go in.

"Nothing had changed. The same good old cook stove and the same pile of wood, the same wonderful odor of meat frying and the fragrance of coffee. In no time we'd be warm, fed, sleepy, and so to bed at the end of a perfect day. The last conscious thought before sleep claimed me was of the wonderful sound of wind through the pine trees. No, I'll never forget moving!"

Grandad Dave Thompson had a sawmill on Iola Gulch. He was a most colorful character, and is remembered fondly by those who knew him. Lucy Jane (Fuller) and Clyde Sievers remember him well, and love to tell his stories. Lucy Jane was raised on the Heights, and spent many good times with the Yeoman family.

Lucy: "I can still see Dave sitting in his rocking chair by the old, long wood stove, telling one of his favorite stories and trying to light his pipe at the same time. His stories were very involved and he told them very dramatically. He would light a wooden match, and then proceed to talk while the match burned down to his fingertips. He would blow it out and lay it on the stove top. Then, he'd keep right on talking and lighting matches and never stop long enough to light his pipe. Pretty soon there was a long line of burnt down matches on the stove – the story wasn't finished, and the pipe wasn't lit!

"One time Matt came home out of breath, telling his dad, Dave, and everyone that he had just encountered a bear in the forest, and it was real close to him. Dave lifted the back of Matt's pants out and pretended to smell. Then, he shook his head in agreement and said, 'Yep, there's no doubt, you were real close to that bear!' "

Clyde Sievers, Lucy Jane's husband, was raised on his father's ranch on what is today Highway 82, between Carbondale and Glenwood Springs. His father's ranch was next to today's Aspen Glen Subdivision.

Clyde remembers the Yeomans and Dave Thompson, "Dave used to get lots of company up where he lived, hunters, vacationers and such. Sometimes they just plain stayed too long, and he'd finally do things to encourage them to leave. He was a bachelor, but he lived clean and kept things fairly tidy One time some people had stayed too long and he was tired of it. One night after supper, he took their dinner plates off the table and proceeded to lay them on the floor for the dog to lick. When he saw they were licked clean he waited until all eyes were on him and calmly put them away in the cupboard. The company left the next morning before breakfast!

"Another time he was tired of another batch of freeloaders and at breakfast

Grandad Thompson clowning with a stuffed bear!

time he found a spider web with a bunch of flies caught in it. He put a few fly legs in the jelly and called it 'Black Fly Jelly,' which he served with hot biscuits. Those people left in a hurry, too!"

One of the big events of the summer for Missouri Heights residents was the annual birthday party which Dave held for his son, Matt. It was always on June 14th, and the women all brought special dishes they had prepared.

Lucy Jane: "The women brought the food and Dave and the men made ice cream. They would ride their horses to the Cardinal Crossing on Basalt Mountain, where the snow still sat from a snow slide. They brought back gunny sacks filled with snow and made the most wonderful ice cream in big ten gallon freezers."

Opal Yeoman: "…in June the big event of Uncle's birthday. Grandma and Grandad were married late in life after they lost their first mates, and, of course, took a lot of kidding by all the neighbors and friends about their first born, and on June the 14th, a year after they were married they presented all the doubting ones with a lovely blond, curly-headed baby boy, much to the consternation of one neighbor in particular, as he had to buy the baby carriage. From that day on, for many, many years the Sunday nearest the 14th of June was set aside for a big neighborhood picnic. People came from ten to fifteen miles away, and in those days that was quite a trip by horseback or team and buggy. The day before the picnic, Daddy would go up in the mountains and bring the horses in so we could ride and show them off. We would keep our eyes glued to the edge of the quakies for the first glimpse of our beloved horses, and when they came in sight, what a lovely thing to see. They had been turned out shaggy and thin from the long winter – they came in shining and fat and heads held proudly high. We would catch them and go with Daddy and Mama up to the 'Cardinal Crossing' to get gunny sacks full of snow to freeze the ice cream the next morning. Then, morning finally came and we were off to the foot of the 'Long Grade' where everyone met for the picnic. There were sack races, foot races, nail driving, tug-of-war and horse shoes, and all the kids with their favorite horses and dogs. What a wonderful day, and Mama would make the best ice cream and cottage cheese in all the state. By late afternoon everyone full, tired, and happy were ready to go home. No, I'll never forget June 14th."

One of the June birthday celebrations.

Vera Schmitell, who lives in Saguache, Colorado, is Opal (Yeoman) Scott's granddaughter. Dave Thompson was her step-great-great-grandfather. Vera remembers one of the stories about Grandad Dave. "Grandad Dave went to a dance down in Carbondale. At that time he was up in age, and most people considered him an old man. There were two young cowboys at the dance, and they were acting up, and being ornery, and Grandad told them to settle down. Well, the cowboys didn't like that one bit, and sassed him back. He took them on, whipped the tar out of both of them, and sent them down the road. That was Grandad Dave!"

Opal and Richard went to school on the Heights, first at the Little Blue Creek School on the Harris place. Ruth (Gould) Zancanella and Rokie Fender were their classmates. Later, the Yeomans went to the Lower Cattle Creek School close to their home on the "Lower Place."

Lucy Jane: "Mattie lived to be 66 years old. She loved cats, and always had a whole house full of them. She suffered terribly from arthritis at the end."

The Yeomans and Grandad and Grandma Thompson are all buried at the Fisher Cemetery.

The exact spot where the Yeomans' cabin was located on Upper Cattle Creek is owned today (in 1998) by Ethel Waters Heuschkel.

The Story Of
THE FISHER CEMETERY
1885

A.J. and Acneth Fisher

The Haff ranch was homesteaded in the 1870s by A.J. and Acneth Fisher. They lost their only son, Billy, in 1885 and buried him on the hill. That was the start of the Fisher Cemetery and its name, and so it will remain because the cemetery is protected forever by the Haff Family Trust.

A funeral procession at Fisher Cemetery in the late 1800s.

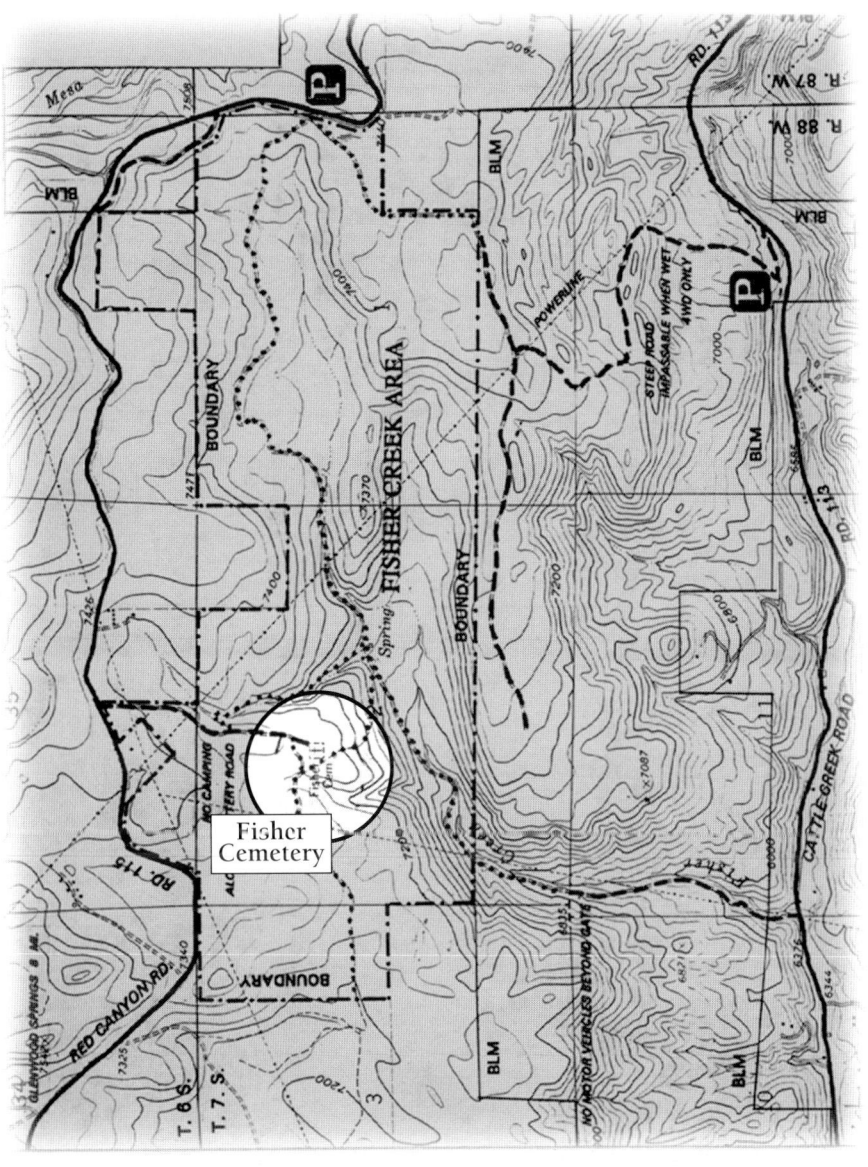

Fisher Cemetery and surrounding area.

The cemetery is located up County Road 114 to County Road 115, and right to the power sub-station. The access road is immediately east of the sub-station.

The Yeoman family graves of David (1901-1930), and two infant girls, Amy Lorraine (1919-1919) and Bonita Ines (1917 - 1918) at the Fisher Cemetery.

Special thanks to Lucy Jane and Clyde Sievers, Carmen Shoup (Opal Yeoman's daughter), Verna Schmitell (Opal's great granddaughter), and the Glenwood Springs office of the Bureau of Land Management.

Fisher family graves of A.J. Fisher.

All day I face the barren waste

Without the taste of water – cool water

Ol' Dan and I with throats burned dry

And souls that cry – for water

Cool, clear water.

The nights are cool and I'm a fool

Each star's a pool of water – cool water

And with the dawn I'll wake and yawn

And carry on – to water,

Cool, clear water.

– Written by B. Nolan
Music of the West
ASCAP
Song Writers Guild of America

THE HOLMES FAMILY – 1911

Harleigh Randall Holmes
1881 - 1963

Katherine L. (Sievers) Holmes
1895 - 1975

THE HOLMES FAMILY

Harleigh R. Holmes loved putting water in places it had never been – to make things grow!

Harleigh R. Holmes was born in 1881, and raised in Newton, Kansas. His father, James H. Holmes, was a water engineer, and also an organizer or colonizer for the Union Pacific Railroad. His job was to actually set up towns every other square mile for the railroad in Kansas and Oklahoma.

Harleigh R. married his first wife, Clara Sill in 1912. She died during child birth.

Katherine Sievers was born in 1895 and raised on her parents' ranch. George and Johanna Sievers owned 643 acres near Carbondale. Half of the ranch is now The Aspen Glen subdivision in 1998, situated on Highway 82 between Glenwood Springs and

1905. Lower Cattle Creek School - District #15. Teacher: Alice Zook (Bennett). Pupils, back row: Johnnie Sievers, Ivan Stanton, Orville O'Neil, Max Sievers. Front row: Helen Doyle (Trout), Irma Kane, Freda Kane, Katherine Sievers, and Sievers' dog, Dick.

1905

Carbondale. The Midland Railroad tracks were to the west side of the ranch, the Rio Grand tracks to the east.

Katherine started school at the Lower Cattle Creek School, when she was six years old in 1901. The Sievers children walked from home, across a swinging foot bridge, and along the Rio Grand railroad tracks to school. George Pearson, Marian (Jacobs) Hotz's maternal grandfather, built the school in 1888. It was located on the south side of what is Highway 82 and Cattle Creek Road today in 1998.

Helen (Holmes) Bond remembers, "My father had finished building a reservoir and irrigation system in Huerfano, Colorado, a town between Trinidad and Walsenburg, and was looking for a new location to build another reservoir. He came to the Western Slope in 1911 with his friend and business associate, Jerome Stovall of Jamesport, Missouri. They saw the need for a water system on the high mesa that would one day be called Missouri Heights, and set their sights on the project. Harleigh R. bought the land for the reservoir from Martin Hotz and Uriah McLean in 1911.

Lee Holmes recalls, "The older maps, and current maps, of the area show the reservoir as being called Spring Park Reservoir. The reason for that name was because of the Spring Park Spring, named by early homesteaders. The spring flowed from Basalt Mountain down into a natural bare basin which was called Spring Park Reservoir. The Hotz ranch was also called the Spring Park ranch. When my father bought the land from Hotz and McLean, he renamed the project 'The Carbondale Reservoir and Irrigation Company.'"

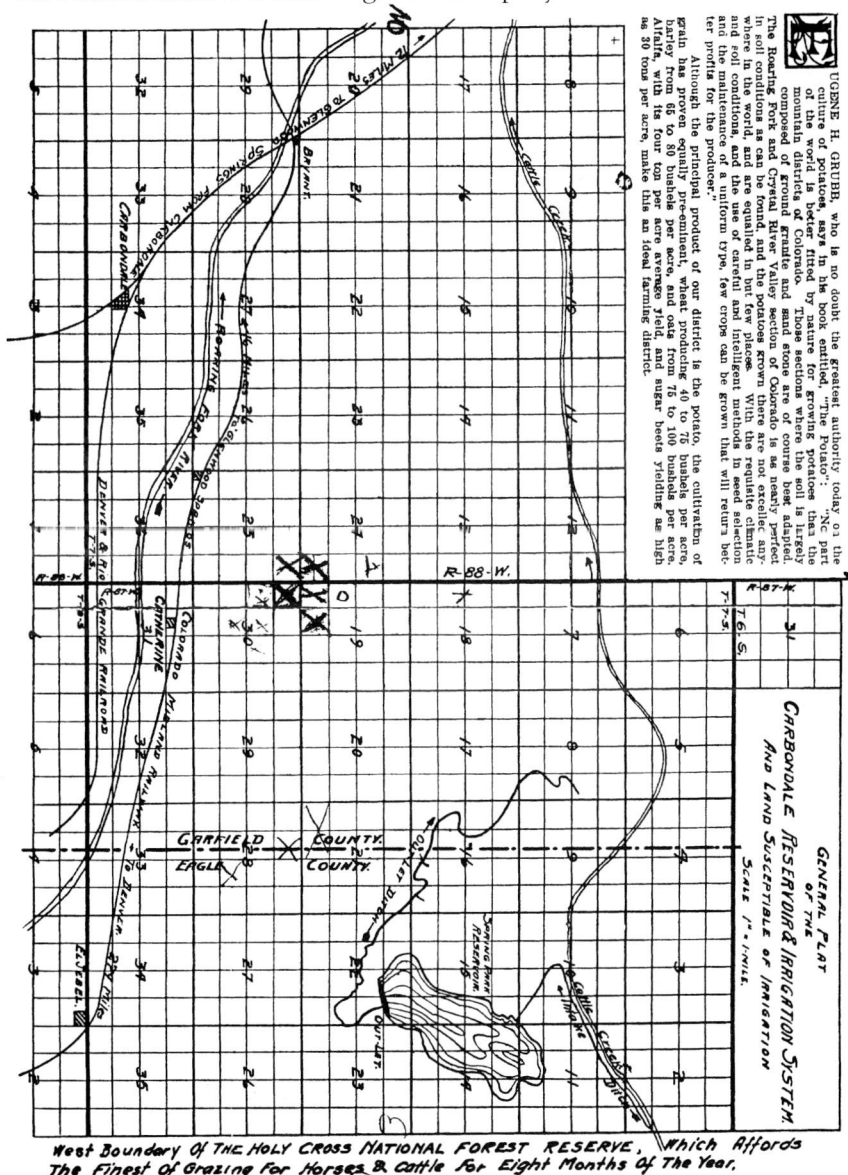

SUDDEN WEDDING SURPRISE TO FRIENDS

Taken from CARBONDALE ITEM, Carbondale, Colorado
Sunday 2 Dec 1917   6 December 1917

That Dannie Cupid a daring little outlaw, is still at large and operating successfully as a matchmaker, was proven Sunday when Miss Katherine L., only daughter of Mr. and Mrs. George Sievers, was united in the holy bonds of matrimony to H. R. Holmes, after a brief courtship.

The romance was a short but pretty one, and extended over but three months time.

But relatives of the bride, and a few of the closest friends of each of the contracting parties, were present when Rev. Dean of the local M. E. Church joined the popular pair into one.

Efforts were made to keep the wedding a close secret, but it leaked out during the day, and you can imagine the surprise of the bridal party when a number of friends from Carbondale were at Sweet Spur, 4 miles out of town, to bid them Godspeed mid a shower of rice and old shoes, when they were boarding No. 6 which they had flagged.

The bride is well known to all of us, having resided in our midst for years. She graduated from the Carbondale High School three years ago with high honors, and has since graduated from the Grand Island Nebraska Business College. Not only has she an enviable education, but also possesses all of those admirable qualities to make her one of the most popular of our young ladies.

Mr. Holmes is the president and general manager of the Carbondale Reservoir and Irrigation Company and holds a like official capacity with the Holmes Motor Truck Company, the latter patent for which he is responsible. During the past seven years he has spent a greater part of his time in Carbondale, and has become well and favorably known throughout the district.

After a short visit in Denver the newlyweds will enjoy an extended honeymoon trip, the full particulars of which they refused to divulge.

They will make their home in Denver during winter months and in Carbondale in summer.

That Mr. and Mrs. Holmes enjoy many years of uninterrupted prosperity and connubial felicity is the wish of Item joined with that of the many friends of each.

"My dad and Jerome Stovall lived at the old creamery [Ed Stauffacher's Dairy & Cheese Factory, started in the spring of 1893, which was later converted to apartments] south of Catherine's Store. My dad rode a motorcycle for transportation around Carbondale and up on the mesa. He caused all kinds of trouble driving that motorcycle by people either riding or driving horses. One day, one of those people on horseback was a young lady named Katherine Sievers. My dad and Katherine always seemed to meet on Road 109, and my dad soon learned to stop the cycle, turn off the motor and let the lady ride by peacefully. That's how they met, and it must have been love at first sight, because they were married three months later!"

Harleigh R. owned a company in Littleton, Colorado, at that time, the Holmes Motor Truck Company. He spent his time between Carbondale and Littleton. While in Carbondale he built the first four wheel drive truck produced by the Holmes Motor Company. It was

Harleigh Holmes Four Wheel Drive Truck. The truck was built in Roy Pattison's Smithy Shop (the building housing the Village Smithy Restaurant in 1998). Left to right: George Sievers, Jerome Stovall, Frank Gertig, an unidentified man, and Harleigh Holmes.

built in the old Carbondale Blacksmith Shop which, in 1998, is the Village Smithy Restaurant, owned by Chris and Terry Chacos.

Helen (Holmes) Bond remembers, "There were no headlights on the original truck because the roads were so bad, no one drove at night."

The reservoir construction began and ended in the summer of 1912. Harleigh's father, James H. Holmes, was the President, Harleigh R. Holmes was the Vice President, and Jerome S. Stovall, the Secretary-Treasurer of the Carbondale Reservoir and Irrigation Company. The address of the company was Suite 810, Continental Building, Denver, Colorado.

Lee Holmes says, "My father advertised in all the bars in Aspen, Glenwood, Carbondale, and Basalt to get men to work on building the reservoir. There were a hundred teams of horses and three crews working continuously; one crew coming to work, one crew leaving, and one crew working, and it lasted until the reservoir was finished in the fall."

| J. H. HOLMES, President | H. R. HOLMES, Vice-President | J. S. STOVALL, Secretary | J. C. STOVALL, Treasurer |

The Carbondale Reservoir & Irrigation Company
Phone Champa 1068

DIRECTORS:
W. H. Dickson
J. C. Stovall
J. S. Stovall
J. H. Holmes
H. R. Holmes

Suite 810 Continental Building

Property located on the Colorado Midland and the D. & R. G. railroads in Eagle and Garfield Counties, Colorado.

Denver, Colorado Feb. 3rd.,1915,

Mr. Fred Holgate
Carbondale, Colo.

Dear Fred;

    We learned yesterday that Davies the fellow that Built Claggetts' house is not going to build Fenders house, so it may pay you to see him, trusting that you will be able to land this job, we remain,

    Very truly yours,

    Stovall & Holmes.

"The land was first cleared of rocks and sagebrush, then it was leveled and dug out with a piece of equipment called a Fresno, an earth digger and mover. The Fresno was pulled by a team and it had a cutting blade which dug up the earth and scooped it into a big bucket about three feet across, 18 inches deep and about 24 inches wide.

"The earth was then transported to the reservoir dam or wherever it was needed, and released with a lever. Then, the team was driven back, and the process repeated. The teams dragged out rocks and took them where they were needed for support and drainage. The Fresno was a small piece of machinery to move a damn little bit of earth!"

A Fresno, used for digging and moving earth.

As mentioned before, Harleigh R. traveled back and forth from Carbondale to Denver, overseeing the reservoir company and Holmes Motor Truck Company. The name of the Motor Company was changed to Plains Motors at one time, and to Coleman Motors when A.E. Coleman came into the business. The company manufactured Coleman trucks and had the patent for four wheel drive. In 1929 and 1930, Harleigh R. built three race cars that the Unser brothers raced up Pikes Peak. He also built race cars for the Indianapolis 500.

In 1937, Harleigh R. bought the stone house that the founder of Littleton, Richard S. Little, had built.

Katherine (Sievers) Holmes traveled with her husband when possible, but she was always the happiest at her parents' ranch on what is today, in 1998, the Aspen Glen subdivision on Highway 82. She kept the ranch as long as she lived.

Helen (Holmes) Bond recalls, "Mother was so happy when she learned that the Lower Cattle Creek Schoolhouse had been moved from the corner where Highway 82 and Cattle Creek Road met up to the Heights. It made her happy because the place she had gone to school for so many years was near the reservoir her husband had constructed."

Don and Anita Witt in front of the Lower Cattle Creek School on Missouri Heights. 1967.

The school was moved to the Witt-Thurman ranch (the old William H. Harris/Sirola place) in 1965 by Donald Witt and George Thurman.

Harleigh R. Holmes died in 1963. Katherine (Sievers) Holmes died in 1975. They are buried in Rosebud Cemetery in Glenwood Springs. Jerome Stovall worked at Coleman Motors until his death and is buried in Denver

Lee Holmes remembers, "My dad was some fellow! He always had some new project going even before he finished the last one!"

Harleigh Holmes, Builder of Carbondale Reservoir, Dies

Harleigh Randall Holmes, 82, builder of the Carbondale Reservoir and Irrigation Project at Missouri Heights, and a retired inventor and general manager of Coleman Trucks, died Wednesday, July 4, at the Carbondale ranch home of his son, Lee Holmes.

Mr. Holmes, in failing health for some time, lived in Littleton for 42 years preceding his death. He was born on February 3, 1881, in Kansas.

He married Katherine Sievers at Carbondale on December 2, 1917. Mr. Holmes was a member of the Presbyterian Church, the Masonic Lodge and the Rotary Club.

Survivors, besides the son and widow, include a second son, Harleigh R. Holmes, Jr., of Detroit Michigan; two daughters, Mrs. By (Dorothy) Weeks, Littleton; and Mrs. Richard (Helen) Bond, Valparaiso, Indiana.

Funeral services were conducted at Littleton, with burial and graveside rites held Saturday, July 27, at Rosebud Cemetery in Glenwood Springs.

Helen (Holmes) Bond shares, "Our father was a unique individual. He loved putting water in places it had never been – to make things grow!"

Author's Note: Lee Holmes passed away October 6, 1997, just weeks after telling me his family history. He was so proud of his father's accomplishments. Lee was such a fine gentleman, so willing to help with this work – I will never forget him.

THE HOLMES FAMILY

Harleigh Randall Holmes
1881 - 1963

Katherine L. Sievers
1895 - 1975

Dorothy
Cyrus Weeks } Carol, Helen

Harleigh
Olive } Harleigh R., Deborah, Holli Leigh

Lee
Elaine } Mary Lee, Jaqueline, Lee Jr., Catherine

Helen
Richard S. Bond } Katherine, Margaret, Julia

Now don't you cry old woman
I know you'll miss your kin
But we're bound for Colorado
To a place you've never been.

I got 160 acres
So we're leavin' ol' Jamesport
And we're gonna' raise potatoes
Up above the Roarin' Fork!

– A.W.

THE IRA FENDER FAMILY – 1914

Ira Fender
1874 - 1950

Renettie Viola (Pease) Fender
1879 - 1956

THE IRA FENDER FAMILY

Ira Fender's parents were Rebecca J. Sloan and William Harley Fender. They were Pennsylvania Dutch, and lived in Illinois, and then Iowa, where Ira was born and lived most of his younger years. He and Renettie (Nettie) Pease were married in 1900 in Liberty Township, Ringgold, Iowa, and had two sons there, Verle and Loren. They moved to Jamesport, Missouri, and had another son and daughter, Eddis and Varoqua (Rokie).

Ira was a farmer but for a short while tried his hand at owning and operating a hardware store in Gillman, Missouri. He sold the store and was once again farming, but times were difficult, and he was ripe for a change. Like other Jamestown residents, Ira became caught up in the hopes and dreams of a new and better life in Colorado, promoted by the two young engineers Holmes and Stovall.

Ira made the trip to Colorado and took home with him a suitcase full of wheat, barley, oats, spuds and alfalfa raised by farmers on the high mesa. Ira's son, Eddis, never forgot the stench that came from the suitcase when it was opened on the kitchen table. Ira's face beamed with admiration as he passed around the grain and hay and large, half rotten Burbank potatoes to show his family and friends. He looked at his wife, Nettie, whose face had fallen with comprehension, and nodded his head with flat determination as he spoke, "We're moving to Colorado!"

Years, later, Nettie would write to her granddaughter Geraldine about the move, "…it was a sad day for all concerned, January 3, 1915, a cold, rainy evening. So hard to bear, leaving my precious mother and father, sisters and brothers. What a sad Christmas, 1914."

Ira and the two older boys, Loren and Verle, left earlier, on December 24, 1914, in a chartered box car filled to the brim with all of their worldly possessions. There was farm machinery, a mower and a binder, a boxed-up piano, and a 1914 model Ford, a few chickens, and one cow, plus the horses and mules, and what furniture would fit.

Eddis remembers that his father had been told, "Horses don't fare well in the high altitude," and had sold all but three: Florie, Lady and Bess, who would make the trip. His father had heard, "Mules would do better in Colorado," and bought four of the strongest he could find: Little Jack, Big Jack, John (a white mule), and Jude (a Jenny).

The brothers Loren and Verle hid inside the Ford the whole trip. Ira made them hide to save on the fare, and throughout the trip the bulls (railroad policemen) would check out the box car, but never found them. Ira rode in the box car, and every 24 hours he had to unload, water, and exercise the livestock. At every stop he would search for food and smuggle it in to the hungry boys.

Nettie, Eddis, Rokie and Nettie's sister, Vera, all rode coach on the train and left January 3, 1915, from Jamestown. Nettie wrote in her letter years later, "We didn't buy Eddis a half fare in hopes of sneaking him through and saving money, but when we stopped in Cameron, the conductor came by and took tickets. He told me I had to walk all the way back to the depot and buy a ticket for him. I was so afraid the train would leave without me."

Rokie Fender was seven years old when the Colorado Midland train arrived at the whistle stop at Catherine. At that time the railroad tracks were where Highway 82 is today in 1998. The dirt road between Glenwood Springs and Aspen was near the tracks at times, but was a twisty, dusty meandering road going from one farm to the next.

Rokie Fender recalls, "Dad and the boys were there to meet us, and the boys were so thrilled with the mountains, they were up on a hill above the railroad tracks waving at us as the train passed by. We lived on the old Ed Stauffacher place for awhile. Matt Stauffacher was still there. We called him 'Uncle Matt' even though he was not related to us. They let us live with them rent-free and gave us potatoes and apples all winter."

The Ed Stauffacher home still stands in its original place, the Blue Creek ranch, owned by Dr. William Gilligan.

Varoqua "Rokie" Fender, seven years old in 1915.

187

Ira had bought 160 acres on the high mesa from Rosetta and Charles Harris who had homesteaded the property. It was all sagebrush, except for five acres which was just roughly broken up so the Harris family could improve it for homestead rights. While the family lived with Uncle Matt at Catherine, Ira, the two boys and a neighbor, Fred Holgate built the house up on the mesa. It was built in a hurry, and the Fenders moved in April of 1915. The 160 acres Ira bought is located up Cattle Creek Road, left on Fender Lane and one mile west on the south side.

An unidentified dog, Rokie, Vera, Nettie and Eddis (left to right) outside the house which Ira, the Fender boys and Fred Holgate hurriedly built in 1914.

Eddis remembers the house, "In those days, they didn't insulate or anything like that. They just put up the outsiding and inside they just used wallboard – tacked it up and covered it with wallpaper, so it didn't take long to set it up."

In her letter to her granddaughter years later, Nettie wrote, "What hard times we had that first year. Sagebrush to be cleared, ground to be plowed, and no water except for the irrigation ditch. Drinking water had to be hauled from Blue Creek, about two miles away. In the winter the stock had to be driven to Blue Creek to drink."

A neighbor, George Hotz (son of Martin G. and Mary Hotz), helped Ira clear sagebrush. A railroad iron was dragged one way across the sagebrush with a team of mules, and going back the opposite way would break most of the plant off at the root. It was then raked into piles with a sulky rack and burned. Ira plowed and put in sixty acres of wheat the first year, and it was the only crop they had. The next year they planted potatoes, had a wonderful crop, and realized the rewards of the rich, black soil Holmes and Stovall had bragged about. Even in the years of water shortages, the potatoes grew well, and the Fenders became a part of the famed Carbondale Valley potato growers.

Loren Fender, son of Ira and Nettie Fender, proudly showing some of the famed Carbondale Valley potato crop. Photo circa 1917.

Eddis Fender recalls, "We were here about three years when Grandma and Grandpa Fender came out. They stayed at our place for awhile. It was 1918 and my dad's brother, Earl, was in the war [World War I] and when he was discharged – we didn't know he was coming – he walked over the hill to our place. Grandma and Grandpa found a place to buy near Carbondale, and he sent for his son Orville to come out from Nebraska. Orville got a farm up by ours."

Ira Fender (left) and Dr. Clagett (right) placing potatoes from the Fender's abundant potato crop in gunny sacks.

Orville Fender bought 360 acres from Dr. Oscar Clagett in 1918.

Rokie Fender remembers, "Some of our neighbors were the Matt Coles, the Clagetts, the Hotz's, the Harris family, the Smiths, and the McLeans. Many were from Missouri and some, like the Clagetts, Hotz's, Smiths, and Fred Holgate, from Denver, had come out before my folks. The high mesa had already been given the name 'Missouri Heights.'"

When they first arrived in Colorado, the Fender children went to school at Catherine, where there was a one-room schoolhouse, until their house was finished on the Heights. After that, the two older boys played hooky most of the time, but once in awhile attended a school in a converted farm house about four miles from the Fender place. It was a house owned by a man named Clauson, and the school district moved in a few desks and found a teacher. After that school closed, the boys went to Crystal Springs School. In the early 1900s, Ira Fender, Ben and Joe Hotz, John McLean, Matt Cole and Dave Thompson furnished the logs and lumber, and all of them built the Blue Creek School. The foundation of this historic school can still be seen on the Witt ranch in 1998.

The Catherine School (on the old road near what is known in 1998 as Highway 82).

Rokie Fender recollects, "I went to the Blue Creek School. Lula Cole and Florence Loesch were the teachers, and the school sat way back up there. When we were little we played all the kid games at school: kick the can, fox and geese, black sheep black sheep, pump pump pullaway, and Annie Annie over. As we got older, we played baseball.

"When the Blue Creek School became too small and deteriorated, the Luby School was built in 1926 on the Sweet place, across the road from the Blue Creek School. Paul Gould and his boys logged the trees from Basalt Mountain to build the school and they installed running water from 'that natural waterway, Blue Creek'."

Eddis remembered when the first telephone line to Missouri Heights was put in, and the first water pipeline which supplied water from Blue Creek to the Fender place. "Dad (Ira), Bill Harris, Verle, Loren and I built the telephone line. We couldn't get any supplies until 1918 when Midland Railroad pulled it up. They were selling telephone poles and wires, and we went down to El Jebel and put them up over the hill to the Heights. I was the only one who had climbing equipment, and I climbed the poles to test the line when there was trouble. We owned the line down as far as El Jebel, then we had to pay 'pole rent' from there to Carbondale to use our old crank telephone."

The first water pipeline from Blue Creek to the Fender place was installed in 1926. As Eddis Fender recalls, "After trying to drill a well with no success, I started thinking about pipe and getting water from Blue Creek, and I got to figuring the distance and what it would cost for buying pipe. I told Dad, 'I think we can put a pipeline in if we can get water from Paul Gould.' Paul Gould didn't like Dad very well, so Dad talked to Frank Sweet and Frank fell for it right away.

"Frank said, 'I think I can get water from Paul.' So he went over and got water from Paul. He (Paul) gave him (Frank) a deed for a tenth of a foot of water. Frank Sweet was supposed to give Dad – and it didn't cost him anything – a deed for half of that.

"We started the pipeline and got it down to Sweet's place and Verle said, 'I'm not going any further until we get the deed for this water.'

"Frank Sweet was up there and he said, 'Oh, don't worry about that, you'll get the deed all right!'

"Verle said, 'When we get it in hand we'll go on with it. You come up with it.'

"He said, 'Don't stop the digging, don't stop the digging, it takes time to get this done and when it's done we'll straighten all this out.'

"Well, when we got it done and Dad went down to straighten it up with Frank, he said, 'No, I'm not going to give you a deed for it.'

"So, Paul Gould heard about it and he said, 'I'll give Ira a deed for a tenth foot of the water with the stipulation that he can't take any more than a tenth foot of the water for the pipeline."

Rokie Fender remembers, "Before we had the pipeline we stored water in the cistern. We had a bucket with a rope to get the water out. You couldn't use the water from there very long because it got stale and wiggle worms got in it. Then we got the pipeline and we did away with that, and turned the cistern into an ice house."

Eddis Fender adds, "We got the ice from the Missouri Heights reservoir, and put ice down there in the old cistern. We put beer down there so we could have ice-cold beer."

Rokie continues, "Mama had an old ice chest to keep ice in, and keep food cool. We used to make ice cream with the last snow that we could get along the ditch. Before we had the ice chest, Mama would use the orange crates that were divided in half. On the top, she'd set a pan of cool water, and a tea towel in front, and wet gunny sacks around the box. It worked as a cooler and kept the butter as hard as could be."

The Fender place had a blacksmith shop, a bunk house, a smoke house, a coal house, a potato cellar, and a garage. When "spud pickers" came to work the fields they stayed in the blacksmith shop until the bunk house was finished. Rokie says, "The 'spud pickers'

Left to right: Lulu Cole, Loren Fender and Rokie Fender.

were Mexican men, and there were usually four or five who came to stay for a couple of weeks with us and picked potatoes."

Rokie Fender was 89 years old on March 30, 1997. From her home in Paonia, Colorado, where she lives with her niece Myrlene (Verle Fender's daughter) she talked about life on the Heights, "My Mama was sick a lot, so I had to do chores and cook quite a bit.

Ira Fender's place; Gary Fender.

A sulky rake, used to rake the dry hay and bunch it for easy handling with a pitchfork.

I remember mixing up the bread and taking the pan in to Mama in the bedroom and showing it to her, asking if it was stiff enough. I did ranch work too, and I drove the team with the sulky rake."

A sulky rake was a long structure with big, round tines – a half circle of steel – that were close together, and when simultaneously lowered to the ground, picked up the hay. When the dump lever was pushed with the operator's foot, the hay was released into windrows (long rows of hay).

The next step was to pick up the hay with a buck rake. Once full, the hay was transported by a team of horses or mules to the hay stackyard. With the buck rake, the hay was put onto a stacker. The stacker was pulled by a single horse, and the machine would raise the hay up and dump it behind the stacker. Then, a man with a pitchfork would finish the stacking by shaping the haystack into a peak so that it would be as water and snow resistant as possible. This is how the hay was stacked until it was used to feed.

Rokie continues, "One time the team ran away with me and Dad, and the boys were running and yelling, 'Jump, jump!', but I couldn't jump forward for fear of falling into the teeth of the rake, so I kicked my feet up and went over backwards and onto the hard ground. I was hurt, but I didn't break anything. The team kept right on going, across the ditch, and finally stopped at the fence line.

A buck rake, for picking up hay from windrows.

Operating a Mormon derrick hay stacker.

"We made our own beer and rootbeer and butter and lye soap, and of course, we had cows and chickens and hogs. We'd sell cream and eggs to Dinkel's Mercantile in Carbondale. Dinkel's had everything in the world in the store: dry goods, groceries, hardware and lumber, machinery, medical supplies, feed and seed – everything you could think of, they had it. We paid our bill at Dinkel's when we harvested. We also sold cream and eggs to the creamery in Glenwood Springs.

"Even though we worked hard, we had many fun times up on the Heights. There was always something going on. The adults had card games nearly every weekend at someone's house. There were dances at the Nelson place, where he had a big barn. Sometimes there was a guitar player and a violin player, and sometimes just the violin player. Everyone brought food and we laughed and danced all night, and didn't go home 'til morning. We had picnics and box socials and fishing parties in the summer, and in the winter we had sledding parties and candy making parties.

"I always loved horses, and I rode every evening. We realized after we moved there that horses lived just fine in the altitude and we had a lot of horses through the years. I had a horse named Topsy and she had a filly named Nancy. Loren bought a horse named Betsy and when she had a colt we named it He-be.

"My father, Ira, was a gentle man, easy to get along with. He never spanked one of us kids, but left the disciplining to Mama. He always said the same thing when we were acting up, 'Old Lady, look at those kids!' Mama was very loving and affectionate. Everyone adored her, and she made us all feel loved and important.

"After we kids had all grown up, we had kids of our own. Verle had a daughter named Myrlene, whom I live with today, and I had a son named Harold. Well, Myrlene and Harold were pals and they had a lot of fun and got into a lot of mischief together. They were ornery as could be, and one time they took rabbit turds and rolled them in warmed up chocolate. They took them to school and passed them around to the kids. It took a minute to soak in, but when it did there was lots of spittin' and screamin' and fightin'!

Loren Fender on his horse, Betsy.

Rokie Fender and her dog Misty, 1996.

"I'm the only one left of my immediate family now... the only one to remember and tell the wonderful stories of life on Missouri Heights."

Ira and Renettie Fender are buried at the Rosebud Cemetery in Glenwood Springs, Colorado.

History of the Land Owners
Rosetta and Charles homesteaded the land.

Ira and Nettie Fender	1913	
Harold and Ruth Fender	1959	
Harold Reese	1962	200 acres
Sirous Saghatoleskami	1998	160 acres
Kip Koski	1998	40 acres

THE IRA FENDER FAMILY

Ira Fender
1874-1950

Renettie Viola (Pease) Fender
1879 - 1956

They both died at age 77.

Children
Verle..........................1900 - 1968
Loren ....1902 - 1949
Eddis..........................1906 - 1989
Varoqua (Rokie) ......1908 -

<u>Verle</u> } Myrlene, Geraldine   Verle } Verle
Bertha Laudenklos   Bessie Peterson

<u>Loren</u> } Betty, Norvel, Gail and Donna
Glafrie Green

<u>Eddis</u> } David and Leroy
Olla Jacobs

<u>Rokie</u> } Harold
Harold Sweet

I'm a-leavin' you, Missouri

Goin' West for the mountain air

Got a farm in Colorado

Gonna' raise potatoes there.

I got a boxcar full of furniture

My wagon and my tools

I'm a leavin' you, Missouri

And I'm takin' my Missouri mules.

– A.W.

THE CLAGETT FAMILY – 1914

Dr. Oscar Frederich Clagett
1881-1954

Effie Orilla (Stevens) Clagett
Lived to be 89 Years Old

THE CLAGETT FAMILY

In 1911 or 1912 two young men, Harley Holmes and Jerome Stovall traveled from Colorado to Jamesport, Missouri, to visit Stovall's relatives. Holmes and Stovall had been working on a project to build a reservoir on the Western Slope of Colorado. The reservoir was being built on one of the high mesas above the Roaring Fork River, about seven miles northwest of Basalt and five miles northeast of Carbondale. The men planned to sell the water by providing an irrigation system to the dozen or so farmers who lived there.

Holmes and Stovall were very impressed by the rich black loam of the cultivated fields, the rolling hills covered with sagebrush, the awesome beauty of the snow-covered peaks of Mt. Sopris, and the surrounding Rocky Mountains. They spoke so enthusiastically to relatives and friends about Colorado that they convinced several Jamesport residents to go see for themselves.

One man had been entertaining thoughts of life in Colorado, even before Holmes and Stovall made their trip to Missouri. His name was Dr. Oscar Frederich Clagett and he had been ill for some time. With his own medical knowledge and that of his colleagues, the problem was diagnosed as "probably tuberculosis." Although modern medicine and remedies were unknown in the early 1900s, Dr. Clagett knew that the dry climate of Colorado might be beneficial. When Holmes and Stovall made their trip to Jamesport, Missouri, and when Dr. Clagett heard their glowing report of the Roaring Fork Valley and the high mesa, he made the trip to Colorado.

Remarkably, during the time he spent in the Rockies, his health improved considerably, and he made the decision to give up his practice and the drugstore that he owned in Jamesport, move to Colorado, and become a farmer!

Dr. Clagett's ancestors were of English descent and he became the third generation of physicians. His grandfather, Dr. Hezekiah Clagett, had practiced in the south in the mid-1800s; his father, Dr. Dudley Malcolm Clagett, practiced in Victoria, Missouri, beginning in the 1870s, and Oscar Frederick Clagett followed in their footsteps.

Oscar Frederick was born August 8, 1881, in Winston, Missouri, and graduated from University Medical College in Kansas City, Missouri, in 1899.

Effie Orilla Stevens was born in Winston, the daughter of John Sylvester Stevens and Betty Burch. Effie went to Northwestern University in Evanston, Illinois. They were married in Winston August 14, 1904, and moved to Jamesport, Missouri, where Dr. Clagett practiced medicine, and owned and operated his drugstore.

Dr. Clagett made the trip out to Colorado in 1913 and bought 360 acres from the McNulty's, who had homesteaded the land. There was a small, rough log, two room cabin and a small barn on the northeast corner of the property, and only about twenty acres had been plowed. There were no fences, but it appeared that except for about eight acres of rocks and trees, the rest of the land could be developed into productive farm land.

By this time the Clagetts had three small children and a fourth on the way. Effie's father, John Stevens, was the president of the Winston Bank, and she had been raised in comfort and luxury. It must have been with great apprehension and difficulty that she accepted her husband's decision to move to the sparsely inhabited virgin land with no electricity, no running water or comforts of any kind.

As her daughter, Betty Burch (Clagett) deBeque, would explain many years later, "My mother came to Colorado because of my father's health. They shared a deep love for each other that withstood all the hardships and heartaches they endured on the Heights and throughout their life together."

Years later, Dr. Clagett's son, Dr. O.T. "Jim" Clagett, would write in his autobiography, "It was decided to make the move to Colorado as early as feasible in the spring of 1914 in order to have as much summer weather as possible to build an adequate house and barn, and to cultivate as much new land as time permitted. There were supplies of all kinds necessary for the new venture that had to be obtained. Father bought a horse and two Missouri mules, a Jersey cow, some pigs and chickens, a farm wagon, buggy, plows, rakes, harnesses, shovels, and carpenter tools."

In February 1914, Dr. Clagett chartered a railroad box car and loaded his newly acquired possessions and animals. Another Jamesport resident, Vic Thompson, left on the same train and shared the box car, taking his possessions and his own team of Missouri mules. Vic Thompson was a brother of Blanch Smith, the new bride of Frank Smith, and the three young people were going to farm the 160 acres directly east of Dr. Clagett's on the high mesa.

Dr. Clagett kissed his wife and children goodbye, with the knowledge that they would follow in a few weeks. He and Vic Thompson rode in the box car to tend their animals, and were, at last, on the way to Colorado.

In 1998 Betty still remembers and laughs about one of the family stories that happened during her father's trip. "My mother, Effie, had shown my father a certain barrel that had been packed with household belongings, and asked him to treat it with care, as it held her fine crystal and china. Father did as he was instructed, marked and loaded the barrel carefully, fussed over it and even sat on it to keep it from rocking during the trip. When it was finally unpacked at the new farm, it was full of metal pots and pans."

Frank Smith, the new groom, joined the men in Colorado a few days later, and at that time, the men from Jamesport – Dr. Clagett, Vic Thompson, Frank Smith, Jerome Stovall, and another Missourian, Carl Hill – named the high mesa above the Roaring Fork "Missouri Heights" in honor of their home state.

In mid-March 1914, Effie, and her four young children, Mary Eleanor (eight years old), John Malcolm (seven years old), Oscar "Jim" Theron (five years old), and baby Helen Louise (two months old), boarded the train to Colorado, accompanied by Oscar's father, Dr. Dudley Clagett. When they finally arrived at the Catherine stop it was ten o'clock at night and quite cold, with snow on the ground. There was nothing in sight, and no one to meet them. The conductor became quite upset, and did not want to leave them standing in the open, stranded on a cold night. It took determined persuasion for Effie to convince him that her husband was far too conscientious and responsible to have forgotten them. Shaking his head with reluctance, the conductor finally moved on with the train. In a few minutes "the clip-clop of horses' hooves and the light from the lantern" was evident, and Dr. Clagett, full of apologies for being late, was thrilled to see his beloved family.

In the days that followed, Oscar's father returned to Winston, Missouri, and the family of four children and two adults moved into the rough log cabin built by the McNulty's. There was no electricity, no water, no toilet, and the only heat came from a kitchen stove which burned coal. Water was hauled from Blue Creek, three miles away.

Jim recalls in his autobiography, "I remember my mother describing the absolute bottom of desolation. One day, after she had done a large washing and hung everything out to dry, the cow got out of the pen and knocked the clothesline down, dropping the entire wash in the mud. It must have taken a special kind of courage to face the problems and difficulties that presented themselves."

The Clagett home in 1914.

The big, red barn built by Dr. Clagett in 1914, called "Clagett's Folly" by neighbors in 1914 still stands in 1998.

As soon as the weather permitted, construction was started on the new house, and the fields were cleared of sagebrush and plowed and disked. As with other families at the time, the young boys, Malcolm and Jim, were responsible for burning the sagebrush. A large piece of railroad track was pulled by the mules, first one way across the field, and then the other way, breaking the sagebrush off at the roots. It was up to the boys to rake the brush into a large pile and keep it burning. When the task was completed, the plow and disk were used and the land was ready to plant. Like others on the mesa, the Clagetts learned that oats, barley, wheat, and potatoes were the crops to raise.

After the house was completed, the family moved in on Thanksgiving Day, 1914.

Jim Clagett: "It was a two-story, with a living room, three bedrooms, a dining room, a kitchen, pantries and closets. We had an outdoor privy, and the only heat in the house came from the kitchen stove and a coal burning stove in the living room. We built a larger cement cistern which held water and produced enough pressure for pipes and taps in the kitchen."

Betty remembers a story, "When the kids took their weekly baths, it was in the kitchen near the hot stove, in a big galvanized tub filled with warm water. One time, Malcolm and Jim got to horsin' around and Malcolm fell backward, butt first into the open hot oven door. For the rest of his life he carried the brand on his hind end.

"Dad was not a farmer or a carpenter, but he decided to build the big, red barn which is still on the place today in 1998. People laughed at his efforts, called it 'Clagett's Folly,' I guess because of the shape and size of it."

In September 1914, the three oldest Clagett children, Mary Eleanor, Malcolm, and Oscar (Jim), who was only five years old, were enrolled in the Catherine School. It was four miles down the hill near the same railroad tracks where the family had arrived from Missouri. The children walked to school and back home, which was not an easy trip for a five year old. Catherine was a one room school with grades one through eight, and had about twenty students in 1914. Vi Patterson was the teacher's name. Eleanor remembers that, "Little Jim would get sleepy in the afternoon, and crawl up on the teacher's lap for a nap, while she continued with her lessons."

Effie constantly worried about her children. Betty says, "She always worried that they were not getting the right opportunities for education and development. She was in agony watching them walk off to school. She organized the first hot lunch program in the area. Each winter dozens of the mothers would make hot soup or stew and take it to the school to serve all the children at lunch time."

Christmas of 1914 was very special for the Clagett children. Effie and Oscar gave them a wonderful Christmas present – a horse to ride to school.

Jim Clagett remembers, "It was a small, white Indian pony that we promptly named George Pokey Legs. George was the most amiable, gentle animal imaginable. He proved this by accepting, without reaction, all the harassments we subjected him to in the year ahead. When we set off to school, my sister Eleanor, being the oldest,

The horse, George Pokey Legs, a Christmas gift to the Clagett children in 1914 from their parents Effie and Oscar Clagett. Seated, left to right: Oscar Theron "Jim," John Malcolm, Mary Eleanor, and baby Helen Louise.

would be in the saddle, my brother Malcolm was just behind her, and, of course, being the youngest, I was on the horse's rump, clinging to my brother. Our six heels kicked George almost constantly, and I wielded a switch from my position in the rear. In spite of all our efforts to increase George's speed, I don't think we ever got him beyond a fast walk under any circumstances. On the other hand, he never kicked or bucked or complained in any way, and we never had any mishaps that could be blamed on George. He was wise and surefooted, and could not be forced by any means to take a route or path that he did not think was safe. Our whole family has happy memories of George, and the pleasure and service he provided. I was certainly pleased not to have to make that long walk to school and back on my own legs any longer. However, riding horseback presented problems, too. On cold winter days we would get so cold and stiff that when we arrived at school the teacher and other students would have to help us get off the horse, and then we would

Clagett potato cellar where the Clagett children sorted potatoes and read books by the light of the lantern. Picture taken in 1998.

have to rub our nearly frozen feet with snow to restore circulation. It was not an easy way to acquire an education."

Life for the Clagett family improved on the high mesa, and the best of all dreams came true as Dr. Clagett lost all signs of tuberculosis.

The potato crop was of utmost importance on the farms of Missouri Heights, and the children of all the families worked at planting, cultivating, and sorting of the crop. Large underground potato cellars were a necessity on each farm. Many potato cellars still stand today (1998) on the Heights. They are all in a state of deterioration.

In his autobiography, Jim describes his memories of the potato crops. "Seed potatoes had been stored during the winter in the underground cellar. It was necessary to cut each potato in such a manner that at least one eye and a generous portion of the potato itself was included in each seed.

"Most potatoes could be cut into six to ten seed potatoes. We children were recruited to help with this effort, and spent many hours in the cold, dark cellar cutting up seed potatoes. In order to relieve the tedium of the chore, each member would take turns reading books by the light of the lantern. This was a wonderfully effective way to make the time pass faster while doing a boring job, and provided entertainment and education for us all as well.

"After planting the potatoes the rows had to be cultivated at least twice, irrigated thoroughly on several occasions, and the most onerous job of all, they had to be weeded. This job fell to my brother and me. We spent many long, hot days trudging up and down the rows of potatoes pulling weeds!"

Effie hated the farm and the difficult life it presented to her, but she dearly loved her husband, and to have him restored to health was worth all the sacrifice. Still, there was many a time when her patience was stretched to the limit.

Betty says, "I remember Mama telling about the Jersey cow and the starch water. She had to heat starch for our clothes in a big galvanized tub of hot water over a fire outside while she washed the clothes. If she went back inside the house for something, the Jersey cow would sneak up and drink the starch water – no matter how hot – she loved it! Poor Mama!"

In 1918 life once again changed drastically for the Clagett family. The United States entered World War I, and suddenly there was a shortage of doctors in Colorado. Dr. Clagett was asked to resume his profession, and he did not decline. The family left the farm on Missouri Heights, sold out to Orville O. Fender, and moved to Carbondale, a town of 300 residents, where Dr. Clagett's practice was most welcomed and soon flourished because of the 1918 flu epidemic.

Jim Clagett recalls, "My father hurried from one patient to another, all over the countryside, at all hours of the day and night. Most of the house calls were made on horseback or sled, and later with his horse and buggy! Baby Helen Louise, four years old, died in the 1918 flu epidemic. Betty Burch Clagett was born in Carbondale November 12, 1921. She was a great joy to all the family and helped make up for the loss of Helen Louise."

In 1923 Dr. Clagett moved his family to Rifle, Colorado, to take over the practice of a Dr. LeRossignol. As the Clagett family lived out their lives in Colorado, there were times of great joy, and times of unbelievable despair.

John Malcolm Clagett died in 1931 from a fall off Flatiron Mountain in Boulder, Colorado, while attending college. The medical career of O.T. "Jim" Clagett made him the fourth generation physician. The magnitude of his accomplishments would have amazed his ancestors. In 1940 as a young surgeon, he was given a position on the surgical staff at the Mayo Clinic in Rochester, Minnesota. His specialty was thoracic and cardiovascular surgery, and he spent his medical career at the Mayo Clinic. He was one of the most highly acclaimed surgeons in the world, receiving honorary membership in

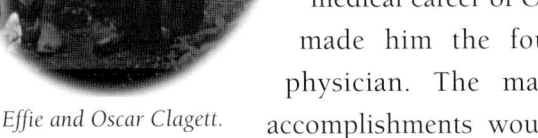
Effie and Oscar Clagett.

The Clagett house in 1998.

all the major important surgical societies in the United States and foreign societies. He was on the surgical staff at Mayo for 32 years, and performed a fantastic number of surgical procedures, helped train hundreds of young surgeons who became outstanding teachers and surgeons, and made very substantial contributions to surgical procedures and techniques.

Jim states, "Eleanor was kind and compassionate, had a wonderful sense of humor and a great imagination. She became a laboratory technician in Denver and married Larry Reed.

"Betty became a teacher and taught school in various places in Colorado. She married Wallace E. deBeque from Carbondale, and taught in the Carbondale schools for some time. In 1998 Betty and Wallace live near Carbondale, not far from Missouri Heights.

Dr. Oscar F. Clagett died January 19, 1954, and was buried at Rifle, Colorado, beside his son Malcolm. The Clagett Memorial Hospital in Rifle is dedicated to his memory. Effie died at the age of 89 and is buried with Oscar and Malcolm.

Jim says, "I learned what a wonderful, wise, kind individual my father really was. He had not had great opportunities. He was always a small town country doctor, and was not able to attend many medical meetings or associate with other doctors, but he always kept up with all that was new in the medical world."

Betty says, "My mother was a very loving, caring person. Every year she would buy five bushels of concord grapes, make grape juice and give it to Father's patients. They were a very affectionate couple, Dad always had his arm around her."

History of the Land Owners

Owner	Year	Acres
Pat and Margaret McNulty		360 acres
Effie and Oscar F. Clagett	1913	360 acres
Orville O. and Orville S. "Bud" Fender	1918	360 acres
Arnold Winters	1964	360 acres
Dick Hunt	1967	360 acres

THE SMITH FAMILY – 1914

Frank Smith
1892 - 1978

Blanch (Thompson) Smith
1891 - 1977

THE SMITH FAMILY

Frank worked at a grocery store in Jamesport, Missouri, delivering groceries to customers' homes, including the Thompsons. Blanch was smitten with him, and began to order more and more groceries. They fell in love and were married in Jamesport on June 5, 1912. The couple moved to Albany, Oregon, where Frank worked as a baggage master for the Southern Pacific Railroad.

Jerome Stovall had been a family friend back in Jamesport, and Blanch's father, Dr. Robert Victor Thompson, bought a relinquishment to a dry land claim in Colorado from him. The land was 160 acres located up on the high mesa, to be irrigated from the reservoir which Jerome Stovall and Harleigh Holmes were building. When Dr. Thompson told Blanch and Frank about the land in Colorado, they were quite interested and soon decided to leave Oregon and move to Colorado. Blanch's brother, Victor Thompson, decided to become partners with Frank in the farming venture, and went with them to Colorado.

Dr. Thompson had a home built on the Colorado property in 1913, before the couple moved. The home still stands today in 1998, on 100 Road.

In 1968 Mike Smith, daughter-in-law to Blanch Smith, encouraged Blanch to write her memories of Missouri Heights.

The Smith home, built in 1913.

The Smith home in 1998, built by carpenters from Denver in 1913.

Blanch: "We sold our house in Albany, and most of our furniture as the freight would be too expensive. I had a piano that I didn't want to part with, and Frank had a Morris chair that he wanted to bring. We shipped a large wooden box and three trunks.

"Father told us that our friends in Jamesport, Dr. Oscar Clagett and his wife, Effie, had bought land right next to ours in Colorado. When we arrived in Jamesport from Albany, Dr. Clagett had a railroad freight car loaded with his and my brother Victor's belongings. The Clagetts had furniture, a team of mules, a Jersey cow, and an old horse. My brother, Victor, had a team of mules that were real gentle and well broke. Dr. Clagett's mules were wild!

"Vic had two sows and some chickens and some furniture my mother had given him. Frank went on to Colorado before me. I wanted to go out on the train with Effie Clagett and help her with her children, but my ticket had to be used before she was ready to leave. So, it was decided

Effie Clagett and children.

that Dr. D. M. Clagett, Dr. Oscar's father, would travel with Effie. I left Jamesport March 28, 1914.

"Frank met my train in Glenwood Springs and we stayed at the Denver Hotel. The next morning we walked around town and gave Glenwood 'the once over' as it has been quite a popular place for honeymooners, like Niagara Falls.

"We went to Farmer's Spur on the Denver Rio Grande and my brother, Vic, met us there with Dr. Clagett's spring wagon. We stopped at Catherine and talked with Mrs. Clara Holmes (Harleigh Holmes' wife). They lived in part of a building which had once been a cheese factory at the Judge Stauffacher's place. There was another apartment in the building where Jerome and Dick Stovall lived, and later on Mabel and Elizabeth (Jerome's wife and daughter) lived there for the summer.

"We started up to the Missouri Heights, and the road was so narrow I said, 'If I ever get there, I didn't think I would ever leave.' The neighbors heard we were coming and were peeking out the windows. I'm sure they took one look at us and said, 'They won't last long!'

"We heard that when the men had arrived from Missouri, Dr. Clagett, my brother, Victor Thompson, Jerome Stovall, and Carl Hill, that they had named the high mesa up above the Roaring Fork 'Missouri Heights.' It was named when we arrived there in 1914.

"My father had already had a house built for us on the property. Some of the neighbors broke sagebrush on part of it and planted oats, which they cut for hay. There were no fences, and it was all sagebrush. Harleigh and Jerome got carpenters from Denver to build the house, and the carpenters boarded with Mrs. George Blue. It was quite a nice little house, with a living room, dining room, two bedrooms, with nice closets, a kitchen pantry, a screened-in back porch, and a basement. They built a cistern up in the field, and the water was piped to the house by gravity flow. The cistern was filled by water from the reservoir, and had a filter box filled with gravel and charcoal.

"That first day, after we had our dinner, the men took me to see where the Clagetts were going to live. It was a three-room house, way back in the field; one large room that they used for a living room, and bedroom combined, a smaller room that was for the dining room, and a smaller kitchen. When the men had unloaded some of their things, they set the barrels that had her dishes out in the yard. The hogs had come along and rooted them over, and her Haviland dishes were in the mud.

"Carl Hill was a young fellow from Jamesport, Missouri, who had bought eighty acres of land and built himself a two-room house across the road from where the Clagetts later built their house. He helped Dr. Clagett to get the place cleaned up. They papered the walls and made flour paste; it was lumpy so they used Mrs. Clagett's flour sifter to strain it. One day after she came, she was wanting to sift some flour, and couldn't find her sifter. Doc said, 'Oh, Carl used it to strain the paste and never cleaned it.'

"The mail box was a mile from our house. I walked over for the mail nearly every day, then would take Clagetts' mail to them. I didn't have much to do but feed our men, as I did not have too much house work. They spent a lot of time building fence. I went out where they were nearly every morning. When it would get about time to eat, I would go in and fix our lunch.

"We did not go to town very often, about each two or three weeks. The only way we had to go was with the big wagon. My brother, Vic, had a nice team of grey mules that Dad had bought for him. Frank bought a team of horses. John, a bay gelding, and Nelle, a black mare that he bought from Mr. Wolf, the conductor on the D&RG train. Vic talked to Mr. Wolf as he came to Carbondale, and told him he would be wanting to buy. John, he got right away, but Nelle was at Silt; she had a colt. My brother went down to Silt on the train and rode Nelle home. He had quite a time, for he couldn't lead the colt and she did not want to follow. They were all about worn out when they finally arrived home.

"Dr. Clagett's place joined ours on the east. That summer the men got the fence built on three sides of our place and Dr. Clagett said they needn't be in a hurry to fence between the two places. The road had gone through our place, so after we fenced there had to be a different road. Harleigh Holmes and Frank made a road along the west side of our place. Harleigh surveyed it, and they used a scraper and mules. The road is in the same place today.

"The boys planted oats and seeded alfalfa along with it. They planted barley and some wheat. It was customary to plow alfalfa ground to plant potatoes. Joe Hotz was living in a house on the Boyle ranch. He sent one of his men to help us cut the seed potatoes. Then, he planted them for we had no potato planter.

"When the grain was ripe, they cut it and stacked it. One Saturday evening, a man came along and said that Mr. E.F. Martin sent word that they would be there to thresh the next day. I said, 'We're not going to thresh on Sunday.' The fellow said, 'Suit yourselves, but they thresh every day that weather is nice.' Frank and I had to go to Carbondale that night to get provisions. I had no idea how much food it would take. Mrs. Clagett and the children came the next morning to help me.

"That fall, Frank got Mr. Fred Holgate, a neighbor and also a carpenter, to build a grainery. It was needed for storage of grain. One room he used for a tool shop. He built a chicken house to the west of the grainery and put up a shed at the east to put up ice. We put up ice every year but the first, until we got an electric refrigerator, which was a long time.

"The first year after the boys got most of the fall work finished, Victor said he believed he would go back to Missouri for the winter. It wasn't too exciting for a young fellow, no place to go and no way to go, except the big wagon.

"Dr. Clagett had carpenters from Carbondale, the Lehows, to build their house and barn. When they got the house finished on the outside they told him they couldn't stay to do the inside finish. Harleigh got a carpenter from Denver named Davies to come to do the finish work. After awhile he said his wife was dissatisfied staying alone in Denver and that he would have to quit. Clagetts were so anxious to get their house finished so they could move in. Doc came to ask us if we would let the Davies live with us, then his wife could come over. We agreed. It was real pleasant having them. We shared the grocery bill. They stayed 'til some time in February.

"Frank and Dr. Clagett agreed that it would be alright to turn the livestock out in the field, they could get quite a lot to eat and it wouldn't hurt them to rustle a little. A short time after they turned them out, Doc came running down to our place and said, 'There's a mule in my cistern!' He didn't say whose. It turned out it was my brother's mule, Kate. He didn't have his cistern fenced, and she

Frank with four hitch of mules.

stepped on the top that closed the opening; it slipped and down she went, rear first. Doc didn't have the cement top on the cistern yet, so they took off part of the top and put poles down in slant-wise, got ropes around her middle and hitched a team to the rope and pulled. They got her almost to the top and she slid back, so it all had to be done over. There were no tractors in those days; Carl Hill had a big team of horses and he pulled her out with them. We were afraid she would contract pneumonia, she had been in the cold water so long. Frank put horse blankets on her and exercised her for some time, then put the other horses in the barn with her and closed it up. She was alright, but we had an exciting few hours!

"As our place was a dry land claim, it had to be in the name of someone who lived there who was at least twenty-one, so it became my responsibility. In the fall we went to Glenwood Springs to the land office to declare our residency and that we had made improvements. Frank and I walked to Farmer's Spur and took the train. The next morning we went to the land office, then came back to Catherine on the Midland Railroad, as it came later in the morning than the D&RG. We walked up the hill home. After three years, we proved up on the place and got a deed from the government. In turn I deeded the place to my father.

"Our neighbors were Fred Holgates, whose place was at the top of the hill, the George Blues, Frank Cox's, the mail box was by their place. The mail carrier came up Missouri Heights hill, from there, on over the hill and down Cattle Creek. The road to our house went east from Cox's. Ed Claussens lived on the Boyle ranch. It was an older and more established place. The only telephone in the neighborhood was there. That place irrigated out of the Needham Ditch, out of Cattle Creek. Cox's, Blues, and Holgates got some irrigating water from Cattle Creek.

"Frank Dyer and his nephew, Bill Rathbun, from Denver, lived across the road west of the Boyle ranch; they 'batched.' One time when the threshers were there, Frank went in to help them get dinner. They opened cans of food and set them on the stove to get hot, and served the food from the cans.

"Dr. Clagett's place was next east from ours. Carl Hill was across the road from Clagetts. Charley Price was south and east from him. Price's half-brother, Mick Southcotte, had a place south of ours. Also, Herman Laudenklos. Bill Arthur lived east of Clagetts and Nathaniel Coles east of them, closer to the reservoir. The property that the reservoir was built on belonged to George Hotz. Their house was still there, but was sold and moved out. People by the name of Tremble bought it and moved it on Cattle Creek. It is the place where Austin Heuschkel lives now.

"One day, Mrs. Hotz stopped to call as she was coming from town. When she got ready to leave, she said she had a bull snake in the back of her buggy. I was amazed that anyone would carry a snake. She said she picked it up along the road, and that it was harmless – they were good to kill mice and gophers.

"There was another older and established place called 'The Basin.' I do not know to whom it belonged, but Rudolph Claussen farmed it the first year we were there.

"In the spring when Victor came back, he brought a saddle that Dad had bought for his twenty-first birthday, so we could go horseback sometimes. One night he went to Carbondale, he talked to the barber. He had a single buggy and harness for sale. We bought them and we could go places easier than with the big wagon.

"Frank had planted one field and was corrugating it. George Blue came along and asked him why he was doing it the way he was. Frank told him that Charley Price told him that was the way it should be. Blue said that wasn't the way at all, so Frank changed and had no trouble irrigating the field. They raised a real good crop. People would tell a tenderfoot anything.

"The Clagett children and the other children from there, Lula

Cole, Maggie Bell Brown, and Daisy Blue, went to Catherine to school the first year we were there. It must have been all of four miles. Most of the time they walked, unless some of the neighbors happened to be going that way and gave them a ride. It would be almost dark when the children would come past our house. I would walk with them until they could see the light in their house. Mrs. Price had told them that sometimes eagles swooped down and picked little children up and carried them away.

"I remember some of the other children who went to school there: the Gilmore children, Bill Patterson's children, the Cerise children, and the Diemoz children.

"At Christmas time they were having a program at the school. We went. Frank fixed the wagon box on the sled runner, put straw in the wagon box. We put covers over the straw and had a sleigh ride. When it snowed it stayed on for quite awhile.

"Clagett's were invited to Pat and Margaret McNulty's on Cattle Creek for Christmas dinner. Martin McNulty, their son, gave the Clagett children a horse he'd had for a long time. They were happy, they called him George Pokey Legs. They then rode to school. Jim Clagett wasn't of school age, but didn't want to stay home, so the teacher said she would take him.

"During the summer, Victor and a friend of his, Guy Conner, went up on Basalt Mountain and cut logs and poles to build a potato cellar. They cut the logs, then chained several of them together and snaked them down to where they could put several on the front running gears of the wagon and drag them down to a level spot and get them on the whole running gears of the wagon, and bring them to the place. They camped on Basalt Mountain while they were doing this work. They became acquainted with birds called 'camp robbers,' they would carry away any food that was available to them.

"To build the potato cellar, they made a frame with large logs, then fastened (I guess nailed) smaller poles all along the sides and over the top, then put straw all over, then used a team and scraper to cover it all with dirt. There were doors on each end of this cellar so they could drive through. It made quite a nice place. In the winter we stored our automobile in it. Fred Holgate helped to build the cellar, or should I say, the boys helped him, for he knew how.

The Smith potato cellar in 1998. It was built in 1915.

"Frank's sister and her husband and little daughter, the Frank Lucas,' came to Carbondale to visit us, and decided to stay there. Frank Lucas was a barber. He got work with Frank Bradley, who had the barber shop.

"That fall, my dad came to Denver on business, so came on over to see us. He drove to Carbondale one morning to visit with Mr. Dinkel, and with Frank Lucas. When he came home, he said he thought I better go back to Missouri with him. Frank Lucas had told him I was expecting a baby later. That was the latter part of September.

"After the boys got the fall work done, Vic said he would stay there and look after the livestock and things in general, and Frank could go back to Missouri. That was around Thanksgiving. Vic was going to stay at the house and 'bach,' but Aunty Clagett had him stay with them.

"Frank worked in Fitters grocery store that winter. Elisabeth was born January 2, 1916. We stayed there until the latter part of February.

"We came to Denver and visited a few days with Dr. Paul Barker's. While in Denver, I telephoned Clara Holmes, who was there for the winter. She told me she was expecting a baby in March, and had been at her mother's waiting. The baby was born, but Clara did not survive. We all felt very sad. She was such a pleasant person, and so good to all of the people on Missouri Heights. Clara Jane was the name of her baby. Her grandmother looked after her when she was little.

"That winter there had been a very heavy snowfall. We went from Denver on the Midland Railroad, which went through South Park. We took a seat in the Pullman car for we thought it would be warmer for the baby. Up in South Park, at a place called White Horse Cut, the wind drifted the snow so that some of the men got out and helped shovel. The engine would take one car through at a time. The snow was so deep in places that it rubbed against the side of the train.

"The train was supposed to arrive at the station in Carbondale at 10 p.m. – it was late and didn't arrive until 5 a.m. The station was about a mile from town. Mr. Hinkle, who had a livery stable, had a conveyance that met the train. The station did not stay open at night. Mr. Hinkle and Frank Lucas went to meet the train at ten o'clock. They had no way of knowing how late the train was. The door was locked – they raised a window and got in to wait.

"My brother came to town the next day with the sled to get us. Mrs. Clagett had our house nice and clean and good fires burning., and there was a baby bed for Elisabeth.

"One day, shortly after we were home, Dr. Clagett came past and said there was to be a wedding dance at George Blue's. Lloyd Blue and Alta Heuschkel, and Lafe Cox and Bessie Blue had been married in a double wedding. Frank said that he wasn't going, he didn't care for dances. Doc persuaded him to go, as it was against the rules of propriety not to go to a wedding dance. There was such a crowd, they moved the furniture out, except in one bedroom, they left the bed where people could leave their wraps. I put Elisabeth up on the pillows so she wouldn't get coats piled on her.

"Victor said he thought he wouldn't stay there and farm – that winter was enough for him – if Frank would buy his part of their equipment and stock and such. Frank agreed to buy Vic's part, if Vic would take his note.

"I was glad Vic went back to Missouri and was home that summer, for in the fall he enlisted in the armed forces and was in France two years. After he came back from the war, he wasn't at home to live any more. Frank paid the note off after Vic was back from the war.

"In 1917 one of Frank's brothers, Lee, came out and helped us. In the fall they were in the potato cellar sorting potatoes. They turned the ignition on the car so they could use the lights to see. I went to the cellar to see when they were coming to eat. When they walked around a little, they were dizzy and had headaches. It would not have been long until they would have been asphyxiated.

"Frank always took grain to be ground for his hogs to Dinkel's Mill. He would sack the grain and load up the sled. He put a cover over the spring seat. We had a two-gallon stone jug; he filled it with hot water and I would get in and put a cover over our laps. We were warm and snug as a bug in a rug. When we started home, he filled the jug at Dinkel's store.

"Dinkel's store had everything – grocery store, hardware, dry goods, lumber, grain mill and all kinds of feed. Most anything one wanted to buy. There was another general merchandise store owned by Mr. W. H. Long. He had quite a supply, but not so much as Dinkel's.

"We bought an Oakland Touring Car on July 1, 1917. Mr. Mansfield, the banker, was an agent for them. He told Frank he would like to keep it so he could demonstrate it at Aspen the 4th of July. The 5th, Fred Blume from the garage brought it to our place. He said Frank would have to take him back to town. Mother Smith was visiting us, so we all went. Frank didn't know a thing about driving an automobile. We went past his sister's house, she begged her mother not to go with us. Mother Smith said she would go with the boys. We had quite a time, killing the engine, but finally got home.

Frank, Elisabeth, Blanch and their dog on Missouri Heights in 1919.

"Mr. Clagett's sister, Bess, and her children came from Trenton, Missouri, to visit them that summer. She was an accomplished musician. They came to our house one evening and Bess played a lot of the current war songs and everybody sang *Over There, Katy, Keep the Home Fires Burning, Long Way to Tipperary.*

"I think it was the spring of 1915 that Ira Fender came out from Jamesport, Missouri. They had bought land south and east of our place from Charles Harris. They had to build a house so they lived temporarily in a small house on the Stauffacher place until their house was built enough that they could get along.

"There was a creek that ran close to where they lived that had trout in it. Ira would go fishing, which was not legal that early in the spring. Dad Patterson, one of his neighbors, warned him, but he paid no attention, so Dad finally had to report it.

"They built a real nice house. Later, they and Sweets, who bought the Basin Place, piped water for domestic use from Blue Creek Spring, located up at the base of Basalt Mountain. They got some irrigating water from the Mountain Meadow Ditch and bought water from the reservoir. Their children were Verle, Loren, Eddis and Varoqua. I don't know, or don't remember, where they went to school; they were in Eagle County.

"The fall of 1918 Frank went to Carbondale one day. He came home and said, 'The flu is getting bad.' He heard of several people who had died, and a great number who were sick. He thought we should go back to Jamesport, and we did, but we didn't escape the flu. While we were there, we all had the flu and Frank had pneumonia. We were glad we were there to have Dad take care of him.

"While we were back in Missouri, the [Spanish] flu was so bad in Colorado, and doctors were very scarce. So some people from Carbondale persuaded Dr. Clagett to move to Carbondale and practice medicine. Dr. Tubbs had been there, but went into the army. Clagetts moved, and soon after, Malcolm and Helen Louise, and perhaps some of the others – I don't remember – contracted the flu.

"Helen Louise passed away from the results of it. It was a terrible shock to us when Dr. Clagett sent us a telegram saying, 'The Grim Reaper has taken our precious Helen.' Malcolm was so low that Doc didn't dare to leave him. Aunty Effie Clagett had to go to the cemetery without any of her folks. Mr and Mrs. Giegel and Mrs. Sweet and Mrs. Debree went with her. She didn't know whether, when she got home, Malcolm would be alive or not.

"That summer my parents came to Colorado. It was decided that we should move to a place that had good domestic water. We had bought more water on the Heights, but it was difficult to transport the water to your land; something happened to it on the way. It worried Frank a lot. We ended up buying two places near Carbondale, the Charles Mow place, and the Darien place.

"We moved into the Mow place on December first. There was so much snow, and it was terribly cold, but we moved anyway. Frank dismantled the hay stacker and the buck rakes so they could be moved. He put a rocking chair in the middle of the hayrack, put a cover on it, and Elisabeth and I sat in the chair, covered with another blanket. No one had been on the road that day, and there was no track, but we got down the hill safely.

"Frances and Clyde Guss, Mr. Mow's daughter, had lived on the place. She was just leaving as we got there. She had left fires in her heating stove and kitchen range, so the house was nice and cozy.

"Little Gid Gerkin, one of our neighbors on the Heights, rode horseback and brought the cows and other horses. Frank went back the next day with the sled and brought the hogs and chickens. We kept our automobile in the potato cellar – when we moved there was so much snow, we couldn't get it out!

"After we moved, we rented our old place to Claude Henderson. They lived there a year. Then, Lester and Julia Taft rented it and lived there several years. If it had been the custom then, as it is now, to drill wells for water, I doubt that we would have left. We had nothing against the place and made pretty good money. Dad had given the place as collateral to secure a note at a bank in Kansas City, and they foreclosed.

"One day in February, Harleigh Holmes was in Carbondale with a truck he had manufactured that had four-wheel drive. It was called a 'Coleman Truck,' and had power to go most any place. He told Frank he would go up and bring our car. His patent for the truck was later used on heavy equipment and highway machinery."

Frank and Blanch had three children: Elisabeth, Mildred "Midge," and Robert F. "Bob."

History of the Land Owners

Jerome Stovall ....early 1900s............160 acres

Dr. Robert Victor Thompson ....1913.................160 acres

Frank and Blanch Smith.....................1914................160 acres
    Claude Henderson
    Lester and Julia Taft ....leased the land

Bailey and Beulah Sterrett ....early 1940s............360 acres
    Arnold Marks ....leased the land

Bud Fender ....1947.................360 acres

Arnold Winters ....1961.................360 acres

Dick and Shirley Hunt.................1967 - 1998..........360 acres

CARBONDALE SEWING CLUB - 1917

Carbondale Sewing Club, 1917, gathered at the Ira Fender home, left to right: Mrs. Lehow, Mrs. Nettie Fender, Blanch (Mrs. Frank) Smith, Johanna (Mrs. George) Sievers, Anna (Mrs. Richard) Lieberman, Emma (Mrs. Frank) Bradley, Francis (Mow) Guss, Katherine (Mrs. Harleigh R.) Holmes, Martha (Mrs. Albert) Witchey, Kate (Mrs. George) Winters, Maude Lucas, Stella (Bennet) Pings, Mrs. Lawver, Kate (Comrie) (Mrs. Joe) Hotz, Ollie Heuschkel, Ruth (Mrs. Emery) Hampton.

THE ULYSSES S. GREEN FAMILY
1914

Ulysses and May beside the spring cabin.

Ulysses Sherman Green
1866 - 1940

May (Johnson) Green
Unknown

THE ULYSSES GREEN FAMILY

Ulysses and May came to Colorado from Oklahoma around 1914, and homesteaded eighty acres up on Missouri Heights. The land was located up 100 Road, one mile north of the Catherine Corner. It consisted of forty acres on the right, and forty acres on the left. The land was mostly sagebrush, piñon trees, and scrub oak, and was not suitable for farming.

May and Ulysses had four children: Ira, Zoe, Bud, and Glafrie. They were all born in Oklahoma, and came to Colorado with their parents.

Ulysses built a home and a spring cabin on the left forty acres. There was a natural spring on the land, but it had to be dug out, and Ulysses, Bud, and Ira dug it out by hand. They laid tracks and used an old ore cart to haul the dirt. The Green family still has the ore cart in 1998.

They piped the water into the spring cabin and called the source "The Green Spring." The water was piped into a wooden box inside the cabin, and flowed back out to the pasture. Combined with a cement floor, the continuous flow of cold water kept the cabin cool all year. It was used for storing meat, dairy products, and other supplies. Cold water was also piped into the kitchen of the house.

The Greens shared their good fortune of having water with their neighbors, and the Hughes family and the Lyons family came to the Greens' for their domestic water. They brought wooden barrels to fill every few days.

Ulysses had been a blacksmith in Oklahoma. He was also a carpenter, and continued that trade in Colorado.

THE BUD GREEN FAMILY

Bud Green
1907 - 1972

Irene (Camden) Green
1919 -

THE BUD GREEN FAMILY

Irene had traveled to Colorado from Allue, Oklahoma, with her two sisters and the older sister's husband. They had moved here searching for a better life. Irene met Bud on a blind date, and they fell in love. They married in 1939 and moved to the Green place on the Heights.

Irene: "We didn't try to farm the land, but I did have a huge garden. I grew everything you could think of and I canned it all, including venison, elk, and chicken. I even canned cabbage. We had no electricity, and the only water supply was piped into the kitchen. Bud had learned carpentry from his dad, and we made a good life for ourselves up on the Heights. We didn't go much of anywhere, but after supper, we would relax and listen to the battery operated radio.

"We had a wonderful Jersey cow named Bossie. She was so good, she'd let me sit on the ground and milk her. She wouldn't move at all, until I was finished.

"In the spring of 1941 Bud wanted to try his hand at farming, so we rented further up on the Heights, on the Orville Fender place. We rented the house that Frank and Blanch Smith had built, by the old potato cellar that is still there today in 1998.

We lived and farmed there for one year, and it was one of the roughest years of my life. I had two little babies to care for and I also irrigated, shocked grain, plowed and mowed and stacked hay. I did it all, and it was difficult. I used to get up at three in the morning to wash clothes and hang them out, and then work in the fields all day. We had an old Ford flatbed truck with sideboards on it. I put my two babies on a pallet on the flatbed and tied blankets across to make shade. Then, I plowed or mowed or whatever and came back every little bit to check on them.

We had a great team of horses: Young Bill and Old Bill. I always laughed because you called one and both came. We planted about ten to twenty acres of potatoes. We had a spud planter that did the planting while I drove the 'Bills.' The planter made furrows, and then dropped the seed potatoes down into the earth, and covered it up. You had to keep the bins full of seed potatoes and keep on movin'.

"It sure was 'Misery Heights' back then. It was the Depression, and we did all that work, and the prices were so low for our crops, there was no way to get ahead. That was when Franklin D. Roosevelt tried to raise the price of potatoes, and painted the potatoes so we couldn't sell them. They ended up going to the pigs. Of course, we were paid a little bit by the government, but it wasn't much. I told Bud I couldn't go on like that, and we moved back down to the old place in 1942."

Georgia (Green) Ochko remembers growing up on the Heights. "In 1948 we moved up to my uncle Loren Fender's place for awhile, and I went to first grade at Luby School. My teacher was Mrs. Elsie Lyons, and she was real nice. Sometimes she let us make papier-mâché flowers out of toilet paper. Then, since my cousin Norval and I were the youngest, we would go lay the flowers on someone's desk for the older kids. I guess it was a girlfriend/boyfriend thing, and we played cupid. I went to school with my cousins Betty-Gail, Norval, and Leroy Fender.

"When we moved back home I went to Carbondale to school and us kids had to walk down to Catherine's Store to catch the bus. On a real cold winter day, Mom would tie handkerchiefs over our noses and mouths to help us keep warm. We looked like bandits. It was half way down the hill to the Hughes house, and we were always welcome to go inside and warm up by the old wood stove. Mrs. Hughes was a wonderful lady, she would put fresh dry hankies on our faces before we left. Then, she laundered our wet ones and had them all clean and ready for us the next day. She was a great neighbor and we loved her. Sometimes in the winter we would sled down to Catherine's and when it was nice, we would ride our bikes. The Harris', Chuck and Bobbie, always put our sleds or bikes where they would be safe until we came back. Then, we had to trudge back up that steep hill with them.

"When Leroy and I were in third and fourth grade, we used to walk a ways down the hill, and then hide behind a tree and watch the school bus come and go. We'd run back home and tell Mom we missed the bus, just as innocent as could be. But, it didn't work. Mom loaded us up in our old 1929 Model A Roadster pick-up, and hauled us to school. It was a convertible pick-up, and so old we didn't want to be seen it it. So, we'd slump down low in the seat and try to hide when we saw anyone. Leon still has that old truck today in 1998, and now we think it's wonderful!"

Irene: "Our neighbors were the Harold Blues, the Hughes, and Lessie and Clarence Lyons. We went to Carbondale once a week for groceries, and shopped at Witchey Mercantile. They carried everything. Even with all our struggles we were a close, happy family on the Heights. We loved our children, and we gave them a good home. After I lost my Bud in 1972, I stayed on the Heights. I watched a lot of neighbors move away, and saw the land sold for subdivisions. I wondered what Ulysses and May would have thought. I left in 1992 and moved to Glenwood Springs. I think about the Heights, and remember the good times."

The Green family, left to right: Bud, Georgia, Deanna, Irene and Leroy.

History of the Land Owners

Ulysses S. Green..................................1915...............80 acres
Bud Green..1940s..............80 acres
Bill Antonides...40 acres
Rim Ledge Uranium and
*   Mining Corporation.....................................40 acres*
Flying Bar Ranch...40 acres
Rim Ledge Area 3................................1997............13.3 acres

Shirley and Thad Englert....................1967...............20 acres
George Temtest....................................1998
Marty Schlein......................................1998
Green Children....................................1998

THE GREEN FAMILY

ULYSSES SHERMAN GREEN
1866 - 1940

MAY (JOHNSON) GREEN
UNKNOWN

Children:
Ira, Zoe, Bud, Glafrie

<u>Ira</u> Ora Kimbrough	Othel, Lowell, Ed, Edna, Faye, Eva
<u>Zoe</u> John Fontz	Edna and Evelyn
<u>Bud</u> Irene Camden	Leon, Georgia May, Deanna
<u>Glafrie</u> Loren Fender	Betty, Gail, Norval, Donna

THE RENFTLE FAMILY – 1916

CHARLES PHILLIP RENFTLE
1890-1976

IMA MAE (MCLACHLIN) RENFTLE
1891 - 1980

THE RENFTLE FAMILY

Merrill H. and Jennie McLachlin.   *Merrill Harvey McLachlin.*

Charles and Ima Mae were married in February of 1914, and they came to Colorado from Audubon, Iowa, in 1916. Ima Mae's father, Merrill Harvey McLachlin, asked the couple to move to Colorado to farm one of his places. McLachlin was from Vermont, and had homesteaded and bought several parcels of land in the Cattle Creek and Snowmass Creek (Old Snowmass) area. Charles had been a cowboy all of his adult life, and Ima Mae had taught school in Iowa.

Ruth (Renftle) Fender remembers, "My grandfather McLachlin was showing my father, Charles, his land up around Snowmass Creek. They stopped to rest, and my grandfather sat down under a tree. He died right there from a heart attack. It was July 17, 1916, and he was 61 years old."

Charles' father, John Renftle, came to the United States from Germany, his mother, Verena, had come from Switzerland. John Renftle ran a mule freight train from Omaha, Nebraska, to Denver, Colorado. It took several weeks to make the trip through hostile Indian country, and John employed a good shotgun rider. He told stories of coming upon smoldering covered wagons arranged to form a circle, and bodies from Indian attacks. His wife, Verena, begged to go on one of the trips. John finally relented, but he instructed his shotgun rider, "If the Indians attack and we are outnumbered, shoot my wife!"

John and Verena had eight children, five girls and three boys. One of the boys was Charles Phillip Renftle.

Charles and Ima Mae moved onto the Cattle Creek land, near Missouri Heights, up 103 Road, and joining the Callicotte land which was to the south. Charles homesteaded more land on Cattle Creek and Mesa Creek, and with the McLachlin land, it all amounted to around 1,569 acres. Charles had never irrigated, and working the land did not come easily to him.

Ima Mae with Harvey and Lillian.

Cassie and Ruth.

Ima had given birth to their first child, Lillian, in Iowa in 1915. After the couple moved into the log cabin on the Cattle Creek ranch, she went back to Iowa to have her second child, Harvey, who was born in 1917. Her two other children were born in the Cattle Creek cabin, Kathryn "Cassie" in 1926, and Ruth in 1928. Dr. Tubbs, from Carbondale, and a neighbor, Alma Pitts, helped Ima Mae give birth.

Lillian in Charles' Model T Ford, on the way to Lower Cattle Creek School, 1929.

Harvey and Lillian first went to the Lower Cattle Creek School, and later to the Crystal Springs School, near the Callicotte place.

*Lower Cattle Creek School, 1927. Back row, left to right:
Opal Yeoman, Richard Yeoman, Eva Cook, Bob Sievers, Rose Trout.
Front row, left to right: Harvey Renftle, Dorothy Sievers, Viola Cook, Lillian Renftle.*

Ruth (Renftle) Fender, "I guess the worst spanking I ever got from my Mom was when I was about four years old. My sister, Lillian, was getting ready for school, so I decided to get ready, too. Each of us only had one good dress and one good pair of shoes, so I got mine on and announced I was ready to go. When Mom said I couldn't go, I sat myself down on a lard can and yelled and kicked and bawled for all I was worth. Well, I got spanked – real good!

"Cassie started school in 1933, and I started in 1934. We rode horseback to school on Dolly and Freckles. Sometimes we rode Jeff, but he was real spooky, he jumped at everything. The boys we went to school with always teased our horses, trying to get us bucked off. It made us so mad, but there was nothing we could do about it. They were so mean, they used to tie our arms behind a fence post and leave us there. We had to stand there until Dad came and rescued us. Dad gave nicknames to Lillian (Lilly-gal) and Kathryn (Cassie). I didn't have one and I was put out. So, he called me 'Ruthie' and I was happy!"

Crystal Springs School. Back row, left to right: unknown girl, Jean Blue, Mrs. Maxfield, Harold Blue. Front row, left to right: Ruth Renftle, Cassie Renftle, Evelyn Cerise, Clifford Cerise.

Lillian (Renftle) Berges: "I remember Mama telling me how one time they were ready to go to town. Cassie was a baby, and they got her all wrapped up to go and laid her on the bed. Then they left and forgot the baby! Of course, they came back and got her.

"Sometimes I would ride to school with Cassie and Ruth. The girls and I would all be on our horse, Jeff, and when we stopped to open the gate I'd be the one to get off. I'd have to poke Jeff with a stick to get him to move over while I opened the gate. A couple of times when I did, Jeff jumped and the girls fell off!

"I had graduated from the eighth grade at Lower Cattle Creek School. There were only three of us in school that year, 1928. Me, Harvey and Bob Siever. For some reason, my dad wanted me to take the eighth grade over, so I went to Crystal Springs School the next year. Maude Maxfield was our teacher. I remember one time she kept Harvey after school and Dad got real mad. He went to see her and said, 'You keep him in at recess, at night he has chores to do'."

Ruth (Renftle) Fender: "Our teachers were Mrs. Maude (Callicotte) Maxfield and Marie Mow. I loved Mrs. Maxfield so much – she was wonderful! Arthur Bogue was a teacher too, and he was my hero.

We had a hot lunch program where everyone took turns bringing lunch. Well, one time my mom put hot soup in a big gallon jar, put it in a sugar sack, and I carried it on my horse. One day after school Arden Reed started teasing my horse with a stick and I swung that sugar sack, hit him in the head, and knocked him flat out cold! The teacher, Art Bogue, saw it happen, and from then on us girls left school thirty minutes early, just so those mean boys couldn't torment us. Yes, he was my hero! I graduated eighth grade from the Crystal Springs School in 1941."

Lillian, Ruth, Cassie and a cousin, Luella.

Lillian: "Charley was hurt in a horse accident when he was young, and it made riding painful for him. So, I became Dad's cowhand, and I was a good one. I helped him round up cattle and take them to summer pasture up Mesa Creek. I also helped him work the land. We raised hay and grain: wheat, oats, and barley. We raised some potatoes and I sure remember picking them. I could harness my own team, and work as well as any farmhand. Dad usually did the plowing and then I harrowed. The plow broke up the land, and the harrow made it even finer. Then, Dad would use the float or leveler. It was a flat, heavy structure that smoothed the land even more and prepared it to plant seed. Then, the drill actually planted the seed. All of this was done with horses until we got our

Harvey on his homemade push rake.

Left to right, back row: Lillian, Ima Mae, Ruth, Cassie; front row: Charles, Charley.

first tractor. Of course, I ran the mower and the buckrake when we cut hay.

"We had milk cows, so we had to milk morning and night. We sold our cream in Glenwood, or shipped it to Denver to be sold. We sold eggs and live hens and chickens to people in Glenwood, and also dressed chickens. I remember one time my Mom was away and I had to prepare the meal for the thresher crew. I was pretty young to do all that cooking, and I remember Emma Marks came over to help me."

Ruth: "Yes, Dad always said he'd rather have Lillian help him with the cattle than any other cowboy. My brother, Harvey, was one of the first men to modernize farm machinery. He used an old truck motor and made a push rake for stacking hay."

In 1943 the schools were consolidated and the Crystal Springs School was closed forever. Charles Renftle bought the school for $100 and Glen Martin moved it over the hill to the Renftle ranch on Cattle Creek. Charles bought the school for his daughter, Lillian, and her husband, Lee Berges, to live in.

Lillian: "We lived in the school from 1943 until 1964, and raised our children, Harold Lee and Stella, there. In 1964 Dad sold the ranch to Norm Sherwood."

Ruth: "My dad had a heart of gold. He trusted everyone and believed that a handshake was enough to close a deal. Of course, sometimes it wasn't, and he got hurt."

Lillian: "My mother was such a hard worker. She was good to everyone and always tried to help others."

Ruth and Bob Scarrow live on Cattle Creek Road on Missouri Heights today in 1998. The house they live in was built by Loren and Ira Fender, who logged the timbers down from Basalt Mountain. Loren and Glafrie Fender lived there first, and sold out to Ruth and Harold Fender in 1953. The land was originally the Mountain Meadow ranch, homesteaded by William H. and Mollie Harris.

History of the Land Owners

Owner	Year	Acres
Mallory	late 1800s	136 acres
Merle Harvey McLachlin	1913	536 acres
Ima Mae Renftle	1916	536 acres
Charles Renftle		
Homesteaded: on Cattle Creek	1918	40 acres
Homesteaded: from BLM	1919	80 acres
Norm Sherwood	1964	800 acres
Dr. Virgil Gould	1964	924 acres
Various Owners	1998	800 acres

THE COWEN FAMILY – 1917

SHERMAN COWEN
1879 - 1937

KATHERINE LEVINA (ROBINSON) COWEN
1890 - 1967

THE COWEN FAMILY

Sherman Cowen was born in Pennsylvania, and was one of eleven children. His father, William Cowen, moved the family to Missouri when Sherman was seven years old.

Katherine was born in Glenwood Springs. Her father was a carpenter and died of tuberculosis when Katherine and her two sisters were quite young. The mother could not cope with raising the three girls, and put them up for adoption. Katherine went to the home of a couple near Carbondale, and she lived with them until she was twenty-one years old. She did not attend school until the age of eighteen, when she borrowed a neighbor's mule and went to the eighth grade for awhile. The next year she tried to go to high school, but was not happy, and soon decided to stay home.

Sherman had come to Colorado, and was working as a farm hand on the place next to Katherine's home. There was a good well on the place where Katherine lived, and the farm hands would stop for water. Katherine and Sherman met at the well. Sherman was

Katherine on a neighbor's mule.

twenty years older than Katherine, but he fell in love with her and soon went courting. He would pick her up in his horse and buggy, and she would go with him to irrigate the fields. Sometimes they went to the picture show in Carbondale, or for rides in the buggy. They courted for six weeks, and on June 17, 1911, the same day as Strawberry Days was being celebrated in Glenwood Springs, they went to Rifle and were married.

Grace Cowen at seven months of age.

Their only child, Grace, was born in 1912 and the family lived on a farm between Glenwood Springs and Carbondale, where the Aspen Glen subdivision is today in 1998. Grace tells about one of her earliest memories, "I was about four years old, and my dad had a load of grain in the wagon. He was going over to another farm where they had a big fan to blow the weeds out of the grain. I wanted to go with him so bad, but he said no, there wasn't enough room. He left and I followed on foot, and walked all the way to the neighbor's. Well, Dad went on to the barn and didn't see me, but the lady of the house did, and took me in for milk and cookies. Then she went out and told my dad, and he couldn't believe I was there, and that I'd walked all that way. He made room for me on the drive home!

"When I was five years old in 1917, we moved to Missouri Heights. My dad bought 640 acres, mostly sagebrush and scrub oak, but we cultivated about ninety acres, and he raised hay and grain. Our place was up above what is Mike Strang's place today in 1998, and at that time the Carl Quakenbush family lived in the old homestead, which is still there today, on the Strang Ranch, near the road.

"I remember they were building the Missouri Heights School, and my dad and I went to look at it. It was just walls and floor joints with cross pieces, and I remember my dad walking across them.

"I started school the next year, and my teacher was Mrs. Jamison. I remember how much I loved her, but I was only there a few weeks when my mother got sick and I had to stay home to help her. I didn't go back to school that year.

"The next year I went back to school, but things weren't good. I had lived on the farm with just my parents, and I had never been around other children. I guess I didn't know how to act around others, and the kids began to tease me and pick on me. Even the teacher, Mrs. Thompson, was mean to me. I couldn't go outside at

The Cowen family: Sherman, Katherine and Grace.

recess or at lunch time. She made me stay inside and eat my lunch at my desk. I was real unhappy and I cried, but I didn't get mad. When I told my mother she said, 'You go back tomorrow and get your books and come home. You don't have to go back!'

"A little while after that my mother got sick again, and she and I went to Grand Junction where she could be treated. We lived there three months, and we went to church there. There was one family at church with kids, and they treated me nice. It was the first time other kids were nice to me. I even became friends with a little black boy whose grandparents were raising him. He and I were good pals, but one day he didn't want to be with me anymore. I think some other kids made fun of him for being friends with me. I was sad, but I didn't get mad at him.

Katherine and Grace had this portrait taken during their stay in Grand Junction.

"We came back home on the Rio Grand and I remember the wind was blowing real hard when we got on, and a cinder got in my eye. I could hardly stand it, it hurt so bad. There was a real nice man and his family on the train. When we got to Glenwood he carried me over to the Denver Hotel where my mother and I were to have a room for the night. The manager's wife looked at my eye, broke an egg, and put the egg white in my eye. It was real slimy, but it felt good. The next morning the cinder was gone, and my eye was well. I remember the manager's wife said she saved the egg yolk to fix for her breakfast!

"We took the Rio Grand to Carbondale, but we had no way to get home. Dad only had a work team of horses, and they had never been on the road. We got a ride almost all the way home with the mail carrier, and walked the rest of the way. We soon saw my dad on his horse, coming to meet us. He was so happy to see us, and couldn't believe how much I'd grown. I was seven years old. I'd learned a lot of lessons in Grand Junction about people and other kids.

"Things were better the next year at school. We had the most kids ever, about thirty, because so many people were renting up on the Heights. A lot of them moved around quite a bit. It was rather entertaining for me that year, I watched all the kids fight!

"We had about twenty-five sheep at one time and about fifty beef cows. In the winter we would butcher a beef and hang it on the north side of the house to keep it frozen. We always had two or three milk cows, and I loved them the best, and the horses.

"My last teacher was Mary Ferguson, and she was so nice to me. There were only three kids in the eighth grade: Loel Green, Edward Blue, and me. Mary Ferguson was a wonderful teacher. She taught me to play marbles, to sew, and embroidery. I completed the eighth grade, but I didn't want to go to high school in Carbondale. Mary Ferguson said, 'You come on back to Missouri Heights School next year and I'll teach you high school.' I was happy about that. My schoolmates where the Swan boys, Ray, Glenn and Carl, the Thomas kids, Alice Turner (who still lives in Carbondale and is a great friend), and Glafrie Green.

"When I was fourteen my mother's stepmother died, and left her the Carbondale property where she had been raised. She even left a little money and we bought a phonograph. I remember how thrilled I was, I had seldom heard music.

"After I quit going to school I just stayed on the ranch and helped my folks. I milked the cows in the morning, took them out to graze, went after them at night, and milked again. I always loved horses, and rode all I could, first on the work horse, and then my Dixie that my dad bought from a neighbor. Dixie was a black. Then, my mom bought a horse for $25 and it was named Dixie, too. I rode down to get the mail through the Quakenbush place. Sometimes my mother and I rode to Carbondale. We rode our horses down to the Carbondale High School graduation, and rode back home. There were no cars on the road at night.

"Another year I rode down by myself to the graduation. Afterwards, Dixie and I started home, down the road where the rodeo grounds are today [100 Road]. I got a little uneasy thinking that someone had seen me start out alone, and I was afraid, so I turned

Grace Cowen in 1998.

around and went back into town. There was a livery stable owned by Burt Hinkel, and I went there and put my horse in the corral and my saddle in the barn. I walked over to the Hotel in the Dinkle Building, and told them my tale of woe. They gave me a room, and I told them my mother would come pay for it when she came to town. I cried because I knew we didn't have money for such foolishness. The room cost twenty-five cents.

"We had no electricity or water on the ranch other than irrigation. I remember we would melt snow on the old coal range for drinking water. We tried to build a cistern once, but the man who built it didn't mix the cement right and it crumbled. In 1931 and 1934 there was a terrible drought. We harvested the wheat and hay in the summer. We would take a wagon load of wheat to the mill in Glenwood Springs and trade it for flour. We also had a real big garden and raised potatoes, carrots and pumpkins, lettuce and squash, corn and beans. We saved the seeds from year to year. My mother sold cream and eggs for grocery money. She rode her Dixie to Carbondale once a week to the cream station. They would test the cream and give you a check right then. One of the creameries was in the house across from the old jail. There's a beauty shop there today. I don't remember how we got it, but my mother had a surrey with the fringe on top. Sometimes we went to town in it, and everyone liked watching us go by. The men building the roads would make room for us to go around them.

"We even went to dances once in awhile at the Missouri Heights School. Sometimes someone would drag me out to dance, but I never learned how. The men would shove all the desks to one side of the room, and the mothers would lay their babies there to sleep. Eddis Fender played the saxophone and Bessie Peterson (who later married Verle Fender) played the piano. There was a little gas stove in the back where they made coffee. At midnight we had coffee and sandwiches before we went home.

"My dad got sick one day, and died not long afterwards. He was only fifty-eight years old. My mother and I knew he had worked too hard. He had lived and worked through the Depression, through the hard droughts, and could never get ahead. He always hoped to do well and pay the mortgage off on our land, but it didn't happen. Mother and I couldn't keep it going either, and we finally lost our wonderful place on Missouri Heights. We had to sell everything to pay our debts, but we couldn't bear to sell my horse, Dixie, and the milk cows.

"We did have some luck because my mother was able to sell the Carbondale property her stepmother had left her. We bought eleven acres, just on the left as you drive from Highway 82 to Highway 133 today. We had apple trees and a couple of sheep, chickens, my Dixie, and three milk cows. We sold cream and eggs. We bought an old Model A for $35, and a friend came to see us, and taught me how to drive. I drove to Glenwood Springs once a week to sell the cream and eggs and get groceries. I would go around to the restaurants and get their scraps for our chickens.

"We had no electricity or running water. Sometimes people would ask if they could leave an old dilapidated car for a few days, and we said yes. They never came back to pick them up, and there were worn out cars all around. Sometimes I slept in the cars with my cats and dogs.

"I kept Dixie and the milk cows until they died, and I always cried when they passed away. It was real sad when my mother died from cancer in 1967. I was fifty-five years old. I lived on the place for fifty-three years, and then people told me I should sell out. I wanted to move back up to Missouri Heights, but it didn't work out!"

Grace Cowen now lives outside of Carbondale, on Willow Lane, just off County Road 100, the same road which she and Dixie took to town and back.

Grace says, "I have wonderful neighbors. Bucky and Cheral Berg take good care of me. They bring me groceries and call to see if I'm alright, and always do nice things for me. I've lived here six and a half years with my dogs, Big Girl and Slim. My good dog, Bud, lived here until he died. I have a big tom cat I call Tom, and one black cow.

"I've learned a lot of lessons in my life. There were fun parts and hard parts, but it's been alright. I never married because my folks always needed me, and the right one never came along. If I could have two wishes, I'd wish that I could stand up straight again, not all bent over; and that I could ride ole Dixie again – up on Missouri Heights!"

The eleven acres of property where Grace and her mother lived is now called the Cowen Business Center. It is at the intersection of Highway 133 and Cowen Drive.

History of the Land Owners

Sherman and Katherine Cowen homesteaded the original 640 acres in 1917.

Grange..
Panorama Estates, John Wix...................1972........640 acres
Sub-Divided, Panorama Ranches............1998.......................

Grace with Slim and Big Girl.

For Grace

I'd love to go out riding
Way up on Missouri Heights
I'd love to ride my Dixie
All around and see the sights.

We'd stop and gaze at Sopris
Ride up by the reservoir
Smell the sagebrush and wild roses
And look down at the valley floor.

I'd see the men out working
Planting spuds or stacking hay
And I'd watch an old spring wagon
Being pulled by dappled grays.

I'd love to watch the magpies
Sailing back and forth on high
And see a herd of white tail deer
Lift their heads as we pass by.

I'd love to go out riding
Way up on Missouri Heights
I'd love to ride my Dixie
All around and see the sights.

– Written by A.W.

THE ORVILLE O. FENDER FAMILY
1918

Orville O. Fender
1886 - 1977

Irene Fender
1896 - 1988

THE ORVILLE O. FENDER FAMILY

Orville O. Fender was Ira Fender's half brother, and was born in Ringold County, Iowa. He followed his brother to Colorado, arriving in 1918. Orville married Irene, who was from Omaha, Nebraska; they had two children: son, Orville "Bud," and daughter, Gene. Orville O. and Irene did not live on the Heights, but owned and worked 320 acres of land there, which Orville purchased from Dr. Oscar F. Clagett. He raised potatoes, hay, grain, and sheep.

Orville's son, Orville O. "Bud" remembers in 1998, "Dad told me that when he was young, he and a friend traveled from Iowa to Bismarck, North Dakota, in a covered wagon, and homesteaded 640 acres there. Dad didn't like it there, so he left and came to Colorado. He would tell us kids about the big mosquitoes in North Dakota. He said they were so big he had to hide under a great big cast iron cooking pot, and when the mosquitoes bored through, he'd hit 'em in the head with a sledge hammer! By the way, Dad sold his land years later, and after he sold it, they struck oil on it!!

"He was a great story teller, and he liked everyone he knew, and never met a stranger. We were the best of buddies, my dad and I, and I went everywhere with him. One time, we were off herding sheep and my horse fell on me and hurt me. He was worried about me and put me on the train from Marble to come home to Mom.

"He was a worker, and didn't know what the word 'quit' meant. My mom was also a worker, and she was very sweet and loving. We used to go to Strawberry Days in Glenwood. I'd have fifty cents to spend. The rides were all just a nickel, so I had lots of fun.

"I remember when the bottom dropped out of the potato market. Dad had two boxcars full of potatoes and shipped them to Denver. He couldn't get much for them there, so decided to ship them on to Chicago, but that didn't work – he couldn't even get enough to pay the freight, so he lost it all.

"I remember Ralph Long, who lived over by Ira Fender's place. The Longs used to keep a car down on Highway 82 in the winter. If they had to go to town, they'd hitch the team up to a sleigh, and come down Catherine's Road to the car."

Orville "Bud" took over the land in 1947 and bought the Sterrett place, which was 160 acres. After he and Alverta Bionaz were married in 1952, they also bought the Francis Young place, another 160 acres, which made their farming operation 640 acres. "Bud" and Alverta moved to the Heights in the fall of 1954, and lived in the house that Dr. Oscar Clagett had built in 1914. They lived there until 1961.

Orville "Bud" recalls, "We raised sheep, cattle, pigs, grain and hay. I've always loved mules, always had one around. I still do today in 1998, in fact, I have three fine looking mules at my place in Sutank!"

From left to right: Orville "Bud," Orville O., Irene, and Gene Fender.

*The Fenders with their granddaughters.
From left to right: Doreen, Orville O., Deborah and Irene Fender.*

Alverta remembers, "We lived on the Heights, and it wasn't easy – it really was called 'Misery Heights.' All we did was work, it was never done, and we just barely got by like everyone else. We were always short of water, had to haul stock and drinking and cooking water from Carbondale, or wherever we could get it."

Bud adds, "I had a big 1,100-gallon tank to haul the water in. In the early spring and winter I'd have to wait until the road was frozen at night to drive up the hill. We finally drilled a well after a few years, and I have lots of money sitting up there in crooked holes, where we tried to find water! One good thing was we had a lot of shares in the reservoir and had good irrigation."

Alhu Bionaz (Alverta Fender's father) hunting on North Thompson with Orville "Bud" Fender (right) and his mules.

"I remember how hard the wind blew on the Heights in the winter. I'd feed stock and the hay would end up at the neighbor's!"

Alverta continues, "Bud taught me to drive the tractor. The first one was an old John Deere with no live power, and I couldn't shift gears fast enough to keep the baler going! I can still hear him yelling at me, 'You're gonna' tear it all apart!' Well, after that, we finally got a brand new Case tractor with power and a wide front end, and things were easier for me. When we baled hay, I drove the tractor and Bud rode on the slip, a platform made of boards. When he got eight bales stacked on the slip, he'd step down and slide them off."

Bud says, "Alverta and I have always been the best of partners, and even though we yelled at each other once in awhile, we were always a team, and we got things done. We baled a lot of hay, and in the spring we had calves and lambing to tend with all night long. Alverta would help the mothers give birth, while I fed stock and cleaned the barn, then we'd trade jobs and keep right on going!"

Alverta adds, "One time I got so mad at him. He promised me he had quit smoking and using tobacco. Well, we were baling and I was on the tractor. I looked back and saw him spitting tobacco juice and I got furious. I jerked that tractor into high gear and took off, and the bales were flying in all directions, and Bud was yelling, 'Slow down! What's the matter with you!'

"I let him yell for a little, then I came to a quick, sudden stop, hopped off that tractor, and grabbed that plug of tobacco out of his shirt pocket and threw it as far as I could. Boy, was I mad!

"There were good times on the Heights, too! We played cards with our neighbors, Ruth and Harold Fender, and Edith and Walter Lawrence (they lived on the Doyle place, where Bill and Diane Teague live in 1998). We also went to dances at the Missouri Heights Schoolhouse, but that sort of faded out around 1958 when everyone got television. Then people wanted to stay home and watch programs. In the summer we had gatherings at peoples' houses, and picnics on Basalt Mountain.

"I'll tell you what the highlight of our week was up on the Heights. It was when we went to Glenwood Springs once a week for supplies and stopped at the A&W Root Beer stand. We had a root beer and a hamburger and it was the best!

"I wish I had a dollar for each time someone came to visit and said, 'Oh, what a beautiful view!' Well, that was nice, but it didn't put the meat on the table!"

Orville "Bud" and Alverta have two daughters, Doreen and Deborah. They sold their Missouri Heights property in 1961, all three pieces, to Arnold Winters. They now live in Sutank with their three mules, Shorty, Porter, and Blackie; a paint horse named Paint and a few cats.

They're my guardian angels

And I know they can see

Every step I take

They are watching over me.

I may not know where I'm goin'

But I know where I come from.

They're my guardian angels

And I'm their special one.

GUARDIAN ANGELS
By: John Jarvis, Don Schlitz, and Naomi Judd
Copyright © 1985 Plugged In Music.
All rights administered by Sony/ATV Music Publishing,
8 Music Square West, Nashville, TN 37203.
All Rights Reserved. Used by Permission.
Copyright © Wynona, Inc. Used by Permission.
Copyright © Harry Fox Agency. Used by Permission.

THE GOULD FAMILY – 1920

Paul Gould
1882 - 1978

Grace G. (Comrie) Gould
1884 - 1939

WHITE AND MORRIS

In the late 1800s, two men, White and Morris, were among the very first homesteaders on the high mesa above the Roaring Fork, which would one day be called "Missouri Heights." Their land, around 600 acres, was to the east, up against Basalt Mountain. At that time the Martin G. Hotz family were their neighbors to the northwest. Very few people remember them today in 1998, but one story cannot easily be forgotten. Rosezella (Rosie Gould) Haff and her sister, Ruth (Gould) Zancanella, whose father, Paul Gould, would one day own the same land remembers, "Morris and White were partners, but they got into a terrible fight over something, and White shot Morris. He left him laying there half dead and the pigs finished him off. It's a gruesome story, but it's what we were told as kids."

THE GOULD FAMILY

George and Sarah Ida (Weaver) Comrie.

Around the early 1900s, White sold his land to George and Sarah (Weaver) Comrie, (Rosie and Ruth's grandparents on their mother's side). In 1920 the land was sold to Paul Gould.

Paul Gould's ancestors came from Ohio, and Adams County, Kansas. Grace's ancestors came from Pennsylvania. They met in Leadville, and were married December 16, 1911, and settled in Carbondale.

Paul Gould and Grace G. (Comrie) Marriage License, married December 16, 1911.

Paul owned 320 acres and leased the rest, which was about 640 acres. There was a one-room cabin on the farm, and Paul expanded it to three rooms, and built a smaller cabin beside it. There, he and Grace raised their family of seven children (in order of birth): Ruth, Archie, Willard, Richard, Rosezella (Rosie), Alice, and Zada.

The Goulds had most of the farm under cultivation and raised oats, barley, wheat, hay, potatoes, and vegetables. Ruth (Gould) Zancanella remembers the potatoes, and the year-round job they represented. "In the spring we cut them up to plant. In the summer we irrigated and pulled weeds. In the fall we picked them, and in the winter we sorted them in the potato cellar. It was a never-ending job."

Rosie remembers, "Like everyone back then, we were poor, and we sold cream and eggs to get a little money. I remember what a wonderful day it was when Mama would go to the Witchey Mercantile in Carbondale, sell her cream and eggs, and buy a pound of baloney. That was a real treat for us kids."

Rear, from left to right: Ruth, Alice and Rosie, with Zada in front.

Paul Gould not only farmed, but he and his sons also logged timber from Basalt Mountain. They lived in a tent on the mountain while they were logging in the winter time. The timbers (logs) were used for building many potato cellars on the Heights, the ranger station in Basalt, several homes, and the Luby School, which was built near the county road on the Sweet land, west of the Goulds in 1926.

The Goulds' potato cellar.

A neighbor, Uriah McLean (left) with Paul Gould and Paul's Indian pony, Bobby.

Ruth remembers, "I tried to help Dad out one day in the fields, but it didn't work. I was supposed to run the stacker, but I pulled the horse up too far, and the stacker threw the hay on the ground past the haystack. Dad said, 'You don't have to come back,' and I worked in the house from then on."

Rosezella (Rosie Gould) Haff was a tomboy and loved working in the fields. "I remember when we threshed the grain. The binder would cut and tie the grain into bundles, and it was my job to stack the bundles properly in to a shock. After the grain had cured for a few days, the

The overshot stacker which Ruth couldn't quite understand.

shocks were pitched onto an open wagon by hand and hauled to the thresher, and the grain was separated from the straw. The thresher blew the straw into big piles – it was real high and slick, and us kids just loved jumping and sliding and yelling as loud as we could. It was great!

"I remember one time Mr. Elzy Rippy came all the way from New Castle with his thresher. It was late fall, and by evening there was a storm coming. Dad asked Elzy to spend the night, but he was worried he might get snowed in. He set off for New Castle with the thresher and told us later he didn't get home 'til 4 a.m.!"

Threshing the grain.

Willard and his colt with Rosie, Zada, and Alice after a water fight.

Rosie and Ruth recall that even though the work was never finished, there was still time for fun. "There was ice skating on the reservoir and the ditches and we had fun on our sleds in the winter. We even strapped on barrel stays to ski, and they worked great. There were Christmas dances and pageants at Luby School, and the people came in their Sunday clothes in horse drawn sleighs with gas lanterns. The music was usually a man on guitar, and sometimes someone played a fiddle or accordion. It was a wonderful and exciting time for all of us."

Archie on the colt he broke and named Buck. The bridle bit was made from a six-shooter, a gun said to have belonged to a gangster!

Rosie continued, "All of us kids rode horses to school. Some of our horses were called: Dixie, Slivers, and Frog. Frog had a crooked leg, and he kinda' hopped, so we called him Frog. In the summer we rode all over the Heights. The mail carrier would drive a team up to deliver mail. If the snow was too deep for the team, he'd walk in, if he could get through."

Luby School on the Sweet place.

The Goulds' neighbors were Uriah and John McLean, brothers whose land was to the north of Goulds'. Other neighbors were Ralph and Alice Harris, Frank and Edna Sweet, Ed and Florence Loesch, the Artaz Family, the Kreutz Family, and Eddis and Olla Fender. Edna Sweet and Olla Fender both taught at Luby School.

Ruth recalls, "My folks were so kind and giving. We could not have had more loving parents. They always took in people who were down on their luck. I can't remember very many meals where the family was alone."

Rosie adds, "Sometimes there were 16 to 17 around the table. My mother fed anyone who was hungry!"

Grace (Comrie) Gould died December 24, 1939. Paul Gould died June 25, 1978. They are buried in Evergreen Cemetery in Carbondale.

As with all farms and ranches, boundaries changed through the years as parcels were sold and bought.

History of the Land Owners

White and Morris – homesteaders ....late 1800s
George and Sarah Comrie ....early 1900s
Paul and Grace Gould..1920
Eddis and Olla Fender..1939
Brice Arlene...1949
Bill Hignet 1981

In 1998, the owners are Jim and Mary Griffith, Amy, Chip and Meg

THE GOULD FAMILY

Paul Gould
1882 - 1978

Grace G. (Comrie) Gould
1884 - 1939

Children

Sarah Ruth	1913 -	Rosezella "Rosie"	1920 -
Archie	1914 - 1964	Alice Grace	1922 -
George Willard	1917 - 1983	Zada May	1926 -
Thomas Richard	1918 - 1964		

<u>Ruth</u>

Lawrence Zancanella
} Elanor, Lawrence

<u>Archie</u>

Lucy (Fuller)
} Robert, Arthur, Hallie, Ruth, Michael

Marie (Johnson)

<u>Willard</u>

Edna Mae (Allen)
} Georgie, Carol

Julie, Mike

<u>Richard</u>

Wilma (Sage)
} Walter, Leslie

<u>Rosezella "Rosie"</u>

Alden Haff
} Richard, Glenda, Donald, Tamar

<u>Alice</u>

Bill Lawrence
} Spencer, Janet, Sarah

<u>Zada</u>

Chuck Ashcraft
} Sharon, Kevin

The Story Of
THE WATSON COLONY
Missouri Heights 1921 – 1922

Alice (Boyd) Turner

When Alice Boyd was twelve years old she lived with her parents, Walton and Anna Boyd, and her brothers and sisters in Pueblo, Colorado. Her father read an ad in a paper telling about a colony that was being developed in a place in Colorado called Missouri Heights. The colony was led by a man claiming to be a millionaire named H.D. Watson, from Kearney, Nebraska. The colony was a communal living situation in which each family who joined would have twenty-two acres on which to live and farm. Watson's plan was that all expenses and profits would be shared, and that all involved would live in peace and harmony.

The land was located due west of where the Mike Strang ranch is in 1998, and south of where Diane and Bill Teague live, at the intersection of County Road 103 and Catherine Store Road.

Alice (Boyd) Turner remembers, "My dad wrote to Mr. Watson asking about the colony, and a little later he received a small check and a note that said, 'Come join us!' My folks sold everything they had and packed our clothing in gunny sacks, and we took the train to the Western Slope. I remember when we arrived in Carbondale. There was no one to meet us, and we waited all day at the depot. It was raining and we were all wet and cold and hungry, five children and Mom and Dad. Finally someone with an old hayrack came and picked us up and we headed up the hill to Missouri Heights.

"There was a house on the property, and a smaller shack, but there were five families already there, and no room for us in either place. So we lived in tents, and I still remember how cold it was in the winter time.

"Mr. Watson was exactly what we imagined him to be, a fine gentleman in every way, very pompous and prosperous looking, and very kind and sincere. He was tall and slender and walked very jauntily with a cane. We couldn't help but believe in him and his ideas. He seemed to have money, and the ability to obtain money. He secured a loan from the bank in Glenwood Springs and bought a small herd of cattle, six cows and one bull, registered Holsteins. He also got enough money to buy a car. He ordered supplies from the May D&F Department Store in Denver, and they arrived and were distributed to all the families. Even with all of this we were still living in tents, and did so for two and a half years.

"My brothers and sisters, Bennie, Jimmy, Catherine, Olive and me all went to the Missouri Heights School, which still stands today. The only teacher I can remember was Bill Tomkin. Some of my classmates were Gracie Cowen (who is still a dear friend of mine), Bob and Cora Holgate, the Grem children, Forby Higginbotham, the Henkes, and the Lawrence children. My family and I walked to school, and that would have been 1921 and '22. My mom would sometimes bring a big pot of homemade tomato soup in the morning, and set it on the old wood stove in the winter time. It would simmer all morning and smell so wonderful, and at noon we would all have soup in our cups. All the mothers took turns, and brought us delicious things to have for lunch. Gracie Cowen's folks had more cattle than we did, and they had meat more often. Sometimes she would bring a nice big steak sandwich, and I would have a peanut butter and jelly sandwich. We loved to trade because the meat was a treat to me, and the peanut butter a treat to her.

"I remember Mr. Watson's wife because she was so strange. We heard that she did not want to come to Colorado. She lived in the house, and never came out of her bedroom. We only saw glimpses of

The Boyd Family at the Watson Colony farm.

Missouri Heights History

Dear Editor,

I was quite interested in the article from the Valley Journal of March 5 titled News Wasn't All That Different in the 20s. The article mentioned the millionaire, H.D. Watson, from Kearney, Nebraska.

We, the Boyd family, lived in Pueblo, Colorado at that time. My father, Walton Boyd, read the ad in the paper then asking families to come to the Watson Colony on Missouri Heights. He applied and was accepted.

We arrived at the railroad depot in Carbondale in the late summer of 1921. That day we waited from 9 a.m. until 4 p.m. when someone from the colony came in an old hayrack, loaded us and our belongings and took us to our destination. We were soaked with rain, cold and tired when we arrived.

There was really no provision made for new arrivals at the Watson Colony. There were only two dwellings there, the main house and the bunk house, which were occupied. There was nothing to do but set up tents. We lived in this arrangement for two winters and one summer.

H.D. Watson, also known as "Alfalfa" Watson, disappeared before farm work began in the spring of 1922, owing banks and merchants far and near. The only families there, Boyd, Layton and Kneutson ran the farm that year.

This union broke up and my father took over a $1,000 mortgage for a small herd of milk cows, a few horses and a few pieces of farm machinery and ran the farm the following year. The Boyd family continued to farm in different areas for the next ten years.

A few families came, looked over the Watson Colony situation and left.

No family was placed on a 22 acre tract of land and helped in any way as described. All soon left but the Boyds. My sister, Mrs. Ray Turner, still lives in Carbondale.

James Boyd,
Denver

her, and everyone wondered about her. We were there two winters and one summer when something remarkable happened. My brother was not there when it happened, but I was, and I remember it well. A big car, which seemed like a limousine to me, drove up to the colony. The men got out and announced that they were the law. They talked to Mr. Watson a short while, and then put him in the back seat. They explained that he was a mental patient and had been living in an institution before he came to Colorado. We found out later that he never paid anyone for the things he bought. He owed the bank, May D&F, and all the merchants, and several neighbors he had swindled. His wife was also taken away later, and we heard she was placed in a home."

Rokie Fender remembers the Watson Colony, "Yes, it was a weird situation. Mr. Watson was a smooth talker, and he liked my dad, Ira. My dad felt sorry for the people and loaned Watson machinery and different tools to help out. Watson was supposed to pay for some things, but never did, and my dad finally knew he was no good. My dad and my brother went over and got our machinery back."

Alice (Boyd) Turner remembers, "Before long, the other families moved away and my dad took over the mortgage on the cattle and rented the colony farm. After a while we moved on and rented the Virgile Holcomb place, and the Wolcott place. When Ben and Olive, my older brother and sister, were ready for high school, Dad rented a little home for them in Carbondale. I remember my mom, Anna, would load two big gunny sacks on the saddle horse and ride down from the Heights to take them food for the week. She took potatoes and beef and bread, and jars of homemade jam, and eggs and butter, and canned buckskin.

"I went to the eighth grade at Luby School over on the Sweet place. I was the only one in the eighth grade, and the county school supervisor came there to give me my exams. The results came in the mail and I graduated from the eighth grade.

THE TURNER FAMILY – 1948

Ray Turner
1916 -

Alice (Boyd) Turner
1908 -

"I was destined to live on Missouri Heights again. Ray and I were married in 1940, and we bought the Holmes cabin in 1948."

The Holmes cabin is west of the Mike Strang place today, and is owned by Laura VanDyne.

"We had forty acres and we raised wheat and oats and alfalfa. We only got one good irrigation in the spring, and that was it. We did have a cistern to store water in, but it was never much water. No one had enough water on the Heights. We raised turkeys and chickens and ducks and had a few horses and cows and sheep. Our neighbors were Edith and Walt Lawrence (who lived where Diane and Bill Teague live in 1998), Quakenbushes (where Strang is today), the Sigler family, the Fenders, Hughes, Lyons, Greens, and the Holgates. Our son, Raymond, went from grade one to eighth grade at the Missouri Heights School in the '50s.

"There were dances at the Missouri Heights Schoolhouse, and in the winter we went with a team and a sled. I remember in the winter the horses' bits would freeze up. The men would bring them inside and pour hot water on them to warm them up before they put them back in the horses' mouths.

"The card parties at different houses were fun. We had two or three tables set up and played different games: poker, sluff, and 500. We bought all our groceries from Chuck Harris at Catherine's Store. One time I had him order a bunch of fresh oysters. It was for a card party at my house (the cabin), and I made fried oysters, buckskin steak baked in the oven, and a big salad. We had a whole bunch over and it was great.

"Before we had a real refrigerator we made our own. It was a wooden box with shelves and a screen in the back. We put a pan of water on top. A gunny sack was partially in the water, and hung down in the back. The front was open, so the air filtered through and the gunny sack kept things cool. Believe it or not, it worked!

"I canned so much buckskin up on the Heights, and most things from my garden, too. We seldom went to Glenwood because it took all day. Once in a while we went to Carbondale, but most of what we needed was at Catherine's Store.

In 1958 we sold the cabin and forty acres to Mr. McCormick, and moved to Carbondale. My husband, Ray, my son, Raymond, and myself have all worked hard. There was always so much to do, but we got it done. We've had a wonderful life, my Ray and I, and we've been so happy together. He is my sweetheart, and always will be."

THE LOESCH FAMILY – 1920

Edward Loesch
1889 - 1952

Florence (Blackmore) Loesch
1891 - 1982

THE LOESCH FAMILY

Edward and Florence lived on Missouri Heights a short time, from 1920 to 1927. Ed was from near Rifle, Colorado, and Florence was from Lincoln, Nebraska. Florence was a teacher before she was married. Their children were: Edward, born 1916; George, born in 1918; Mary Idelle, born 1924, Russell, born 1929, and Lois, born in 1930.

Florence was given the teaching position at Blue Creek School for the year 1920, and the family moved from Rifle to the William Harris land on Missouri Heights. The place where the Loesch family rented from William Harris was across the road from Paul Gould then, the Witt ranch in 1998.

George: "My brother and I went to the school with mother even though we were not of school age; I was only two years old, and Ed was four. Our house and barn and the school were all close together by the county road. I can barely remember that the school was made out of old logs. My sister, Mary Idelle, was born in that house in 1924. I think Dr. Clagett was there to help my mother.

"We lived on the Heights until I was eight or nine years old, so I don't remember too much. I do remember learning to herd cows for

George and Edward riding Roxie and Dan. Missouri Heights, 1922.

Horse at left: George and a friend; horse at right: baby Mary Idelle and Edward. 1924.

my dad, and I remember him riding horseback down to Basalt to the Oddfellows Lodge. We moved back to Rifle when I was about nine, and I do recall the trip. We drove our cows, about twenty-five head from the Heights to southwest of Silt. Ed drove the team and wagon and my dad and I rode our horses to herd. We made it to east of Carbondale the first night, then on to New Castle the next day and put our cattle in the stock yards, and our team in the livery. The next day we reached our old home place southwest of Silt."

Florence and Ed Loesch are both buried in Rifle, Colorado.

The Loesch family with relatives on the Heights in 1925.
Edward in overalls, Florence holding baby Mary Idelle.

THE ARTAZ FAMILY - 1922

Peter and Zorine, on Missouri Heights, 1943

Peter Constantin Artaz
1885 - 1979

Zeasarine "Zorine" Tersil (Darien) Artaz
1896 - 1983

The Children of Peter and Zeasarine Artaz:

1. Nino .... 1915 - 1917
2. Nettie .... 1916 -
3. Elvera "Tootie" ... 1918 -
4. Louise .... 1919 -
5. Lucille .... 1920 -
6. Souvenir "Bob" ... 1922 - 1997
7. John .... 1925 -
8. Hank .... 1927 -
9. Alice .... 1929 -
10. Irene .... 1932 -
11. Aileen .... 1934 - 1937
12. Betty .... 1936 -
13. Evelyn .... 1937 -

THE ARTAZ FAMILY

Peter Constantin Artaz was born on November 13, 1885, in St. Marcel (Torino) Italy. He came to the United States in 1907, when he was 22 years old. He came just for a visit, but liked it so much, he stayed and never returned to Italy. He always wanted to go back to see his family, but never had the opportunity. He first worked as a farmhand for Frank Berthod. He met Zorine at a neighborhood dance.

Zorine Tersil Darien was born May 25, 1896, in Ollomont (Torino) Italy, and came to the U.S. in 1904 with her mother, sisters, and brothers. Her father, Roger Darien, had arrived earlier, in 1900.

Nettie Artaz, daughter of Peter and Zorine: "I remember Mama telling me how she and her brothers and sisters went to school in Basalt, and how the other kids made terrible fun of them because they couldn't speak English."

Peter and Zorine were married November 28, 1914. They lived with the Dariens for awhile, then moved to Leadville, where Peter worked in the mines. They lived in Buena Vista, then back to Leadville, as well as various Colorado locations including Alma, Stringtown, Como, and Olmont. In 1922 they moved to the Sweet ranch on Missouri Heights.

Left to right: the family dog, Nettie, Louise, Lucille, and Tootie Artaz.

They lived in several places for the following few years: the Ben Hotz place by the reservoir, back down to Hook's Spur, and then up to the Ross Long ranch on the Heights, and finally the Harris place in 1929. In 1998 the Harris place is located at the corner of Cattle Creek Road and Fender Lane.

Souvenir "Bob" remembers, "My parents were from Italy, and they gave me the name Souvenir, which means 'treasure' in Italian. I was about seven years old when we moved to the Harris place on the Heights, and plenty big enough to work. We raised hay, oats and wheat, alfalfa, potatoes, and barley. We had about ten to twelve acres in potatoes, forty to fifty acres in hay. We worked ten to twelve work horses, had milk cows, pigs and chickens and rabbits, and also tended a great big garden. I remember Brownie and Prince were two saddle horses we rode to school. My sisters worked in the fields and knew how to do everything as well as any man. Dad always started the little ones out learning how to operate the hay rake."

Elvira "Tootie": "Nettie and I did the plowing, the disking, raking and mowing of the hay and everything. We could both drive a two or four horse team, and I sang the whole time I was driving those horses. I'm sure they heard me a mile away singing for all I was worth. I sang *Red River Valley, Home on the Range*, and *The Yellow Rose of Texas* at the top of my lungs.

"We planted lots of potatoes. Dad drove the planter with the team, and Nettie or I rode on the back and made sure the seed potatoes went down the tube and were planted correctly. If not, Dad would get real unhappy.

Nettie and Tootie on a potato planter in 1997.

"Souvenir fed the stock, cows and horses, and all of us learned to milk when we were big and strong enough. Mom and Dad did the irrigating. All of us girls took turns working in the fields, and in the house. Mama said she never had to scold, we all had our job to do, and we did it. We even helped Mama deliver her own children. We never had a car or a telephone when we lived on the Heights, and there was no way to get a doctor in time, so we helped her give birth. Hank was the only one of us born in a hospital, all the rest were born at home.

"We made cheese and butter and saved the cream to fill five and ten gallon cream cans, and took the cream to Carbondale to sell at the creamery. Cream is the yellowish part of milk which contains from about eighteen to forty percent butterfat.

Sears, Roebuck and Co. cream separator.

"I spent many an hour turning the handle on the old black cream separator! The handle of the separator had to be turned fast enough to let the disks of the machine twirl fast enough to separate the milk from the cream. Dad said it had to be turned sixty RPMs, rounds or revolutions per minute, to work. As this was being done, the skim milk drained from the machine into a can from one spout, and the cream drained into a bowl from the other spout. It would take about ten to fifteen minutes to separate the cream from the milk of two milk cows.

Sears, Roebuck and Co. milk cans.

"We didn't drink the skim milk like people do today, we drank the whole milk, just as it came from the cow. We fed the skim milk to the hogs, and the calves. The calves were weaned when they were two or three days old, and we taught them to drink the skim milk. What we did was put our hand down in the bucket of skim milk and, with the other hand, held the bucket up to the calf's head. You'd stick your finger up through the milk and get the calf to suck on it. after a couple days of sucking your finger, they would go ahead and drink on their own.

"The cows had to be milked morning and evening. Of course, before they were milked they had to be gone after in the pasture and brought in, all before and after school. At the creamery, a five-gallon can brought in $2, and a ten-gallon can, $4."

Tootie: "I'll explain to you how we made our own cheese. We saved each milking in separate containers until we had about two-thirds of a washtub full. Then we skimmed the cream off the top with a utensil called a skimmer. It just took the cream off the top of the milk. The last milking was mixed in with the rest without skimming. We heated the washtub on the wood stove until it was just luke warm, then we added one rennet tablet that had been soaked and dissolved first. It only took one tablet to a tub, then we took it off the heat and let it set and cool until it was a little solid. Then, we took a wooden stick and stirred it. This made the whey (liquid in the milk that separated from the curds) rise to the top. The curds were the solid part. After it set and settled after the stirring, we poured the whey off. Now, the whole thing was ready for the cheese press.

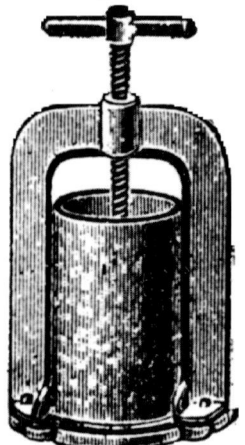

A Sears, Roebuck and Co. cheese press.

"We put a cloth inside the press and put the cheese mixture in. The cloth sort of shaped the cheese. Then, we folded the cloth all around the cheese and tightened the lid down. It all set 'til morning, and what moisture was still in the cheese drained out through the cloth. In the morning we undid the cloth, turned the cheese over, put it back in the press just like before, and let it set and drain one more night.

"Next morning, we took it out and rubbed it all over with regular salt, and it was ready to put down in the cellar, which kept it cool. Once a week it had to be checked because mold would form on it. The mold was rubbed off with a cloth on all sides. Then it cured for the rest of the year. You could eat it in about a month, but the longer it sat, the better it was.

"It was kind of fun making the cheese. Us girls loved to do one thing: just before we put the cheese in the press, we formed some of it into a ball with our hands and ate it. This was the curds, and it was just like cottage cheese. We liked that part.

"In the evening after dinner, and all the chores were finished, we could play 'til dark with our friends. We played hide and seek, red line, and fox and geese. For red line, we drew a big, long line in the dirt, and everyone had to run back and forth across it without getting caught. The one who was 'it' had to stay on the line."

Nettie: "Everyone back then made their own soap. It wasn't soap for taking a bath, but was used to wash clothes and even clean house. We had to make soap because we couldn't afford to buy it. It was soap-making time when Dad butchered a hog. Soap came from the fat on the hog. After Dad cut up the hog, he peeled the fat off it. It was called pork rinds. The rinds were the skin of the animal. We put it all in a big roaster pan and put it in the oven of the wood stove. We had to watch it carefully, and soon the fat melted, turned clear and the rinds shriveled, then you took out what rind was left and you had all liquid fat, which looked like cooking oil.

"We put the liquid into a tub and heated it up. When it was pretty hot we added one can of lye. It was in powder form, and you had to stand back a bit because the fumes were strong. We stirred the mixture with a stick until it got thick and then somewhat solid. Then we let it set until it was just solid enough to cut into bars. Then, the bars sat until they were good and solid. They were the size of bars of soap today. When they were good and solid we wrapped them in cloth. Some people added a little perfume to their soap. It was used for all our cleaning, clothes, woodwork, floors, blankets, and everything. It sure is a lot easier to go to the market today and buy a box of soap. We did buy bars of soap we used to wash our hands and take baths with."

Souvenir: "I did something real bad once, but I was little and didn't know any better. Mama came home and found little dead baby chicks laying all around the yard. She asked me what happened and I told her I was just trying to teach them to fly. Those poor little things – I threw them all up in the air!

"We had no water and no electricity. We hauled water from the Harris place.

"I remember my first real job, when I got paid, was over at the Jammarons,' who lived on the Edna Sweet place. I drove the stacker team and the dump rake for Mr. Victor Jammaron. I made fifty cents a day. That was when I was ten or eleven. My second job was herding pigs. There were thirty or forty of them, and I had to move them around to eat, and keep them all together. I did this up at Snowmass and got fifty cents a day for that, too. It was big money!

"My brothers and I made our own fun. Sometimes we would saddle up the horses and ride all over the Heights. Other times we'd get the dogs and go chipmunk hunting in the rocks. The dogs loved that!

"My folks only went to Glenwood Springs at Christmas time. Our Christmas presents were little homemade wooden trucks, and one year a toboggan Dad made for us. Then, there was fresh fruit and homemade candy from our grandparents.

"My brother, Johnny, still has a scar that happened when we rode the toboggan one winter day. The snow was real deep on the road, which is Cattle Creek Road today. There were six or eight of us on the toboggan and we had started up the road a ways and were coming down at a pretty fast pace. I was steering and when we got near the corner where the mail boxes were, everyone started yelling, 'Make the turn! Make the turn!' They knew if we didn't we'd go down the road and all the way to El Jebel. Well, I tried my best to make the turn up but we slammed into the mail boxes and Johnny got a nail pushed into his head about a fourth of an inch deep. I guess it wasn't at a delicate spot because Mom doctored it and he was alright – but he still has that scar.

"We went to school at Luby School, next to the Paul Gould place. We rode Brownie or Princess, or we walked. I remember when I was in the fourth grade, my teacher was Margaret Darien. I got my hands paddled with a ruler once. I was taking books home at night, and getting too far ahead. She didn't want me to be ahead of the others, so I had to stop. Our school friends were: Rosie, Alice, Zada and Dick and Archie Gould; Desmond Harris; the Dupires; and the Bogue family. School was from nine 'til four."

Tootie: "My teacher at Luby School in the seventh grade was Mrs. Quinlan, and in the eighth grade was Olla Jacobs, whom I adored. Miss Jacobs would take us all outside to the ditches to catch bullfrogs. Then, we would have fried frog legs for lunch. I went to school with the Goulds; the Bogues, Bulah and Bruford; Alice Turner; and Ed and George Loesch. Nettie and I both graduated eighth grade from our one-room school, Luby.

"When all of us girls were older, we not only worked at home, but we worked out at various farms and homes, too. We worked for other people in the fields and did housework. We all learned how to make money. Dad was not harsh, he just taught us to work, but he also insisted that everyone take Sunday off. It was wonderful to look forward to. We would go visiting, and see our neighbors."

Souvenir: "I used to love chasing my sisters around the barn with a pitchfork. One time I got all carried away and threw it. The tines landed right between one of my sister's toes. Boy, was I lucky about that! I just stayed near home and worked mostly. I didn't go to town until I was fifteen or sixteen, when I went to Glenwood Springs and saw my first movie. That would have been about 1938."

The Artaz family left the Heights in the late 1930s, and moved to Capitol Creek, where they lived and worked on what is now the McCabe ranch.

Souvenir: "The winter I was sixteen or seventeen years old, we lived in Capitol Creek. They were having the annual Christmas party

The Artaz family, 1953. Back row, left to right: John, Bob, Louise, Hank, Tootie, Irene, Lucille. Center: Peter and Zorine. Front row, left to right: Evelyn, Alice, Betty, Nettie.

at Luby School up on the Heights, and I wanted to go and see my old friends. I rode my horse all the way. When the party was over, it was late, and freezing cold. I started home and got to Basalt about two in the morning, and rode on home. It was a great party!"

Tootie: "When I was seventeen years old, we traveled from Snowmass to Glenwood Springs and I saw my first movie. It was a real thrill for me! Our parents were so wonderful. They dearly loved each other and treasured each one of us kids. Our lives were hard but we were a happy family."

Peter and Zorine were married 64 years. They are buried at the Rosebud Cemetery in Glenwood Springs.

Author's Note: Souvenir "Bob" Artaz passed away September 17, 1997, just days after telling me his boyhood stories. I will never forget his sweet smile as he spoke so lovingly of his parents, his brothers, and sisters, and their life on the Heights.

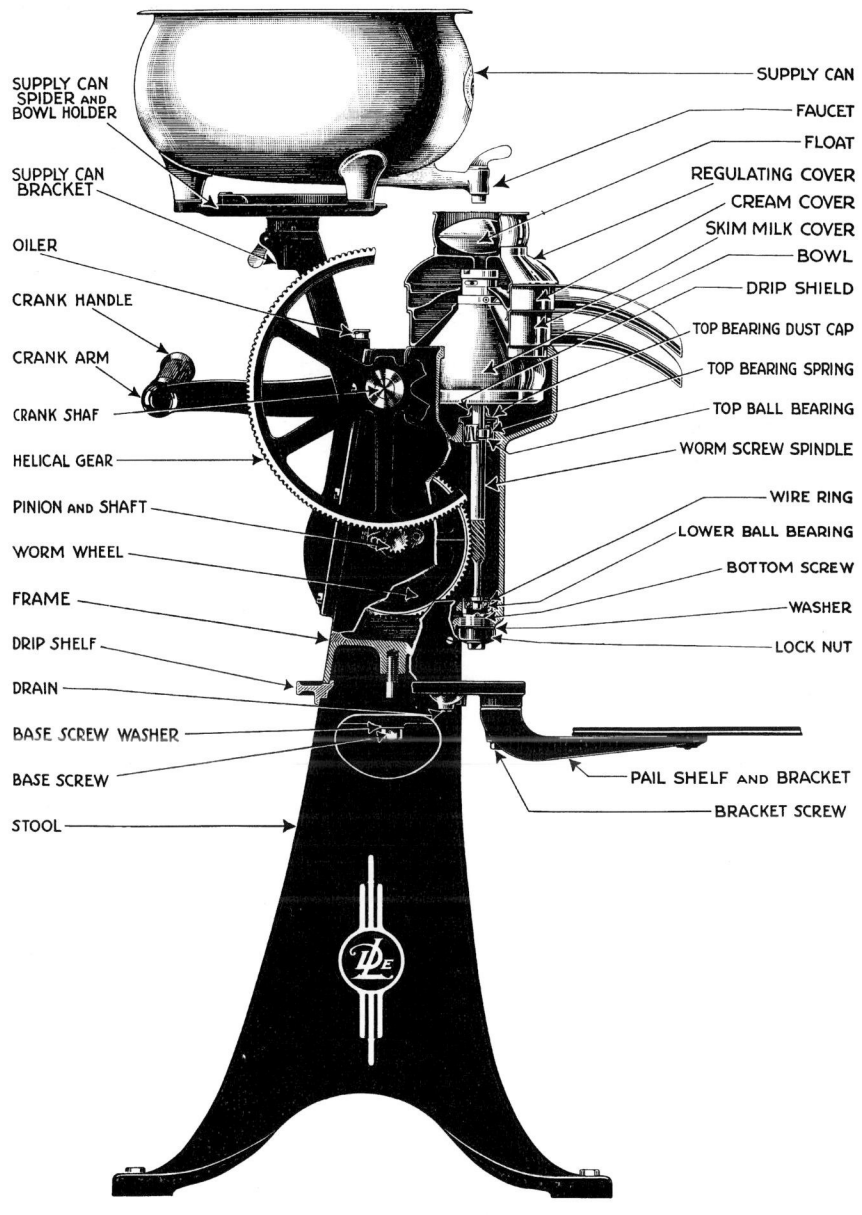

SECTIONAL VIEW OF CREAM SEPARATOR

Figure No. 15

I'd love to be there watching

Early in the morning

The sun comes up and

Crowns the mountains king

And if by chance you dare to be

High upon the mountain

I swear that you could hear the angels sing.

Have you ever been down to Colorado

I spend a lot of time there in my mind

And if God doesn't live in Colorado

I bet that's where he spends most of his time.

– *Written by Dave Kirby*

THE KREUTZ FAMILY – 1926

Carl Kreutz
1894 - 1971

Mary Leona (Lewis) Kreutz
1889 - 1979

THE KREUTZ FAMILY

Carl Kreutz was born in 1894 in Westboro, Missouri.

He enlisted in the Army in 1912 and served under Pershing at the Mexican border against Pancho Villa. He served in World War I from 1917 to 1919 at the Meuse Argonne.

Mary Leona "Lee" (Lewis) was born in Jamestown, Indiana, in 1889, and was raised in St. Joseph, Missouri.

Carl's father met Leona "Lee" first, and told her his son was in the war. He asked if she would write to him. Carl and Mary Leona corresponded for some time, and became attached, sight unseen. After the war Carl moved to Denver to work for Harleigh Holmes at his company, Coleman Motors, and Lee moved to Denver to be treated for asthma. They found each other, saw each other for just one week – and got married July 28, 1919. Their first daughter, Betty Jane was born in Denver on August 22, 1920.

Carl Kreutz (above and below).

Their second daughter, born October 30, 1921, Helen (Kreutz) Dupire recalls, "We moved from Denver to Missouri Heights when I was six years old. I went to Luby School for just the first six weeks of the term in 1927. Arthur Bogue was the teacher.

"We walked to school and had to go through the brush, and we got wood ticks on us. For some reason the ticks loved me! I was blond haired, and Mom poured iodine on my head to get the ticks off. I ended up with black and white hair, but it did get the ticks off.

"Lee" and Carl.

"At home we had no water or electricity, and I remember how wonderful it was to have Blue Creek water in Luby School. It tasted so good!

"We moved back to Denver for awhile, but when I was ten years old, we moved back to Missouri Heights, and my dad worked for Harleigh Holmes and ran the Carbondale Reservoir and Irrigation Company. I started Luby School again in the fifth grade. None of us had any money, but we didn't know we were poor, because everyone else was the same. We kids all stayed all night with each other, and had so much fun. We didn't have electricity at our house until 1950. We walked everywhere we wanted to go. The Gould kids had horses, but we didn't. I remember the first time I was given bread and butter with sugar on top. It was at Grace and Paul Gould's house, and I was so thrilled. I never had that before in my life, and it was so wonderful! Grace Gould always fed anyone who was hungry.

"We lived up above the Frank Sweet place. On Saturday nights everyone went to Carbondale, and us kids couldn't wait. Sometimes we had a nickel to spend. One of the best things was the Vaudeville

Carl and Betty Jane with a 1922 Dodge.

show put on in the building where the Near New is today in 1998. They had entertainers who put on a stage show. There were also stage plays in the little park next to the Near New building. The plays were given from the back of a big truck. They sold patent medicine, and we'd sit on logs to watch. It cost fifteen cents to see it all.

The Kreutz family: Carl with Betty Jane on his lap, "Lee" and Helen.

"For fifteen years my father Carl ran the Carbondale Reservoir for Harleigh Holmes. He had to fill the reservoir from the intake ditches in the spring, and then govern the outlet, which was no easy job. He walked the ditches all summer and controlled the water. Every few weeks we would send out postcards for a ditch meeting, and everyone met at the Missouri Heights Schoolhouse, and voiced when they wanted their water on and off. I used to get up at 6 a.m. and walk the ditches with my dad every morning. I remember I was so hungry when I came home, and then around 10 a.m. at school I could hardly keep my eyes open.

"My dad also farmed. We raised hay, oats and potatoes. We had milk cows, and a big strong team of horses named Bess and Flo. Our closest neighbors were the Goulds and the Fenders. The kids I went to Luby School with were Dick and Rosie Gould; Souviner, Louise and Lucille Artaz, and Desmond Harris. Olive Jacobs was my fifth grade teacher.

"I remember Rosezella "Rosie" Gould and my sister, Betty Jane, used to catch big frogs at the reservoir. They would crack the frogs' heads on the wagon tongue, cut off their legs and fry them. They tried to get me to eat them, but I wouldn't.

"Us girls used to swim in the ditches when they were running. We didn't have cute bathing suits like kids have today. We just swam in our undies, and if we heard a car coming, we'd all scream and go hide behind a ridge.

"One time we saw a great big bull snake with a frog in its mouth. Rosezella "Rosie" Gould wasn't afraid of anything. She grabbed that snake and took the frog away from it – so she could fry its legs!

"My sister and I walked to Luby School, but in the winter we pushed each other on a sled. After we got up the road so far from our place, it was a down hill coast clear to school. I only went to Luby for the fifth grade. After that I went to the Carbondale School.

"I remember the mailman, Ray Swagart. In the good weather he drove an old car, but when the mud was too much for the car, he used a horse and buggy.

"This was my life on the Heights."

Leona and Carl Kreutz are buried in the Littleton Cemetery near Denver. Helen lives in Carbondale in 1998, and Betty Jane lives in Littleton, Colorado.

THE KREUTZ FAMILY

Carl Kreutz
1894 - 1971

Mary Leona (Lewis) Kreutz
1889 - 1979

Children

Betty Jane.................1920 -   Helen.....................1921 -

Betty Jane..................... ⎫
                                 ⎬ Janice, Carla
Clayton Floyd..............   ⎭

Helen .... ⎫
                                 ⎬ Barry Lee, Susan Adair
Augustine Dupire ....   ⎭

Carl Kreutz dies after heart attack

Carl Kreutz, 76, of 2576 W. Alamo Avenue, died Saturday in Rocky Mountain hospital after his third major heart attack in seven years. He was a resident of Littleton from 1921 to 1950, and again from 1959 to 1971.

Mr. Kreutz was born in Westboro, Missouri, on May 24, 1894. He enlisted in the Army in 1912, serving under Pershing at the Mexican border against Pancho Villa. He served in World War I from 1917 to 1919 at the Meuse Argonne.

He worked at Coleman Motors at its inception with H. R. Holmes, founder. Then, in 1930 he began work for the Carbondale Reservoir Company for Holmes and remained in the Carbondale area. He married Mary Leon Lewis of St. Joseph, Missouri, in Denver on July 28, 1919.

Enlisting in the Navy's Seabees in 1943 in World War II, he served in Hawaii. Following his service he returned to the Carbondale area, where he remained until he came back to Littleton to live.

Mr. Kreutz was a life member of the Carbondale Masonic Lodge; a 50-year member of the VFW; past commander of the Veterans of World War I; and a member of the Littleton Elks Lodge. He always prided himself on his military service. His hobbies were history and reading. He also loved hunting and fishing and enjoyed this in the years he lived in Carbondale.

In addition to his widow, he leaves two daughters, Mrs. Betty Jane Ford Floyd of 2100 W. Pine Ridge Avenue, and Mrs. Helen Dupire of Snowmass, Colorado; two sisters: Mrs. Betty Garrett of Kaycee, Wyoming, and Mrs Theo Wardell of Rexburg, Idaho; four grandchildren and three great-grandchildren.

Services were held Tuesday at 1 p.m. at Drinkwine Mortuary. Burial was in Littleton Cemetery.

The Story Of
"Misery" Heights
Franklin Delano Roosevelt And The New Deal

Some people believed that an over-abundance of agricultural products which began in the 1920s was the cause of the Great Depression, which hit the nation full force after the stock market crash in October of 1929. Colorado farmers soon felt the effects with virtually no market, and the lowest prices ever for all their efforts.

Franklin Delano Roosevelt (F.D.R.), Democrat of New York, was inaugurated as 32nd president on March 4, 1933. Roosevelt's New Deal took drastic measures to reduce farm production and raise prices for the struggling farmer. The Agricultural Adjustment Administration, nicknamed the Triple A, was established in 1933, giving the government authority to buy crops and destroy them, in high hopes of raising prices. Corn, cotton, wheat, potatoes, and hog production were drastically reduced and farmers were given crop reduction contracts. The contract provided a meager monetary compensation, and farmers suffered terribly along with the rest of the nation. The farmers accepted the crop reduction contracts because it was their last hope.

Across Colorado, on Missouri Heights, and in the whole Roaring Fork Valley, the famed potato crop was destroyed. Government representatives came to each farm and painted the potatoes, using sprayers filled with paint or dye, and ruined perfectly fine potatoes so they could not be sold. Farmers stood by helplessly and watched, as an entire year's worth of backbreaking work was destroyed in a matter of moments. They wondered how they would pay the bills and hang onto their mortgaged farms.

In 1932, five million young men were unemployed in the nation, and as a part of the New Deal, F.D.R. established the Civilian Conservation Corps (CCC), which organized young men all over the country into camps and paid them to work for the government. Some of the projects they worked on were: prevention of soil erosion, forestry, upkeep of National Parks, and construction of dams and waterways. Nearly 32,000 young men in Colorado were in the CCC, with one camp in Glenwood Springs. The camp was located on Grand Avenue, where Sayre Park is today in 1998.

The CCC contributed more than $56 million to Colorado's bleak economy at a time when its crop land value had declined to the lowest on record. The CCC earned the reputation as the most successful and popular of the New Deal Relief Agencies.

On January 6, 1936, the Supreme Court declared that the Triple A was unconstitutional, and the government developed new measures to help the farmer, many of whom were on the brink of foreclosure. For some, it was too late, and the hard times continued through the 1940s.

On December 8, 1941, the United States declared war on Japan, and the CCC was disbanded, as young men went to the aid of their country. 2,700 Colorado men and women gave their lives in the war from 1940 to 1946. The Colorado Selective Service system inducted 73,664 young men into the Armed Forces. When the war was over, the CCC camp in Glenwood Springs was used to house German prisoners of war, who were brought to the area to pick potatoes in the Roaring Fork Valley.

By the late '40s and early '50s, the production of potatoes was no longer profitable in the Roaring Fork Valley or on Missouri Heights. The end of an era was brought about through a combination of circumstances: potato blight (a disease affecting the potato crop), lack of pickers, and not enough profit for the work involved.

THE JAMMARON FAMILY – 1930

Victor Jammaron
1886 - 1968

Sidonia (Ronc) Jammaron
1899 - 1984

THE JAMMARON FAMILY

Victor Jammaron came to the United States in 1907 from Etroubles, Italy. Etroubles is located near the border between Switzerland and Italy, near St. Bernard Pass. Victor came to this country because his father and uncle, Leonard Jammaron, had spent time in Colorado in the 1880s and had returned to Italy with stories of the rich silver and gold mines, and the beauty of Colorado. They had both worked in the mines at Aspen, and the uncle had worked in one of the kilns near Sellers, which produced charcoal for the smelter in Leadville.

Victor was twenty-one years old when he came to the "Land of Plenty" with dreams of becoming prosperous. He went to night school to learn to read and write and speak English. When World War I erupted, Victor became an American soldier. His ability to speak and understand French, Italian, and English made him valuable as an interpreter. At that time immigrants were given points toward U.S. citizenship if they enlisted in the armed services. He was in France during most of his stint in the army.

In 1924 he returned to Italy and intended to stay. He married Sidonia Ronc, and in 1925 changed his mind and decided to return to Colorado. He was ready for a new life, and conditions in Italy were not as rewarding as he had remembered them. Victor and Sidonia came to the Roaring Fork Valley, and he worked for Frank Sweet as an irrigator on Sweet's Crystal River ranch.

His son, Joe, remembers, "My dad was a first rate irrigator. He could make water go anywhere. It was always difficult for me, but for him it was easy!"

The Jammarons lived and worked in various places in the valley. Emma was born

Victor, Emma, Sidonia and Joe.

THIS LEASE, Made and entered into in duplicate this 10th day of February A.D. 1930 by and between H. A. Laudenklos party of the first part, and Victor Jammaron, party of the second part, Witnesseth;

That the said party of the first part leases unto the party of the second part the following described premises situated in the County of Garfield and State of Colorado, to wit; The ranch known as the H. A. Laudenklos ranch ranch situated in that section of the county known as Missouri Heights and under the water system known as the Carbondale Reservoir and Irrigation Company supplying irrigation water for the said ranch. Together with the improvements thereon except as hereinafter reserved, for the term of three years commencing February 1930 and ending Mar. 1, 1933.

The party of the first part reserves one frame house on hill east of main buildings.

The party of the first part pays one-third water maintenance under said reservoir system, furnishing water to the land for eighty (80) acre feet.

The party of the first part pays one-third of threshing bill, furnishes all grass seed, all fencing material, and pays the party of the second part for rebuilding potato cellar, as follows:

Three dollars per day for single man, and five dollars per day for man and team, and said party of the first part furnished all lumber necessary for said cellar that party of the second part may need. As part payment for cellar work, party of the first part gives the party of the second part one-half interest, to the value of one hundred ($100.00), in one John Deere binder. And if said amounts not sufficient to pay for the labor on said cellar, the party of the first part permits the party of the second part to hold out for balance due from cellar work money that the party of the second part receives for the party of the first part's share of the crop.

All present pasture land is to be used as such by the party of the second part.

The party of the second part agrees to farm all land in a farm-like manner, and furnish all seed for the crop years of 1930, 1931, and 1932, except grass seed as above mentioned.

The party of the second part is to market and sell all grain and potato crops at his discretion, and to pay to the party of the first part as rent for above mentioned premises one-third of net proceeds except as otherwise herein mentioned.

All hay is to be divided in stacks and two-thirds to be the property of the party of the second part, and one-third the property of the party of the first part. The party of the second part has the option to buy the one-third hay crop of the party of the first part at the agreed market price of hay in the stack.

All straw and fall pasture is to be the property of the party of the second part.

The party of the first part is to furnish one-third of all twine and one-third of all sacks for grain and potatoes necessary for harvesting and marketing, and in the event that the party of the second part furnished the party of the first part's share of twine and sacks, the party of the first part agrees to allow the party of the second part to hold out of the share of the cop of the party of the first part any such amount necessary to reimburse the party of the second part.

The party of the second part agrees to furnish all machinery and livestock.

IN Witness Whereof the parties hereto have executed these present.

Party of the first part _H. A. Laudenklos._

Party of the second part _Victor Jammaron_

This lease, Made and entered into in duplicate this 15th day of February, 1933 by and between Edna D. Sweet, party of the first part, and Victor Jammaron, party of the second part witnesseth.

That the party of the first part leases unto the party of the second part the following described land situated in Eagle County, Colorado, to sit: S.W. 1/4 of S.E. 1/4 Section 21/----S.W. 1/4 of S.W. 1/4 Section 22. ----N.W. 1/4 of N.W. 1/4 Section 27. N.E. 1/4 of N.E. 1/4 of Section 28, Township 7, South Range 87 West. With all the water from the Monarch Ditch and the Carbondale Reservoir Company, together with all the improvements thereon for the term of three years commencing March 1st, 1933 and ending March 1st, 1936, for one third of the crops raised on the above described land,

The party of the first part agrees to pay the water maintenance under the Carbondale Reservoir Company and to furnish to the party of the second part all the materials to be used on the Monarch Ditch in case of break or to replace the old flumes and all the materials for fencing hay stalks. The party of the second part furnishes all labor necessary for above.

The party of the second part agrees to farm all land in a farm-like manner and furnish all the seed for the crop years 1933, 1934, and 1935, except grass seed, which will be furnished by the party of the first part. Each party will pay for his share of twines and sacks for harvesting and marketing grain and potatoes. All land now in cultivation and used by the party of the second part for pasture during the crop season shall be paid by the party of second part in proportion to the average of the hay raised on the farm. The party of the second part will pay two thirds of the threshing bill and own all the straw. All grains to be divided at threshing, two thirds to the party of the second part and one third to the party of the first part.

All present pasture land will be used as such the party of the second part. The has to be divided in stacks and two thirds to be the property of the first part. The party of the second part will have the option to buy the share of hay of the party of the first part for the market price of the locality for cash. The fall pasture will be the property of the party of the second part, unless sold with the hay, then party of the first part shares one-third.

The party of the second part is to market the potatoes any time he may see fit, and pay to the party of the first part one third of the proceeds. The party of the first part will pay to the party of the second part five cents per hundred pounds for his share of potatoes and grain to be delivered to the closest railroad point. The party of the first part will let the party of the second part use all the working horses harness and plows until June 15, 1933. If the party of the second part furnish the party of the first part sacks, twines, grass seed or any materials or bills mentioned in this ease to be furnished by the party of the first part, the party of the first part agrees to allow the party of the second part to hold out of the share of the crop of the party of the first part, any such amount to reimburse the party of the second part.

All machinery belonging to party of the first part, of which list is attached, shall be stored behind fence, and shall not be used by party of the second part except as above specified. Party of second part shall not be held responsible for said stored machinery, and shall not store said machinery, except by written order, from party of first part.

Maintenance of the telephone and pile line to be kept by party of the second part, such material as required to be furnished by party of the first part.

Harold E. Sweet

Victor Jammaron

in Carbondale in 1926, and Joe in 1928, when they lived in Basalt.

They also rented the Flynn place outside of Carbondale, which is the Winter Eagle Ranch in 1998. In 1930, they moved to Missouri Heights and rented the Laudenklos place until 1933. Leo was born in 1932. They moved to the Edna Sweet place on the Heights in 1933. Ida was born in 1934.

Joe, Baby Leo, and Emma Jammaron.

Joe: "My dad raised alfalfa hay with a little Timothy grass mix, wheat and, of course, potatoes. We raised Burbanks and Pontiacs. Pontiacs were a cross-mix of two potatoes, a Bliss Triumph and an Early Ohio. This cross produced a better red potato. The potato cellar was up on a hill, back of the house. I remember I had to weed the potatoes, and ten acres seemed like a million to me back then. We took our potatoes to the railroad at Hook's Spur and to Catherine. Sometimes we had a thousand sacks of potatoes. I remember in '37 or '38 the government men came out and painted the spuds with blue dye to try to stop the glut on the market.

"Planting potatoes was a job I'll never forget. I was about ten years old, and first we had to cut seed potatoes into pieces to plant. Each little piece had to have and eye or two on it, and the piece weighed about an ounce. This was all done in the potato cellar. When we were ready to plant, Dad drove the team, and I sat

Properly cut seed potatoes. Each piece has two good eyes and is about the size of a hen's egg.

behind on the seat in back. Right in front of me was a wheel, sort of like a pizza pan with divisions between the pieces, like this:

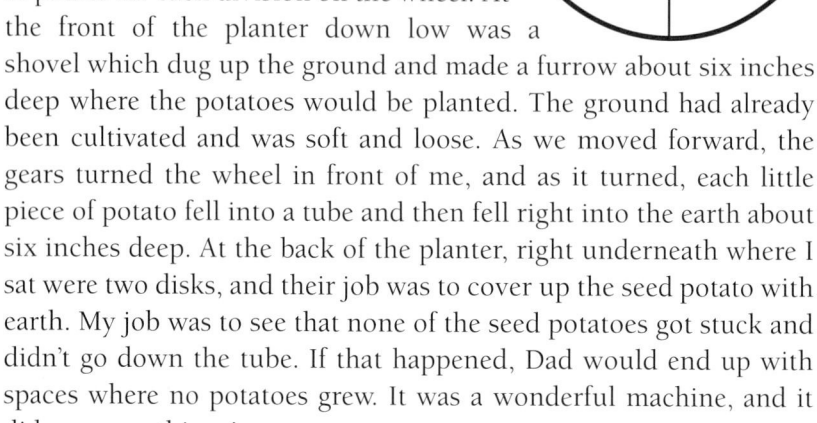

"The pieces were dumped into the box on the planter and as the horses were moved forward the pieces of potatoes would fall into the wheel, just one piece of potato for each division on the wheel. At the front of the planter down low was a shovel which dug up the ground and made a furrow about six inches deep where the potatoes would be planted. The ground had already been cultivated and was soft and loose. As we moved forward, the gears turned the wheel in front of me, and as it turned, each little piece of potato fell into a tube and then fell right into the earth about six inches deep. At the back of the planter, right underneath where I sat were two disks, and their job was to cover up the seed potato with earth. My job was to see that none of the seed potatoes got stuck and didn't go down the tube. If that happened, Dad would end up with spaces where no potatoes grew. It was a wonderful machine, and it did so many things!

"Making straight furrows across a field was an art in itself. Farmers took great pride in a field of perfectly straight furrows. It was something that had to be learned."

A potato planter.

Rosie (Gould) Haff lived on the Heights at the same time, and remembers her potato planting days well. "The land was well prepared before the potatoes were planted in the spring. First, it was plowed, and then harrowed. A harrow was an implement with spikes or disks that pulverized the soil until it was real smooth with no lumps in it. Of course, the plow and the harrow were pulled by teams of work horses.

"While Dad and the boys were getting the land prepared, my mom and my sisters and I cut up potatoes for planting. My father had a cutting place all set up for us in the garage and he brought in sack after sack of spuds. They were poured into a box-like container and came down a shoot to the cutting table. The cutting table had razor-sharp knives embedded in the top of it with the cutting edge up. Mom taught us to take each potato and run it across the knives, cutting them into small pieces with one or two eyes. When planted into the earth, the eyes would grow into potato vines. After they were cut into pieces, they were placed in wire baskets and dipped into a mild formaldehyde mixture to fight disease. Then, they were ready to plant. It took us about two weeks to cut up, dip and finally plant. Dad and the boys did the planting, anywhere from forty to sixty acres. We planted Russets and Red McClures.

The Jammaron family on Missouri Heights, Back row: Emma, Sidonia, and Victor. Front row: Leo, Ida and Joe.

Victor Jammaron on a potato digger on Missouri Heights.

"That was just the beginning! As the vines grew and produced potatoes we had to weed and cultivate. The cultivator was an implement that moved between the rows and pushed dirt up around the plant. If this wasn't done, the potatoes would get sunburned and you couldn't get a good price. We would harvest the potatoes in late fall, well into October after a good freeze or two had frozen the vines."

Joe: "Yes, we harvested in the late fall and the potato digger was a wonderful machine, too. It was pulled by four horses, and it had a shovel down low on the front which dug under the potatoes as the horses pulled forward. The forward motion forced the potatoes and dirt surrounding them into an apron. The apron was made out of rods which formed a chain-like belt. The dirt would sift between the rods and the potatoes stayed on top until they were dropped back on the ground. Then they were picked up by hand and either put into sacks or a wagon. I never liked that job – it was hard work!

"We didn't go to Carbondale very often, and to go to Glenwood Springs was a real big excursion. The roads were all dirt, only some had gravel. I remember the Glenwood Grand Avenue was paved just out to the cemetery, and it was dirt from then on. It was terrible in the spring, with all the mud. We had a 1927 Model T truck with twenty-inch wheels.

"The Sweet place was the first place we lived that had running water. It was just piped into the kitchen sink, we had no bathroom, just an outhouse. We didn't have electricity the whole time we lived there.

"We had six work horses (three teams), and one saddle horse. The teams were: Nancy and Blue; Kate and Bill; Chub and Bird. Our saddle horse was named Rusty.

Emma, Joe, and Leo on Bird.

Teacher at Luby School, Eva Ravoux, with Joe (left), Emma and Leo.

"I went to Luby School on the Sweet land over by Paul Gould's. I started fourth grade there. My teacher's were Eva Ravoux, Mrs. Schotz, and Lillian Brickta. My classmates were Desmond Harris, the Gould girls: Rosie, Alice, and Zada, Harold Fender, Lawrence Sirola, Myrlene and Geraldine Fender; and Ilene, John, and Clayton Ages."

A lot of families

Headed West

With no more than

Bedding, buckets, Bibles,

and high hopes –

That's a pretty good start.

– Used with the permission of Gladiola Montana
"Never Ask a Man the Size of His Spread"
Gibbs Smith, publisher ©1993

THE LYONS FAMILY – 1934

Ezra Lyons
1880 - 1955

Elsie Lyons
1887 - 1972

THE LYONS FAMILY

Ezra came to Colorado alone, around 1930 from Ulysses, Kansas, to prospect for gold. He had several mining claims around the Redstone area, and up on Basalt Mountain. With no success at mining, he obtained a permit to build a saw mill on Basalt Mountain. In 1934, Elsie and her son, Clarence, and his wife, Lessie, came from Kansas to join Ezra. Clarence worked the saw mill with his father and they built a log cabin on Basalt Mountain where they lived.

Elsie and Ezra had four children: Clarence, Lulabelle, Hazel, and Nellie.

Elsie taught school at Luby School for a few years. She lived in a room in the schoolhouse during the week and went up to the saw mill on Basalt Mountain on the weekends.

Elsie at the saw mill on Basalt Mountain.

Ezra logging on Basalt Mountain.

THE LYONS FAMILY

Clarence W. Lyons
1911 - 1985

Lessie (Duncan) Lyons
1915 -

Children

Clara	1935	Ann	1945
Donald	1936	Robert	1947
Leroy	1938 - 1991	Danny	1949
Harold	1943		

THE LYONS FAMILY

Lessie and three of her children: baby Leroy, Don (left) and Clara (right) at the saw mill.

Lessie and Clarence had seven children: Clara, Donald, Leroy, Harold, Ann, Robert, and Danny.

Lessie Lyons remembers, "We lived in the cabin on Basalt Mountain for three years. The folks, Elsie and Ezra, stayed there and we moved to Leadville, where Clarence worked at the Climax Mine. We then came back to the area and Clarence worked awhile for John McNulty as a farm hand. We lived in Carbondale for awhile, and then we bought our land, 40 acres, on Missouri Heights from Lloyd G. Blue, Jr. in 1945. We sawed the logs for the house that I still live in (in 1998),

Three of the Lyons children (left to right) Donald, Clara, and Leroy.

up on Basalt Mountain. Clarence became a fence builder, and put up fences all over the area. He was the best fence builder in Colorado.

"Clarence taught Leroy to build fence and they worked together for many years. We didn't do much farming, just a little hay and grain. I was busy with my family, and didn't have time for much more. Of course, we did have fun once in awhile going to the dances at the schoolhouses, and playing bingo.

"Our neighbors were the Higginbothams, the Fenders, and the Holgates. I knew Victoria Sirola, who lived over by the reservoir. She was a hard worker and a very thoughtful, compassionate lady.

"I'm very proud that in 1998 my grandchildren, Crystal and Eric (Leroy's daughter and son), carry on the Lyons' fence building business. Like their father and grandfather, they know how to build good fences, and have trouble keeping up with all the work they are offered.

Leroy's daughter and son, Crystal and Eric.

History of the Land Owners

Patent dated August 15, 1921 to Erwin O. Emerson

Warranty Deed to John R. Handy ....September 27, 1927

Warranty Deed to J.L. Loansbury.....................April 5, 1932

Warranty Deed to Lloyd G. Blue, Jr..............August 23, 1940

Warranty Deed to Lessie May Lyons.......September 24, 1945

THE LYONS FAMILY

Ezra Lyons
1880 - 1955

Elsie
1887 - 1972

Children

Clarence	1911 - 1985	Lulabelle	1917 -
Hazel	1909 -	Nellie	1923 -

Ezra, Elsie
- <u>Clarence</u> → <u>Clarence</u>
  - Clara } Mike, May Ellen
  - Marjorie (Elliot) / Don } Wendy, Doug, Tinker, Terry, Donnie
  - Nancy (Liggett) / Leroy } Alex, Eric, Crystal
  - Marianne (Flasche) / Harold } Julianne, Suzanne, Marianne, Andrew
  - Marion (Samuelson) / Ann } Jamie, Jodi, Jerod, Joel
  - Berniece (Garcia) / Robert } Bruce, Chamaigne
  - Danny } Brenda, Carrie
- Lessie (Duncan)
- <u>Hazel</u>
- <u>Lulabelle</u>
- <u>Nellie</u>

THE HUGHES FAMILY – 1934

The Hughes with their 1919 Model T Ford Touring Car.

Harry Elmo Hughes
1881 - 1961

Martha Hulda (Gross) Hughes
1901 - 1994

THE HUGHES FAMILY

Lael Hughes, "My father, Harry Elmo, was born and raised in Belknap, Illinois. He always told us that he was of Scotch, Welsh, Irish, English, and Dutch descent. We think that he moved to Denver around 1920. He was a Pentecostal preacher at one time and he also was an iron worker who made railroad spikes."

Clement Hughes: "My great aunt on my mother's side and uncle came to Colorado first, in the late 1800s. Aunt Emilie was from Weida in Thur, Germany, and Uncle Dave Rizzoli from Tyrol, Italy. Uncle Dave was a stone mason and I remember him telling that he helped build the foundation, made out of slabs of marble, for the Catholic church in Marble. It was never completed, probably because of lack of money. The foundation can still be seen today in 1998 in Marble."

In 1911 Uncle Dave went to Germany to bring my mother, Martha, and her brother, Frank, to the United States, and then to Carbondale. It was just before World War I started, and I'm sure my mother's parents sent the children over to keep them safe."

Martha (Gross) Hughes told of her journey to the United States from Germany in an interview with Mary Ferguson on Carbondale's KDNK radio in 1984. "We left Germany in January of 1911, when I was ten years old. My Uncle Dave came after my brother Frank (who was fourteen) and I, and we sailed from Germany on the steamship President Grant. It took us fourteen days at sea, and it was a terrible trip,

Anna Gross, Martha and Frank's mother. Photo taken at Weida in Thur, Germany.

with bad waves all the way. Almost everyone was sick but me. We landed at Ellis Island and had to stay there three days as there were so many people, and so much red tape to go through. I had never been around that many people, and it was so confusing. I remember a man was giving out crackers to the crowd, and I didn't know what they were, so I wouldn't take one.

"I didn't much like school in Germany, so I looked forward to coming to the 'Land of Opportunity.' Of course then I didn't know that I would never see my parents again.

"We took the train to Carbondale, and I thought we would never get there. It was decided that I would wait a year to start school as I could not speak English. For some reason English was not difficult for me to learn, and I did well when I started school. Frank felt he was too old to go to school, and worked with Uncle Dave.

"When I was fifteen, I was the May Day Queen in Carbondale. I saw the first airplane to come to Carbondale. It landed at the Frank and Edna Sweet ranch, where I picked potatoes. My friend, Eva Ravoux, was with me when the airplane landed, and I remember she walked right up to it.

"I walked from my aunt's home in Carbondale every morning to pick potatoes. I got twelve cents a sack, which was a lot of money; then, dead tired, I walked all the way home at night.

"I remember the old Stauffacher cheese factory at Catherine. I also remember when Katherine Cowen and Gracie would come to town in the surrey with the fringe on top. It was something to see, and they would stop at my aunt's place for a visit and coffee. I remember the men who were building the roads in Carbondale would move the Fresnos and teams out of the way so the Cowens could pass by."

Martha graduated from the eighth grade in Carbondale and went to Denver to work around 1920.

Myrna: "I remember my mother telling how she did housework and babysitting work for a family in Denver. She decided to save all her money so she could go back to Germany to see her family. She had saved quite a bit, and was almost ready to go, when the family she was working for suddenly needed money for something. She gave them all her hard earned money, and they never paid her back, and she never went back to Germany."

Harry Hughes with his 1919 Liberty 6 Model 10-B Touring Car.

Martha met Harry E. Hughes, in Denver. They fell in love and were married June 10, 1923. They lived in Denver for several years where Thecla, Harry, and Lael were born, then Grand Junction where Clement was born, and then Glenwood Springs where David was born.

Clement: "My father was a carpenter, a painter, a paper hanger – he did everything he could to make a living. My mother made donuts, and my dad sold them door-to-door in Grand Junction and Glenwood Springs. He worked for the W.P.A. and the CCC camps (prisoner of war camps)."

Martha (Gross) Hughes in her 1984 interview: "We moved up to the Heights in 1934. We had about eleven acres located up 100 Road on the first crest of the hill, on the right. We lived in a tent at first, and eventually had a house. I had no furniture at all when we moved in. Martha and Myrna were both born in that house. There were only about twelve families on the Heights then, all farmers, who raised potatoes, grain, and cattle. There was no electricity and no water. We hauled our water in, and kept warm by the old wood stove. There were no water rights with the land."

No. 34 County Treasurer, Garfield
Doc. #156871 County, Colorado

Treasurer's Deed

to
Martha Hulda Hughes

Dated April 5, 1946
Acknowledged April 5, 1946 before
Charles S. Keegan, Notary Public,
Garfield County, Colorado

Conveys 11.8 acres in Section 30, Tp 7 S., R. 87 W., 6th P.M.

Recites that said property was subject to the general taxes for the year 1930. That the taxes remained due and unpaid at the date of sale, and whereas, the County Treasurer did on Dec. 17, 1931 at (an adjourned sale) the sale begun and publicly held on Dec. 14, 1931 expose to public sale as required by law, the real property above described for the payment of the taxes, interest and costs then due and remaining unpaid.

That at said sale property was re-offered from day to day, as the statute provides, and no bids were offered or made by any person or persons for side property and one offered to pay the taxes, interest and costs on said property, amounting to 1.73 and the Treasurer having become satisfied that no sale of property could be had, therefore, said property was on Dec. 17, 1931 struck off to Garfield County, Colorado, and a certificate of sale was duly issued therefor,

And Whereas, said Garfield County did on Dec. 4, 1945 duly assign the certificate of sale of said property and all its right, title and interest therein to Martha Hulda Hughes and whereas Martha Hulda Hughes has paid subsequent taxes on said property to the amount of $65.99 being all of the subsequent taxes on said property with the interest and costs, and more than three years redeemed according to laws, the same is hereby conveyed to Martha Hulda Hughes, subject to the right of redemption by minors, insane persons or idiots, provided by law.

Cert. #218, year 1931.

Filed for record April 5, 1946 at 10:15 o'clock A.M., and recorded in Book 211 at page 469 thereof.

Myrna: "I remember we hauled water in big wooden vinegar barrels from Witchey's Mercantile in Daddy's pickup. Mom would clean them out once a week with Clorox. One time Martha fell in one when she was little, trying to get a drink! We got our water from our neighbors, the Greens, or from Jack McCan's filling station in Carbondale.

"Our neighbors were Mark Lounsbury (a bachelor), Fred Holgates, Virgle Holcombs, Mick Southcotte, the Lyons, the Greens, and Buster and June Blue."

Clement: "We walked a mile to Catherine School down on the main road, where Highway 82 is today in 1998. The school was where Catherine Court Trailer Park, owned by Ed Dreager, is today. My first grade teacher was Mrs. Lewis, and my second grade teacher was Mrs. Mow. We went to school with the eight Green kids, who belonged to Ora and Ira Green: Othel, Lowell, Ed, Edna, Faye, Vada, Eva, and Bill."

Martha and Myrna talk about their memories of school at Catherine, "We went to school with the Green kids, Richard Cerise, and Rita and Delpha Wherham. We were the youngest so we went to the lower grades at Catherine until it closed in 1945, and then we were bussed into Carbondale.

"One time Eva Ravoux was the teacher at Catherine. Someone had a boiled egg and was playing with it when they weren't supposed to. Well, Eva took it away and tossed it in the old pot bellied stove. She sat back down on her chair next to that hot stove, and when that egg exploded like a bomb, she jumped a mile off that chair. Of course, us kids thought that was the funniest thing ever, but Miss Ravoux didn't appreciate our laughter."

Myrna: "I was the youngest and I only went to the first grade at Catherine. There were only two of us in the first grade, me and Glen Barksdale. One time my brother, Harry, was out playing with the goats before school. He only had one pair of good jeans to wear to school. Well, he came in all smelly from those goats, and there was no time for Mama to wash his jeans. Dad got Mom's perfume – it was Lorna Gay perfume – and rubbed it on Harry's jeans. You can imagine what he smelled like then, but he went on to school!"

The Catherine School in the late 1930s, on the road that would become Highway 82.

Lael: "I was almost expelled once at Catherine School. The outhouse was old and dilapidated with cracks in the sides of it. One time I waited until the teacher had gone in and sat down, and I fished a little willow branch in there and tickled her butt! She came out screamin' and I was in big time trouble!"

Martha: "There were double desks at school, and my brother, Harry, and I sat together so he could help me with my ABC's. Well, one time Harry got in dutch with the teacher, Margaret Darien. He brought a black walnut to school, and just to be ornery, he was rolling it back and forth with his foot on that old hardwood floor, and making an irritable racket. The teacher got so mad she hit him over the head with a yardstick and broke it in two. Of course, we laughed.

"One time we all played hooky! We were walking to school and decided we just didn't want to go, so we made a big circle around the field close by and took off. We went to see the Greens and played around all day. Later on, Dad came and picked us all up in the pickup and took us home. School was still in session, and when we drove by all of us yelled and screamed. We didn't get in trouble at home, but we sure did the next day at school. Margaret Darien made us all write a hundred times that we wouldn't do that again. So, we waited 'til she wasn't looking, held two pencils at one time and wrote it all out."

Clement: "All of us kids were taught to work, and we did, doing anything to make a little money. My brothers and sisters and I picked lots of potatoes. We picked right alongside the German war prisoners during World War II at the Leonis Chuc ranch. We also had all kinds of animals to tend to: cows and goats, pigs and sheep, and chickens and rabbits. They all had to be fed before and after school. We also

The Hughes family on the Heights.
Back row, left to right: Harry (Dad) Martha A., Martha (Mom) Harry, and Lael.
Front row, left to right: Myrna, Clement, and David.

needed a lot of firewood, and spent many hours chopping wood."

Martha: "Us girls would have to take Mama's wooden clothes basket and scout for sticks for starting fires in the old wood stove. We kept all the hillsides up there picked clean. We also had to graze the cows, four or five of them all summer. Mama told us we could only graze from Catherine Store to the school and back, on our side of the road. We didn't have watches, of course, but we knew when the cows had taken their time and grazed up and back we could head for home. It was from about 8:30 a.m. 'til noon. On the way home we herded them by the Green place for water.

"I remember two things that happed to our brother, Lael. One time he was getting dressed for school in front of the old wood stove. He either fell or got pushed, and he had a brand, a star on his butt for years. Another time Harry was pushing a hand lawn mower and Lael decided to sit on it. Well, it took a minute but he yelled and jumped when the blades tore into his hind end."

Clement: "We finally got electricity on the Heights in 1954, and then we dug a well in 1960. That made things a lot easier for Mom. After all of us had left home and married, Lael and his wife, Eddie,

Potato Day 1983, Queen Martha Hulda Hughes, and King John Nieslanik.

Martha with her crown of potatoes, Carbondale's Potato Day 1983.

(Harris) Hughes lived on the property. They still do today in 1998, and they own Catherine Store down on Highway 82."

In 1983, when Martha Hulda Hughes was 84 years old, she was Carbondale Potato Day Queen. The King was John Nieslanik. It was a great honor paid to the little girl who came from Germany in 1911.

History of the Land Owners

Homesteaded by Maria McCarthy in 1901.

Samuel Geigel	1904	
Edward Stauffacher	1914	
Ernest and Lester Stauffacher	1920	
Martin Hotz	1920	
Samuel Geigel	1925	
Mary Blue	1925	
E.O. Emerson	1926	11.8 acres
Emilie Rizzoli	1926	11.8 acres
County Treasurer	1931	
Martha Hulda Hughes	1945	11.8 acres
Lael Hughes	1964 - 1998	17 acres

THE BAIR FAMILY – 1934

Elmer and Ida Bair's wedding day, October 21, 1921.

Elmer Bair
1899 -

Ida (Smith) Bair
1899 - 1995

THE BAIR FAMILY

Elmer: "I was one of fourteen kids, so I tell everyone, 'I'm one of fourteen bears in the same trap – and the same man set the trap'."

Elmer and Ida lived on the Heights from 1934 to 1936. They lived on what is today in 1998 the Mike Strang ranch, in the old homestead house built by J. Needham, up Catherine Store Road to 102 Road, on the left. When the Bairs lived there, Charlie Oliver leased the place from the owner, William Prechtel.

Elmer was a sheepman, and he bought Oliver's hay and pasture for his sheep in the winter time. He ran about 2,500 mother sheep at Oliver's in the winter, and up on Cottonwood Pass in the summer. He homesteaded land on Cottonwood Pass, and at the peak of his sheep business ran close to 5,000 head.

Elmer: "We shared the homestead house with another family, the Walter Barkers. Poor ol' Walter liked to hit the bottle when he could, and we felt sorry for his wife and kids. I tried to teach him to hunt to provide meat for his family, but he couldn't get the hang of

The old homestead house; on the Strang Ranch in 1998.

it, so I did the hunting. I'd have him tend my sheep, and I'd go get an elk for them. One time I got two elk, and of course we all poached, that was the only way we could keep eating. Well, I had the two elk hung up by the house when a neighbor came by and said the game warden was coming. I had to move fast, so I loaded the elk in the wagon. It was winter time, and the snow was deep, but I got them up to the barn and hid them in the manger. Then I covered them all up with straw, and just in the nick of time, because here came the game warden. I guess I did pretty well, because he looked around and didn't find them!

"One time ol' Walter got all tanked up in town, and got in a fight. He came back all bruised and scratched up. Charlie Oliver happened to see him and said to me, 'I can't believe he lived through it, but I think a wild cat attacked Walter.'

"John McNulty always liked the taste of buckskin [deer] best if they were shot and butchered during the month of June. I still think of him in that month, when he got his 'June buck.'

"Charlie Oliver was a real good farmer and I always appreciated the fact that he was good to his animals. He had beautiful teams of work horses. They were a Belgian and Percheron mix, and he always treated them well."

Elmer and Ida had two daughters, Laura and Lois. The girls went to the Missouri Heights School which was just a short distance from the ranch.

Laura: "I went to the sixth, seventh, and eighth grade up on the Heights. My teachers were Miss Roberts and Eva Ravoux. Leona Nelson, my friend, and I rode our horses all over Missouri Heights. We loved to ride up by the reservoir."

Lois (Waller) Bair: "We had a lot of fun at the Missouri Heights School, and were so ornery to the teachers, Eva Ravoux and Miss Roberts. At recess time in the winter, we'd build a big snow house and make a tunnel way back inside it. Then, when the teacher called us to go back for school, we'd pretend we couldn't hear her from the tunnel. Our classmates were the Fullers, the Holgates, the Fenders, the Tafts, the Henkes and Ray and Roy Hoovies."

Elmer: "I had an Indian man work for me. His name was John, and the man stuttered somethin' awful. We could hardly communicate when he first came, but after a while we got better. I had several men working, and they would all tell me what supplies they needed and I'd go to town and get them. Ol' John tried to tell me, but couldn't get it out, so I had him write a list. Sometimes I turned around to try to talk to him. He could do a little better talking to my back.

"The men ate in the house with us when they were close enough. Well, John didn't know much about religion, and I guess you'd call him an atheist. I always had everyone bow their heads at the table for a blessing. John couldn't say 'Elmer' for some reason, and he said, 'M-M-Mister Hel-Helmer t-t-talks to the pl-pl-plates!'

"I moved my sheep all over Missouri Heights, but I had a reputation of taking care of the range. We were at the Olivers, Goulds, Fenders, Sirolas, Jammarons, and the Kreutz places.

"I remember one incident with the Black family who lived up on the Heights. He hated sheep, and one day I let my sheep graze up next to his alfalfa field. He had three teenage boys, and they decided to cut a few of my sheep out of the herd. Well, I came along on my horse about that time and calmly took my sheep back. Mr. Black didn't like that at all, and he came after me with a club, calling me an S.O.B., and saying how he was gonna kill me. He didn't really scare me, I just stepped off my horse and got him down and straddled him. But, about that time the three boys jumped me, and of all things, started pulling out my hair – by the roots! I had my hands full, keeping the old man down, and fighting off the kids. Ol' Black also had a nephew visiting, a big strong Marine, and he came out of the house ready to fight, too. About this time one of my hired men, an Indian half-breed, came looking for me, and he took care of the Marine. By this time, ol' man Black and the kids were all worn out, so I left and went on my way; but that wasn't the end of it. Black called the sheriff and out he came, with a posse of three men. I went over with Charlie Oliver and we all met. We talked 'til 2 a.m., and we kept burning sagebrush to keep warm. Well, we finally got it all talked through and settled and things were all right, except for one thing: my bald head!

"Hunting season always came at the same time farmers picked potatoes up on the Heights. They didn't have time for both, so I just hunted for them.

"We had terrible hard winters up on the Heights. The mailman, Louie, had a terrible time getting around. He was stuck all the time, but he got out and kept going. Then, if anyone else got stuck he'd help them, too."

Ida died in 1995 at age ninety-five. She and Elmer had been married seventy-five years. She is buried in Glenwood Springs at the Rosebud Cemetery.

Elmer: "I always told my Ida that she set a record.

"She said, 'What do you mean?'

"Well," I said, "you're the only woman in the world who walked into a bear den, stayed with the bear, and asked for more.

"Ida and I had great, great-great, and great-great-great grand kids, so you see, the older you are, the greater the kids!"

THE HOLCOMB FAMILY - 1935

Virgil Holcomb
1891 - 1978

Blanche (Smith) Holcomb
1885 - 1965

THE HOLCOMB FAMILY

Virgil was born and raised in Gallatin, Missouri, and moved to Rifle, Colorado, in 1908. For one winter he drove a mule team which pulled an ore wagon from Ouray to Telluride, Colorado. He was also a forest ranger on Taylor Creek near Gore Pass for several years. He then became a lineman for Public Service Company in Meredith, Colorado. Blanche's parents were John and Adelaide Smith, from Dillon, Montana. In 1892 they came to Basalt, Colorado, where John and his brother, Basil, ran the Smith Mercantile on Railroad Street for many years.

Blanche was a telephone operator at the telephone office in Carbondale. She had three young daughters: Helen, Hilda, and Irene, from a previous marriage at the time she and Virgil met in Carbondale. They married March 28, 1928, and lived in Meredith for a short while, and then moved to Carbondale. Later, Virgil and Blanche had one daughter, Lois.

During their time in Carbondale, around 1935, Virgil bought the Earl Blue ranch on Missouri Heights. It was located up 100 Road, across from the old Fred Holgate place, on the right. The family lived in Carbondale, but Virgil ran sheep on the ranch in the summer, and up near Lilly Lake, around Marble, in the winter. He had a large

Holcomb house on the old Blue place.

The house Holcombs built on the Blue place.

The Cox ranch house.

sheep operation, and lambing and shearing time was the busiest of the year.

Lois (Holcomb) Reynolds: "I used to ride with Dad when he moved the sheep up to Marble. We would herd them from the ranch to Carbondale, which took a good part of the day. Then, the next day, take them on up near Marble. It was such a beautiful ride, I loved it!"

In 1945, the Holcombs sold their place in Carbondale and bought another place on the Heights, the Cox ranch, located up Catherine Store Road, at County Road 102, on the left. They lived in the large house, which still stands in 1998, until a home was built on the Blue place. On the Blue ranch, they had a beautiful view of Mount Sopris.

Lois: "My dad dearly loved his horses, and always had three or four special ones on the ranch. They were used for riding and packing up in the high country. I remember, he had a big, beautiful stallion named Red Bird. No one could handle him but my dad."

The Holcombs sold out and moved to Wheat Ridge, Colorado in 1960. Both Virgil and Blanche are buried in the Crown Hill Cemetery at Wheat Ridge.

Virgil and Blanche Holcomb in 1940.

THE HOLCOMB FAMILY

Virgil Holcomb
1891 - 1978

Blanche (Smith) Holcomb
1885 - 1965

Children of Blanche: Helen, Hilda, Irene

Children of Virgil and Blanche: Lois

Lois
Clinton Reynolds } Connie, Steve

THE DIEMOZ FAMILY - 1938

Adolph and Edith Diemoz
The Sweet Place
1938 - 1939

Adolph and Edith remember the two years they lived on the Heights. They rented the Sweet place, owned by Edna Sweet. Before Edith and Adolph rented in 1938, the place had been rented by the Victor Jammaron family.

Adolph raised hay, oats, barley and, of course, potatoes. Adolph remembers, "We grew New Yorkers, Red McClures, Peoples, and Burbank potatoes. You had to know how to irrigate properly or the potatoes wouldn't grow right. Too much water meant too many vines, and not enough meant not enough vine or potatoes. Also, you had to know just exactly when the plant needed the water to grow and produce. I learned all of that from my dad, Clement.

"We shipped out from Emma, and the potato buyers were John Ritter, Frank Alton, and Caesar Vallet (Edith's brother) in Glenwood Springs. The potatoes were inspected and you would get so much for the number ones, and so much for number twos."

Adolph talks about the 1930s, when the potato market went bad. "I had three railroad cars filled with 300 sacks each. The buyers offered me twenty-five cents per 100 pounds, and the sack to put them in cost me ten cents, so we couldn't make any money after paying the pickers. We chopped the potatoes up and fed them to our cows. I remember one old cow got choked trying to eat them, and died.

"Then, President Franklin Roosevelt tried to relieve the decline in prices by passing a decree to destroy the potato crop, and try to raise prices up. The government sent men to come to the farms and spray the potatoes with paint, so we couldn't try to sell them. We just dumped those sprayed potatoes in a hole on the ranch. Like most farmers, I was a Democrat before Roosevelt did that. Afterwards, I became a Republican. I remember my dad saying, 'Democrats are for poor people, Republicans are for the rich' Well, I wanted to be rich."

Edith remembers life on the farm, "Sometimes it was lonely up there. It would rain for days, and the winter was so long! Edna Sweet owned the place, so when we had our hay cut and stacked, she would come up and measure the stack to determine her share of the crop. They'd throw a measuring tape over the top and down the sides, and measure that. Then, they measured the base to figure how many tons there were."

Floyd Diemoz at the Sweet place in 1938.

Adolph adds, "I had about 100 to 120 head of beef cattle, and I'd herd them up to the West Sopris crown near Dinkle Lake to graze. Then, in the winter we fed hay at the ranch.

"In '38 and '39 Carbondale had a drugstore, Witchey Mercantile; Dinkle (general merchandise); Ping's for groceries, and Bagget's butcher shop."

Edith remembers, "We didn't go to town unless it was necessary. If it rained, the roads were so muddy we couldn't get out."

Frank and Edna Sweet, owners of the Missouri Heights ranch rented by the Diemoz family.

"Our neighbors were John and Victoria Sirola, the Fenders, the Goulds, and Ralph and Alice Harris."

Adolph recalls, "I was credited with saving a man's life on the Heights once. A Mr. Bair was thinning his horse's tail with a sharp knife one winter day when his hand slipped and he stuck the knife deep into his groin. His wife got him in the car, but the snow was deep, and she was so upset she got stuck right away, so here she came, runnin' and yellin' for help, tryin' to get to our place. I hurried and got the car out and got to him. I had to drive with one hand and hold the wound as tight as possible with the other to stop the blood flow. I was afraid he would bleed to death. I thought we'd never make it fast enough to Carbondale and Dr. Tubbs, but we did. Then, I had to hold both of his arms tight so he couldn't jump while Dr. Tubbs searched for the vein with a pair of tweezers. He finally got the bleeding stopped and Mr. Bair was down for a long time, but he got well. He always said to me, 'Adolph, you saved my life'."

Adolph slaps his knee, shakes his head from side to side and laughs, "Boy, those were the good ol' days!

"One time I was herding cows up on the Sopris Range. By then, there were lots of sheepherders in the valley, and, of course, we cowmen

Adolph on his horse Sunny.

didn't like them or their sheep much! I headed up the mountain and ran into this sheepman who proceeded to tell me I couldn't take my cows any further! Well, a good argument developed and all of a sudden this sheepman drew his gun and aimed it right square at me. Well, I didn't waste any time, I jumped from my horse, grabbed him by the collar, and took that gun away from him in a matter of a few short seconds. I fired one bullet into the air, emptied the gun, put the bullets in my pocket, and gave him his gun back. He went on his way, and so did I. Yes, those were the good ol' days!"

History of the Land Owners

Mary Strepley homesteaded the original 160 acres on May 16, 1892

Mary Hotz	1899	160 acres
Joe Hotz	1911	160 acres
Lloyd Edgearton	1918	160 acres
Frank & Edna Sweet	1920	160 acres
Dorothy (Sweet) McHenry		160 acres
Grange		160 acres
Aspen Mountain Subdivision - The Ranch	1998	

Elijah was a farmer,

He knew how to make things grow,

And Granny swore to follow him

Wherever he would go.

As things turned out, they had to leave

Their small Missouri farm,

But he kept her fed

And she kept him warm.

GRANDPA (TELL ME 'BOUT THE GOOD OLD DAYS)
By: Jamie O'Hara

Copyright © 1985 Sony/ATV Tunes LLC.
All rights administered by Sony/ATV Music Publishing,
8 Music Square West, Nashville, TN 37203.
All Rights Reserved. Used by Permission.

THE LONG FAMILY – 1941

Ralph Long
1916 - 1997

Alvera "Tootie" (Artaz) Long
1918 -

THE LONG FAMILY

Ralph's father, Ross James Long, came to Colorado from Missouri. His place on the Heights had been homesteaded by T.J. Heuston.

Ralph and Tootie met when Tootie was in high school at Carbondale, and Ralph was working on the Joe Fiou ranch. They were married in 1937, and in the spring of 1941 moved to Missouri Heights. They rented the Ralph Harris home on the Harris place, which would later be the Sirola place. They farmed 240 acres, raising oats and wheat, alfalfa, potatoes, pigs and beef and dairy cattle.

Ralph and Tootie had three children: Ralph Douglas, born in 1937; Eunice Marie, born in 1940; and Bernard Ralph, born in 1941.

Tootie: "We had such a large family that we mostly got together with them on weekends and holidays. We did go to dances at the Missouri Heights Schoolhouse and the Oddfellows Hall in Basalt.

"Later on in 1944 we bought the Gus Hotz and the old Long place and some Jack Russell land, giving us about 600 acres all together. We bought it all for $9,000. We were south of Ira Fender's and our land was 'L' shaped. Ralph and his brother Clarence were always partners on the land.

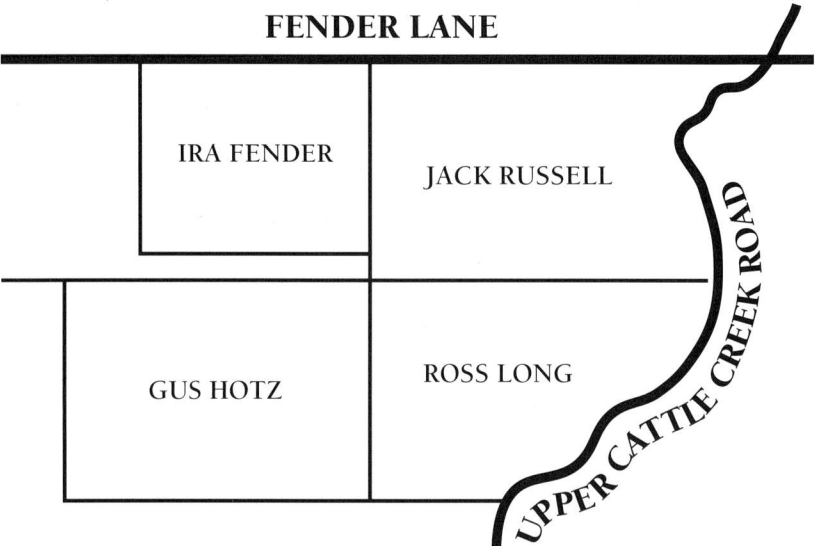

"Our kids went to Luby School. Doug had Edna Sweet for a teacher and Eunice and Bernard had Elsie Lyons."

Eunice: "I remember my first year at Luby School in 1946. We had to pump water, and of course the outhouses were in the back. We rode our horses to school. Bell was a mare and we also rode Pinkie. Two of us would ride on one horse in the winter to keep warmer. I remember on a cold winter day when school was over we would get on the horse and lay forward, over the animal's shoulders. Then, the teacher would cover us with big, heavy coats. In a blizzard, we didn't even look up, we just kept warm next to the horse and each other. The horses went home all by themselves because they knew Dad had oats waiting for them. One year I was the only girl at school. I went to school with Leroy Fender and the Goulds."

Tootie: "Later on, in 1952, we moved to the Orville Fender place and the kids went to the Missouri Heights School. Their teachers were Mrs. Brogan,

Ralph with his bull elk in 1950.

Ralph with his horse.

Vesta Chamberlain, and Mrs. Velma Willy. Doug graduated from the eighth grade there in 1952.

"In 1954 we left the Heights for awhile, and moved to Carbondale, where Ralph worked in the mines. But, we went back and lived on the Hotz ranch again, and Ralph worked the land for Courtney Barns. Eunice was married when we lived at the Ira Fender place in 1958; Doug married when we were at the Barns place in 1967.

Ralph loved the Heights, always talked about the fields and the earth and his joy of working the land. Like most farmers, he loved his horses and his dogs."

Eunice: "When someone found out that either my dad or his brother, Clarence, had broke a horse to ride, they knew right away that it had been done well. They were the best!"

Tootie, "We sold out in 1959. We sold all three places, 600 acres – the old Gus Hotz place, the old Jack Russell, and the old Long place – to the Aspen Mesa Subdivision. I lost my beloved Ralph a few months ago, but I'm a realist, and life goes on. I remember with great happiness my life on Missouri Heights."

THE BIANCO FAMILY - 1942

Mike and Stella (Carturier) Bianco
Prechtell Place
1934 - 1956

Mike Bianco's father, Joe, came to the United States in 1910 from Undine, Italy. Three of his brothers Pete, Mike, and John, preceded him to Colorado, and all four brothers pursued mining claims in Leadville, Silverton, Telluride, and Cardiff. As a young man Joe had fought in the Italian army. After living in Colorado a few years, he voluntarily joined the U.S. Army in 1917 when he was thirty years old, to serve during World War I. His wife Louise (Magnal) came to the U.S. in 1920 from Italy, and they met in Colorado and married. They had four children, Adelle, Mike, Lena, and Dan.

Mike was raised on his father's homestead, 160 acres on Four Mile Road. His father had milk cows and sold sweet cream to Parkinson's Drugstore in Glenwood Springs to make ice cream.

When Mike was five years old, he learned to make a loop and throw a rope, and he roped everything he could on the ranch: goats, sheep, hogs, and even chickens. Skim milk calves were orphaned calves raised on milk from a bucket. The milk had the cream taken out, which made it skim milk, and was perfect for raising calves. One time Mike roped a skim milk calf, but it was bigger than he was, and it took off running with Mike dragging behind. He was determined not to let go, but he did yell for his mom. She ran out of the house and saved him, yelling, "Don't do that again!"

He also drove the stacker team for his dad at five years old, and remembers when they ran away with him. His dad, Joe, was a meat cutter and sausage maker, and also made real good Zinfandel wine.

Mike went to school at Lower Cattle Creek School, located on the south side of what is the intersection of Highway 82 and Cattle Creek Road today. His schoolmates were the Siever children, Clyde and Dorothy; Austin Heuschkel and his brother and sisters, Verne, Christine, and Peggy. His teachers were Mrs. Marie Roberts, Florence Beck, and Mrs. LaForce.

In 1942 Mike and his sister, Lena, moved up to Missouri Heights and farmed the Virgle Holcomb place of 160 acres. Mike was twenty-two years old, and Lena was twenty-one. (The Holcomb place is partly owned by Carolyn and Jake Stoner in 1998.) They were there only one year. In 1943, Mike, his brother, Dan, and his father, Joe, took over the 500-acre Henry Prechtell ranch, which had previously been leased by Charlie Oliver. Kit and Mike Strang own the land in 1998.

Stella Carturier was born on her parents' ranch on East Sopris Creek Road, three miles south of Emma, in 1927. Her parents, James and Berlena Carturier, were from Italy. Her father came to the United States first, and worked in the Leadville smelter, then on a ranch near Basalt, before he bought the land on East Sopris Creek. Her mother,

Mike and Stella Bianco, married March 15, 1947.

Berlena, came to the U.S. from Italy in 1904, when she was four years old. Berlena's family settled in Snowmass.

Mike Bianco and Stella Carturier were married in Denver in 1947. Mike brought his bride up to the Missouri Heights ranch to live.

Mike remembers, "We had about thirty to forty acres in potatoes, about eighty to ninety acres in grain (wheat, barley, and oats), the rest being alfalfa and pasture. We had thirty milk cows, Holsteins, Short Horns, and Brown Swine. I always said, 'Milk cows paid the grocery bills, set the table, and bought the clothes on our backs!' We also had 125 head of Black Angus beef cattle at one time. We sold our cattle in Rifle, Glenwood, and Denver.

"We didn't have electricity the first two years on the Prechtell place. It was put in in 1949 and we were happy to get our first refrigerator. We had to haul all our drinking water from Carbondale. It was good water, we hauled it in cream cans. It didn't last very long, then we had to throw it out and go get more. Our animals were watered from the Needham ditch, which originated on the place. We had 255 acres under irrigation. In the summer time we drove our cattle up to Cottonwood Pass to pasture.

"Potatoes were a good crop for awhile. We raised Russett Rules and Burbanks. My dad always liked Burbanks best. We used Mexican pickers and then German war prisoners as pickers in '45 and '46. We hauled our sacks of potatoes to the whistle stop at Catherine's Corner to the box cars off and on through the years of the late '30s and early '40s. President Franklin Delano Roosevelt would try to raise the price of potatoes by destroying our crops. Government people painted them so we couldn't sell them. I took many a truck load of painted potatoes over to John McNulty to feed to his pigs. Then, sometimes the potatoes would just turn black for reasons we never understood. Everyone's potatoes turned black with little black spots all inside. I guess it was the blight. There finally came a day when they weren't worth all the trouble and work of raising, and we all quit in the early '50s.

"We had wonderful work horses on the ranch before we could afford modern machinery. There was a team of Belgians, full brothers, named King (a roan) and Gerry (a white). Another team of Belgians

Mike, Dan and Dan's wife, Sarah, on the Prechtell Ranch, with Gerry and King pulling.

was Molly and Nellie. Prince was a loner, he only worked well alone, and two other teams were Rock and Rye, and Nellie and Owen. I remember I had a fine saddle horse, a mix between a Morgan and an Arab named Tommy.

"My dad, Joe, was sixty years old when he drove his first tractor.

"The baler was quite a marvelous machine. One man drove and while it was moving, the baler pushed wire through the blocks and around the bale. The second man tied the wire around the bale."

Stella (Carturier) Bianco recalls, "There wasn't much time for fun on the ranch. All we knew was work. I did enjoy the ride when we took the cows to pasture up on Cottonwood Pass. We'd leave in the early morning and get there about 2:30 in the afternoon. It was a beautiful ride, and I loved it."

Stella and Mike had two children, Michael James, born in 1950, and Lois Eileen, born in 1953.

The baler.

Joe with the combine.

Dan with the combine.

"Once in awhile we'd go to a dance over at the Missouri Heights School across the road. I remember Rose and Alex Cretor. Alex played drums and Rose played accordion. Walter Lawrence played banjo and his wife, Edith, played accordion."

Mike said, "I did love hunting with my dad. We would go up Thompson Creek or Cottonwood Pass. My dad, Joe, worked for Jess Callicotte, and helped him build the Park ditch which took water to Cattle Creek. We stayed on the Prechtell place until he died, and then his children wanted the ranch. I had to move, and in 1957 we left Missouri Heights and moved to Emma. That year was about the last of the potato crops."

Mike and Stella Bianco's 50th wedding anniversary, 1997.

History of the Land Owners

J. Needham homesteaded the land..1882

Carl Quakenbush ....1917..........483 acres

Henry Prechtell ....1934..........483 acres

Charlie Oliver..⎫
Mike and Stella Bianco ..1943-1956...483 acres ⎬ worked and leased the land
Stecklein ....1956-1965...483 acres ⎭

Mike and Kit Strang ....1965 - 1998..........483 acres

Oh, Shenandoah I'm goin' to leave you,

Away – you rollin' river.

Shenandoah – I'm goin' to leave you,

Away – I'm bound away,

Across the wide Missouri.

THE STERRETT FAMILY - 1943

Bailey Sterrett
1897 - 1945

Beulah (Supineer) Sterrett
1900 -

THE STERRETT FAMILY

Bailey Sterrett was from Rockbridge Baths, and Beulah was from Raphine, Virginia. The Sterretts moved from the Shenandoah Valley in Virginia to Carbondale, Colorado, shortly after they were married on January 7, 1920. The Sterretts had three children: Annie Wallace, Bailey, Jr., and Virginia.

According to their daughter, Virginia, "Many people moved to Carbondale from Virginia and Mississippi in the 1920s. We always wondered why all the Missourians moved to the Heights with no water and such difficult living conditions, when they could have settled in Carbondale."

Beulah, who is 98 years old in 1998, remembers, "When I came to Colorado I was twenty years old, and newly married, and terribly homesick for my family in Virginia. If I saw a cowboy walking down the

The Sterretts' Missouri Heights house in 1998.

The Sterrett potato cellar in 1998.

street in Carbondale, I would cross quickly to the other side. We had been warned that cowboys and Indians were dangerous."

The Sterretts bought land up on Missouri Heights, 160 acres, which had been homesteaded in 1914 by Frank and Blanche Smith.

Beulah: "We bought the land and rented it to the Arnold Marks family.

"The agreement was that all farm production of any kind be split fifty-fifty with us. We kept our own cows up there, so we got half of all the dairy products, and even half the eggs the chickens laid. Mr. Marks kept honest records of all the grain, hay, and potatoes, and we settled up at the end of the year. Even if they slaughtered a hog, we got half of it. Mrs. Marks was Theo (Waters), and I remember going up to visit and she'd be cleaning the cream separator. It was a tedious job, cleaning all those parts, and oh, how she hated it!"

Virginia: "I remember, during World War II, when F.D.R. issued each family War Ration Books. The books were distributed from a government office in Glenwood Springs. The amount of rationing stamps you were given depended on the size of the family, and each person in the family got a book. The stamps had printed on them certain weapons that the country needed, like tanks, fighter planes and war ships. By rationing what and when we bought things like meat, sugar, tires, gas, and cars, we helped our country have more of

Ration stamps from War Ration Book #3

INSTRUCTIONS

1. This book is valuable. Do not lose it.
2. Each stamp authorizes you to purchase rationed goods in the quantities and at the times designated by the Office of Price Administration. Without the stamps you will be unable to purchase those goods.
3. Detailed instructions concerning the use of the book and the stamps will be issued. Watch for those instructions so that you will know how to use your book and stamps. Your Local War Price and Rationing Board can give you full information.
4. Do not throw this book away when all of the stamps have been used, or when the time for their use has expired. You may be required to present this book when you apply for subsequent books.

Rationing is a vital part of your country's war effort. Any attempt to violate the rules is an effort to deny someone his share and will create hardship and help the enemy.

This book is your Government's assurance of your right to buy your fair share of certain goods made scarce by war. Price ceilings have also been established for your protection. Dealers must post these prices conspicuously. Don't pay more.

Give your whole support to rationing and thereby conserve our vital goods. Be guided by the rule:

"*If you don't need it*, DON'T BUY IT."

16—32299-1   ☆   U. S. GOVERNMENT PRINTING OFFICE : 1943

UNITED STATES OF AMERICA
OFFICE OF PRICE ADMINISTRATION

421546 DX

WAR RATION BOOK No. 3 *Void if altered*

NOT VALID WITHOUT STAMP

Identification of person to whom issued: PRINT IN FULL

Bailey D. Sturrett
(First name)   (Middle name)   (Last name)

Street number or rural route _____

City or post office _____   State _____

AGE	SEX	WEIGHT Lbs.	HEIGHT Ft. In.	OCCUPATION

SIGNATURE _____
(Person to whom book is issued. If such person is unable to sign because of age or incapacity, another may sign in his behalf.)

WARNING
This book is the property of the United States Government. It is unlawful to sell it to any other person, or to use it or permit anyone else to use it, except to obtain rationed goods in accordance with regulations of the Office of Price Administration. Any person who finds a lost War Ration Book must return it to the War Price and Rationing Board which issued it. Persons who violate rationing regulations are subject to $10,000 fine or imprisonment, or both.

OPA Form No. R-130

LOCAL BOARD ACTION

Issued by _____
(Local board number)   (Date)

Street address _____

City _____ State _____

_____
(Signature of issuing officer)

War Ration Book #3

those things for the fighting troops, and the ability to manufacture and use weapons.

"It wasn't a terrible sacrifice, and we were lucky to have the farm products from the Marks family. We wanted to help our country, and our men at war. Since we were somewhat of a farm family, we didn't need meat stamps as much as we needed sugar stamps. Mom made lots of jams and jellies. So, we traded our meat stamps with our relatives in Denver, who really needed the meat. The stamps could be used at any of the Carbondale or Glenwood stores."

The Sterretts kept the acreage on the Heights for several years, and sold out to Bud Fender in 1947. In the early '40s they bought the Sweet place, on 109 Road, outside of Carbondale, which had been owned by Frank and Edna Sweet, early pioneers, who were also a part of the Missouri Heights history. The wonderful farm house which Frank Sweet built still stands today in 1998. It is the home of Beulah Sterrett-Wilson, called the Sterrett-Wilson ranch.

The Sterrett-Wilson Ranch in 1998, Carbondale, Colorado.

History of the Land Owners

Jerome Stovall..........................early 1900s...........160 acres

Dr. Robert Victor Thompson....1913......................160 acres

Frank & Blanch Smith............1914......................160 acres

Dr. Robert Victor Thompson ....160 acres

    Claude Henderson ....leased 160 acres

    Lester and Julia Taft ....leased 160 acres

Bailey and Beulah Sterrett.......early '40s ....160 acres

    Arnold Marks ....leased 160 acres

Bud Fender ....1947......................160 acres

Arnold Winters ....1961......................160 acres

Dick and Shirley Hunt.............1967 - 1998 ....160 acres

the turn-of-the-century Sterrett-Wilson Ranch · Carbondale, Colorado   ceceivett

THE MARKS FAMILY – 1944

Arnold "Slim" Emerson Marks
1909 - 1985

Theo Leone (Walsh) Marks
1915 - 1985

THE MARKS FAMILY

Arnold "Slim" Marks was born at Calhan, Colorado, to Zeno William and Maude (Wigger) Marks. Zeno and Maude worked a dry land wheat farm near Calhan. Theo Leone Walsh was raised by her mother, Nellie, and Patrick Waters on Cattle Creek, near the Missouri Heights reservoir.

When Slim was sixteen years old, he and his father farmed on Missouri Heights on land located at the corner of 100 Road (Catherine Store Road) and Crystal Springs Road 103. In 1998 the land is owned by Bill and Diane Teague.

Slim married Theo on January 11, 1932, and their first child, Margaret Irene, was born in the original log and sod house which had been built when the land was originally homesteaded.

Theo, baby Margaret and Slim in 1932, in front of the log and sod house built when the land was homesteaded.

The family lived in various places during the Depression years, and returned to Missouri Heights in the spring of 1944. They leased the Bailey Sterrett place, where they lived and also farmed part of the Cowen place (which had once belonged to Sherman and Katherine Cowen).

Margaret (Marks) Harris: "I was eleven years old when we moved to the Sterrett place. My dad raised alfalfa, grain, potatoes, sheep and cattle, and seven children! My brothers and sisters were: Nellie Louise, Arnold Gene, Ethel Marie, and a baby girl who died at

Left to right: Slim, Margaret, Theo, and Nellie.

three days old, Harold Ray, Patricia Lee, Linda Jo, and Danny Allan. The baby girl and my brother, Harold Ray, both died quite young.

"We had several milk cows and sold our cream and eggs, like everyone else, for money to buy beans and flour. Our cistern was filled by a ditch from the reservoir, and the reservoir was usually dry by early August. When that water was gone, my dad took a large wooden water tank over to Verle Fender's place to fill up. It was an every day occurrence in fall and winter.

"My father hosted many fall elk barbecues for family and neighbors, using oak cut from the farm for firewood. My uncle John (Dad's brother) brought in California hunters for many years.

One time a woman was exclaiming over Mount Sopris and the view. My dad looked her right in the eye and said, 'You can't eat the goddamned scenery!' No, life wasn't easy for Missouri Heights farmers. My father was a member of the Missouri Heights School Board, and the R.E.A. [Rural Electric Association] board."

The Marks lived on the Heights until February of 1952, when they moved to Brush Creek Valley at Eagle. They ranched there for twenty-five years, until they retired.

Arnold "Slim" and Theo both died in 1985, and are buried at the White Hill Cemetery near Carbondale. Margaret Marks married Desmond Harris, son of Alice and Ralph Harris, in 1951.

To Victoria

It must have been quite difficult
To come here long ago
To learn the language and the ways
Of a place you didn't know.

You married young and lived your life
Without one luxury,
You lived right here on Missouri Heights
In a world with little ease.

You plowed the land and planted,
Worked your fingers to the bone,
Made your bread and your polenta
And you made a happy home.

You had your share of heartaches,
Lived with pain and grief and tears,
Outlived four of your own children,
Persevered through troubled years.

Yes, I think of you, Victoria,
And even though you're gone
Here on the land where you once walked
Your strong spirit lingers on.

– A.W.

THE SIROLA FAMILY – 1944
"Sherola"

John Sirola
1884 - 1947

Vicenca "Victoria" (Juricic) Sirola
1894 - 1991

THE SIROLA FAMILY

John Sirola was born in 1884 near what is now Zagreb, Yugoslavia. Prior to 1918, the area of his birth was within the country of Austria, and he was of Austrian descent.

He served in the Yugoslavian military, and later, at age twenty-two, immigrated to the United States. He never saw his parents again. Upon immigration, his last name was changed from "Sherola" to "Sirola." John settled in Aspen, Colorado, joining the small community of Austrian miners living there.

Vicenca Juricic was born in Mali doyl, Austria, near the Adriatic coast, an area which would later become part of Yugoslavia. When she was thirteen years old her family immigrated to the United States and also settled near Aspen. Her first name was changed to Victoria. She had two sisters, Mary and Margaret.

John and Victoria were married October 22, 1912. John became a share cropper in the Aspen area, and they lived in several places, including Wild Cat and Woody Creek. Their children were, in order of birth: Rudolph, Mary, Francis "Fanny," Milton, Alvina, and

The Sirola children on Missouri Heights.

The Sirolas, left to right: John, Victoria, Lawrence, Mary, Fanny, Alvina, and Milton.

Lawrence. Their first child, Rudolph, drowned in an irrigation ditch at age two.

Debbie (Sirola) Bryan: "My father, Lawrence, suffered severe facial injury at the age of eighteen months. He was crawling behind his mother as she chopped wood, and the blade of the axe hit his nose. No medical care was given, and he lived his life with a diagonal scar that ran the length of his nose."

Victoria was also severely injured. She fell from a wagon and broke a leg, which never healed properly, leaving her crippled for the rest of her life. On November 16, 1944, the Sirolas bought 160 acres on Missouri Heights from Ralph Harris. The Sirolas moved into the home at the top of the hill up Cattle Creek Road from Highway 82, where Ralph and Alice Harris had lived. In 1998 it is the home of Caroline and Patrick Murphy. To the north on Sirolas' land was the crumbled foundation of the Blue Creek School, which had been built in the early 1900s.

The Sirolas raised hay, oats, and potatoes on the land, and owned cattle and horses.

Filed for Record the 1 day of December A.D. 1944 at 1:15 o'clock p.m.   Mae Cox, Recorder

No. 72511

Warranty Deed

THIS DEED, made this 16th day of November, in the year of our Lord one thousand nine hundred and forty-four, between Ralph Harris, also known as **RALPH C. HARRIS**, of the County of Garfield and Sate of Colorado, of the first part, and **JOHN SIROLA**, of the County of Eagle and State of Colorado, on the second part:

Witnesses that the said party of the first part, for and in consideration of the sum off … Dollars and other good and valuable considerations, to the said party of the first part in … paid by the said party of the second part, the receipt whereof is hereby confessed and acknowledged, … granted, bargained, sold and conveyed, and by these presents does grant, bargain, sell, convey and confirm, unto the said party of the second part, his heirs and assigns forever, all the following described lots or parcels of land, situate, lying and being in the County of Eagle and State of Colorado, to-wit:

The Southwest Quarter of the Southeast Quarter (SW1/4SE1/4) the Southeast Quarter of the Southwest Quarter (SE1/4SW1/4), Section Twenty-two (22); the Northwest Quarter of the Northeast Quarter (NW1/4NE1/4), the Northeast Quarter of the Northwest Quarter (NE1/4NW1/4), Section Twenty-seven (27), all in Township 7 South, Range … West of the 6th Principal Meridian, together with all ditch and ditch rights, water and water rights used thereon or in connection therewith.

TOGETHER with all and singular the hereditaments and appurtenances thereto belonging, or in anywise appertaining, and the reversion and reversions, remainder and remainders, rents, issues and profits thereof: and all the estate, right, title, interest, claim and demand whatsoever of the said party of the first part, either in law or equity, of, in and to the above bargained premises, with the hereditaments and appurtenances.

TO HAVE AND TO HOLD the said premises above bargained and described, with the appurtenances, unto the said party of the second part, his heirs and assignees forever. And the said party of the first part, for himself, his heirs, executors, and administrators, does covenant, grant, bargain and agree to and with the said party of the second part, his heirs and assigns, that at the time of the ensealing and delivery of these presents, he is well seized of the premises above conveyed, as of good, sure, perfect, absolute and indefeasible estate of inheritance, in law, in fee simple, and has good right, full power and lawful authority to grant, bargain, sell and convey the same in manner and form as aforesaid, and that the same are free and clear from all former and other grants, bargains, sales, liens, taxes, assessments and encumbrances of whatever kind or nature soever

(Documentary Stamps $4.40)
(Cancelled 11/24/44 RH)

and the above bargained premises in the quiet and peaceable possession of the said party of the second part, his heirs and assigns against all and every person or persons lawfully claiming or to claim the whole or any part thereof, the said party of the first party shall and will WARRANT AND FOREVER DEFEND.

IN WITNESS WHEREOF, the said party of the first part has hereunto set his hand and seal the day and year first above written.

Signed, Sealed and Delivered in the   )   *Ralph Harris*   (SEAL)

John Sirola, far right, with his children in the field. This piece of machinery is a binder, and it was pulled by three horses. The metal can on the left held string, which would automatically bind the bundles of grain, then kick off the bundles to be picked up by hand.

Debbie (Sirola) Bryan: "My father's sister, Mary, once wrote of her father, John, that he had eyes as blue as the Colorado sky. She also said of her father that he was a mild man, kind, and had a pleasant humor. He was about 5' 9," and was quite husky, or 'on the athletic side.' He was not a good rancher, as he could not find the heart to slaughter the livestock. His children called him 'Papa,' and from stories told by my father, Lawrence, my sense is strong that he was an extremely gentle and nurturing father. He spoke fluent Austrian and Italian.

"Because of her early marriage to an Austrian, my grandmother, Victoria, never gained control of the English language, and I had trouble understanding her. Her sisters, Mary and Margaret, were modern women, but Victoria remained very 'old world' throughout her life. She was a good mother and a hard working woman. She lacked refinement, but no one's flower garden was more spectacular, and no one made better polenta. Alvina once told a story about how the men in the community would gather and collectively work to harvest each other's crops. The women prepared the meals and Alvina was troubled about how her mother would perform this task. Alvina said there was nothing fancy about the feast that ensued, but that the men raved about how Victoria was the best cook in the community."

Gerry McLaren, Victoria's niece, remembers, "Aunt Victoria was such a hard worker. She had a big garden, chickens, turkeys, a milk cow, and also worked the fields. She made sauerkraut and polenta, but most of all I remember her wonderful homemade bread. It was the best I ever tasted! Even today, some people still remember seeing Victoria walking through the scrub oak, gathering firewood and carrying it tied in a bundle on her back."

John Sirola died on July 21, 1947, and is buried beside his son, Rudolph, in the Red Butte Cemetery in Aspen. When Lawrence returned to Carbondale from military service, he carved a marble headstone for his brother Rudolph's grave, which can still be seen today in 1998. Victoria outlived four of her six children. She died in November of 1991 at the age of 97, and is buried in Perris, California.

Milton went to college in Boulder, and became an engineer. He died of cancer in 1960. Francis "Fanny" married Jim Hovis. They had

Left to right: Teresa Juricic (Victoria's mother), Milton, and Victoria.

John Sirola's potato planter in 1998.   *John Sirola's double furrow plow in 1998.*

two children, and she died in 1985. Lawrence became a professional carpenter in Southern California, and helped build the famous Matterhorn at Disneyland. He died in 1991. Mary married John Bono, who died in World War II. She devoted her life to taking care of her mother in California. Mary died in 1997. Alvina never married and is living in Springfield, California, in 1998.

John Sirola's farm machinery is still on the land, which is the Witt ranch in 1998, on Upper Cattle Creek Road.

History of the Land Owners

William H. Harris homesteaded the land in the early 1900s.

Ralph Harris	1919	160 acres
John Sirola	1944	160 acres
Don Witt and George Thurman	1963	160 acres
Anita L. Witt	1998	120 acres

THE HIGGINBOTHAM FAMILY
1946

Forbes "Forby" Higginbotham
1900 - 1986

Olive (Prickett) Higginbotham
1900 - 1984

    Forby and Olive Higginbotham were both raised near Vernon, Colorado, on the Eastern Slope. They had three children, Willa, George, and Forby.

    Their son, George, says, "They came here simply because my dad hated the Eastern Slope and always wanted to live over here. I felt the same way, and my brother, Forby, and I came to Missouri Heights with them.

"My dad bought 200 acres in 1946 from Mick Southcotte, up Catherine Road to the top and on the right. Although it was 200 acres, only fifty acres had irrigation. My dad farmed a little, had milk cows and pigs, and raised barley and hay. I worked out on various ranches and never had any trouble finding a job. I was a typical young guy back then, when I wasn't working, I hung out in the bars and got crazy.

"My dad was a member of the Oddfellows Club in Carbondale, and mother was in the Rebekah Lodge. Our neighbors were Verle and Bud Fender, Ray and Alice Turner, the Holgates, the Hughes, the Lyons, and the Biancos."

Forby and Olive sold the 200 acres to John Stirling in 1966, and bought a three-acre piece with a cabin from Laudenklos'. The cabin still stands in 1998, and is owned by Laura VanDyne. Forby went to work for Courtney Barns, helped build the Barns' home, and was their caretaker for many years. He retired in 1973 and he and Olive moved to Greeley, Colorado. Olive died in 1984, and Forby, in 1986. They are both buried in Greeley.

History of the Land Owners

Mick Southcotte ....1937....................200 acres
Forby and Olive Higginbotham........1946....................200 acres
Phillip B. Klein................................1964....................200 acres
Gene and Rebecca Stirling ....1966....................200 acres
John Stirling.....................................1966 - 1998 ....200 acres

History of the Cabin Owners

E. F. Martin

Laudenklos

Alice and Ray Turner

Higginbotham

Jake Stoner

Laura VanDyne - 1998

Obituary
George Higginbotham

George Higginbotham, 71, of Carbondale, died Monday, January 26, 1998. Memorial services will be held Saturday, January 31 at Farnum-Holt Mortuary in Glenwood Springs. Visitation hours will be 9 am to 11 am on Saturday.

George was born May 1, 1936 in Vernon, Colorado. His parents were Lee Forby and Olive Pickett, both deceased. George served in the US Navy in World War II from 1944-46. He then moved to Carbondale with his family and began working for Peter, Leonis, and Caesar Chuc on their ranch. In 1951, George started work for Bob and Ruth Perry on the Mt. Sopris Hereford Ranch. George worked for the Perrys for 47 years, until his death Monday.

George is survived by his sister, Willa Nadine Kercher of Greeley, his brother, Lee Forby, also of Greeley, four nephews, four nieces, two great nephews, and three great nieces.

George took much pleasure in getting new calves started in the spring. He spent his summers in cow camp irrigating, maintaining fences, and looking after the cows. He enjoyed the wildlife that would come to the cabin door. George never judged anyone. He was a loyal friend and will be truly missed.

Donations may be sent to Carbondale Fire and Ambulance at 300 Meadowood Drive, Carbondale.

THE YOUNG FAMILY – 1946

William Young
1885 - 1949

Lizzie (Gant) Young
1892 - 1975

THE YOUNG FAMILY

William Young was of Irish descent, and was born and raised in Breckenridge, Colorado. Lizzie's ancestors were English and her parents lived all their lives in New Castle, Colorado. William and Lizzie had four children: Mary, May, Bessie, and Francis.

The children were all grown when Lizzie and William moved to the Heights from New Castle in 1946. They bought 160 acres from Kate Robinson in 1944. Kate was an heir to J.F. White, who homesteaded the land in the late 1800s. A description of the land follows: "For the North half of the SW quarter and the North half of the SE quarter of Section 21, in Township 7 – So. of Range 87 W. of the 6th Principal Meridian, Colorado containing 160 acres." Frederick W. Sovereign bought the land in 1917 and President Woodrow Wilson signed the deed.

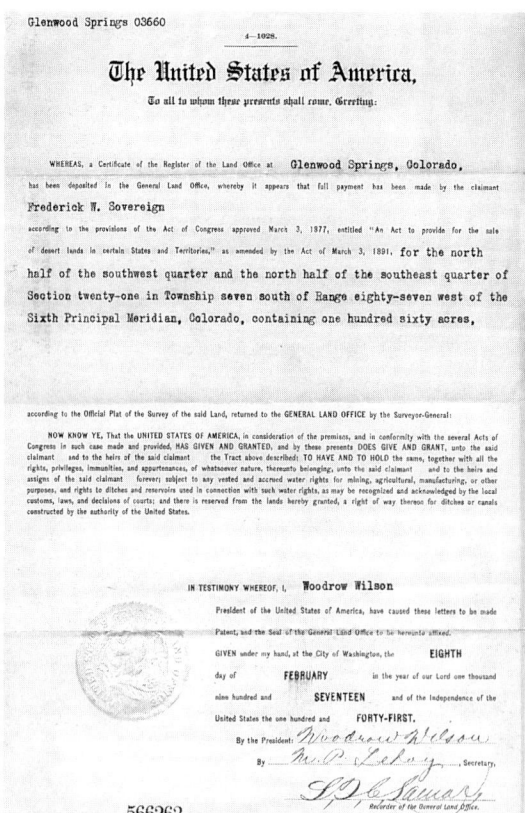

Francis: "I was in World War II in the Army, when my folks moved on the Heights. I served as a medic in the South Pacific in New Guinea and the Admiral Ty Islands. I came home and helped Dad farm.

"We didn't have a well, just a cistern, and our domestic water had to be hauled in. Dad raised grain and alfalfa, and about four or five acres of potatoes. We also had some beef

The Young family cabin in the 1940s.

and dairy cattle. The cabin still stands today, up on the Heights at the intersection of Fender Lane and 102 Road. The ranch was half in Eagle County and half in Garfield County.

"Of course, all of Dad's farm machinery was horse-drawn. We had a one-man potato planter called a 'Pick Planter.' One person could drive the team, and as long as you kept the bin full of seed potatoes, the machine dug the furrow, dropped in the potato, and covered it up. There were one-man planters and two-man planters back then, the other being the one where someone sat on the back and fed the potatoes onto the wheel. My dad didn't ship his potatoes anywhere, he sold locally.

"I also made $5 a day cleaning out irrigation ditches in the spring. A lot of us younger fellows did, and it was pretty good money, considering a farm hand made from $1.25 to $1.50 a day.

Lizzie and William on the ranch with a two-way plow pulled by a three-horse team: Silver, Coalies, and Ribbon.

I picked lots of potatoes at different farms. I'd get four cents a sack, and it took about four baskets to a sack. I also worked baling hay over at the Sterrett place for Arnold Marks.

"My folks worked mighty hard up on the Heights. Yes, they called it 'Misery Heights' back then, but my folks were a very loving, happy couple. They took time out for dances at the Missouri Heights Schoolhouse, and had card parties with the neighbors. We sold out to Bud Fender in 1958."

The Youngs, William and Lizzie, are both buried in the New Castle cemetery.

Francis Young lives in Carbondale with his dog, Fritz. Fritz meets visitors at the door, and likes to have her belly scratched.

Francis Young in the 1940s.

Francis on his horse, Brownie. "Brownie was a wild horse. Albert Dwere sold him to me for $35."

History of the Land Owners

J.E. White homesteaded the original 160 acres in the late 1800s.

Frederich W. Sovereign.................1917...................160 acres

Harleigh Holmes........................1919...................80 acres

H.W. Robinson – executor of the estate of J.E. White, to Adella D. White and Katherine Robinson (heirs).

Lizzie and William Young...........1944...................160 acres

Bud Fender.................................1958...................160 acres

Arnold Winters ....1961...................160 acres

HAROLD FENDER – 1950

"I remember when I was a kid up on the Heights during the Depression. We fed our hard-earned potato crop to the cattle and hogs because we couldn't sell them. Things were a little better later on, and we raised some spuds for the next few years, but by the '50s most of the Fenders were out of the potato business. The schools no longer let kids out to pick, and it just didn't pay.

"So, we went into the sheep business in the late '50s and on

Harold and his son, Gary, in the '50s.

into the '60s. At one time, I had 1,700 ewes. A thousand sheep were called a band. We had about 1,050 little ones each year, and lambing time in February or March was a rough three weeks. Many of the ewes had twins and they needed constant attention at birth. My family all took shifts to work with the sheep, and shifts to sleep.

"When a ewe has a lamb, she and the lamb have to be separated from the other sheep. A ewe will kick off her own lamb and take someone else's if she isn't isolated, especially if she has twins. So, we had to put the ewe and her lamb or her twins in a little pen about four feet square until they would bond. So, it's a lot of work, and each one has to be put in the pen to keep nature straight. We were in the sheep business until the '70s.

I used to raise potatoes up on Missouri Heights
I could plant those spuds, and pick 'em in my sleep
But, real bad times and the Triple A
Stepped in and changed my plans,
So, by God, I just started raising sheep.

I was with 'em in the mornin,'
I was with 'em noon and night,
Had to teach those silly ewes
Which lamb to keep
And in a while I began to smell –
And act like one myself
And I wish I'd never seen a goddamned sheep.

– A.W.

SECTION III

ONE-ROOM COUNTRY SCHOOLS

CATHERINE SCHOOL - 1886

District 8. 1886 - 1945.

Catherine School was built in 1886, and the land was deeded to the School District by Thomas McClure. The McClure land was to the north of the Judge Ed Stauffacher land, where the Blue Creek ranch is today in 1998. Thomas McClure was the man who developed the well known McClure potato during the potato heyday in the Roaring Fork Valley.

The school was built by the men of the community, and was originally located near the old, meandering road which connected the farms in the area.

In 1925 the school was moved near the new road, which would one day become Highway 82. Oscar Cerise, who is 91 years old in 1998, went to the original Catherine School in 1913, and completed all eight grades there.

Oscar: "I remember some of my teachers at Catherine. There was a Miss Sandusky, Miss Ethel Chisum, Margaret George from

Catherin.

The Catherin school will give an entertainment at the school house Friday, April 22, beginning at 8 p.m. The purpose of the entertainment is to procure funds for the purchasing of an organ for the use of the school. Come and assist us with your presence and the small admittance fee of 15 cents.

– *From the Glenwood Post, April 16, 1898.*

Rifle, Stella Sherwood from Carbondale, Beth Harris, and Edna Sweet. It took me longer than eight years to graduate because we didn't go to school if there was work to be done at home on the farm. When the work was done, then Dad said, 'Go to school.'

"We took instruction in arithmetic, penmanship, language, agriculture, and other things. Most of the kids walked to school, but in the winter they rode horses. I remember one year we had about eighteen students, and another year just three. The teacher had a hand bell she called us in with.

"I remember Ben Darien moved the school to its second location in 1925. He used a steam engine to pull it on some sort of a platform he built."

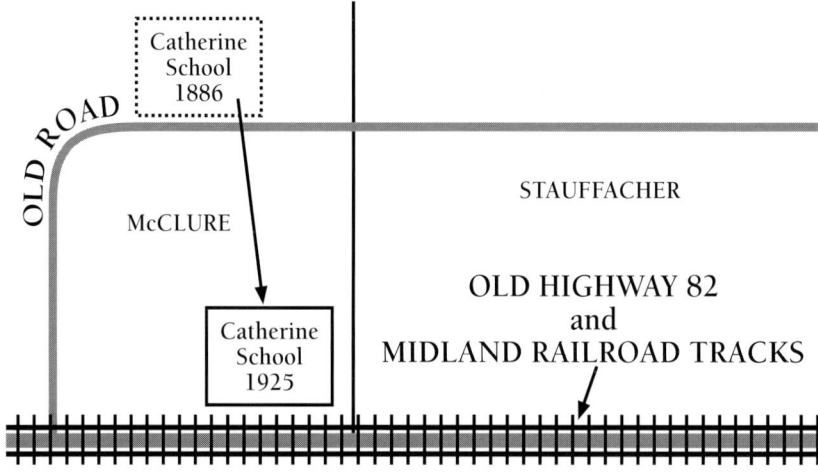

Oscar's son, Clifford Cerise, went to the school for two years in 1935 and 1936. Clifford: "I remember my teacher was Miss Hemphill. I only went to first and second grade there, but my brother, Richard, went to all eight grades. We used to get in trouble for laughing and giggling all the time. The teacher would daw a circle on the blackboard and put a dot in the middle of it. Then, we had to stand there and put our nose on the dot. After awhile we'd look at each other at each end of the blackboard and get tickled all over again.

"The school was closed in 1945 and the Cerise family bought the land, 150 acres, and the school, in 1951, from Margaret Phipps, who the land had reverted back to.

Student chairs from Catherine School, owned by Eddie and Lael Hughes in 1998.

"In 1954 we sold the school and one acre of land to Lon and Esther Herwick. The school was sold again and moved up near Ashcroft. It was lived in as a home for several years. It was there twenty years ago, but I think it's been torn down now."

Lael Hughes went to school at Catherine in the '40s. He and his wife, Eddie, still have the small chairs that were once used for students at Catherine.

Lael: "Before there were desks, the kids sat at tables in chairs. We still have several of them today.

"I guess we were pretty bad kids there at Catherine. I remember the school superintendent said once that we were the roughest school in Garfield County. In one year we had six teachers!

"We had an old pot bellied stove of course, and us boys used to fit two empty cartridge jackets together, filled with water. We would throw them in the old stove when the teacher wasn't looking, and wait for them to explode. One time I snuck one in but it didn't explode. A little later, Elmer Roberts opened the stove and threw in a big piece of charcoal at the teacher's request. The cartridge exploded with the door open, and there was soot all over the school – and the kids. It was great!

Lael Hughes, 1998.

"Another time six or seven donkeys got loose from someone and came down the road right at recess time. All of us boys caught them and penned them in the school yard. We decided to ride them and they bucked for a few days and then they were pretty tame. I remember that one got poked with a stick and the teacher put iodine on the wound!

"Then there was a teacher named Mrs. Gott. To discipline us she made us stand and hold a real big, heavy dictionary. She made us hold it a long time, and pretty soon your arms began to hurt. Ed Green and Elmer Roberts and I came up with a plan. The next time I got in trouble, I waited just until she was handing me the dictionary, and let it slip out of my hands, right on her foot! We never had to hold it again.

"We did all the usual things, like putting mice in the teacher's desk, and tipping over the outhouse. One time we tipped it over when Richard Cerise was in it. We did anything to try and get sent home. We'd eat garlic until the whole school reeked with it, and we'd try our best to find a skunk on the way to school and get him to spray us. It was wonderful if we got sent home!"

In 1998 the Catherine Court Trailer Park, owned by Ed Dreager, is where Catherine School was located from 1925 until 1945.

Susorine (Diemoz) Bon
1909

1927.

Susorine was born in 1909 to Ernest and Rosia Diemoz from Aosta, Italy. Her parents' ranch was situated where the Ranch at the Roaring Fork on Highway 82 is located today in 1998.

Susorine rode her horse from the ranch to school at Carbondale Union High School. Susorine: "It was mighty cold in the winter time, getting to school. I'd wrap a big blanket over me and the saddle and down over my legs. Back then almost everyone had a shed or a barn on their property, so I rented a barn near the school to keep my horse in."

She graduated from high school in 1927, passed the State Teacher's Exam, and that summer started her college education at Gunnison State College. Susorine taught in the winters at several one-room schools in the Roaring Fork Valley, and attended classes at Gunnison during the summers.

Her first teaching position was at Catherine School in 1927. By that time, her parents had sold their ranch and moved to Carbondale, so she rode her horse from Carbondale to Catherine to teach her pupils. Susorine: "My parents moved in late winter, so I didn't have to ride too long in the cold before it turned nice. I had to get up pretty early to get to school before the kids. Of course, when it was cold, I had to get there early enough to start a fire and get the school warm." Some of her students at Catherine included her brother, Julius Diemoz, Alex Creton, and the Henke children.

The second year she taught at Catherine, Susorine bought her first car, a 1928 Model A Ford. She drove it to teach at Catherine for the next three years, and also to Gunnison to attend summer classes.

Susorine, her 1928 Model A Ford Sports Coupe, and college friends, left to right: Vera (Kiner) Patterson, unknown, Susorine Diemoz, unknown, Olla Jacobs, unknown; Gunnison, Colorado, 1928.

Eva Ravoux.

Eva Ravoux, Susorine, and Margaret (Letey) Darien.

Susorine: "There weren't so many people back then, and, of course, we knew everyone. My friends were teachers, too: Vera Patterson, Olla Jacobs, Margaret (Letey) Darien, and Eva Ravoux.

After teaching four years at Catherine School, Susorine taught three years at Emma, a year at Carbondale, and two years in Basalt. She was also a substitute teacher at the Missouri Heights School and Luby School in the late '30s and early '40s.

The wedding day of Arthur and Susorine (seated), with brother Julius and Eva Ravoux standing.

Susorine: "I was a strict teacher, we all were, but the children really never gave me trouble. If I substituted up on the Heights, it was always easy. I just continued on with lesson plans, and had the children show me their assignments. I enjoyed my teaching years."

Susorine married Arthur Bon in 1934. She lives by herself in Carbondale in 1998. She is 89 years old, is still driving, and does all her own yard and house work, and enjoys her flowers.

Susorine (Diemoz) Bon and students of Catherine School, February 16, 1929.

Catherine School picnic, May 15, 1931. The cars are 1930 Model A Fords.

Margaret Darien

Margaret's parents were Major and Pascaline Letey. They came from Aosta, Italy, located at the base of the Alpine mountains in northern Italy. Major came to the United States as a young boy. Later, he went back to Italy, where he met Pascaline. He returned to the United States, and when Pascaline was twenty-one years old, he sent for her. When she arrived they were married.

The Leteys owned a ranch where the Aspen Glen Subdivision is today in 1998, and Margaret was born there on July 24, 1908. When Margaret was four years old, in 1912, they moved to another ranch near Emma. Margaret went to school at El Jebel and graduated from the eighth grade. She then went to Basalt for three years and then to Garfield County High School in Glenwood Springs, where she graduated in 1926. She was awarded a scholarship to Gunnison State College, but she didn't get to use it.

Back row: Marian (Jacobs) Hotz, Steve Diemoz, Ollie (Glassier) Cerise, Alma Olsen, Fred Glassier, Amie Diemoz, Margaret (Letey) Darien.

Third from front row: Oscar Berthod, Adolph Diemoz, Leo Berthod, Pete Glassier, Louie Glassier, Pat Letey, Albert Cerise, Miss Almstead (teacher).

Second from front row: Freeman Nash, Joe Nyberg, John Ronce, Emily Letey, Adriene Nash, Edith (Glassier) Letey, Olla (Jacobs) Fender, Gus Darien, Jim Darien, Don Nyberg.

Front row: Vinance Favre, Arnie Favre, Ruth (Gould) Zancanella, Oscar Diemoz, Keith Jacobs, Orsula (Letey) Cerise, Zella (Olsen) Eisworth, Archie Gould, Amos Nash.

Margaret: "I was so excited about going to college at Gunnison, but it wasn't meant to be. Of all things, I got the measles, and I was so sick, I had to come home. After that I went to Greeley Teachers' College and in twelve weeks, got my teaching certificate in 1927.

"My first teaching position was at Emma; a one-room schoolhouse, for $75 a month. I was there one year and then offered the position at my old school, El Jebel, for $125 a month. I had about thirty-three students there.

"After that I taught at the Snowmass School for a few years, and then to Catherine on Highway 82. At the Catherine School, I had about fifteen students. I liked being there because it was an easy drive from Basalt and the roads were always plowed. I had a nice group of

*Catherine School students, left to right:
Lael Hughes, George Cummins, Harry Hughes, Clement Hughes, and David Hughes.*

kids there, the Mumbert Cerise kids, the Hughes, the Holgates, and a few others.

"I remember one time the kids accidentally put the flag up – upside down. Ed Gregier was driving by on Highway 82 and saw it. He came running in thinking there was an emergency. I said, 'No, everything's fine,' and the kids went out and put the flag up correctly.

"We had an old coal stove, no electricity, and of course, two outhouses. By this time kids no longer rode horses to school. When we had a school program, I'd bring gas lanterns to school, and we'd put up sheets to make a stage. Each day, after school, I'd get two buckets of coal and stoke up the stove for the morning. I took a five gallon cream can of water from home each morning. Then, I put the water in a container with a spicket. Each child had their own cup, which we hung up on nails on the wall. I put each one's name beside each cup.

"I closed the Catherine School in 1945 when the schools were consolidated and the students were bussed to Carbondale. After that I went to Carbondale and became the school librarian. Then, I taught in Basalt until I retired in 1979. I just thought I retired – I substituted every day for five years."

Margaret married Ben Darien in 1929. She and Ben ran the Basalt Supply Company, a grocery and mercantile store where the Basalt Post Office is today in 1998. They ran the store for 24 years, but Margaret still found time to serve on the Basalt Town Council for sixteen years. She was the mayor of Basalt at one time, and also served on the Library Board for fifteen years. Margaret still lives in the Basalt Post Office building in 1998, and keeps the adjacent property beautiful with her flowers and yard ornaments. Margaret taught school on and off for over sixty years.

Margaret: "I think my kids at the country school got just as good an education as they do here in town... maybe a little better."

UPPER CATTLE CREEK SCHOOL
1888   District 6

Upper Cattle Creek School in 1998.

The Upper Cattle Creek School, or Coulter Creek School, as it was originally called, appears on the 1888 Government Land Survey Map. In the early days it was customary for land owners to take their time in deeding the land over to the school district. In this case, the deed was not recorded until 1895. Frank Heuschkel and Patrick Waters helped build the school around 1888, and their children attended classes there.

The first teacher was J.T. Stump, and the first class consisted of twelve pupils, grades one through eight, and included Thomas and Mary McNulty's children: Jim, Tom, John, Margaret, and Anna; Grace and Nellie Miller; the Heuschkels: Ellen, William, John, Ernastina,

The 1895 deed and legal description of land donated by Albert L. Coulter to Garfield County School District, for the Upper Cattle Creek School.

*Coulter Creek School in the late 1800s.
Left to right, back row: Lewis, Susan Aceneth, teacher, unknown, Harry Clark, Bertha Heuschkel, hidden boy.
Third row: Lewis child, Josephine McNulty, Ernastina Heuschkel.
Second row: Ray Cantrell, Alta Heuschkel, Loren Cantrell, Tom Heuschkel.
Front row: three unknowns, Katherine McNulty.*

Alta, Bertha, and Tom; and the Pat and Margaret McNulty children: Catherine, Mary, Martin, and Josephine.

Viola (Miller) Waters went to the school from 1927 until 1935, from the first to the eighth grade. The Millers lived a half mile north of the school, and several of the teachers boarded with them.

Viola: "We walked to school, as we lived just a half mile away. I remember my teachers were Claudine Colburt, Roberta Funk, Edwina Sheehan, Sylvia Shellhamer, and Mildred Prine. Miss Sheehan, Miss Shellhamer, and Miss Prine boarded with my family when they were teaching.

"I went to school with the Royce children; the Blues: Billy, Margie, and Lila; the Grems: Nellie, Mildred, Oliver, and Laura; the Blacks: Carmen, Neil, and Barbara; Roy Staples, Roy and Henry Sonnleitner, Eulala Mocks, Alden Haff, Pat Coryell, and my brother, Harold Miller.

"I remember when the boys all got caught smoking cigarettes out behind the barn. The teacher sent me home to get a bar of soap. She proceeded to make the boys chew pieces of it, and they got mad at me for going after it.

"Of course, many of the kids rode horses to school, and at lunch time the horses had to be watered at the creek. Well, there were some wild, fast horse races seeing who could get there first.

"We used to play tag while running on the rafters in the barn. They were really high rafters, and it's a wonder we all lived to tell about it. There were two outhouses, a coal shack close to the road, and the fairly big barn. My father, C.W. Miller, installed the merry-go-round and the flagpole."

Parents, teachers and students gathered for a school program at Upper Cattle Creek School, 1926.

Left to right, back row: Mary McNulty, unknown, Katherine Boyd, Jim Blue, Mrs. Boyd, Nellie Waters, Susan Miller, unknown, Clement Miller, Bob Leyerely.

Third row: Pat Waters, baby Jerry Waters, Mrs. Grems, Laura Grems, two unknowns.

Second row: Alden Haff, unknown, Lila Blue, Theo Marks, Henry Sonnleitner, Gene Leyerely.

Front row: Mildred Grems, Billy Blue, two unknowns, Viola Miller, Margaret Blue, Ethel Waters, and Andy Waters.

Upper Cattle Creek School. Photo courtesy of Andy Guliford.

Pat Coryell went to the school from 1926 until 1931 or '32. His parents, Charles and Josephine (McNulty) Coryell, lived in a cabin on the Burley Miller place. Pat was the youngest student at the school in 1926, when he started first grade.

Pat lived with his grandmother, Margaret McNulty, part of the time. His grandfather, Pat, was no longer living. (His grandparents were not related to the Thomas and Mary McNultys, although the two families had come from Ireland to the United States around the same time). Pat and Margaret McNulty had four children, Mary,

Upper Cattle Creek School students, 1927.
Left to right: back row: Gene Leyerely, three unknown girls, and Roberta Funk (teacher).
Third row: Roy Staples, two unknowns, Lila Blue, unknown.
Second row: two unknowns, Tom Waters, unknown, Alden Haff.
Front row: Harold Miller, Viola Miller, unknown, Oliver Grems, unknown, Roy Miller.
The unknown children are believed to be children of the Grems, Royces, and Blues.

Catherine, Martin, and Josephine. Mary taught school at Upper Cattle Creek around 1927.

Pat Coryell: "Roy and Henry Sonnleitner, two of my schoolmates, and I all lived with my grandmother, and we rode horses to school. I was pretty little in the first grade, and those horses were awfully big. I fell off twice, and broke an arm each time. I went to school with Andy and Ethel Waters, Alden Haff, the Grems, Viola Miller, and Roy and Henry Sonnleitner.

"Our close neighbors were the Miller brothers, Burley and Clement, the Cocquits, and of course, my uncle Martin McNulty, who lived on my grandmother's place."

Ethel (Waters) Miller-Heuschkel went to the school from 1934 until 1939, grades four to eight. Ethel: "My folks wouldn't let me go there earlier because they thought I was too fragile to ride the horse, and it was too far to walk, so I went to school in Glenwood Springs, where my great aunt lived, until I was big and strong enough to ride. My family rode three and a half miles from home, and our horses were Scraggles, Strip, and Rusty. John McNulty lived about half way, and we would stop there to warm up. Johnnie or whoever was there would have hot chocolate ready for us. We would warm up by the coal stove, and then Johnnie would boost us back up on our horses, and we'd ride on to school.

"The horses had a nice barn to stay in, and all the parents brought hay. In the spring when the grass was green, we let them loose to graze in the schoolyard which was fenced in.

"School was from 9 a.m. until 4 p.m. and we learned spelling, grammar, reading, writing, arithmetic, and history. I remember I loved the Colorado history. Our teachers were Edwina Sheehan,

Upper Cattle Creek School in the 1930s or '40s, taken by teacher Roberta Ogden. Photo courtesy of Andy Guliford.

Sylvia Shellhamer, Mrs. Katherine Senor, and Roberta Ogden. Only one teacher taught each year. I remember I loved Mrs. Senor so much.

"We had wooden desks with ink wells, and a little cubby hole for our books. The textbooks were furnished by the school district, but we could take them home at night to study. There was a small library, a coal stove, and blackboards and maps on the walls. There was also a piano, and every teacher could play just enough for us kids to sing along. In the morning we started out with the Pledge of Allegiance, and sometimes the teacher read from the Bible, and we said the Lord's Prayer.

"There were classes from grade one through the eighth. The teacher would start with the lower grades first, and while she worked with them, we older ones worked on our own lessons until it was our turn. Even though there was talking, it didn't bother us, we got used to it and just paid attention to our own studies.

"Most of the time we took our own lunch to school, but sometimes the teacher made lunch. Each child was told to bring a certain ingredient and the teacher would make a big, delicious stew.

"We played games outside at lunch time: hide and seek, kick the can, and as we got bigger, we had a continuous softball game. In the winter we loved jumping off steep hillsides into the snow, and sledding. When it was time to go back inside, the teacher rang the bell, and we filed in orderly and took our seats. The teacher would read us a good story for fifteen or twenty minutes, until we settled down, and then we would have class again.

"At Christmas time we had plays and sang Christmas carols, and all the parents came. We celebrated each holiday and decorated the school room.

"I remember one time a farm hand was working nearby and gave some of the older boys cigarettes. They got in bad trouble with the teacher and had to chew soap!

"We girls wore dresses to school, but because we rode horses, we wore overalls over our dresses, and took them off when we got to school. In the winter, we wore long stockings or long underwear.

"I went to school with the Grems, Alden Haff, Pat Coryell, and the Mocks family.

"There were School Board meetings held in the school at night, and there were gas lanterns for light. The dances were usually held about once a month, and everyone looked forward to them. The women made sandwiches and pies and cakes, and it was a real party. We started to dance from about the third grade on. First the girls danced with each other, and then one special night your first official dancing partner was your dad. The music was someone on piano, maybe a guitar, or an accordion, all local people and friends.

"There was a shooting once at the school during a dance that was held one night. I don't remember the names, but some fellow stole another man's wife, and the husband got plenty mad. He went home and got his gun, and came back and shot him. It didn't kill him, but he was wounded, and I remember they wound up in court.

"Then, there was the Halloween night that Johnnie McNulty, John Walsh, and John Nickeles put a whole spring wagon up on top of the school. I don't know how they got it up there, but it was a sight to see.

"Graduation time was very important and everyone came to congratulate us. We received a very good education at our little one-room schoolhouse, and had no trouble at all fitting in and keeping up when we went to high school. Our Upper Cattle Creek School closed forever in 1947 and the children were all bussed to Carbondale or Glenwood Springs, depending on where they lived."

Special thanks to Raul Laurence.

As noted, photos courtesy of Andy Guliford are used with permission; taken from his book America's Country Schools, *third edition, published by the University Press of Colorado ©1996.*

In 1977, the Garfield County School District sold the Upper Cattle Creek School to the Upper Cattle Creek School Association, a Colorado nonprofit corporation, for $4,000.

Recorded at 9:00 o'clock A. M. FEB 1 4 1977 BOOK 493 PAGE 398
Reception No. 276906   Ella Stephens, Recorder

WARRANTY DEED

STATE DOCUMENTARY FEE
FEB 1 4 1977
$ .40

WHEREAS:

1) Roaring Fork School District RE-1, in the County of Garfield and State of Colorado, is the owner of certain property described below and conveyed by this instrument;

2) At its regular meeting held October 13, 1975, the Board of Education of Roaring Fork School District RE-1 passed a formal resolution that the property conveyed below will not be needed by Roaring Fork School District RE-1 in the County of Garfield and State of Colorado in the foreseeable future for school purposes;

3) The property conveyed below will not be needed by Roaring Fork School District RE-1, in the County of Garfield and State of Colorado in the forseeable future for any lawful purpose;

4) Roaring Fork School District RE-1 in the County of Garfield and State of Colorado, also known as Garfield School District No. RE-1, is the successor in interest of School District No. 6 of Garfield County, Colorado, which was dissolved and became a part of Roaring Fork School District RE-1, in the County of Garfield and State of Colorado, that the property described below is embraced within the boundaries of said Roaring Fork School District RE-1, in the County of Garfield and State of Colorado, and School District RE-1, in the County of Garfield and State of Colorado, is the successor in interest of School District No. 6 of Garfield County as to the property described below.

THEREFORE, Roaring Fork School District No. RE-1, in the County of Garfield and State of Colorado, whose address is 1405 Grand Avenue, Glenwood Springs, Colorado, for $4,000.00 hereby sells and conveys to Upper Cattle Creek Schoolhouse Association, a Colorado non-profit corporation, whose address is 0114 Woods Road, Woody Creek, Colorado, 81056, the following real property in Garfield County, Colorado;

    A tract of land in Lot 10, Section 5, Township 7 South, Range 87 West of the 6th P.M., described as follows:

    Commencing at the Southwest corner of said Lot 10, thence North along the West line of said Lot 20 rods, thence East 8 rods, thence South 20 rods to the South line of said Lot 10, thence West on said South line 8 rods to the place of beginning.

with all of its appurtenances and warrants title to the same, subject to:

    Right of the proprietor of a vein or lode to extract and remove his ore therefrom, should the same be found to penetrate or intersect the premises hereby granted as reserved in United States Patent recorded March 15, 1898, in Book 12 at Page 476 and re-recorded March 15, 1898 in Book 12 at Page 478.

BOOK 614 PAGE 619

STATE OF COLORADO)
) ss.
COUNTY OF GARFIELD)

Recorded at _____ o'clock __ P.M. DEC 13 1982
Reception No. 335136 MILDRED ALSDORF, RECORDER

At a regular meeting of the Board of County Commissioners for Garfield County, Colorado, held at the Commissioners' Annex in Glenwood Springs, Colorado on __Monday__, the __13th__ day of __December__, A.D. 19__82__, there were present:

    Flaven J. Cerise _____, Commissioner Chairman

    Eugene "Jim" Drinkhouse _____, Commissioner

    Larry Velasquez _____, Commissioner

    Earl Rhodes _____, County Attorney

    Stan Broome _____, County Manager

    Mildred Alsdorf _____, County Clerk

when the following proceedings, among others were had and done, to wit:

RESOLUTION NO. 82-308

RESOLUTION CONCERNED WITH AMENDING THE LEGAL DESCRIPTION CONTAINED IN RESOLUTION NO. 82-220

WHEREAS, the Board of County Commissioners of Garfield County adopted Resolution No. 82-220, which had to do with a correction of a real property tax roll in regards to certain property in Garfield County;

WHEREAS, the legal description contained therein was not complete, and the Board now desires to more accurately describe the subject property.

NOW, THEREFORE, BE IT RESOLVED by the Board of County Commissioners of Garfield County that the description of the real property contained in Resolution No. 82-220 shall be as follows:

  Section 5, Tract A in Lot 10 Cont 1 A Beg. at SW Cor of LT 10 the N 330 Ft, the E 132 ft., the S 330 ft., the W 132 Ft. to POB 10A, all in Township 7 South, Range 87 West of the 6th Principal Meridian in the unincorporated area of Garfield County.

ATTEST:

_____
Clerk of the Board

BOARD OF COUNTY COMMISSIONERS
OF GARFIELD COUNTY, COLORADO

By: _____
  Chairman

Upon motion duly made and seconded the foregoing Resolution was adopted by the following vote:

    _____, Aye
    _____, Aye
    _____, Aye
              Commissioners

STATE OF COLORADO)
COUNTY OF GARFIELD) ss.

I, _____, County Clerk and ex-officio Clerk of the Board of County Commissioners in and for the County and State aforesaid do hereby certify that the annexed and foregoing order is truly copied from the Records of the Proceedings of the Board of County Commissioners for said Garfield County, now in my office.

STATE OF COLORADO
County of Garfield

Recorded at 11:14 o'clock A.M. OCT 7 1982
Reception No. 333585 MILDRED ALSDORF, RECORDER

At a regular meeting of the Board of County Commissioners for Garfield County, Colorado, held at the Court House in Glenwood Springs on Monday, the 16th day of August, A.D. 19 82, there were present:

Flaven Cerise, Commissioner Chairman
Eugene Drinkhouse, Commissioner
Larry Velasquez, Commissioner
Earl Rhodes, County Attorney
Leanne Cleland, Deputy, Clerk of the Board

when the following proceedings, among others were had and done, to wit:

RESOLUTION #82-220

RESOLUTION CONCERNED WITH THE CORRECTION OF THE REAL PROPERTY TAX ROLL OF THE GARFIELD COUNTY TREASURER TO REMOVE FROM SAID TAX ROLLS REAL PROPERTY INCORRECTLY AND ERRONEOUSLY PLACED UPON THE GARFIELD COUNTY TAX ROLL

WHEREAS, the Upper Cattle Creek Schoolhouse Association did acquire real property located in Garfield County, Colorado, which was and is exempt from taxation since the property is owned and used solely and exclusively for tax-exempt educational purposes and which is legally described as follows:

Sec 5 A Tract in LT 10 Cont 1 A Beg. at SW Cor of LT 10 th N 330 Ft, th E 132 ft., th S 330 ft., th W 132 Ft to POB 10A.

WHEREAS, the above-described real property was incorrectly and erroneously listed on the real property tax roles of the Garfield County Treasurer for the year 1981, and continues to be so listed as being subject to property taxes when such property was declared previously to be tax-exempt, and such exemption has been ordered to continue for the tax year 1982 by order of the Colorado Property Tax Administrator entered on July 15, 1982;

NOW, THEREFORE, BE IT RESOLVED THAT:

The Garfield County Treasurer shall remove from the property tax roles of Garfield County, effective January 1, 1981, the real property described above, the titleholder of which is the Upper Cattle Creek Schoolhouse Association, pursuant to the determination of the Colorado Property Tax Administrator.

BOARD OF COUNTY COMMISSIONERS
GARFIELD COUNTY, COLORADO

Chairman

ATTEST:

Deputy Clerk fo the Board

Upon motion duly made and seconded the foregoing Resolution was adopted by the following vote:

Flaven Cerise .... Aye
Eugene Drinkhouse .... Aye
Larry Velasquez .... Aye

Commissioners

STATE OF COLORADO
County of Garfield

I, ..., County Clerk and ex-officio Clerk of the Board of County Commissioners in and for the County and State aforesaid do hereby certify that the annexed and foregoing Order is truly copied from the Records of the Proceedings of the Board of County Commissioners for said Garfield County, now in my office

IN WITNESS WHEREOF, I have hereunto set my hand and affixed the seal of said County, at Glenwood Springs, this .... day of .... A.D. 19.......

County Clerk and ex-officio Clerk of the Board of County Commissioners

Cattle Creek cowboys Alden Haff, left, and Billy Blue, right.

LOWER CATTLE CREEK SCHOOL
February 19, 1888 – 1998   District 15

Lower Cattle Creek School was built in 1888 on the south side of where Highway 82 and 113 Road intersect in 1998. The school was built by George Pearson, who was Marian (Jacobs) Hotz's grandfather on her mother's side.

Marian: "My grandfather was born in England and came to the U.S. in the middle 1800s. After traveling to other places in the U.S., he settled in the Roaring Fork Valley, and became a carpenter. Many of the buildings, including the Lower Cattle Creek School that he built, are still standing today in 1998."

The first teacher was Mrs. Gardner; in 1905 Alice (Bennett) Zook was the teacher; and the last teacher was Mrs. Pegg, who taught in 1949.

Lower Cattle Creek School in 1905.

Opal Yeoman was a student at the school in the early 1920s, and remembers it in her book *My Corner of Colorado*. "We would ride horseback four miles to and from the 'Little Red School House' at the mouth of Cattle Creek, where it joined the Roaring Fork River. There was a barn for our horses so they would be protected from the weather. All grades from the first through the eighth were taught there, and I still admire those teachers. They would brave the early morning cold to get there early and build the fire so the schoolhouse would be nice and warm for us. We enjoyed school and studied hard.

"And the fun we had going home – racing our horses, exploring the gypsum hills where we found a deposit of sulphur so pure you could ignite it with a match."

The school closed in 1949 and sat empty until 1959, when Alden and Rosie (Gould) Haff moved into it while they were remodeling a larger home across the highway. Ironically, the house they were remodeling was the original Luby School building from Missouri Heights (it had been moved down from the Heights to the Haff property). So, for several years the two one-room country schools were situated across the road from one another.

Rosie (Gould) Haff: "We lived in Lower Cattle Creek School while our home was under construction across the highway. My dad, Paul, Alden, and my brothers had moved Luby School down from the Heights. I had gone to school in Luby as a kid, and now it was to become our home.

"There were still desks and books in the Lower Cattle Creek School when we moved in. We called the School District, and they came and picked them up. Then, Alden built partitions in the big room and made smaller rooms. We lived there with our four children, Richard, Glenda, Tamar, and Donald.

"I remember the electricity was always going out. One Thanksgiving Day, it went out, and didn't come back on. But, we had a gas stove, so I was able to cook, and we kept nice and warm. We lived there the year of 1959, and moved into our new place in 1960."

In 1964 the Lower Cattle Creek School was sold to Donald H. Witt and George Thurman. The school was raised and moved up to Missouri Heights, to the old William Harris/Ralph Harris/John Sirola/Witt Thurman land. Oddly enough, the Lower Cattle Creek School would rest only a short distance from the deteriorated foundation of the old Luby School.

In the Harleigh Holmes history, it is noted that Helen (Holmes) Bond remembers how pleased her mother, Katherine (Sievers) Holmes, was when the Lower Cattle Creek School was moved to the Heights. "It made her happy because the place she had gone to school for so many years was near the reservoir her husband had constructed." (Harleigh Holmes built the reservoir in 1912.)

In 1998 the Little Red School House where so many children spent their youthful years pursuing an education is still on Missouri Heights, and is the home of David and Ellen Anderson.

Details from the history of the Lower Cattle Creek School were taken, with permission, from the newspaper, "The Carbondale Echo," 1893, and Opal Yeoman's book My Corner of Colorado, *©1967.*

CRYSTAL SPRINGS SCHOOL
1889 – 1944   District 26

Steve Callicotte: "The land where the school was built was homesteaded by Harry Harding. He was an old cow puncher who ran cattle with my grandfather, William Riley Callicotte. Harding sold out to A.W. Sharpe and he and Sharpe deeded the land to the School District in 1889. The school was located about one and a quarter miles up from what is today Highway 82, right where the County Road 103 is located."

Early history of the school comes from the Curtis family history. James William Curtis and his wife, Elizabeth, were Steve and Virginia Callicottes' maternal grandparents. Elizabeth Anne "Lizzie" (McCansland) Curtis was the first teacher at the Crystal Springs School in 1889. Before the school was built, she taught students in her home at her Crystal Springs ranch. She had received her teaching degree at Colby University in Watterville, Maine.

Lizzie's daughter, Judith Ann, followed her mother's footsteps and received her teaching degree in California. She returned to Colorado and married Jesse Callicotte.

Elizabeth "Lizzie" Curtis.

Judith Ann (Curtis) Callicotte.

No. 21858

This Deed, Made this fourth day of May in the year of our Lord one thousand eight hundred and ninety nine, between A. E. Sharp and Harry Harding of the County of Garfield and State of Colorado, of the first part, and The Directors of School District No. twenty six (26) of the County of Garfield, and State of Colorado, of the second part,

WITNESSETH, That the said parties of the first part, for and in consideration of the sum of Twenty & no/100 DOLLARS, to the said parties of the second part in hand paid by the said party of the second part, the receipt whereof is hereby confessed and acknowledged, have remised, released, sold, conveyed and QUIT-CLAIMED, and by these presents do remise, release, sell, convey and QUIT-CLAIM unto the said party of the second part, forever, all the right, title, interest, claim and demand which the said parties of the first part have in and to the following described real estate situate, lying and being in the County of Garfield and State of Colorado, to-wit:

A certain parcel of land situated in the North west corner of the east half of the South west quarter of Section numbered twenty four (24) in township seven (7) South of Range eighty eight west of the Sixth Principal Meridian in Colorado and bounded as follows to wit: On the north by North line of the East half of the South west quarter of said Section twenty four; on the west by the west line of the said East half of the South west quarter of said section twenty four township seven (7) South of Range 88 W. 6th P.M. On the South by the County road as now constructed in what is known as Spring Gulch and on the east by a line running parallel with the west line of the East half of the South west quarter of the said Section twenty four aforesaid and the said East line shall be at a point (10) ten feet east of the school house of the aforesaid School District twenty Six Garfield Co. as now built located and constructed and shall run to the said County road on the South and to the said North line of the East half of the South west quarter of the aforesaid Section twenty four, township seven S R 88 W 6 p m

TO HAVE AND TO HOLD THE SAME, Together with all and singular the appurtenances and privileges thereunto belonging or in anywise thereunto appertaining, and all the estate, right, title, interest and claim whatsoever of the said parties of the first part, either in law or equity, to the only proper use, benefit and behoof of the said party of the second part, heirs and assigns forever.

IN WITNESS WHEREOF, The said parties of the first part have hereunto set their hands and seals the day and year first above written.

Signed, Sealed and Delivered in Presence of

A. E. Sharp (SEAL.)
Harry Harding (SEAL.)
                    (SEAL.)
                    (SEAL.)

STATE OF COLORADO,
County of Garfield } ss.

I, Edw'd D Landy in and for said County, in the State aforesaid, do hereby certify that A E Sharp and Harry Harding who are personally known to me to be the persons whose names are subscribed to the foregoing Deed appeared before me this day in person and acknowledged that they signed, sealed and delivered the said instrument of writing as their free and voluntary act, for the uses and purposes therein set forth.

Given under my hand and Notarial seal, this 11th day of May 1899.

My commission expires April 1, 1900.

Edw'd D Landy
Notary Public

Filed for Record the 1st day of July A. D. 1899 at 8:20 o'clock A. M.
J. O. Hourr, Recorder
Deputy

Steve Callicotte: "My mother taught school at the Crystal Springs School before she was married in 1912. After her marriage, she taught as a substitute once in a while.

"I was born in 1917, and when I was six years old, I started school there, and went through all eight grades. My first teacher was Mrs. Roach.

"I think Mrs. Roach taught for a few years and then my Aunt Maude (Callicotte) Maxfield. After Maude was Mary Ferguson, Mary Weller, Miss Haley, Miss Keys, Maude again, and then her son-in-law, Art Bogue. After that I think it was Mrs. Maxine Mow, Bernice Perry, and I believe the last teacher was Agnes Ferris.

Ella Barrett at the Crystal Springs School's original location, 1934.

"I remember one time Mary Ferguson decided I was in bad need of a good strapping! She proceeded to spank me with a belt, but I had on a pair of great, big, oversized overalls, and the belt just knocked

Mary Ferguson.

the dust off of me and never landed home. I started laughing and so did the whole school, and Miss Ferguson was mad as a wet hen. I remember my Mom went to school and talked to her later.

"In the winter, my sisters and I rode a sled to school. It was all downhill and those roads were pure ice. One time the girls got

Miss Mary Weller.

too far back on the sled and in a minute were going fifty miles an hour down the road. The wind was whizzing around us and we were sailing. The only way we could stop was to crash, and it was a real wreck. The girls ended up with burnt legs – it's a wonder we weren't killed!"

In 1943, the schools were consolidated and the Crystal Springs School was closed forever. The school bus had replaced the riding horses, the teams and wagons, the sleds, and sheer leg power, and children were bussed to Carbondale. It was the end of an era. Charles Renftle, the father of Ruth (Renftle) Fender, bought the Crystal Springs Schoolhouse, and Glen Martin moved it up over the hill to the Renftle ranch on Cattle Creek.

Charles bought it for his daughter, Lillian, and her husband, Lee Berges, to live in. The Berges' lived there from 1944 until 1964, and raised their two children, Harold Lee and Ellen, in the old school.

In 1998 the old schoolhouse is still in the same location on what is now called Cotton Hollow Lane. The Teri and Allen Harelson family has added to the original structure, and the Crystal Springs Schoolhouse is their home.

Crystal Springs Schoolhouse on the Charles Renftle Ranch, 1944.

Crystal Springs Schoolhouse in 1998.

Maude (Callicotte) Maxfield
1882 - 1943

Maude (Callicotte) Maxfield, shown in her high school graduation photograph, taken when she was twenty years old, at East High School in Denver.

Maude's parents were William Riley and Duley Ann Callicotte. She was born in Leadville, where her father was a school teacher. When Maude was very young, the family moved to Aspen. When Maude was twelve years old, the family moved to Denver, where Maude began to study piano. She was quite gifted musically, and became a brilliant pianist. Her daughter, Lucille, still has her mother's piano in her California home in 1998.

Maude graduated from East High School in Denver, and did not attend college, but did pass the Colorado State Teacher's Exam. Her first teaching position was at a one-room country school up the

Crystal River on the Western Slope. She boarded at the Grubb's ranch, and taught for two years.

Maude moved from the Western Slope to Salt Lake City, Utah, to study music with an accomplished teacher, Mr. McClelland, who played the tabernacle organ. After hearing her play, he told her that she was so advanced that he could not teach her more, and he asked her if she would consider teaching some of his students. She accepted, and taught there for three years.

During this time, she met Roy Maxfield. They fell in love, and were married. Roy was a tile setter who, in 1911, built the white marble floor in the Hotel Utah on the corner of South Temple and Main Streets. The marble floor is a very beautiful work of art, still appreciated today in 1998.

Maude and Roy moved back to Colorado and lived on the Callicotte home ranch for several years. Then, in 1918, Roy homesteaded his own place, 160 acres on the mesa between Cattle Creek and Crystal Springs. The young couple proved up the land and built a house, and added one room at a time. There was no water, and no electricity. Water was hauled in wooden barrels from the Crystal Springs, three miles away. They had two daughters: Lucille, born in 1911, and Vernice, born in 1912.

Maude Maxfield calling children in at the Crystal Springs School.

Vernice Maxfield, Lucille Maxfield, Ruth Sultsenburger, Ralph Callicotte, Dale Callicotte, and Martha Huntington, all students at Crystal Springs School.

Maude taught school at the Crystal Springs School from 1921 until the late '30s. She drove a buggy three miles to school in the fall and spring, and in the winter, she and her girls moved into a little house on the E.F. Martin ranch to be closer to school.

Lucille (Maxfield) Bogue: "We used to sled to school from the Martin place, my Mom and my sister and me. It was perfect sledding – down hill all the way. We would get to going so fast, the only way to stop was to roll off into the snow. It was great fun, but then we had to scramble around and retrieve our lunches, scattered all around. It wasn't all that easy going home, trudging uphill, pulling our sleds all the way.

"I was mother's pupil for five years in the little school. Sometimes there were only ten or so of us, one or two in each grade. The older ones always helped the younger ones with their lessons. We studied arithmetic, reading, phonics, history, geography, and music. With my mother, it was a lot of music. She played the piano every morning and we knew every song in the book. I can still hear us singing our hearts out on *Swanee River*.

"We put on wonderful plays and school programs. One time we made apple blossoms out of tissue paper, and painted the tips pink.

Maude and Roy D. Maxfield, with their 1922 Model T Ford, in 1931.

We attached them to branches and used them in our program. We also had beautiful Christmas pageants, and all the parents came dressed up in Sunday clothes.

"I remember one time, Aunt Judith Ann played Santa Claus. When she passed out presents, her skirt slipped down and was showing out the bottom of her Santa drawers. Her little two year old daughter, Virginia said, 'Oh, look! Santa has a skirt on just like Mama's!'

"Mother's students absolutely adored her. She was so gentle and sweet, and cared so much for each and every one of them.

"One time, we were taking the buggy to town for groceries at threshing time. We had to cross some bumpy ditches, and I bounced right out. The wagon wheel rolled over my head. I was unconscious, and mother was frantic. She got me to Dr. Tubbs in Carbondale as fast as she could – and I was alright!

"My father was a stern man, but very honest, and good to all of us. My mother was the most loving woman, a wonderful teacher and mother."

In 1930, the ranch went into foreclosure, and the family moved to Glenwood Springs. In 1998 the 160 acres is owned by the Sutey brothers. Maude died in 1943. She and Roy are buried in the Rosebud cemetery in Glenwood Springs.

Special thanks to Lucille Bogue: author, poet, and playwright.

Arthur Bogue
1909 - 1979

Arthur's early years were spent in Cardiff, near Glenwood Springs. His father died when Arthur was quite young, and shortly after his death, Arthur and his mother, Annie (McCarthy) Bogue moved to Basalt, where Annie was the town's postmistress.

Arthur's wife, Lucille (Maxfield) Bogue remembers how they met. "They were having a Christmas party at the Missouri Heights School, and I was just home from my first year in college. For some reason, my family went to the party, and my sister and I couldn't help but notice this handsome guy. We kept acting so silly over him – that was Arthur."

Arthur and Lucille were married Christmas Day in 1935. Arthur had received his teaching degree from Western State College in Gunnison. His first job was as principal of the elementary school in Creede, Colorado. Later on, the young couple returned to the Maxfield home ranch, and Arthur taught for a short time at the Crystal Springs School.

He was well loved by his students, who still remember him today in 1998.

Crystal Springs School outing.
Left to right, back row: Opal Cline, Ima Mae Renftle, and teacher Art Bogue.
Front row: Kathy Renftle, Dan Bianco, Ruth Renftle, and Art's wife, Lucille Bogue.

Later, he was the superintendent of schools for six years in Yampah, Colorado, where the couple's daughter, Sharon, was born. Arthur then taught in Steamboat Springs for two years before becoming the head of the Federal Land Bank. Arthur and Lucille's daughter, Bonnie, was born in Steamboat Springs.

Arthur spent the rest of his life working for the Federal Land Bank. He enjoyed working with ranchers and loved the land.

Teri Harrelson's wedding day in the schoolhouse, January 21, 1994.

In 1889, who would possibly have imagined that a hundred years later, the one-room Crystal Springs Schoolhouse would be seen in a Hollywood movie? It was used in the 1989 Paramount Pictures production of *Flashback*, starring Dennis Hopper and Kiefer Sutherland, a spoof about the 1960s radical Abby Hoffman, and his escape and adventures in the Colorado mountains. Portions of the movie were filmed at the old Charles Renftle ranch on Cattle Creek, where the Crystal Springs Schoolhouse was moved in 1943.

Allen Harrelson bought the schoolhouse from Gailen Smith in 1989. On January 21, 1994, Allen and his bride, Teri, were married in the Crystal Springs School, which is their home today in 1998. The Harrelsons have enlarged and remodeled the school, but the original hardwood floor is still in use, and in places ink stains and marks from the old woodburning stove are visible. The Harrelsons are very proud of their beautiful home and its history.

The Crystal Springs School (above) and the Renftle barn (below) as they appeared in the 1989 movie Flashback.

BLUE CREEK SCHOOL
1903 - 1926

Florence (Blackmore) Loesch.

Blue Creek School was built around 1903. The land was donated by William H. Harris. The school was a log structure, one room, with no running water, and a wood stove for heat.

Ruth (Gould) Zancanella, who was born in 1913, went to the school when she was nine years old. Her father, Paul Gould, owned the ranch directly across the road from Blue Creek School, to the east and up against Basalt Mountain.

Ruth: "We all rode horseback to school. There were two privies [out houses] outside, a wood shed, and a barn for the horses. By the time I went there in 1921 - 22, the school was pretty dilapidated. Our teachers were Florence Loesch and Lula Cole. I think Helen Peterson and Catherine Ross taught there, too. Also, Kathleen Oroke, who later became the County Superintendent of Schools. They all taught grades one through eight.

"I remember the Loesch family had a home real close to the school. They rented it from William H. Harris. The children I went to school with were: the Loesch boys, George and Edward; Theo and John Waters; Bill and John McLean; Vincent and Irena Harris; Opal Yeoman, and my brother, Archie Gould.

"We had a bucket filled with fresh water each morning, which we all drank from, using the same dipper! Lula Cole was a real pretty girl, and all the boys were in love with her. Mrs. Loesch didn't put up with any nonsense, and the boys were real ornery. Almost every morning she lined those boys up and paddled them good – just to get things off to a good start! My, what a different world we live in today! Believe me, I was always real careful, and I never got paddled!"

George Loesch was only two years old in 1920, when his parents Edward and Florence moved from Rifle, Colorado, to Missouri Heights. His mother, Florence, was given the teaching position at Blue Creek School in 1920.

George: "We left Rifle and moved to the William Harris place near Blue Creek on the Heights. The school was right by the cabin we lived in, which was near the county road. My brother, Edward, and I went to school with our mother, even though we were little. I was two or three and Edward was four or five years old. I can barely remember a log frame with a pitched roof, the inside about half as wide as it was long. I can remember the Gould kids, Vincent and Irena Harris, and the Long kids. Mother must have taught from 1920 until 1924, because I think she quit teaching when my little sister, Idelle, was born in 1924. I do remember two young ladies who taught after that, and boarded with us: Miss Jessie and Miss Oroke.

The foundation of the Blue Creek School is still on the Witt ranch in 1998.

Lula Cole

Lula Cole lived on the Heights with her parents, Mr. and Mrs. Matt Cole. They lived near the reservoir, close to the Carl Kreutz family.

Rokie fender remembers Lula. "Lula was older than me, but she was my best friend. She went to school at Western State College in Gunnison. I'm not sure if she graduated or passed the teacher's exam, but she taught at the Blue Creek School on the Heights around the same time as Florence Loesch. We had such a good time with her, she was real pretty and all the boys liked her. The kids who went to school with me were the Goulds, the Yeomans, the McLeans, and I remember a girl named Hazel Root.

"Lula and I loved to ride our horses. I remember she told me how she snuck out from home one night to meet a boy in Carbondale. She had her horse all saddled in the barn, and waited until her parents were asleep. I guess she got back home, and they never knew.

"Another time, when I was in the eighth grade, we rode our horses to Carbondale in the late winter. We went to a play and a dance, and it was freezing all the way home.

"Then, one time one of the Comrie boys wanted us to help him break a horse by riding with it snubbed up close to one of ours. We rode to Basalt on the snow and ice. I couldn't hold my horse back, and Lula couldn't hold the green broke horse back. We had quite a ride and we never told our parents.

"I graduated the eighth grade at the Blue Creek School in about 1919 or 1920, and Lula was my teacher. Later on, the Coles moved to California, Lula married and had a child. She came to see me in 1970, and it was a wonderful reunion."

LUBY SCHOOL - 1926

District 7. 1926 - 1959.

John M. Luby: "My father, Bill Luby, was a stickler for detail, accuracy, proper form, spelling, etc. He was District Attorney for twelve years, then served thirty-five years on the bench in the Fifth Judicial District in Eagle, Lake, and Summit counties. He served at the pleasure of the people, and once was a candidate of both parties, as the Democrats refused to let a man run that wanted to. He believed you should give a firm handshake and look a person in the eye!" The Luby School was named after Judge William Luby.

When the Blue Creek School became too deteriorated, it was decided by the community and school board to build a new school across the road on the Frank and Edna Sweet land, to the south of Paul Gould's. Frank Sweet donated the land. Paul Gould and his sons logged trees off Basalt Mountain, and with the help of neighbors, they built the school in 1926. Some of the logs were salvaged from the old Blue Creek School for the new building.

Judge William Harold Luby, Eagle County Fifth Judicial District.

Luby School students in 1931.
Left to right, back row: teacher Olla Jacobs, Louise Artaz, Tootie Artaz.
Middle row: Dick Gould, Souvenir "Bob" Artaz, Rosie Gould, Helen Kreutz, Betty Jane Kreutz, Alice Gould, Lucille Artaz.
Front row: Harold Fender, John Artaz, Desmond Harris.

Rosezella (Gould) Haff went to Luby School. "My dad and brothers, and other men in the community built the school in 1926. It had another wooden building beside it, one end was a coal shed, and the other end a barn for the horses. It was large enough to hold six or seven horses. There were two privies outside, and I remember how cold they were in the winter. At first the school was just one big room, but later on, it was partitioned off to make a cloak hallway and a living quarters for the teacher. For awhile it was called Blue Creek School, and later on named for William Luby.

"My dad put in running water from Blue Creek and everyone was so happy. Some of the kids had never seen running water inside.

"School was taught there until the late 1950s. In 1959 it was closed, and the school district put the building up for bid. My husband, Alden, and I wanted it so we put in our bid. Several people

bid on it, and it got up to $250. I told Alden to go one dollar over the top bid. He did, and we bought it for $251.

"Alden and I tore the building down, piece by piece, nail by nail, and moved it to our land, down on Highway 82 at the intersection of Highway 82 and Cattle Creek Road. We painstakingly put it back together, but not exactly as it had been. We added on rooms and porches, and made a beautiful home out of it for our family. We lived there from 1960 until 1980. In 1998 our old home belongs to the Don Waechtler family, and is Slim's Taxidermy. The old foundation of Luby School is still on the Jim and Mary Griffith ranch on Missouri Heights in 1998."

Students at Luby School.

The old Luby School, 7916 Highway 82 in 1998.

LUCY JANE FULLER

"My parents were Bob and Harriet (Raley) Fuller, and we lived in the Sweet cabin, which is still on the Jim Griffith place today. In 1932, when we lived there, there was only one cabin and an outhouse. There were four of us kids, myself, Laura Bell, Milton, and Dixie, and we all walked to Luby School. Olla Jacobs was the teacher. We went to school with Helen and Betty Jane Kreutz, the Artaz kids, the Goulds: Alice, Rosie and Zeda, and Desmond Harris.

"Later on we moved to the Sandy place, and rode to school, all four of us, on one horse, bareback. The teacher would help us get off the horse in the barn. We would step off, onto the manger, and she helped us so we wouldn't fall."

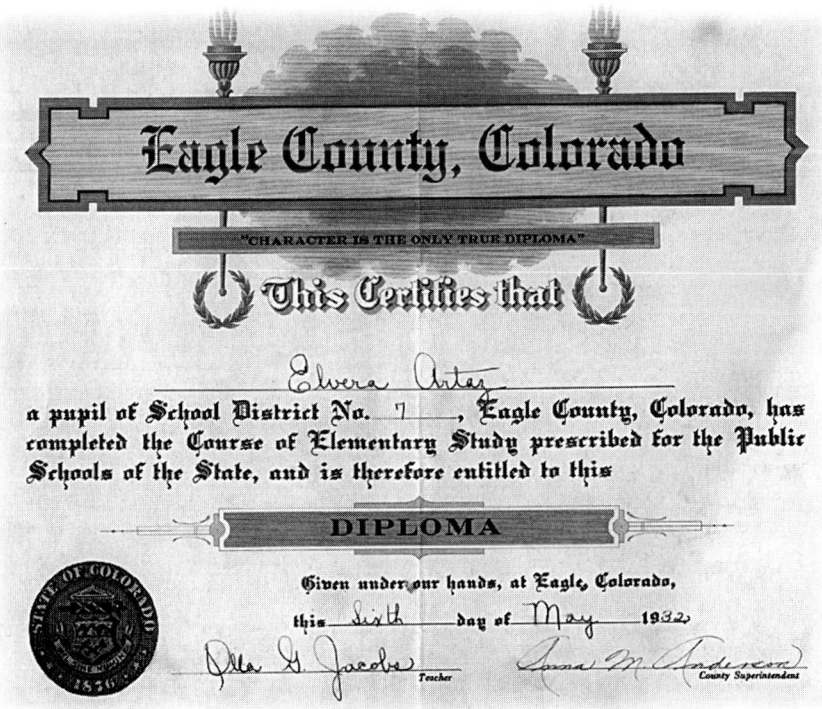

Eighth grade diploma of Elvera "Tootie" Artaz, from Luby School, 1932.

Olla Jacobs
1912 - 1979

Olla Jacobs was born in 1912 to Marian and Ed Jacobs. She graduated from Basalt High School and received her teaching degree from Western State College in Gunnison. The following two years, 1931 - 1932, she taught at Luby School, the only years she taught school. She boarded with the Ross and Maude Garret family, who lived on the Edna Sweet place, not far from the school.

Her sister, Marian (Jacobs) Hotz remembers Olla. "She walked to school from the Garret place, rain or shine. Sometimes the mud was knee-deep, but Olla walked! She was a fun-loving person, just like one of the kids, that's why they all loved her. She so much loved the out-of-doors, held classes outside, and took her students on many hikes across the countryside. She was also very artistic, and even though she never had a lesson, she painted many beautiful paintings which I have in my home today in 1998.

"Olla loved the American Indians, and the Indian way of life – even wished she had been born an Indian. She spent much of her spare time hunting for Indian artifacts, which she collected. In her day there were still Indian camps and burial grounds to be found. If Olla came upon a place she considered sacred, she would not disturb it. It was the correct thing to leave it untouched, and Olla was a very spiritual person."

Olla married Ira Fender's son, Eddis, in 1932, and they had two children, Leroy and David.

Students at the Luby School, 1931. Olla Jacobs, teacher at far right, rear.

Betty (Fender) Prichard
School Years 1940 - 1947

Betty Fender was born in 1934 to Loren and Glafrie Fender, and was raised on Missouri Heights. She remembers her school years when she was a student at Luby School, located on the Frank Sweet place. "My first teacher was Mrs. Elsie Lyons, who was married to Ezra Lyons. Mr. Lyons ran the saw mill way up on Basalt Mountain. Mrs. Lyons, my teacher, would live in a room at the school during the week, then go up to the saw mill on weekends to be with her husband and family.

"I remember Mrs. Lyons had a glass eye, and I was her pet, so of course I loved her, glass eye and all. I rode my horse, Foxie, to school, and Mrs. Lyons would let me ride after the mail during school hours. I rode to the fork of the road where the mail boxes were and brought back the mail for Luby School.

A young Elsie Lyons.

"All the kids rode horses to school. I remember one time, Sonny Long and I tried riding Foxie double. Well, she didn't like it one bit, and reared up and hit me in the nose with her head. She almost lost both of us but we managed to stay on 'til I got her settled down. Dad bought Foxie at an auction for me to ride. She was skinny and puny, but I loved her, took good care of her and made her beautiful.

"Another teacher was Francis Domka, and she roomed with my parents, Loren and Glafrie Fender. I was so ornery to her, but it sure was great fun. One time I caught a mouse in Dad's grainery, put it in a match box and snuck it in the top drawer of Francis Domka's desk. I couldn't wait for her to let out a blood curdling scream and have the whole place in an uproar, but, darn, it didn't ever happen, so I just had to imagine that she found it all by herself. Another time I put a tack on her chair, but she never let on like it was there. Oh, what she must have gone through with all of us.

"There were only six or eight pupils all together at school. My schoolmates were: the Long children, Eunice and Doug; and the Kelly kids, Glen and Earl and their two sisters.

"School started at 9 a.m. and got out at 3 p.m. I remember when kids accidentally wet their pants, they had to stand in front of the wood stove until they dried out, while the rest of us snickered and made faces at them when the teacher wasn't looking.

Elsie and her dog.

Message.

Your hearty co-operation is solicited in the endeavor to secure the best development of your child. If a pupil receives failing grades in any subject, it may be attributed to lack of study, too many outside activities, irregular attendance, or poor health. Therefore, you should make immediate inquiry concerning your child's work. Your visits to the school-room will help give inspiration to both pupils and teacher.

Signature of Parent or Guardian.

This Card Must Be Signed and Returned Promptly.

1st Period *Loren Fender*
2d Period   *Loren Fender*
3d Period   *Loren Fender*
4th Period *Loren Fender*
5th Period *Loren Fender*
6th Period ....
7th Period ....
8th Period ....
9th Period ....

EAGLE COUNTY PUBLIC SCHOOLS

19..40..-19..41..

Report of

Betty Fender

School .... *Luby* ....

Dist. No. ..... *7* ....

Grade ... *1* ...

ENTERPRISE PRINT, EAGLE, COLO.

Methods of Grading.

A—93-100
B—85-92
C—78-84
D—70-77
F—Failure

Attendance and Studies	1	2	3	4	5	6	7	8	9	Average
Days taught	25	27	31	30	30	30				
Days absent	3	6	16	15	8	5				
Times tardy	0	1								
Reading	B	B	B⁺	A	A	A				
Spelling				A	A	A				
Arithmetic	A	A-	A	A	A	A				
Penmanship	C⁺	C⁺	C⁺	C⁺	C⁺	C⁺				
U. S. History										
Colorado History										
Hygiene	B	B	B	A	A	A				
Agriculture										
Science										
Geography										
Civics										
Language	C	C	C	C	B					
Art	C	C	C	C	C					
Music										
Phonetics	B⁻	B	B							
Seatwork				B	A	A				

Character Traits.

S—Satisfactory.
I—Improvement.
X—Pupil not co-operating sufficiently.

PERIODS	1	2	3	4	5	6	7	8	9
Attitude toward work	S	S	S	S	S				
Manners toward teacher and others	S	S	S	S	S				
Promptness in attendance and assignments	S	S	S	S	S				
Obedience to rules, respect for authority	S	S	S	S	S				
Thrift, respect for school property	S	S	S	S	S				
Personal habits in school and on school grounds	S	S	S	S	S				

Certificate of Promotion.

THIS CERTIFIES THAT *Betty Fender*

has completed the work of the *1st and 2nd* Grades

and is hereby promoted to the *Third* Grade.

Frances Domka
Teacher.

Date *May 9* 19 *41*

Edna Sweet with some of the Luby School students.

"We took our lunches to school, and I had a little square lunch bucket. Mama would fix me my favorite once in awhile: a baloney, lettuce and mayo sandwich, and a banana. I remember how wonderful it smelled when I opened up my lunch bucket.

"We had a library full of books on shelves on the east side of the room. It held books on science, civics, and history. Also, short stories for kids like Peter Rabbit, and one with a beautiful bluebird on the front. I think the school district sent some books and others were donated by the community.

"We hung our coats and hats in a long hallway at the front of the building. There was a coal shed out to the side and the old stove burned coal or wood. My dad, Loren, and his brother, Uncle Eddis, built the shed to stable our horses in. They always made sure the horses had oats and water. They also built the shelves for the library, and brought in books. The teacher's room was on the left-hand side as you walked in the door.

"Edna Sweet was my teacher in fifth grade, in 1943 - 44.

"We raised the flag of the United States on a flagpole outside every morning, and lowered it every night. I remember being so careful when it was my turn to fold and unfold it correctly, never letting it touch the ground.

"We played hide-and-seek, and fox-and-geese at recess. There were Christmas pageants and parties and plays. All the grandparents and parents and aunts and uncles came, and they were so proud of us. I can remember myself on stage once, looking at all the faces and Mama and Daddy smiling at me from the back."

Message.

Your hearty co-operation is solicited in the endeavor to secure the best development of your child. If a pupil receives failing grades in any subject, it may be attributed to lack of study, too many outside activities, irregular attendance, or poor health. Therefore, you should make immediate inquiry concerning your child's work. Your visits to the school-room will help give inspiration to both pupils and teacher.

Signature of Parent or Guardian.

This card must be signed and returned Promptly.

1st Period *Loren Fender*
2d Period   *Loren Fender*
3d Period   *Loren Fender*
4th Period *Loren Fender*
5th Period *Loren Fender*
6th Period ....
7th Period ....
8th Period ....
9th Period ....

EAGLE COUNTY
PUBLIC SCHOOLS

1943 - 1944

Report Of *Betty Fender*

School *Luby*

Dist. No. 7

Grade 5

ENTERPRISE PRINT, EAGLE, COLO.

Methods of Grading.

A—93-100   C—78-84
B—85-92   D—70-77   F—Failure

Attendance and Studies	1	2	3	4	5	6	7	8	9	Average
Days taught	29	28	25	30	29	30				
Days absent	1	3	2	6	0	1½				
Times tardy	0	0	0	0	0	0				
Reading	A	A	A	A	A	A				
Spelling	A	A	A	A	A	A				
Arithmetic	B	B	B	B	B	B				
Penmanship	B	A	A	A	A	A				
U. S. History	B	B	B	B	B	B				
Colorado History										
Hygiene										
Agriculture										
Science			B	C	A	B	B			
Geography			B	B	A	B	B	A		
Civics										
Language			B	B	A	A	A	A		
Art			B	B	B	B	B			
Music										

Character Traits.

S—Satisfactory.
I—Improvement.
X—Pupil not co-operating sufficiently.

PERIODS	1	2	3	4	5	6	7	8	9
Attitude toward work	I	I	I	S	S	S			
Manners toward teacher and others	S	S	S	S	S	S			
Promptness in attendance and assignments	S	S	S	S	S	S			
Obedience to rules, respect for authority	S	S	S	I	S	S			
Thrift, respect for school property	S	S	S	S	S	S			
Personal habits in school and on school grounds	S	S	S	S	S	S			

Certificate of Promotion.

THIS CERTIFIES THAT *Betty Fender*

has completed the work of the 5th Grade

and is hereby promoted to the 6th Grade.

Edna D. Sweet
Teacher.

Date May 13 1944

Bernie Smith and Eunice (Long) Smith

Bernard "Bernie" Long: "I was a student at Luby School in the first, second and third grades, from about 1947 to 1949. Elsie Lyons was my teacher, and I remember she was real strict, and we were pretty careful not to get in trouble.

"I remember one time I got one of the girls, Betty Antle, real mad at me. I stuck a stick in the front wheel spokes of her bicycle and made her crash.

"I also remember Mrs. Lyons kept a .45 Colt revolver in her room at the school, and I'm sure she knew how to use it. Sometimes my parents would pick Mrs. Lyons up and take her with us to the movie in Glenwood Springs. When we took her back to the school, she would ask my dad, Ralph, to come in and make sure no one was hiding inside. My dad would check all the rooms and even under the bed, and then Mrs. Lyons would feel better about being there alone.

"We rode our horses to Luby and I remember we rode Bell and Pinky, and Brownie, who was blind in one eye. We also rode ol' Jerry. He was a big, wide work horse, and he was so comfortable, it was like sitting on a big, overstuffed recliner."

Luby School teacher, Anna Schotz.

Eunice Long: "The two of us would ride on one horse in the winter to keep warmer. I remember on a cold winter day when school was over, we would get on the horse and lay forward, over the animal's shoulders. Then, the teacher would cover us with big, heavy coats."

GRAPHING THE GRADE

EAGLE COUNTY
PUBLIC SCHOOLS

1947 — 19 48

∴

Period, Semester and Annual Report

of

Eunice Long

Grade, Year or Class 3

Dist. No. 7

CITIZENSHIP ATTITUDES

Objectives as an Individual	Periods					
	1	2	3	4	5	6
Dependableness						
(a) *Days Absent (Unexcused)	0	0	0	0	0	0
(b) *Days Absent (Excused)	1	3	6	6	5	3
(c) *Times Tardy	0	5	9	9	9	10
(d) General Dependableness	+	+	+	+	+	+
School Attitude	+	+	+	+	+	+
Promptness	+	+	+	+	+	+
Effort	+	+	+	+	+	+
Courtesy	+	+	+	+	+	+
Self-Reliance	+	+	+	+	+	+
Initiative	+	+	+	+	+	+
Thrift	+	+	+	+	+	+
Self-Control	+	+	+	+	+	+
Good Workmanship	+	+	+	+	+	+
Objectives of Group Membership						
Good Sportsmanship (Complies with Group Dec'sns)	+	+	+	+	+	+
School Service (Makes worth-while contrib's)	+	+	+	+	+	+
Takes Criticism Profitably	+	+	+	+	+	+

(*) Statistics from School Register.

(†) Excused Absence should be given very sparingly.

On other objectives, if the pupil excels, mark (+). If he is in much need of improvement, the objective is marked (O).

SUBJECTS	MARKS	1st Period	2nd Period	3rd Period	Examination	Sem. Average	4th Period	5th Period	6th Period	Examination	Sem. Average	Year Average
Music	+											
	S	—	—	—			—	—	—			
	O											
	F											
Art	+											
	S	—	—	—			—	—	—			
	O											
	F											
Pen'- ship	+											
	S	—	—	—				—				
	O											
	F											

Comments on Achievement Tests:

Date given

Date given

Date given

Edna (Denmark) Sweet
Pioneer Teacher • Historian • Writer

From her book *Carbondale Pioneers, 1879-1890*; © 1947:

"When Horace Greeley uttered the words 'Go West, young man, and grow up in the country,' my father, C.E. Denmark, with countless others took him quite literally and started westward in 1880. After spending three years in Crested Butte, he journeyed to Aspen in the fall of 1883. In March of 1885, my mother with her two children, undertook the trip by stage. We left Leadville at daylight with three heavily loaded stages. At Twin Lakes we were transferred to sleds and crossed Independence Pass without mishap, arriving at Weller, eight miles east of Aspen at nine o'clock at night. After having dinner, we were transferred again to wagons. The stage driver announced that it was a corduroy road the rest of the way in to Aspen, and the mud so deep the bottom had dropped out.

"One of the two wagons broke down, so the other two had to divide the passengers. There were fifteen in our wagon. After we

Edna Sweet with students at Luby School.

climbed in I was terrorized to see my first drunken woman, standing up and brandishing her bottle and screaming!

"The driver announced that if anyone would get out and stay at the station overnight, they would be taken to Aspen the next morning. On account of my baby brother, who was only two years old, my mother decided to stay. Two or three others stayed. The wagons which had gone ahead were all night getting in to Aspen. One wagon upset and the occupants were thrown into the river and several were injured.

"My mother and baby brother and I went back into the dining room and sat down by the stove. Mr. Weller came in and said he had no extra beds, so we would have to sit by the fire all night. Two men, freighters, came forward and kindly offered their bed, saying that they would sleep in the stable on the hay. There were two beds in the room with two strange men occupying the other bed, but we were so dead tired, we thankfully accepted and were piloted through the loft of the log building where fifty freighters had rolled up in their blankets, and were peacefully sleeping on the floor.

"We started for Aspen the next morning at nine, and did not reach our destination until 4 p.m. Aspen was in the midst of one of the biggest silver booms the United States had ever seen. Ten thousand people roamed the streets.

"In July 1885 my father purchased the right of Ben Banning, a hardy pioneer, to ranch on the Roaring Fork near the town of Carbondale for $200."

Edna Denmark grew up in Carbondale. It is not known where she was educated, but she became a teacher. Her husband, Frank Sweet, came from Hartford, Connecticut, in 1882 to the Roaring

Fork Valley. Edna: "He had loved the green valleys of Connecticut, and when he viewed the barren wastes around Carbondale, was imbued with the idea of making the desert bloom like a rose."

Frank Sweet, Lafayette Girdner, and William Dinkle formed a partnership and started the Dinkle Mercantile in 1887. They sold everything from threshing machines to needles.

The Sweets owned land throughout the area, around Carbondale, and up on the Heights. They had five children: Irene, Walden, Julian, Dorothy, and Harold. Edna taught school at Luby on Missouri Heights. The land had been deeded to the school district by Frank and Edna on their property next to Paul Gould in 1925 or 1926. The school was built in 1926.

Edna was a historian and a gifted writer, as is evident in her book *Carbondale Pioneers* (which can be found today in 1998 in the Carbondale Library).

Edna: "In the early days he [Frank Sweet] served as city councilman in Carbondale. He, with Mr. Tandy, fought for the town to set out trees. It was a bitter fight, but they won, and they lived to see the result of their labor in the town's shaded streets. When I climb the East Mesa and view our little village lying so peacefully at the foot of Mount Sopris, with its beautiful homes, trees and flowers, then go back in memory to my first glance of the treeless desert, I feel that we have rubbed Aladdin's wonderful lamp and that the valley and mountain is, indeed, one of the scenic spots of the world, worth all the toil, the strife and tears that went into the building of it."

Frank and Edna are both buried at the Carbondale White Hill Cemetery.

The ranch house built by Frank Sweet in the late 1800s, on the Sterrett-Wilson ranch in 1998.

MISSOURI HEIGHTS SCHOOL
1917 – 1998   District 48

The Missouri Heights School in 1998.

The land, 158 acres, was first homesteaded by David James in 1897, Patent 1203 Ute Series.

History of the Land Owners

Edward J. Taylor .... 1898 .... 158 acres
George C. Banning .... 1898 .... 158 acres
James O Needham .... 1898 .... 158 acres
Jessie L. Needham .... 1903 .... 158 acres
Orville A. Boyles .... 1904 .... 158 acres
Henry Prechtel .... 1930 .... 158 acres
Obscure records:
W.M. Quakenbush .... 1950s .... 158 acres
Missouri Heights
    Community League .... 1963 - 1998 .... 75/100's acre

A description of the school land: 75/100's of an acre: Section 20 – a corner line in the NE corner of the NW1/4 SW1/4 of Section 20, Tp. 7 S., R. 87 W., 6th P.M.

Book 352
Page 488

Recorded at 1:55 o'clock P.M., Sept. 4 1963
Reception No. 222663 Chas. S. Keegan Recorder.

THIS DEED, Made this 12th day of July in the year of our Lord one thousand nine hundred and Sixty-three between
------- W. M. QUACKENBUSH -------
of the County of Potter
and State of ~~Colorado~~ Texas, of the first part, and
---- MISSOURI HEIGHTS COMMUNITY LEAGUE, -------
of the County of Garfield
and State of Colorado, of the second part,

WITNESSETH, That the said party of the first part, for and in consideration of the sum of ONE DOLLAR and other good and valuable considerations -------------------- DOLLARS, to the said party of the first part in hand paid by the said party of the second part, the receipt whereof is hereby confessed and acknowledged, ha s remised, released, sold, conveyed and QUIT CLAIMED, and by these presents doe s remise, release, sell, convey and QUIT CLAIM unto the said party of the second part, its heirs, successors and assigns, forever, all the right, title, interest, claim and demand which the said party of the first part ha s in and to the following described real estate situate, lying and being in the County of Garfield and State of Colorado, to-wit:

The Corner Square Acre lying in the Northeast Corner of the NW¼SW¼ of Section 20, Tp. 7 S., R. 87 W., 6th P.M.

TO HAVE AND TO HOLD the same, together with all and singular the appurtenances and privileges thereunto belonging or in anywise thereunto appertaining, and all the estate, right, title, interest and claim whatsoever, of the said part y of the first part, either in law or equity, to the only proper use, benefit and behoof of the said part y of the second part, its heirs and assigns forever.

IN WITNESS WHEREOF, The said part y of the first part ha s hereunto set his hand and seal the day and year first above written.

Signed, Sealed and Delivered in the Presence of

W. M. Quackenbush [SEAL]
.... [SEAL]
.... [SEAL]
.... [SEAL]

STATE OF ~~COLORADO~~ TEXAS } ss.
County of Potter

The foregoing instrument was acknowledged before me this 5th day of ~~July~~ Aug. A.D. 19 63, by* W. M. Quackenbush

My commission expires June 1, 1965. Witness my hand and official seal.

Lillian Steele
Notary Public.

*If by natural person or persons here insert name or names; if by person acting in representative or official capacity or as attorney-in-fact, then insert name of person as executor, attorney-in-fact or other capacity or description; if by officer of corporation, then insert name of such officer or officers, as the president or other officers of such corporation, naming it.—Statutory Acknowledgment, Session 1927.

No. 933. QUIT CLAIM DEED.—Bradford-Robinson Printing Company, 1814-46 Stout Street, Denver, Colorado

The old homestead on the Strang Ranch in 1998.

A few people remember that school was first held in the old homestead house built by James O. Needham around 1882. The homestead house still stands in 1998, near the intersection of 102 and Catherine Store Road, on the Mike Strang ranch, and is the home of his son, Michael Lathrop Strang.

In 1913, Frank and Blanch (Thompson) Smith, from Jamesport, Missouri, homesteaded land near the place where the Missouri Heights School would be built. In her memories of life on the Heights written in 1968, Blanch remembered how the school was started. "It was a problem to get the children to school, so some of the patrons from that part of the district (we were in the Crystal Springs District) applied to the County Superintendent of Schools to get a school on Missouri Heights.

"The Boyle ranch donated an acre of ground for a site, and men were elected to be the building committee. Each ranch donated work. I suppose they borrowed money to buy materials. Frank and others took a team and hauled lumber from town.

"When they got the building finished, they had dances every once in a while and donated the money they raised to the building fund. We never went to the dances, as Frank did not like dances. He always sent his dollar and I baked a cake for the refreshments.

"I do not remember who the first teacher was; one year there was a teacher from Leadville, Miss Jeanne Lindsey. She stayed with us.

Frank Smith hauling lumber for the construction of the Missouri Heights School.

"One Sunday during the summer there was a benefit picnic for the school at George Sievers' place on the Roaring Fork. They had a nice picnic place with a pavilion for dancing. The people had a number of things to sell, such as hamburgers, hot dogs, and pop. Then, they charged so much each dance."

Cora (Holgate) Natal recalls her memories of the building of the school. "The community of farmers built the Missouri Heights School in 1917, under the guidance of my father, Fred Holgate, who was a carpenter. Later, they built the teachereage [teachers' living quarters] and then a coal storage unit. Some of our teachers were Vera (Paterson) Kyner, Mary Ferguson, Eva Ravoux, and Susorine (Diemoz) Bon."

Grace Cowen: "When I was five years old, we moved to Missouri Heights where my father, Sherman, had 640 acres up above what is the Mike Strang ranch today in 1998. I remember it was 1917, and they were building the Missouri Heights School. My dad and I went to look at it and it was just walls and floor joints with cross pieces, and I remember watching my dad walking across them."

The Missouri Heights School teachereage (teacher's quarters) at right.

Adventure at the Missouri Heights School – 1931
By Lucile (Maxfield) Bogue

When I got home for Christmas vacation, the family made a momentous decision. We would celebrate by all going up to the Missouri Heights Schoolhouse for their Christmas program, Mom, Dad, Vernie, and me. Why such a decision was made, I can't say. We'd heard of Missouri Heights all our lives, but had never been so adventurous as to drive that ten or so miles to see it.

It was a crisp, cold night just before Christmas, with a huge, white moon. Even though I'd survived all the ups and downs of the first semester of college, I was thrilled as though just breaking out into society for the first time.

The school program was over quickly, not nearly as good, we privately decided, as the ones Mom used to put on every Christmas at the Crystal Springs School. Hers were always huge, dramatic successes, for she made costumes and played wonderful, spirited piano music. But, the dance was the reason we had come all this way anyway, for their community dances were legendary. Soon, the dance band tuned up and the fun began.

Just the usual crowd of country folks, some we knew and some we didn't. But one tall, handsome, laughing young man caught our eye immediately.

"Who is that fellow?" Vernie and I kept whispering to everyone we knew. No one seemed to know. Then I asked the teacher who had been in my first grade in Carbondale years ago. Apparently, she still didn't feel very friendly, remembering when she had kicked my shins because I was a frightened, timid "hillbilly" and, at Mom's urging, had pulled her long hair in self defense.

"Go ask him!" she flipped over her shoulder. "He's the new professor at Basalt!" But that's as far as we got.

Mom, who was sitting on the sidelines, motioned me to her.

"Annie," she said to the woman she sat with, "this is my older girl, Lucy, just home from Colorado College." I could hear her pride. Then to me, "Remember my telling you about my playing for Annie McCarthy's wedding years ago?" I involuntarily laughed aloud at the memory, for when asked without warning to play 'a wedding march' all she could think of was the thundering *Ben Hur Chariot Race*! As the three of us laughed together, the woman motioned to someone behind me.

"Now, I want you to meet my little boy!" I turned around to find the handsome "professor" at my shoulder! Our mothers introduced us!

The evening floated by on dancing feet, as though in a dream. Art Bogue, the dashing stranger, asked to take me home. Me! With Vernie, my beautiful little sister at the dance! And he asked me!

The world was a mass of glittering diamonds all the way home that night. The most beautiful night in the world!

Four years later there was another big dance at Missouri Heights. It was a shower dance, preceding our wedding! 1935! Missouri Heights is special!

Betty-Jane (Kreutz) Floyd
Teaching Years 1939 - 1941

Betty-Jane was born in 1920 in Denver to Carl and Mary (Lewis) Kreutz. The family lived in Denver and also on Missouri Heights during the 1930s and '40s. Carl worked for Harleigh Holmes in Denver at the Coleman Motor Company, and on Missouri Heights he ran the Reservoir and Irrigation Company which Harleigh had built in 1912. While on the Heights, they lived about one and a half miles east of the reservoir.

Betty-Jane and her sister, Helen, attended Luby School in 1931 and '32, and Olla Jacobs was their teacher. Helen Kreutz: "We walked to school in good weather, and in the winter we took turns pushing each other on a sled."

Betty-Jane graduated eighth grade from Luby School in 1932, and then went to Carbondale Union High School where she graduated in 1936. She began her studies at Western State College in Gunnison, Colorado, and passed the State Teachers' Exam. Her first teaching position was at the Missouri Heights School in 1939 for $80 a month. The following is an article published by the *Valley Journal* newspaper in Carbondale about her first year at the school on the Heights:

Valley News
During Missouri Heights School Days
It was a time of the "Ditch Bank Contract Summit"
By Betty-Jane Floyd

Editor's Note: A couple of weeks ago, the Valley Journal ran a story about the one-room schoolhouse on Missouri Heights. Now used as a community center by the Missouri Heights Community League, the one-room schoolhouse was the historic social and educational focal point for the Heights farming community until the 1950s.

In response to that piece, we've received a letter and short story from Betty-Jane Kreutz Floyd, who taught there some fifty years ago. She notes in her letter:

Dear Friends:

I taught at the Missouri Heights School in 1939-39 and '39-'40. My home was a nearby ranch.

I wrote this story several years ago; it was about my first contract at Missouri Heights and the interesting situation surrounding it! I was nineteen years old and very excited and thrilled (and poor!) at the time.

The children in the picture are Myron and Donna Thrasher; Lorraine Kissee; Barb, Bob and Keith Black; Jackie Peterson, and Nadine and Robert Reser. They represented five grades. I am now retired after 32 years of Colorado teaching. I as a reading supervisor in Englewood, Colorado at the time of my retirement. I am a 1936 graduate of Carbondale Union High School.

We had a little school newspaper available to the community, and it was a scream... I did have some outstanding and very sharp students!

Ditch Bank Contract Summit

I walked along the ditch bank near the headgate, the often-opened and well-creased teaching contract in my hand. It was a one-page document made out with the carefully described requirements of School District 48, Garfield County, May 27, 1939, written in longhand. Best of all, the words "Eighty dollars a month for nine months" were very clear.

The president of the school board was just ahead, his irrigating shovel in his hand, working at the beginning of the potato rows as the ditch water turned in to his field. He didn't look up but kept forming the tiny forks, his overalls damp and slightly muddy. I knew the importance of the timing when "the water was on," and I knew it had to be utilized when the reservoir was opened for use on dry Missouri Heights. He had work to do.

While waiting for President Southcotte's attention I unfolded the white sheet again. I had it almost memorized. It had been put in my rural mailbox two weeks before, and I had shivered with relief and excitement when I read it. However, it had been unsigned and evidently hurriedly stuffed into an envelope without noticing that the signature was left off. I was due to go to summer school at Western State in Gunnison the following week, and I was anxious to have it signed before I left.

I looked down at the strictly worded directives, but they didn't bother me at all, as I was thrilled to have the job prospect: "Teacher to do own janitor work or hire it done, paying for it herself. Teacher to be at school at 7:45 in cold weather and prepare to heat the building. Teacher will teach all holidays except Thanksgiving and Christmas. One week of vacation at Christmas. Teacher not to be married during the school term." The word "teacher" was repeated four times and I doted on that!

Mr. Southcotte looked up momentarily from his irrigating. I spoke out quickly, "I wonder… wonder if I could get this signed. I do thank you for bringing it by to my mailbox."

"Yuh got plenty of time… all summer: I've been busy. don't worry about it," he answered.

"I'll be leaving for Gunnison on the bus. I'd really appreciate..." I persisted.

"I'll get around to it," he muttered, leaning his chin against the shovel handle. "I've been wonderin' if you're old enough. You won't be nineteen until August. It's a big job, that school. Thirteen kids and six grades comin' up."

I had been on this same ditch bank just four days before and had heard an almost similar statement when he had said, "Our board secretary went 'tuh West High School in Denver for a year and a half. Maybe he could help 'yuh a little."

I decided to stick it out and didn't move from my grassy place. "You have all my credentials. The board said they were very fine."

"Lemme have it. It's a-gettin' chilly and I have to finish here," he said as he took the paper, put it on a large rock by his foot and scratched out his name.

"Thank you, thank you," I murmured as I turned to go, tucking the contract into its envelope. He grunted, his knee-high rubber boots moving toward the ditch.

Eleven months later, at four o'clock on a Friday afternoon, I locked the wither frame door on my little schoolhouse. The interior had been prepared for the coming week of school, the floor cleaning compound swept up and out, the stove cleansed and the ashes emptied, the coal and wood stacked inside. I heard a noise behind me and turned to see Mr. Southcotte approaching on his horse, shovel stuck behind his saddle. His head went down when he saw me, but he said "Here's your contract for next year. It's signed." He smiled a little when he said that.

Then, looking straight at me, he said, "Yuh done real good. We're glad we had yuh."

It was enough.

A young Mick Southcotte (right) with Tom Heuston, an early Missouri Heights homesteader (center), and an unidentified man (left).

Betty-Jane received her teaching degree in 1939.

Some of her class activities at the Missouri Heights School:

- Monthly Newspaper.
- Cloud Coast - a Chapter of Colorado Young Citizen's League.
- Annual Book - Books left at school and shared by everyone.
- Language Experience Approach to Reading (Reading Method).
- Participation in Garfield County Scholastic Contests (Won three first places, and four second places with her fifth and sixth grade classes).

Years later, after a Carbondale High School reunion in 1985, Betty would write of earlier days on Missouri Heights in the *Littleton Times Weekly*. "The sheep wagons and bunkhouses of my western slope were filled during long winter evenings with cowhands reading anything they could get their hands on, classics and catalogs alike. My sister and I would later go over to the spot where a wagon had been moved, or where a cabin was vacated, and find a wealth of reading material, ranch romances, word puzzles, and sports magazines. Later, we passed them to the neighboring kids, who read them avidly, also. Now various reading centers in universities throughout the U.S. stress promoting reading of all kinds, not just fine literature. Honestly! We were way ahead of that game."

Betty-Jane Floyd was a well respected and honored teacher for 33 years, teaching in a variety of settings ranging from the Missouri Heights School to Arapahoe County.

Betty-Jane: "Although I hated Missouri Heights and its isolationism, I loved its children. They had a rough time, picking potatoes, skimping on clothes, and managing their meager resources carefully. However, they were very intelligent, very creative, and just plain nice. I truly enjoyed my years of teaching on Missouri Heights."

Colorado governor, Richard Lamm, presenting Betty-Jane Floyd with the Colorado Teacher of the Year Award in 1981.

Eva Ravoux
1902 - 1989

Eva Ravoux's father, Anthony Ravoux, was from Beseges, France, near Paris. In 1859, he came to America with his parents at age five, and they settled in New Shanic, Pennsylvania. New Shanic was a coal mining town. Young Anthony, age nine, worked in the mines with his father and went to school in the winter.

The Ravouxs came to Leadville, Colorado, in 1882 in hopes of striking it rich. In 1884, Anthony settled for farming and sold wild hay to the Dow Sebree livery stable for $40 a ton.

Anthony met Justine Letty in Aspen. They married and moved to Carbondale in 1909 and purchased the Dow Sebree ranch. They had two daughters, Mary and Eva, who both graduated from Carbondale High School. Eva graduated from Western State Teachers' College in Gunnison in 1933. She taught in Basalt, Spring Valley,

Luby School, and Missouri Heights from 1933 to 1947.

Eva married Fred A. Needham on December 24, 1945.

After leaving the Roaring Fork Valley, Eva taught in Grand Junction, Colorado, for 27 years.

At right: Eva in 1933.

Obituary – Eva M. Needham

Funeral service for Eva M. Needham will be Wednesday, April 5, at 2 p.m. in the Callahan-Edfast Chapel in Grand Junction.

The Rev. A.J. Bertrand will officiate. Burial will follow at Memorial Gardens in Grand Junction.

Mrs. Needham died in her Grand Junction home Saturday, April 1, 1989, of cardiac arrest. She was 86.

She was born November 20, 1902, in Aspen, to Anthony and Justine (Letty) Ravoux.

She spent her childhood in Carbondale and graduated from high school there.

She graduated from Western State Teachers' College in Gunnison in 1933. She taught school in Basalt, Spring Valley, and Missouri Heights from 1933 to 1947. She then taught with the Redlands School District in Grand Junction for 27 years.

She married Fred A. Needham December 24, 1945. He died in 1972 in Grand Junction.

She was a member of St. Joseph's Catholic Church in Grand Junction.

Survivors include a stepdaughter, Jean Wigger of Hotchkiss; three step-grandchildren and nine step-great grandchildren.

Memorial contributions can be made to the charity of choice.

Callahan-Edfast Mortuary of Grand Junction is in charge of arrangements.

Missouri Heights School, 1947. Left to right, front row: Arnold Gene Marks, Douglas Ralph Long, Louise Mary McNulty, Eunice Long, Forby Higginbotham, Charlene Lawrence, Ray Turner; back row: Jackie Shipley, Nellie Marks, Kenneth Holgate, Delmar Lawrence, Ethel Marks, Claude Holgate, Miss Velma Willey, teacher (1944 - 47).

Missouri Heights School, 1950 - 1951.

Left to right, front row: Ray Pettigrew, Verle Fender, Ethel Marks; middle row: Dorothy Long, Linda Marks; back row: Dixie Stott, Forby Higginbotham, Eunice Long, Lonnie Stott, Doug Long, Ray Turner, Grace Brogan (teacher), Nellie Marks, Charlene Lawrence.

School was held at the Missouri Heights School until 1956. After that year, students were bussed to Carbondale.

In 1998 the Missouri Heights School is owned by the Missouri Heights Community League, and is used for community events.

Vesta Chamberlain, the last teacher at Missouri Heights School, 1951 - 1956.

Missouri Heights School eighth grade graduation, 1954. Left to right: Ray Pettigrew, Vesta Chamberlain, Eunice Long.

PARENTS OR GUARDIAN PLEASE READ

On or before the first Wednesday of each school period this report will be filled out by the teacher and sent to you for inspection. If this report is not presented at the proper time, kindly notify the teacher.

If a pupil receives F P or M on any subject it should be made a matter of immediate inquiry. Possibly it is to be attributed to the lack of study, to too many outside engagements, irregularities in attendance or to some cause which can be removed.

Special attention is called to the serious consequences of IRREGULAR ATTENDANCE. It is important to remember that the loss of even a portion of a school session often proves to be a serious interruption to progress, and tends to produce a lack of interest in the school work. Excuses showing good cause for the absence or tardiness should always be sent promptly to the teacher on the return of a child to school. Neglect of this may cause the child to be sent home after the excuse.

We suggest that you talk over this report with your child each time it is received, and if it has any peculiar needs which are indicated to you by the marks on this card, that you confer with the teacher or superintendent regarding it.

If parents could show their interest in the child and school by occasional visits to the school it would prove a great source of inspiration and help to both pupil and teacher.

Your hearty co-operation is solicited in the endeavor to secure the best development of your child.

Miss Velma Willey .... Teacher

.... Sup't.

ESPECIALLY GOOD IN { Reading / Numbers }

ESPECIALLY POOR IN { .... }

Certificate of Promotion May 8th 1947

I CERTIFY that Eunice Long is eligible to promotion to Second Grade

Mrs. Elsie Lyons
.... Supt. or Teacher

Missouri Heights School

GRADE REPORT

PERIOD, SEMESTER AND ANNUAL REPORT

of Eunice Long

Grade, first one

for the School Year 1946-47

Miss Velma Willey .... Teacher

TO THE PUPIL

1. Be clean in person, dress, habits, thought and speech.
2. Be dutiful, polite and respectful to parents, teachers and all whom you may meet.
3. Be earnest in play in the time for play, and equally earnest in work in the time for work.
4. Cultivate promptness, energy and patient industry. They are worth more to you than money or influence in securing success in life.
5. Be studious and industrious, attentive, earnest and obedient if you would win the highest esteem of your parents, teachers, schoolmates and the general public.

PLEASE KEEP THIS REPORT NEAT AND CLEAN

Parent or Guardian is requested to examine this report carefully, each page, and acknowledge its receipt by signing below. Kindly return at once.

1st 6 weeks ... Mrs. Ralph Long
2nd 6 weeks ... Mrs. Ralph Long
3rd 6 weeks ... Mrs. Ralph Long
1st Semester ... Mrs. Ralph Long
1st 6 weeks ... Mrs. Ralph Long
2nd 6 weeks ....
3rd 6 weeks ....
2nd Semester ....

Form 14 Omaha School Supply Co.

METHOD OF GRADING
- A — Admirable. Grade 95 to 100
- B — Excellent. Grade from 85 to 95
- C — Fair. Grade from 75 to 85
- D — Poor. Grade from 60 to 75
- M — Very Poor. Grade below 60

Any grade lower than FAIR will not be honored by promotion

ATTENDANCE CONDUCT STUDIES	1st 6 Weeks	2d 6 Weeks	3d 6 Weeks	Exam.	1st Se. Gd.	Second Sem Gd	Exam.	2d Se. Gd.	Year's Av.
Times Tardy	1	1			0	0			
Days Present					15	19		4	
Days Absent	2	1½			0	1		3	
Conduct	B	A	A		A	A		A	
Effort	A	A	A		A	A		A	
Arithmetic	A	A	A		A	A		A	
Language									
Grammer									
Geography									
History									
Physiology									
Spelling	A	A	B		A	A		A	
Drawing	B	B	A	B					
Reading	A	A	A		A	A		A	
Penmanship	B	B	B		B	B		B	
Music									
Citizenship									
Science					B	B			
Phonics					B	A			

	1st 6 Weeks	2d 6 Weeks	3d 6 Weeks	1st Sem.	1st 6 Weeks	2d 6 Weeks	3d 6 Weeks	2d Sem.
ATTITUDE TOWARD SCHOOL WORK								
Indolent								
Wastes Time								
Work is Carelessly Done								
Copies; Gets too much help								
Gives Up Too Easily								
Shows Improvement								
Very Commendable	X	X	X		X	X	X	
RECITATIONS								
Comes Poorly Prepared								
Appears Not to Try								
Seldom Does Well								
Inattentive								
Pro notion in Danger								
Capable of Doing Much Better								
Work Shows a Falling Off								
Work of Grade too Difficult								
Absent Too Much								
Showing Improvement								
Very Satisfactory	X	X	X		X	X	X	
CONDUCT								
Restless; Inattentive								
Inclined to Mischief								
Rude; Discourteous at times								
Annoys Others								
Whispers Too Much								
Shows Improvement		X			X			
Very Good	X	X	X		X	X	X	

N. B.—This Mark X is placed opposite trait to which attention is called.

Mary Ferguson
1906 -

Mary Ferguson's father and mother, John Lamprecht and Marianna (Primocio), came to the United States in 1906 from Ziri, Austria. John came here because the U.S. was "The Golden Land." His brother, Louis, had arrived first, and John and Marianna followed, and they all homesteaded on Thompson Creek, near Spring Gulch. Mary was born in Spring Gulch in 1906. Her father later bought property in Carbondale, where the family settled.

After graduating from Carbondale High School in 1924, Mary went to Greeley, Colorado Teachers' College, which is now the University of Northern Colorado. She was only able to attend classes in the summer. At that time, the state of Colorado gave a state teaching exam; those who passed it could teach school for one year. The exam had to be taken again each year. Mary took the exam and taught for a few years, until she graduated college with a teaching degree. She then taught at several schools: Larson School on Divide

Creek, Crystal Springs, Lower Cattle Creek, Missouri Heights, and, finally, 27 years in Carbondale. The salary of her first teaching job was $75 a month.

Mary Ferguson: "I remember up on the Heights when my students were Gracie Cowen and Olive Boyd, who still live in Carbondale in 1998. There were also the Quakenbush children, Owen Holgate, and the Tackers. The kids all rode horseback to school.

"I only had ten or twelve students in the one-room schoolhouse, all in grades one through eight. I taught reading, math, history, phonics, music and geography, and we took field trips. We always walked on our field trips. First graders read their lessons to the eighth graders, and everyone helped each other. There was no water in the school, so we all brought fruit jars filled with water, and our lunch. In the winter time I would bring a big pot of cocoa to keep warm on the wood stove. School started at 9 a.m. and was over at 4 p.m.

"We had wonderful Christmas pageants, and the parents would come to the school in horse-drawn sleighs. They would wear their good clothes, and everyone looked marvelous. Of course, we also had graduation exercises at the school, and that was always an important event. We had great dances at Missouri Heights School. The men would move all the desks to one side to make room, and the wooden floor made a wonderful dance floor. Sometimes there would be a fiddler and someone to play the piano. Virginia Long was the fiddler, Mary Blue played piano, and Frank Williams was the announcer.

"After I started earning a salary I bought a Model A Ford and drove to the Heights from Carbondale. I'd have a terrible time in the winter on those muddy roads. I'd invariably get stuck, jack up the wheel, poke some sagebrush under it, and keep on going! Some days I had to poke a lot of sagebrush to get to school.

"One time Olive Boyd asked me to help her make her graduation dress. She came home with me to work on the dress that evening in Carbondale. Well, for some reason the lights in Carbondale went out, so we finished the dress by candlelight.

"Children were taught fine manners back then; they called every adult 'Mr.' or 'Mrs.'

"When I couldn't drive to school I boarded with the closest neighbors to the school, the Quakenbushes, who lived where the

Strang ranch is today. I also boarded at Lester Taft's. Some of the other teachers were Olla Jacobs, Keith Jacobs, and Edna Sweet.

"I married Melvin Vernon Ferguson in 1927. Melvin and I had four sons: Jack Harvey, Kaye Donne, Richard Noren, and Marvin Vernon. In the early '40s we had to move to Los Angeles for one year for the war effort. My husband worked for Lockheed, the airplane manufacturing company, and I taught extended day school. Extended day school meant that when parents were kept at their jobs for extended hours during the war, the children stayed at school until their parents got off work, and came after them. When we came back to Colorado, we lived up on Crystal Springs. We were the first place on the left, just past the springs.

"In 1987 Eddis Fender and I were the Carbondale Centennial King and Queen. I was also Potato Day Queen.

"Today, in 1998, I have the distinction of being the oldest woman in the U.S. with a live radio talk show. It's on KDNK, community radio for the Roaring Fork Valley, out of Carbondale, on Sunday nights at 6:00 to 6:30, called 'This I Remember.' I've had the show for fourteen years. *U.S.A. Today* did an article on me about my show. I had people calling me from all over the world at all times of night to ask me about it. Sometimes they called at 3 a.m.! Well, I just woke right up and talked to them."

Eddis Fender and Mary Ferguson as Carbondale's Centennial King and Queen; 1887 - 1987. Mary has received countless awards and honors for her many years of dedication to community service.

SECTION IV

MISSOURI HEIGHTS WATER

MISSOURI HEIGHTS WATER
1880 – 1998

In the beginning, a natural spring flowed into a natural basin at the base of Basalt Mountain. The spring was named Spring Park Spring in the early 1800s by one of the first homesteaders. It might have been the Hunt Brothers, A.P. Spraunkle, Eliah Miller, or John Strepey who lived nearby. It was a natural, crude reservoir of water for farmers on the high mesa that would one day be called Missouri Heights.

Several ditches were constructed from the reservoir by the first homesteaders using teams and Morman ditch diggers (plow like implements), plows, shovels, and painstaking hours of slow, tedious progress.

The Coulter Ditch (Cattle Creek)	June 1, 1882
The Heuschkel and Chapman Ditch (Cattle Creek)	June 20, 1884
The Needham Ditch (Cattle Creek)	July 11, 1884
The Martin Ditch	June 16, 1885
The Monarch Ditch (Cattle Creek)	July 31, 1885
The McNulty Ditch (Cattle Creek)	September 15, 1885
The McNulty Ditch #2	September 20, 1886
The Blue Creek Ditch (Blue Creek)	April 14, 1888
The Mountain Meadow Ditch	May 31, 1902
The Park Ditch	September 12, 1904

An attempt was made around 1905 or 1906 to unite the farmers and improve the outlets and inlets of the reservoir, but it did not materialize, and in 1911, Harleigh Holmes, from Denver, began to buy the surrounding land and draw plans for the project. The new reservoir was completed in the summer of 1912 using 100 teams, fresnos, and three crews of men working around the clock. Harleigh formed the Carbondale Reservoir and Irrigation Company and named the project the Spring Park Reservoir.

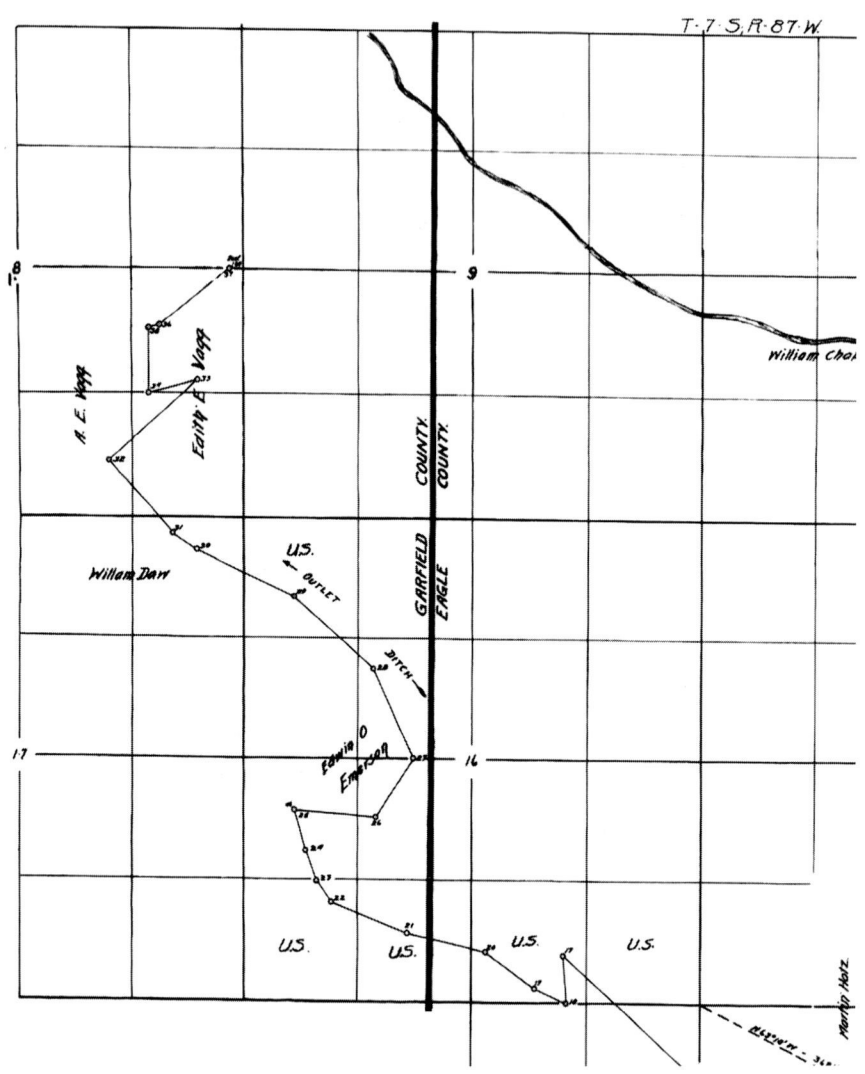

Page one of Harleigh Holmes' construction map for Spring Park Reservoir.

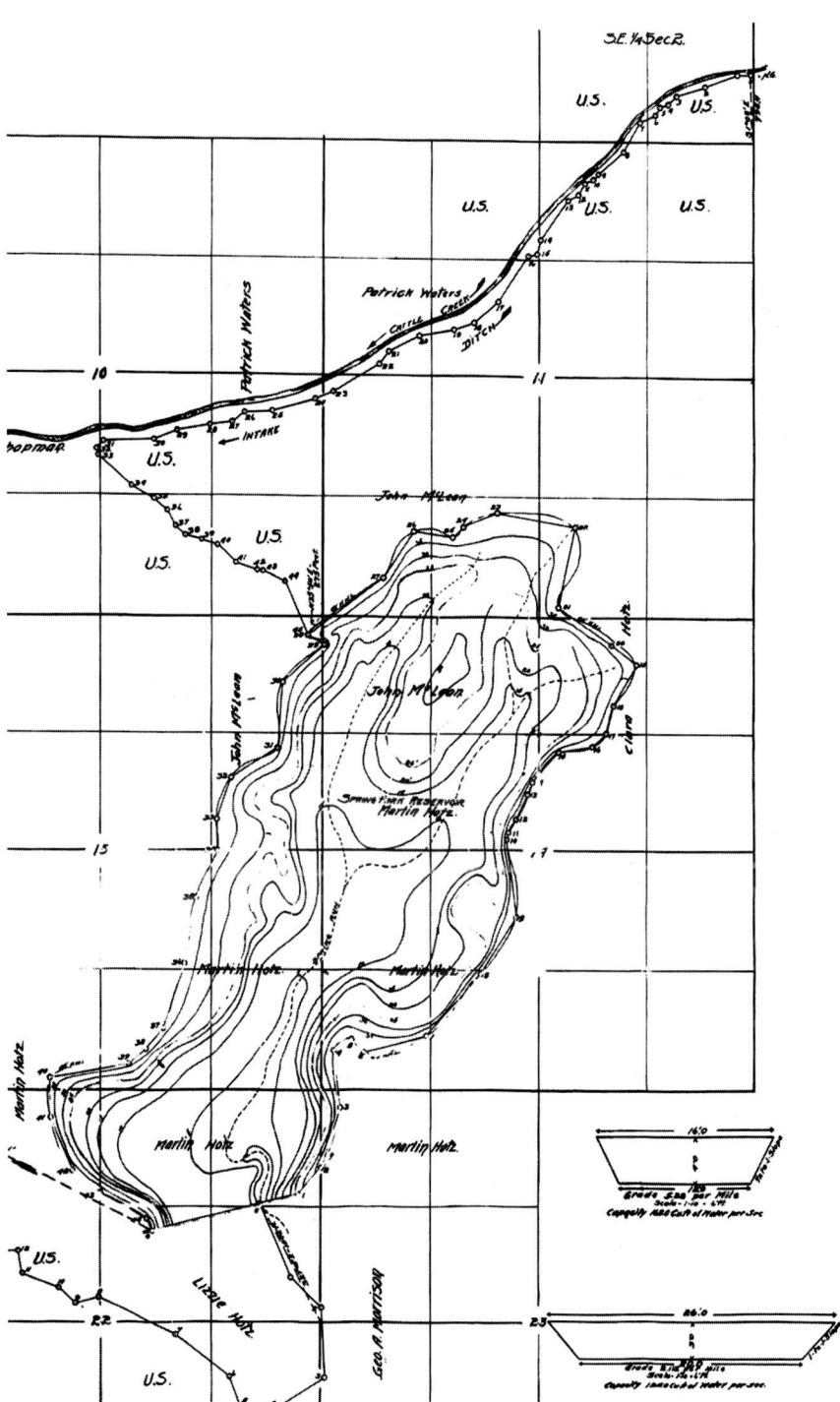

Page two of Harleigh Holmes' construction map for Spring Park Reservoir.

Know all men by these presents; That the undersigned J.H. Holmes and H.R. Holmes claimants, whose post office address is 206 M°Phee Bldg, Denver, Colorado, have caused to be located the Spring Park Ditch consisting of the Intake, and Outlet ditches, as hereinaftermentioned, have made these several statements relative thereto, and filed the same in compliance with the law of the State of Colorado. The accompanying map which shows the location of said ditch, form a part of this filing 1st. The headgate of said ditch is located at a point on the South bank of Cattle Creek, from which it derives its supply of water, whence the S.E. corner of sec 27-T.7S, R.87.W of 6° P.M. bears S1°08'E-7454 feet

2nd. The depth of said Intake Ditch is 3.0 feet
   " Width " " " - 15.260 feet on top
   " " " " " - 20.0 " - Bottom
   " Grade " " " - 0.4 - per 1000 feet
   " Length " " " - 12,913 feet

The depth of said Outlet Ditch is 4.0 feet
   The Width " " " - 16.0 feet on top
   " " " " " - 12.0 " - bottom
   " Grade " " " - 1.0 - per 1000 ft
   " Length " " " - 26,497 feet

3rd. The carrying capacity of said intake ditch is 16.0 cubic feet of water per second of time and the carrying capacity of said outlet ditch is 124.0 cubic feet of water per second of time, and claim is hereby made for 120.0 cubic feet of water per second of time for irrigation purposes.
4th. The estimated cost is $ 7,500.00
5th. Work was commenced by survey on the 11th day of November A.D. 1911.

                J. H. Holmes
                Claimant
                H. R. Holmes.
                Claimant

    Know all men by these presents, that the undersigned J.H. Holmes and H.R. Holmes claimants, whose post-office address is 206 M°Phee Building, Denver, Colorado, have caused to be located, The Spring Park Reservoir: have made these several statements relative thereto and filed the same in compliance with the laws of the State of Colorado. The accompanying map which shows the location of The Spring Park Reservoir, with intake and outlet ditches form a part of this filing and is hereby made a part thereof.

First   The height of Dam of the Spring Park Reservoir is 47' feet.

Second   The initial point of survey is located at a point whence the S.W. Corner of sec 22-T.7S; R.87-W of the 6th P.M. bears N-6340'W-3681-feet

Third   The accompanying table gives the area and capacities for each foot in depth from the bottom of the outlet tube up to and including the High Water Line.

Fourth   The total capacity of The Spring Park Reservoir is 522,662,775 cubic feet of water, for which claim is hereby made for irrigation purposes.

Fifth   The source of supply of said reservoir is Cattle Creek.

Sixth   The estimated Cost of said reservoir is $ 88,750.00

Seventh Work was commenced by survey on the 9th day of November A.D. 1911.

                J. H. Holmes
                claimant
                H. R. Holmes.
                Claimant

State of Colorado   } ss
City & County of Denver}

The Spring ~~Park~~ Glen A. Izett being duly sworn on his oat deposes and says that he is the engineer of the Spring Park Reservoir, that the survey of the same and the map there of were made under his instructions and that such survey is accurately represented upon this map; that he has read the statements thereon, and that the same are true of his own knowledge

                Glen A. Izett
                ENGINEER

Subscribed and sworn to before me this 23 day of November A.D. 1911.
    My commission expires Aug 5 - 1915.

                Elizabeth F. [illegible]
                Notary Public.

Page three of Harleigh Holmes' construction map for Spring Park Reservoir.

Table of Areas and Capacities

Depth in ft.	Area in sq. ft.	Capacity in cu. ft.	Depth in ft.	Area in sq. ft.	Capacity in cu. ft.
Bottom Outlets	116,500		21	14,126,692	136,765,746
1	360,720	238,610	22	14,822,784	150,840,430
2	604,940	721,440	23	15,518,976	166,011,314
3	849,160	1,448,490	24	16,215,168	181,878,386
4	1,093,380	2,419,760	25	16,911,360	198,441,060
5	1,337,600	3,635,250	26	17,618,288	215,706,474
6	2,251,520	5,429,810	27	18,325,216	233,678,226
7	3,165,440	8,134,290	28	19,032,144	252,356,906
8	4,079,360	11,760,630	29	19,739,072	271,742,514
9	4,993,280	16,297,010	30	20,446,000	291,835,050
10	5,907,200	21,747,250	31	20,997,696	312,556,898
11	6,841,600	28,121,650	32	21,549,392	333,830,442
12	7,776,000	35,430,450	33	22,101,088	355,656,682
13	8,710,400	43,678,650	34	22,652,784	378,032,618
14	9,644,800	52,851,250	35	23,204,480	400,261,250
15	10,579,200	62,963,250	36	23,408,608	424,383,263
16	11,149,440	73,827,570	37	24,149,732	448,680,442
17	11,719,680	85,262,130	38	24,628,852	472,622,807
18	12,289,920	97,366,930	39	24,024,044	497,410,235
19	12,860,160	109,841,970	40	25,400,120	522,663,740 High Water Line
20	13,430,400	122,987,850			

Field Notes of The Spring Park Reservoir
beginning at Sta. 0, whence the N.W. Corner
of Sec. 22, T.7 S., R.87 W. of the 6th P.M. bears N 65°40'W,
3681 feet.

Thence	N 77°55' E	1817	Feet to Station	1
"	N 42°15' E	418	" "	"	2
"	N 10°25' E	726	" "	"	3
"	N 6°35' W	668	" "	"	4
"	N 62°50' E	240	" "	"	5
"	S 45°30' E	191	" "	"	6
"	N 75°30' E	761	" "	"	7
"	N 42°00' E	454	" "	"	8
"	N 33°20' E	702	" "	"	9
"	N 7°40' W	887	" "	"	10
"	N 12°45' E	69	" "	"	11
"	N 31°15' E	179	" "	"	12
"	N 27°00' E	310	" "	"	13
"	N 21°50' E	157	" "	"	14
"	N 41°25' E	454	" "	"	15
"	N 03°20' E	412	" "	"	16
"	N 46°55' E	224	" "	"	17
"	N 16°05' E	325	" "	"	18
"	N 30°55' E	560	" "	"	19
"	N 53°05' W	378	" "	"	20
"	N 54°45' W	767	" "	"	21
"	N 13°10' E	948	" "	"	22
"	N 79°30' W	932	" "	"	23
"	S 68°45' W	425	" "	"	24
"	S 44°50' W	170	" "	"	25
"	N 72°50' W	457	" "	"	26
"	S 33°30' W	648	" "	"	27
"	S 54°20' W	1102	" "	"	28
"	S 60°10' E	223	" "	"	29
"	S 50°10' W	660	" "	"	30
"	S 4°45' W	760	" "	"	31
"	S 59°40' W	664	" "	"	32
"	S 20°30' W	506	" "	"	33
"	South	360	" "	"	34
"	S 27°00' W	600	" "	"	35
"	S 10°20' W	766	" "	"	36
"	S 20°10' W	788	" "	"	37
"	S 41°30' W	304	" "	"	38
"	S 51°00' W	283	" "	"	39
"	S 80°45' W	957	" "	"	40
"	S 1°30' E	469	" "	"	41
"	S 23°40' E	654	" "	"	42
"	S 52°45' E	720	" "	"	43
"	S 61°15' E	646	" "	"	44
"	S 31°00' E	120	" "	"	0

Page four of Harleigh Holmes' construction map for Spring Park Reservoir.

Special thanks to Jim Griffith for Harleigh Holmes maps.

Field note of the Outlet Ditch
beginning at Sta.0, whence the East ¼ Cor.
of Section 22-T.7-S; R.87 W. of the 6th P.M.
bears, S 27°16' E, 1842 Feet.

Thence	S 22°30' E	928	Feet to Station	1
"	S 47°30' E	500'	" "	"	2
"	S 1°30' E	816'	" "	"	3
"	S 39°00' W	712'	" "	"	4
"	N 84°30' W	408'	" "	"	5
"	N 21°15' W	368'	" "	"	6
"	N 51°30' W	810'	" "	"	7
"	N 64°30' W	1026'	" "	"	8
"	S 76°35' W	285'	" "	"	9
"	N 47°10' W	260'	" "	"	10
"	N 69°25' E	466'	" "	"	11
"	N 9°20' W	277'	" "	"	12
"	N 63°15' W	312'	" "	"	13
"	N 67°10' W	791'	" "	"	14
"	N 18°20' W	242'	" "	"	15
"	N 41°30' W	840'	" "	"	16
"	N 48°10' W	1928'	" "	"	17
"	S 4°15' E	554'	" "	"	18
"	N 66°10' W	406'	" "	"	19
"	N 37°00' W	700'	" "	"	20
"	N 76°20' W	940'	" "	"	21
"	N 68°30' W	972'	" "	"	22
"	N 35°15' W	300'	" "	"	23
"	N 43°00' W	368'	" "	"	24
"	N 16°05' W	468'	" "	"	25
"	S 64°50' E	356'	" "	"	26
"	N 33°20' E	787'	" "	"	27
"	N 24°25' W	1118'	" "	"	28
"	N 49°06' W	1241'	" "	"	29
"	N 66°30' W	1300'	" "	"	30
"	N 89°10' W	326'	" "	"	31
"	N 42°20' W	1136'	" "	"	32
"	N 50°10' E	1400'	" "	"	33
"	S 76°25' W	595'	" "	"	34
"	N 10°00' E	738'	" "	"	35
"	N 75°00' E	132'	" "	"	36
"	N 53°00' E	1040'	" "	"	37

Whence the E ¼ Corner of Sec-8-T.7-S, R.87 W.
of the 6th P.M. bears East 180 feet.

Accepted for filing in the Office of the
State Engineer of Colorado on the 1st day
of Dec. A.D. 1911.

Chas. W. Comstock
State Engineer

By _____
Deputy

9294

State of Colorado
County of Garfield, SS.   in the District Court

Statement of Claim
to
The Spring Park Reservoir
In the matter of the adjudication
of the priorities of water rights in
Water District No. 38.

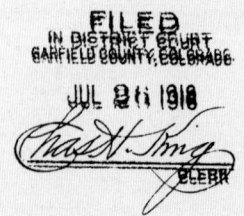

The undersigned, herewith make states of claim for use in the above entitled matter, for purpose of securing the benefits of the laws of the State of Colorado, relating to the adjudication of priorities of water rights for irrigation, as well as for any beneficial purpose other than irrigation, applicable to this claim of right.

1. The claim is made for the right to store water from Cattle Creek in the Spring Park Reservoir and to use the water so stored for irrigation.
2. The name of this reservoir is the Spring Park Reservoir.
3. The name of the owner of the said Spring Park Reservoir is The Carbondale Reservoir and Irrigation Company, a corporation.
4. The Post Office address of said owner of said reservoir is Carbondale, Colorado.
5. The Spring Park Reservoir is situated in Sections 11, 14, 15, 22, and 23, in Township 7, S. R. 87 W. 6th P.M., the initial point of survey beginning at station 0 whence the N.W. corner of Sec. 22, Tp. 7 S.R. 87 W. bears North 63° 10' West 3681 feet.
6. The drainage area to said reservoir is about 60 square miles.
7. The source of supply of water for said reservoir is Cattle Creek... to a... 1-3/4 enlargement of this Mountain Meadow Ditch no. 21.7 B.B....
8. The feeder or intake ditch to said reservoir is the...; the intake of said ditch is situated on the south bank of Cattle Creek at a point whence the S.w. Corner of Section 1, Tp. 7 S. R. 87 W. 6th P.M.
9. The dam of said reservoir is situated on the southerly side of said reservoir; height of dam at crest is 27 feet; depth of water in said reservoir at dam, at high water line, which is the 20 foot contour line of said reservoir, is 20 feet; Length of dam 1664 feet; width of dam on bottom, 133-1/2 feet; width of dam on top 12 feet; said dam is built of earth and clay.
10. The area of said reservoir at the 20 foot contour line is 309 acres.
11. The spillway of said reservoir is located at easterly end of dam, width of spillway 40 feet; said spillway is sufficient in carrying capacity to carry the excess waters that may flow into said reservoir.

12. The outlet ditch from said reservoir is the Spring Park Reservoir Outlet Ditch, the connecting point from said reservoir into said outlet ditch being 15 feet below the high water line, or 15 feet below said 20 foot contour line of said reservoir; the outlet from said reservoir into said outlet ditch being through a pipe controlled by a valve and stem, with scale showing depth of water and amount of water released from said reservoir into said outlet ditch; thence the waters are conducted through said ditch in a southeasterly, southerly, southwesterly and northwesterly direction to the lands and used for irrigation. The said outlet... intercepting the East and West... of this said Mountain Meadow Ditch and a portion of said Waters... are used through... for irrigation.
13. The amount of water hereby claimed for storage from Cattle Creek, in the Spring Park Reservoir, is, 122,987,250 cubic feet of water for irrigation purposes.
14. The date of appropriation of storage water hereby claimed from Cattle Creek, for storage in said reservoir is December 28th, 1911.
15. The said ditch is 13 feet wide on top, 10 feet wide on bottom, grade 8 feet to one mile, and has a carrying capacity of 103-1/2 cubic feet of water per second of time.
16. The said outlet ditch is 11 feet wide on top; 8 feet wide on bottom, grade .05 per 100 feet, and has a carrying capacity of 40 cubic feet per second of time.
17. The number of acres lying under said reservoir irrigated and proposed to be irrigated thereby is 5000 acres.

The Carbondale Res. & Irri. Company Seal.

H. R. Holmes Seal.
Vice Pres.

State of Colorado,
County of Garfield, SS.

H.R. Holmes, being first duly sworn, deposes Carbondale Reservoir and Irrigation Company, a corporation, named as the petitioner, and owner of the above named Spring Park Reservoir; that affiant is personally conversant with the matters and things contained in the foregoing Claim Statement and with the facts as they exist on the ground, and that the matters stated in the foregoing Claim Statement are true to the best of affiant's knowledge, information and belief.

H. R. Holmes,

Subscribed and sworn to before me this 26th day of July, A.D. 1918.

Chas H. King,
Clerk of the District Court

by _____ by *E. Bernice King*
Deputy.

District Court December 29, 1898

Martin Hotz - Plaintiff
vs.
John McLean, Mary McLean
John McLean Jr., E.U. Miller } Defendants
John M. Strepy, Harvey White

...plaintiff further alleges that at various times during the past three years the said defendants have unlawfully and maliciously conspired together for the purpose of harassing and annoying this plaintiff and interfering with his use and enjoyment of his said interest in said ditch and the said laterals therefrom, and have repeatedly threatened this plaintiff and his family and used vile and opprobrious language towards him and them and endeavored to frighten plaintiff away from said ditch and said laterals and from using or going upon the same at all, and during the latter portion of the irrigating season of 1898 and on or about the 27th day of September, A.D. 1898 the said defendants or some of them turned the water into said ditch and prevented this plaintiff from doing work thereon and by threats of violence drove the plaintiff from said ditch, and at other times the said defendants or some of them have threatened to shoot him if he used this ditch at all and have driven him from said ditch with guns and more especially on or about the 14th day of November, A.D. 1898, the said defendants John McLean and John McLean, Jr. drew a gun upon this plaintiff and threatened to kill him and blow the top of the head off of his wife and son if they ever went onto that ditch again, and the said defendants have severally and collectively terrorized over the plaintiff and his family to such an extent as to prevent him from using his said ditch and laterals and water rights and he dare not and cannot go on said ditch or use the same without coming in conflict and either being shot or beat or committing a breach of the peace in defense of his life and person and said property; that the said course of said defendants is a continuing and insufferable nuisance to this plaintiff...

Discussing water rights, a Western pastime. (Used by permission, Paul Stanton ©1974.)

Helen (Kreutz) Dupire: "My dad, Carl, ran the Carbondale Reservoir for Harleigh Holmes. I remember one time when I was about ten years old, we were all asleep, when someone came pounding on the door, cursin' and yellin' for my dad. It was Victor Jammaron, and he was boilin' mad, yellin' that he was going home to get a gun and kill my dad because he didn't get his water! Mr. Jammaron took off runnin' toward his home where the Sweet place was, and my dad took right off after him. Well, I took off right after my dad in my night gown and bare feet. We all hit the Sweet place and my dad tackled Mr. Jammaron, and then here came Mrs. Jammaron out of the house and she tackled my dad, too. I jumped right in on top of them and all four of us were yellin' and fightin' for all we were worth. Pretty soon, I guess everyone wore out, and we stopped. Mr. Jammaron calmed down and so did the rest of us. They finally talked it out, and we went on home. My dad and Mr. Jammaron were always good buddies before, and even after that, but when it came to water, friendship was forgotten!"

Blanch Smith, homesteader on Missouri Heights, 1914: "That summer my parents came to Colorado. It was decided that we should move to a place that had good domestic water. We had bought more water on the Heights, but it was difficult to transport the water to your land; something happened to it on the way. It worried Frank a lot."

Carbondale Reservoir and Irrigation Company dam under construction with partially filled reservoir, wheelbarrows, and other equipment, water pipe or outlet valve, and a tripod wooden structure. Photo taken between 1900 and 1919 by photographer Louis Charles McClure (1867 - 1957), courtesy of The Denver Public Library, Western History Division.

Betty (Fender) Prichard: "I remember when I was about six years old, and I went irrigating with my dad, Loren. We walked up over a hill and we saw Lawrence Sirola with a shovel doing something at the ditch. Well, Dad flew into a rage and started yelling and all of a sudden they ran at each other and started fighting. They were grabbing and punching and rolling on the ground, and I was so scared, and my heart was beating so fast. I picked up Dad's shovel and I swung it as hard as I could and somehow I hit Mr. Sirola right on the head. I yelled, 'Leave my dad alone!' It startled both of them and they quit fighting. My dad couldn't believe I did that!"

Someone (who asks not to be named) remembers that Victor Jammaron used to sit at the headgate at night with a shotgun. He also remembers that Earl Oliver snuck up one night and hit Mr. Jammaron over the head with a shovel. We don't know what happened next!

Dick Haff, son of Alden and Rosie (Gould) Haff: "I remember one time my Grandpa got in a fight with Kreutz's over water. There was a team standin' nearby, hitched to a mower. When Kreutz and my grandpa started throwin' punches, the team bolted and ran off through the fields and right through the fences. They tore that mower all to pieces.

"Another time three or four men were having a big, loud water argument. I was over the hill a ways, haulin' some logs with the horse. Well, my horse spooked and ran off, and I yelled real loud to my uncle, who was helpin' me, 'Archie, if you can't catch him, just shoot him!' All of a sudden the men in the argument all took off runnin' in all directions. I didn't even know they were there!"

Rosie (Gould) Haff: "My dad had the complete water right to Blue Creek, which was a blessing in some ways, and a curse in others. Boy, there were lots of water fights! People cut fences in the middle of the night to let stock in to drink. There were even instances of some people sneaking into houses and poisoning food. They even poisoned dogs to keep them quiet. My dad met most of them with a shotgun."

William H. Harris: "Paul Gould wouldn't give me a drink of water if I was dyin'!"

Paul Gould: "I'll put a jug of water in his coffin!"

Ruth Fender: "One time John McNulty called the *Glenwood Post* and asked if a photographer would come meet him at his place. They met, and John walked him to Cattle Creek. John laid down in the creek to show there wasn't much water in it, and had the man take his picture. When the picture came out in the paper John was quoted as saying, 'See, the Missouri Heights Reservoir Company is hogging all the water'!"

Today, in 1998, the Missouri Heights Reservoir and Irrigation Company, a corporation of stockholders using the water, is the owner of the reservoir.

Special thanks to Lawrence Mincer, attorney, and Gary Fender.

SECTION IV

SUBDIVISIONS – 1998

SUBDIVISIONS – 1998

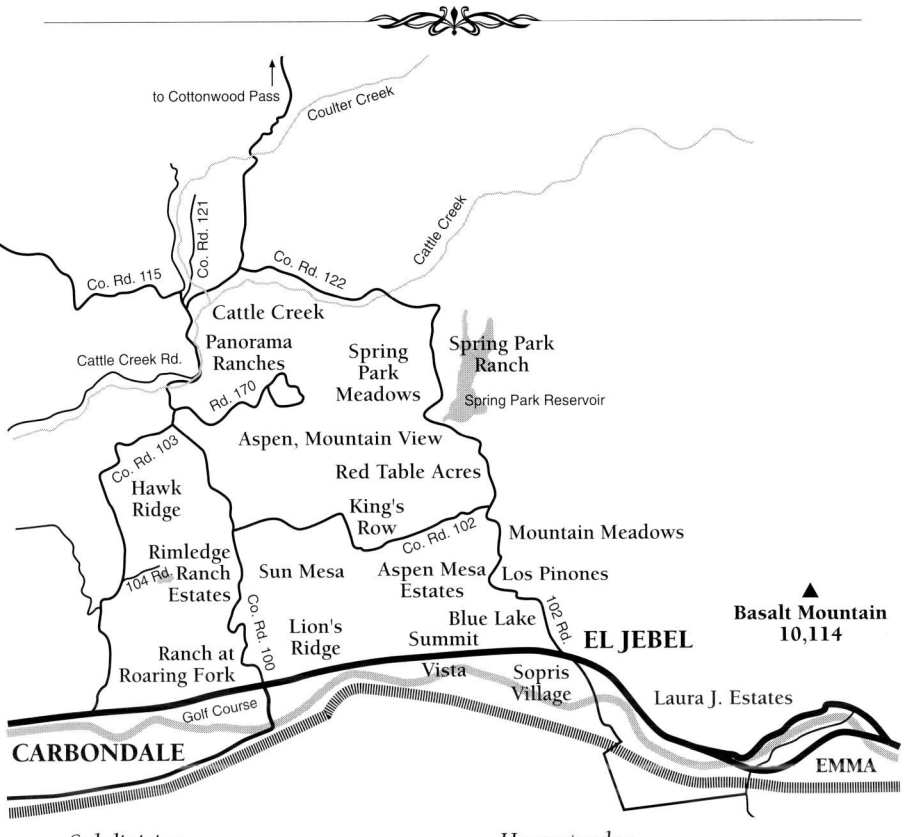

Subdivision	Homesteader
Los Piñones	William Harris
Aspen Mesa	T.J. Heuston/Augustine Hotz
Mountain Meadows	Fred Shehi/William Harris
King's Row	Raymond Harris (son of William)
Red Table Acres	William Harris
Aspen Mountain View	Harleigh Holmes/Hunt Brothers
Panorama Ranches	Sherman Cowen
Hawk Ridge	James William Curtis
Rimledge Ranch Estates	Ulysses S. Green
Sun Mesa	Mick Southcotte
Spring Park Ranches	Ben & John Hunt
Spring Park Meadows	Ben & John Hunt

Remember

I still ride my pony, up on Missouri Heights,
I try to keep away from cars and dogs,
There's bikers and there's runners, and traffic everywhere,
And I pick my trail around the whole barrage.

I ride up by the reservoir, and I think of Harleigh Holmes,
And how he loved to make the water flow,
And I hear children laughing in the yard at Luby School,
And I feel the quiet peace of long ago.

I ride by every homestead, and I see them standing there,
They wave and tip their hats and fade away,
And I recall their faces, and the lives that they once lived,
Those sturdy pioneers of yesterday.

Yes, I still ride my pony, all around up on the Heights,
And I see things that others just don't see,
But now, you've been there with me,
And I hope you won't forget,
Missouri Heights and all its history.

– A.W.

*The author with her favorite quarter horse, Hezzie.
Photo by friend and neighbor, Stephanie Monk.*

Anita McCune Witt is a long time resident of Missouri Heights, moving there in 1967, when most of the land was still open ranch land. A former trick rider in rodeos, she still enjoys riding her horses on the trails of nearby Basalt Mountain.

She is also an entertainer, playing guitar and singing standards and Western songs to audiences throughout the Roaring Fork Valley. She also performs fancy rope tricks while delivering humorous quotes from Will Rogers.

Anita has always enjoyed writing, preparing her manuscripts in longhand at her kitchen table. Her work has appeared in numerous magazines and newspapers, including *Western Horseman, Country Living, Destination, Reminisce, Horse Illustrated, Woman's Day,* and *The Rocky Mountain News.*

GUARDIAN ANGELS

By: John Jarvis, Don Schlitz, and Naomi Judd

Copyright © 1985 Plugged In Music.
All rights administered by Sony/ATV Music Publishing,
8 Music Square West, Nashville, TN 37203.
All Rights Reserved. Used by Permission.
Copyright © Wynona, Inc. Used by Permission.
Copyright © Harry Fox Agency. Used by Permission.

Copyright © 1989, New Hayes Music/New Don Songs
(administered by Copyright Management, Inc.), Kentucky Sweetheart Music,
Plugged In Music and BMG Music.
All Rights Reserved. International Copyright Secured. Used by Permission.